TOWERS

OF

GOLD

Isaias Wolf Hellman

TOWERS

OF

GOLD

How One Jewish Immigrant Named
Isaias Hellman Created California

FRANCES DINKELSPIEL

 ST. MARTIN'S GRIFFIN 🐾 NEW YORK

To Gary, who said I could, and Warren, who said I should

www.stmartins.com

Design by Susan Walsh

The Library of Congress has catalogued the hardcover edition as follows:

Dinkelspiel, Frances.
   Towers of gold : how one Jewish immigrant named Isaias Hellman created California / Frances Dinkelspiel.—1st ed.
       p.   cm.
   Includes bibliographical references.
   ISBN: 978-0-312-35527-2
   1. Hellman, Isaias W. (Isaias William), 1842–1920.   2. Jews—California—Los Angeles—Biography.   3. Jews, German—California—Los Angeles—Biography.   4. Jewish bankers—California—Los Angeles—Biography.   5. Capitalists and financiers—California—Los Angeles—Biography.   6. Banks and banking—California—History—19th century.   7. Banks and banking—California—History—20th century.   I. Title.
   F869.L89J5345 2008
   979.4'940049240092—dc22
   [B]

2008025264

D 10 9 8 7 6

CONTENTS

THE HELLMAN FAMILY

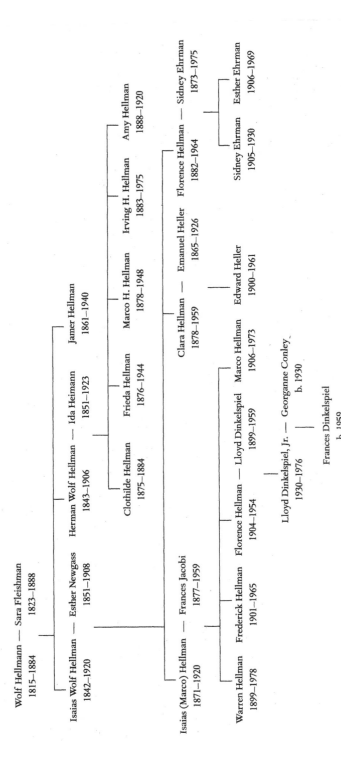

Wolf Hellmann — Sara Fleishman
1815–1884   1823–1888

Isaias Wolf Hellman — Esther Newgass   Jamer Hellmann
1842–1920   1851–1908   1861–1940

Herman Wolf Hellman — Ida Heimann
1843–1906   1851–1923

Clothilde Hellman   Frieda Hellman   Marco H. Hellman   Irving H. Hellman   Amy Hellman
1875–1884   1876–1944   1878–1948   1883–1975   1888–1920

Isaias (Marco) Hellman — Frances Jacobi
1871–1920   1877–1959

Clara Hellman — Emanuel Heller   Florence Hellman — Sidney Ehrman
1878–1959   1865–1926   1882–1964   1873–1975

Edward Heller   Sidney Ehrman   Esther Ehrman
1900–1961   1905–1930   1906–1969

Warren Hellman   Frederick Hellman   Florence Hellman — Lloyd Dinkelspiel   Marco Hellman
1899–1978   1901–1965   1904–1954   1899–1959   1906–1973

Lloyd Dinkelspiel, Jr. — Georganne Conley
1930–1976   b. 1930

Frances Dinkelspiel
b. 1959

INTRODUCTION

On my thirteenth birthday, my father took me to lunch at the Poodle Dog, one of San Francisco's oldest restaurants, the kind of place with red leather banquettes and smoke-stained walls. It had been part of the city's fabric for so long that no one cared any longer that it had once been a notorious "French" restaurant, with rooms upstairs rented by the hour. I loved the Poodle Dog for its name and its creamy vichyssoise sprinkled with delicately cut chives.

My birthday present was a checking account, which might seem an unusual gift for a young girl. But my parents had decided that learning to manage my money was a quick route to maturity, and I looked forward to having control over my small savings. When my father and I finished eating, we walked down Montgomery Street to the main office of Wells Fargo Bank, where crystal chandeliers hung from a high ceiling and tellers waited on customers from behind marble counters. We headed straight to a gentleman at a desk in the back. Dad said a few words, and the elderly banker pulled out a thick white card embossed with a gold stagecoach. He signed my name to it and then looked at me with a grave expression. "Don't lose this," he said, explaining it was identification for my checking account. "It's not replaceable."

The first time I pulled the card out of my wallet at a branch of Wells Fargo Bank, I was amazed at the reaction I got. Even though I was too young to drive and could barely see over the counter, the bank teller treated me with exaggerated courtesy. She didn't ask to see a picture ID. She didn't have to check with the manager when I wrote a check. She just gave me my money.

The carte blanche was the first clue I had that my family held special status at Wells Fargo Bank—yet I had only the vaguest notion of why that card got me VIP treatment. I was aware that my great-great-grandfather, Isaias Hellman, had something to do with Wells Fargo Bank, but the exact relationship eluded me. My family had been in California for five generations and we were well-to-do, but my relatives rarely discussed our past.

It was not until twenty-seven years later, after I had worked as a reporter for newspapers across the country and had two children of my own, that I finally understood why a descendant of Isaias Hellman commanded so much respect at the bank. I had taken a leave of absence from my newspaper job to write personal essays. I needed more material, so on a bright spring day in 1999 I went to the California Historical Society in downtown San Francisco, where I knew some of Hellman's papers were kept. I thought I would look at a few letters, and was amazed when the archivist explained that the society had more than forty cartons filled with Hellman material.

She brought me the first box. I opened a folder to find it crammed with letters written in old Germanic script. They were brittle and musty, but the ink on them seemed as dark and clear as the day they had been written. One appeared to be a report card from 1854. The next folder revealed contracts that seemed to refer to the buying and selling of properties. Then came an 1869 letter from a Herman, referring to a book he had borrowed from Hellman.

I had gone to the society not even knowing the name of Hellman's siblings but soon realized that the clues to his life lay hidden in more than fifty thousand pieces of paper—business ledgers, letter books, telegrams, grocery bills, newspaper clippings, and many personal letters. Before long, I was spending day after day in the windowless reading room intent on deciphering ornate handwriting and obscure business deals. It was like chipping away at a column of marble. Each letter revealed a small detail about Hellman, which alone did not provide a portrait. But the facts accumulated over many months, and the more I read, the more intrigued I became. I soon realized that I had stumbled on every reporter's dream: an unknown story about a critical chapter in the country's history.

Isaias Wolf Hellman was California's premier financier in the late nineteenth and early twentieth centuries, a man whose financial acumen catapulted the state into the modern era and laid the groundwork for one of the world's most dynamic economies.

In a time of unsophisticated financial markets, when banks minted their own money, bankers like Hellman were the men who smoothed the rough edges of the economy. They offered credit, invested in companies, and issued debt. During financial panics—which happened roughly every ten years in the nineteenth century—bankers provided stability. The chaotic markets and industrial boom after the Civil War created a new class of capitalist, men who accumulated gargantuan fortunes in a relatively short time span. Men like Jacob Schiff and J. P. Morgan forged financial dynasties and networks that were in some ways more powerful than the central government. As the age of the independent financier evolved into the age of the corporation, those nineteenth-century titans helped lead the United States from an agrarian-based economy to an industrial one.

Bankers in California were too far from the financial centers of New York, London, and Paris to equal the significance of their East Coast counterparts, but they were instrumental in helping transform California from an isolated outpost where capital was measured in animal hides and gold nuggets into an economic powerhouse driven by mining and agricultural interests. And no banker in California was more critical in this change than Isaias Hellman. "No one man in California has left an impress upon the financial affairs of the state in so many different communities and in such an unquestioned manner as I. W. Hellman," Ira B. Cross wrote in his four-volume *Financing an Empire: History of Banking in California.*

Hellman was both builder and financier. He was a major investor and promoter of at least eight industries that shaped California—banking, transportation, education, land development, water, electricity, oil, and wine. In a classic American rags-to-riches story, he came to Los Angeles from Germany in 1859 with nothing and went on to build up three of the West's most important banks—the Farmers and Merchants Bank in Los Angeles, the Nevada Bank in San Francisco, and the Wells Fargo Bank. He was president or director of fourteen other banks. At the height of his power at the end of the first decade of the twentieth century he controlled more than $100 million in capital, equivalent to $38 billion in 2006 currency. His business partners were some of the most influential men of the time—Collis Huntington, Edward Harriman, Meyer Lehman, and John Mackay.

Hellman started buying lots in Los Angeles in 1863 and before long was one of the largest landowners and land developers in the region. He was a pioneer in transportation, helping bring the Southern Pacific Railroad to Los Angeles and creating trolley lines that crisscrossed the city. He was a major owner and financial backer of the municipal water systems of Los Angeles and San Francisco and dominated the wine industry until Prohibition. In addition, he donated the land that helped create the University of Southern California and he served as a regent of the University of California for thirty-seven years.

Hellman's genius lay not only in investments in companies. He also backed people, much like today's angel investors in Silicon Valley, and his support paid off for California many times over. Hellman helped Harrison Gray Otis acquire full ownership of the *Los Angeles Times,* a newspaper that indelibly shaped southern California. He funded Henry Huntington's rail lines—a force that arguably transformed Los Angeles. He gave Edward Doheny and Charles Canfield the funds to help them drill for petroleum—a personal loan that directly led to the discovery of California's massive oil deposits.

The newspapers called Hellman the richest man in the West, and at one point in 1890 estimated his fortune at $40 million. This was an overstatement, but it expressed the common sentiment that Hellman's investments were everywhere.

Hellman was not without his critics. He was so closely entwined with the politics of Los Angeles in the 1870s that newspapers talked of a "Hellman machine." He resisted turning control of the privately owned Los Angeles water company over to the city, ostensibly because he thought his representatives could better manage it than corrupt political officials. And Fremont Older, the crusading editor of the *San Francisco Bulletin,* held up Hellman in 1907 as an example of the type of businessman who thwarted municipal reform, preferring instead to do business in backroom deals. Even his younger brother, Herman, once his closest confidante and business adviser, turned against him.

Hellman's life also illuminates another story—that of the Jewish contribution to the settlement of California. When people think of Jewish immigrants, they generally think of the eastern European Jews who crowded into the Lower East Side of Manhattan or other urban areas. These Jews faced discrimination in housing and jobs, and it often took a generation or two to rise out of modest circumstances.

But the story of the Jews of California is different. Many of them fled the discrimination of their homelands in Germany, France, and Poland, and headed in the 1850s to California and its promise of gold. While a few became miners, most became merchants who catered to the miners' needs. And from the start, these Jews were accepted and integrated into society. They were elected to public office, built their homes alongside their Christian neighbors, and became the established mercantile elite. In both San Francisco and Los Angeles, Jews were community leaders. It was not until the 1890s that intransigent anti-Semitism gripped California. And while barriers were erected after then, the Jews had already indelibly shaped the state.

Hellman exemplified the almost unfettered access Jews had to power. Other Jewish businessmen who made indelible marks include Adolph Sutro, who engineered a tunnel that was critical to the growth of the Comstock silver mines in Nevada. At one point Sutro owned one-twelfth of the land in San Francisco. He later became mayor.

The story of Levi Strauss, a young Bavarian immigrant who turned a bolt of canvas into one of the world's great clothing companies, is well known. But fewer people know about the Haas family, who came from the same small town in Bavaria as Hellman. They started out in California as dry-goods dealers and liquor merchants, and one of their descendants took over Levi Strauss & Company in the twentieth century. Today, the Haases rank among the top philanthropists in the country. The Sloss and Gerstle families had a virtual mononoply on the Alaskan seal fur trade. When Secretary of State William Seward acquired Alaska from Russia in 1867 for $7.2 million, the deal was so derided it was nicknamed "Seward's Folly." But Louis Sloss and Lewis Gerstle soon demonstrated there was money to be made in that vast and frozen wasteland. After acquiring the rights to take the fur of one hundred thousand seals a year, the company paid more than $10 million in taxes for the pelts—far more than the original cost of the deal.

Hellman was so famous in his lifetime, that newspaper reporters regularly asked his opinion about the economy or world affairs. They followed the construction of his many mansions as closely as they did his bank acquisitions. News of his death was bannered at the top of newspapers around the state.

Despite this fame, Hellman is not widely remembered today. As I went from library to library around the state trying to cobble together a chronology of his life, I found myself alternately fascinated by his accomplishments and puzzled by his relative anonymity. What does it say about legacy when a man as rich and powerful as Hellman is virtually forgotten less than one hundred years after his death? Even I, his own great-great-granddaughter, was unaware of his achievements.

My carte blanche was stolen in 1975 when I left it in my wallet behind a wall in a local park, naively thinking it would be safe while I played with my friends. I was sad at its loss, but it didn't really matter. Within a few years, the card was obsolete, for banks started issuing ATM cards for identification.

But I never forgot the feeling of power the card gave me. And when I combed through the papers at the California Historical Society and other libraries around the state, I got a glimpse of how Hellman steadily accumulated influence over a sixty-year period. He was able to pair his particular financial genius with a time of enormous opportunity. For almost 160 years, California has been a wealth engine for the country, yet only the stories of the gold rush, and now the Internet boom, are well known. As Hellman's great-great-granddaughter and a reporter, I decided I wanted to illuminate the forgotten part of this history, the story of a man who played a critical role in the creation of one of America's most astounding economic miracles—California.

ONE

PANIC

1893

The mood was ebullient in the California Pavilion at the 1893 Chicago Exposition. The mission-style building, rumored to have cost $100,000, was finally set to open. Scores of California boosters sporting grizzly-bear-shaped badges clustered in the massive structure, eager to hear their governor, Henry Markham, extol the virtues of their state.

Examples of California's bounty lay everywhere. The hall, lavishly decorated with flowers and flags, was landscaped with ancient date palms and other semitropical plants. A fountain sprayed red wine, and mounds of raisins glistened in bowls. No display was more showstopping than the thirty-five-foot-tower built entirely of oranges. Laborers had worked for days to carefully layer the 18,873 pieces of fruit on top of one another, creating a bright orange column that sent a delicious fragrance floating through the air. The only other exhibit that rivaled the orange tower was a life-sized knight built entirely of prunes.

Millions of people from around the world were expected to visit the exposition, and California had spared no expense to show them that it was a state rich in land, crops, and innovation. While officials were proud that the gold rush had generated hundreds of millions of dollars in ore, they wanted people to know that the state was also an agricultural powerhouse, an important trader with the Far East, and a good place to do business. As Governor Markham snipped the ribbon that opened the pavilion, he boasted to the crowd that fruit production generated $3 million a year alone for the state. Wheat, grapes, and wine brought in millions more, creating a robust economy. California's population was growing rapidly, and its financial institutions were "in splendid condition," he enthused.

As Markham delivered his sunny remarks, he had no idea that Los Angeles's financial condition was rapidly disintegrating.

Few could have predicted that Los Angeles was about to be plunged into a crisis. The weather in the waning days of spring had been glorious, hot and sunny without a cloud in the sky, typical of the region's blessed climate. In 1876, just seventeen years earlier, Los Angeles had been a speck of an outpost on the edge of a continent, but now it boasted amenities as modern as those of any American city. Streets that were once notorious for their thick dust in the summer and heavy mud in the winter were now covered with asphalt. Wooden sidewalks had given way to stone, while electric lights illuminated the newly erected buildings in the downtown.

As the sun rose on June 20, Los Angeles residents dressed for work and school, thinking perhaps only of the day ahead. Few were focused on the ongoing debate in faraway Washington, D.C., as to whether to remain on the gold standard or tie America's currency to silver. More likely, they were absorbed by news from the Chicago Exposition or by the debate about the advisability of widening First Street.

European investors, however, were so worried about the uncertainty of the U.S. monetary system that they had been steadily withdrawing their gold for the last few months. The exodus of capital had sent stock prices plunging, and suddenly all the financial machinations of the last twenty-five years—the massive expansion of railroads, the mismanagement of those companies, rampant stock manipulation, and monopolistic practices—came to an abrupt halt. By June, gold was scarce—and that meant everyone wanted some. Unstable banks began to fail at an alarming rate.

Los Angeles had always considered itself protected from the country's financial vicissitudes. The last major upheaval in the U.S. economy had been twenty years earlier, and its effects had taken two years to travel the three thousand miles west from New York. Even after two banks in nearby San Bernardino shut their doors, the *Los Angeles Times* reassured readers that the city's banks were strong, routinely handling 66 percent more funds in 1893 than they had three years earlier. "Los Angeles has her financial house in good order and has no reason to fear contagion from the prevailing epidemic," said a June 19 article. "To use an expressive phrase of the day, 'Los Angeles is all right!'"

But the soothing words of the newspaper did no good. On the day after Governor Markham gave his speech on the glories of California, Los Angeles investors developed an irrational, almost unexplainable, fear that their local banks were running out of gold coin. No one event triggered the panic, but all of a sudden hundreds of people became convinced they might lose their savings unless they immediately withdrew their money from the town's vaults.

They rushed in frenzy toward the junction of Temple, Spring, and Main streets, home to most of the city's financial institutions. They surged into the banks, desperate to hold their cash and make sure it was safe. The First National Bank had recently installed a curved mahogany counter that let tellers serve several customers at a time. What had seemed like a business innovation in good times was a detriment now, as the clerks doled out pile after pile of $20 gold pieces at a rate that threatened to deplete the bank's money supply.

Nearby, so many worried depositors had swarmed the City Bank that its president posted a sign saying it would "temporarily suspend" paying depositors. An hour later, the University Bank drew curtains across its windows and posted a notice: "Bank closed. Depositors will be paid in full."

By dawn the next day, scores of men in dark suits and bowler hats and women in mutton-sleeve dresses were lined up along Main Street, jostling one another as they tightly clutched their bank books and watched for signs that the banks would open. Within a few hours the crowd was so thick there was no room to walk on the sidewalk. Blue-suited police officers herded clusters of people against a bank building, where many peered anxiously through the arched windows to see if there was any activity inside. The clock on the wall of the nearby Nadeau Building tolled ten o'clock, but the banks remained ominously closed.

It seemed like most of Los Angeles's fifty thousand residents had come to the financial district either to withdraw their life savings or to gawk at desperate faces. "It was not the usual morning-go-to-work crowd, but a strange race of people who seemed to have taken possession of the city," one paper commented.

The doors of the City Bank and the University Bank remained shut. When the president of the Los Angeles National Bank opened the bank's iron gates, he was met by a cheer, but the joy was short-lived. Moments after he went back inside, a clerk slapped a sign on the front door announcing that those wishing to withdraw their money would get only a portion of what they were owed. The Farmers and Merchants Bank, the city's oldest and biggest bank, on the corner of Main and Commercial streets, opened on time, but so many people crowded inside that the bank paid out $400,000 by noon, leaving just $43,000 in its vaults. By the early afternoon, customers had taken $3 million out of the city's nineteen banks, forcing six to shut their doors as demand was outstripping supply.

Around one o'clock, just as it seemed the frenzy would only escalate, a rumor began to spread downtown that Isaias Hellman, one of the founders of the Farmers and Merchants Bank, was coming to Los Angeles. Hellman's reputation in Los Angeles was legendary. He had gotten his start as a clerk in a dry-goods store back in the days when Los Angeles was more Mexican pueblo than American city, and had risen to be California's richest and most influential financier. He was now the president of the Nevada Bank in San Francisco and had investments in water, gas, and rail lines up and down the state. Most important, his reputation as a conservative banker, one who insisted on keeping large gold reserves on hand at all times, was impeccable. Old-timers still remembered how Hellman had smoothed over the last bank panic back in 1875.

"Hellman is in town, Hellman is in town!" people shouted as they streamed toward the San Fernando Depot, just a few blocks from downtown. As they reached the train station, they encountered a most unusual scene. Hellman, a short, austere-looking Jewish man with gold-rimmed glasses and a dark Vandyke beard, dressed in a black frock coat and a top hat, stood by the tracks. A cadre of guards surrounded an armored rail car and watched carefully as workers heaved bags of gold into a Wells Fargo Express wagon.

The wagon laden with gold lurched forward and started its trip to the Farmers and Merchants Bank just a few blocks away. Isaias and his brother Herman, the bank's vice president, rode ahead, their grim faces reflecting the seriousness of their mission. Shortly after the bags were brought inside the bank, the two men started to heap mounds of gold coin on the mahogany counter, in plain sight of the worried customers. Hellman had brought more than $500,000 from his personal account in San Francisco (about $11 million in 2006 dollars), and all that coin soon became towers of gold stacked on the counter, a testament to the financial strength of the Farmers and Merchants Bank.

The sight of that shiny metal was a tonic. As the frantic crowd watched the golden towers grow, its panic subsided. Many customers redeposited the funds they had withdrawn in such frenzy. By the end of the day, Farmers and Merchants' coffers were replenished; in fact, deposits were up by $100,000.

As the word of Hellman's gesture spread, frightened customers at other banks calmed down. It soon became clear that the crunch was just temporary and that there really was enough money to go around. The panic ended.

Never before had the California economy depended so much on the actions of one man. It would not be the last time.

TWO

NEW NAMES, NEW LIVES

1817–1859

On January 12, 1817, six men walked slowly through the frozen dirt streets of Reckendorf, a small valley town nestled by the Baunach River in Bavaria. It was the dead of winter and the sun cast a feeble light as the men trudged toward the mayor's office, adjusting their pace to that of seventy-three-year-old Mordel Hellmann and his sixty-seven-year-old brother, Jesaias. The men passed familiar landmarks—a church, half-timbered houses, a brewery, the ruins of a castle—on their way to swear allegiance to a new king.

The Hellmanns had made this pilgrimage before. Over the centuries, Reckendorf had been ruled by a succession of masters, some tolerant, others greedy, a few ruthless. The village, with 950 residents clustered in worn-stone-and-red-roofed houses, was too insignificant to be the prize in any fight, but its history had been entwined with the wars, battles, and rivalries that had swept central Europe since the eighth century. Bishops, monks, knights, and princes had all ruled the village. One law, however, had always remained constant: Jews were categorized as foreigners.

Jews had first come to Reckendorf around 1644, refugees from the devastating Thirty Years' War. So many people had died from plague, famine, and warfare that villages across the region, then part of the state of Franconia, resembled ghost towns, with scores of empty, burned houses, rotting fields, and decaying corpses. The knight ruling Reckendorf invited the Jews to take over the deserted homes because he could levy extra taxes on them that he could not demand of his Catholic subjects. It was an offer the Jews found hard to refuse, for they were prohibited from living in cities.

Over the years, the Jews never forgot that they were not citizens of Franconia, but guests who could be expelled at a moment's notice. Franconia's rulers imposed a series of laws meant to tightly control its Jewish population. Every year, Jews had to pay a lord for a letter of protection, or *Schultzbrief*, to live in Franconia. They had to pay taxes when they married, when they died, and when they were buried. Each time Jews traveled to a new town they paid an entry fee. They had to ask the town council for permission to change occupations or to shift from selling one kind of ware to another.

Reckendorf's Jews and Catholics lived side by side in an uneasy alliance, one that barely veiled the threat of violence simmering below the surface. In 1692, the Catholics, who made up two-thirds of the population, went on a rampage, killing and maiming their Jewish neighbors. Then in 1746, when Mordel Hellmann was just two years old, Reckendorf's Catholics accused the Jews of kidnapping an eight-year-old boy, purportedly to extract his blood to make Passover matzos. Angry mobs gathered along the village's narrow streets and under the spire of its church and yelled to their Jewish neighbors that they would riot against them if the boy was not returned by a certain time.

The boy's body was discovered just moments before the deadline, and his death turned out to be accidental, and not caused by the Jews. The Jews of Reckendorf were spared that day, and for decades to come they celebrated their narrow escape by fasting on the anniversary of the boy's disappearance.

As the Hellmann men walked to the mayor's office that cold winter day, they had reason to believe that life for Jews might be getting better. In 1813, after Napoleon's armies had swept through Germany, spreading notions of freedom and equality gleaned from the French Revolution, Franconia fell to Bavaria, and the new king issued an edict that promised additional freedoms. For the first time Jews were allowed to enter a trade, join a craft guild, farm, attend university, and own land, although the law banned them from peddling, their traditional occupation, and denied them the vote. They would no longer have to pay a protection tax to a lord and would now be ruled by the laws of the kingdom rather than by religious law.

While the new king wanted to bring the Jewish population into the modern era, he still wanted to limit its growth and where Jews lived. He issued an edict requiring Jews to be entered on a *Matrikel*, or list, kept by town authorities. No Jew could move into a town until another Jew died, keeping the population constant. A young man growing up in a town could not establish legal residency when he matured unless he replaced a name on the *Matrikel*, making it almost impossible for the young of the town to marry and raise families. Reckendorf's list permitted only seventy-eight Jewish families to reside in the town. If Bavarian Jews couldn't accept these new rules, they would be classified as foreign and expelled from Bavaria.

The Hellmanns' trek through Reckendorf's rutted streets was another attempt at survival in an inhospitable land. The six men would have to swear their allegiance to Maximilian I and sign their names attesting to their loyalty. For the first time, they would have to adopt surnames and no longer be known as "the son of someone." Mordel would no longer be Mordel ben Lazurus, son of Lazarus.

The clan had chosen the surname Hellmann, or light man, as its new, common last name. As the men crowded into the house of the mayor, the place where all official city business was conducted, they pledged their fealty and then signed their names. Mordel and Jesaias could not write German and used Judendeutsch, a blend of Hebrew and German, to make their mark. But their sons and nephews, Lazarus, Solomon, Marx, and Lob Hellmann, already preparing for future changes for Jews, signed their names with German script.

It was a time of light for Germany's Jews. Change was coming, and as Mordel Hellmann wrote his new name in the town register, he had reason to believe that Jews might finally be accorded respect.

Two years later, in 1819, Jesaias Hellmann died at the age of sixty-nine, leaving behind a wife, Voegele, four children, and a meager inheritance. In an attempt to help feed her family, Voegele opened a small store in her home where she sold salt, sugar, pepper, shoelaces, and matches.

Her oldest son, Maier took over the support of the family. At twenty-seven, he already was a successful cattle dealer. He bought young cows, raised them to maturity, and then sold them in markets around the region.

Cattle trading was a popular Jewish profession in Bavaria. For decades, Germany's rulers had forced Jews to work in jobs that didn't compete with the livelihood of Catholics or Protestants, who were mostly craftsmen and farmers. So most Jews went into some sort of trade. Many became exporters who bought grain, skins, and wool from farmers and sold their goods at large regional markets. Others were peddlers who bought finished products in the towns and cities and sold them to farmers in the countryside.

All of these traditionally Jewish occupations involved the issuance of credit to poor Catholic and Protestant peasants, making Jews essential to economic life in Bavaria. Non-Jewish traders often refused to deal with farmers who could not pay in cash, so the poorer peasants did business with Jews. Traders would often pay farmers cash for their crops or goods, but sell to them on credit and collect funds after crops were harvested. Cattle dealers would often rent a cow to a peasant, who would then use the animal's milk and work power in exchange for letting it graze on his pasture. The cattle dealer would then sell the cow and share a portion of the profits with the peasant. In these ways, Jews served as middlemen between rural areas and the cities, and between the peasantry and the merchants.

Voegele's second-oldest son, Solomon, became a weaver after his father's death, and in 1827, when Wolf turned twelve, he joined his older brother at the loom. The Hellmanns made woolen cloth for clothing and also wove elaborate brocade fabrics to sell.[1]

The textile trade had always been strong around Reckendorf, as many Catholic farmers raised sheep and sold the unprocessed wool to Jewish weavers, who spun it into thread and then wove it into cloth. Many weavers set up looms in their bottom floors and enlisted family members to make cloth. The more successful weavers also hired workers to make shirts or other clothing.

The nearest market for cloth was Bamberg, a beautiful walled city on the Main River about ten miles away from Reckendorf. Solomon and Wolf would take their finished goods there to sell, often spending the entire week away, returning home in time for the Friday evening Sabbath. Despite the indignities of having to pay a toll when entering a new town or having to search for lodgings that would accept Jews, weaving earned the men a decent living.

That soon changed. Weaving was one of the first crafts to be mechanized during the Industrial Revolution, and by the mid-1840s Wolf and Solomon found it increasingly difficult to compete with the price of factory-made cloth. The erosion of their livelihood forced them to try to expand the wares they sold, but their attempts were rebuffed by Reckendorf's town council, which had the right to regulate Jewish commerce. Wolf repeatedly applied for permission to sell scissors, knives, and other metal hand tools, but he was always turned down. The council stated that there were already too many other Jews selling similar items, and another vendor would saturate the market.

In December 1841, when Wolf was twenty-six, he married seventeen-year-old Sara Fleishman. The couple had known each other most of their lives, for they had grown up three houses away from each other. Sara's father was a successful cattle trader, and she brought a dowry of 700 gulden to the marriage, as well as an offer to live rent-free in one of her father's houses for ten years. With Wolf's 500 gulden in savings, the couple was fairly comfortable.

On October 3, 1842, in a stucco house on a rutted side street in Reckendorf, Sara gave birth to her first son, Isaias Wolf Hellmann. Less than a year later, on September 25, 1843, Sara had another son, Herman. Being so close in age would be both a blessing and a burden to the two brothers, who resembled one another with their round faces, brown hair, and large brown eyes. They were ready-made playmates who confided in each other, but they also sparred for dominance. Isaias, as the first born, demanded his brother's respect, a patronizing attitude Herman grew to resent. He was also brilliant, with a mind adept at math and languages, and had little patience for those he considered less clever. Herman, in contrast, was genial and easygoing and made friends easily. The two brothers complemented each other, yet frequently found their differences a source of anger.

Sara would go on to have eleven more children, although only seven of her offspring would live past infancy. Bertha was born in 1845, followed by Flora in 1846, Regina in 1848, Ernestine in 1853, and James in 1861.

Life in Reckendorf for two little boys was filled with diversions. The town sat by the banks of the Baunach River, which regularly overflowed, creating a fertile plain that was well suited for crops. The villagers both depended on and feared the flooding, and they named their church after Saint Nicholas, the patron saint of ferrymen and fishermen, in hopes he could help them navigate through the angry waters.

The river provided a wonderful place to swim in the summer and to ice-skate in the winter. The hills above the valley were dense with oak and fir, and the fields were planted with hops, offering lots of places to explore. Geese wandered freely on the dirt streets, and the boys took delight in chasing them until they squawked in protest.

Reckendorf sat in the heart of southern Bavaria's beer industry. Bamberg was famous for its smoke-flavored beer. Reckendorf's oldest brewery, the Schlossbrauerei, founded in 1597, produced both dark and light ales called

Recken Bier. Four other breweries made their own types of beer. Another of the town's main industries was the production of a particular type of tile. It was red and flat, with a curved edge that could be laid out in a pleasing scallop pattern. Houses all around Reckendorf were roofed with this trademark red tile, which contrasted nicely with the half-timbered and plastered houses.

For the Jewish community, the center of life in Reckendorf was the synagogue, an unimposing sandstone building constructed in 1727. For generations, Reckendorf's Jews had worshipped in the temple, the men coming twice daily to pray and staying all day on Saturday. The town's young boys read from the Torah in the sanctuary when they turned thirteen, their mothers and sisters listening from the women's balcony upstairs. A flat stone outside the synagogue's door was worn from the force of all the glasses broken on it during Jewish wedding ceremonies.

The Reckendorf Jewish community numbered around three hundred at its height and was one of the more prosperous Jewish communities in the region. Most Jews living in rural villages in Franconia or Bavaria relied on local cantors or traveling rabbis to lead religious services, yet Reckendorf could afford its own rabbi as early as 1762. The same year, the congregation raised enough funds to remodel the synagogue, adding an apartment for the cantor, and a *mikvah,* or ritual bath, in the basement. In 1798, after decades of being forced to carry their dead seven miles north to Ebern, the Jews of Reckendorf were finally permitted to open their own cemetery about two-thirds of a mile out of town.

By the time Isaias was born, the Hellmann clan was one of the largest of the Jewish families in Reckendorf and among the most prosperous.[2] There were about sixty-five Hellmann cousins in the town of slightly more than 1,100, with the most prominent being Wolf's older brother Maier, a successful cattle trader and an elder in the synagogue. Maier lived across the street from Wolf in a double house that had an attached barn large enough to accommodate his cattle herd in the winter.

There were other large Jewish clans in Reckendorf, and Isaias and Herman played with boys from these families, forming relationships that would survive immigration and distance. One of these clans was the Haas family, who lived in a caramel-colored, low-slung house just a few steps from the synagogue. The family dealt in cotton and textiles. Another family, the Walters, lived in a large half-timbered home with blue-green shutters near one of the town's restaurants. They traded hops for a living, doing a brisk business in this brewing region.

When Isaias started school in 1848, his classmates were all Jewish. Nine years earlier, town officials had decided that Catholics and Jews should not attend school together, so the Jewish community constructed its own building across the street from the synagogue. In the morning, the children studied reading, writing, spelling, and singing. After he turned nine, Isaias and the older boys would walk to the synagogue three afternoons a week to study Hebrew, German, and mathematics with the rabbi. Isaias was an exceptional student. One teacher characterized his intellect as "excellent."

Isaias's parents were so impressed by their son's academic abilities that they decided he should continue his studies after he turned twelve instead of starting an apprenticeship. In 1854, they enrolled him in a commercial school in Marktbreit, a mostly Protestant town on the Main River thirty-nine miles away. The school, started in 1849 by Solomon Wohl, a charismatic cantor and religious teacher, was well respected enough to attract Jews, Catholics, and Protestants. Wohl characterized the school as a place to study the science of commerce. His advertisements promised to plant "the seed of all good and noble" in its students and have the boys study religion "without pedantry."

Only half of the 108 students were Jewish, and it was the first time Isaias had ever been in such close proximity with boys of other religions. Since the students were the sons of bankers, farmers, brewers, shipowners, teachers, parsons, and small merchants, Wohl set out to train them for professional lives. The boys studied German, English, French, Italian, algebra, geometry, bookkeeping by single and double entry, music, drawing, and sports.

Learning with a man like Wohl in a sophisticated city must have opened Isaias's eyes to the possibilities of the future. It presented him with an opportunity to break away from the cloistered, regulated Jewish world of Reckendorf and join an intellectual community that was focused on the world, not just making a living. It was an exciting time to ponder the issues of the larger world, as Europe was undergoing major changes that would have a direct impact on Isaias's life.

By the time Isaias started secondary school, it was clear that the future was still limited for Jews in Bavaria. The Catholic population had rebelled against the new liberties given to Jews in 1813, because they feared losing their livelihoods. In 1819, Catholics rioted in Würzburg, a city north of Reckendorf. For two days they ran through the city streets, attacking Jews and smashing the windows of Jewish institutions. The police did little to quell the violence, and two men were killed and more than twenty others were injured. The unrest soon spread to other parts of Bavaria, including Bamberg. Hundreds of other Catholics signed petitions decrying the emancipation of Jews, starkly illustrating that Jews continued to be regarded as foreign.

By 1849, the Jewish community had new evidence that its full participation in society was a long way off. A year earlier, students, teachers, intellectuals, and others throughout central Europe had revolted against their leaders, calling for increased civil liberties, freedom of the press, and a lessening of the power of kings and the aristocracy. Full emancipation for Jews was included in the demands. Representatives from the thirty-six independent states that made up the German confederation gathered in Frankfurt to adopt a constitution for a more representative government. But the members of the parliament disagreed on too many issues to come to a consensus. The region's kings finally grew impatient with their rebellious subjects and sent in troops and police to reassert their authority.

The clampdown prompted hundreds of thousands of Germans to leave the country, including many Jews. From 1840 to 1870, more than 20,000 of Bavaria's 59,000 Jews emigrated, drastically transforming rural Jewish life. They sold their possessions and goods, and walked or rode from their tiny villages to the harbors that beckoned them—Bremen, Hamburg, Le Havre in France. They spilled into New York, Baltimore, and New Orleans and then fanned out across America, becoming peddlers, merchants, farmers, and miners.

The Bavarians joined thousands of other Jews from Prussia and France, part of a mass movement that would triple the United States' Jewish population from 50,000 in 1850 to 150,000 by 1860. Two decades after that, the Jewish population would nearly double again to 280,000.

Members of the Hellmann family and other Jews began leaving Reckendorf in large numbers in the mid-1840s. From the time Isaias and Herman were toddlers running around the house of their parents, they had watched relatives and friends pack up their bags, hug their families good-bye, and depart, rarely to be seen again. News of the missing cousins would come in snatches, as the travelers' letters were passed from house to house. At first the boys heard about ocean crossings, stormy seas, and food that went putrid. "We did not see any land for 26 days," one cousin, Louis Hellman, wrote his family in 1846. "I was seasick for three days. The food was plentiful but very bad." Then the letters relayed tales about America, about learning English and eking out a living.

On August 31, 1857, when Isaias was just fourteen years old, he and his father went to court in the nearby town of Baunach to apply for permission for Isaias to emigrate. The official in the office grilled Isaias, telling him life was tough in America. Was he sure he was ready to go? Isaias said he was certain and indicated that he had relatives who would help him financially.

It would be another nineteen months before Isaias would finally leave. He was probably waiting for Herman, who had his own visit to the district court on February 9, 1859. Before Herman was allowed to go, he had to prove he was unfit for military service. A doctor testified that Herman had a weak physique, his chest was slim and flat, and his shoulder blades were protruding. The ball of Herman's left foot was swollen because it had been frozen, meaning the youth would never qualify for the military.[3]

The court decreed that the two brothers were free to leave the land of their birth.

Hamburg in the winter of 1859 was cold and damp, and the wind blowing off the Elbe River could penetrate through thick layers of cloth. But for two boys who had traveled hundreds of miles, the lure of the harbor easily outweighed the inconvenience of the temperature. Ships of all kind bobbed in the water, flying flags from nations around the world. Huge smoke-belching ocean steamers capable of carrying hundreds of passengers were tied up near clipper ships that thrust acres of sails, masts, and rigging in the air. Smaller boats darted around the harbor, ferrying passengers and supplies to the vessels that were still waiting to anchor at a dock.

Isaias, sixteen, and Herman, fifteen, had never seen anything like it. While they had traveled with their father to Bamberg and other small cities in Bavaria, Hamburg was different. Hamburg was huge. It bustled. It heaved. In 1859, the city was more than a thousand years old, and its exchange, where merchants and financiers gathered from all over the world to do business, was regarded as an important center for commerce. Hundreds of men traded goods and money in the massive building every day, and the profits from that enterprise spilled out into the streets.

If Isaias and Herman were like most visitors, they went to the Stintfang, the hill tourists climbed to look at the Hamburg port, one of the busiest in Europe. From there, they could have caught a glimpse of the ship that would take them across the Atlantic to a new home, to a place they hoped would give them a chance to work hard and prosper, and to escape the continued indignity of being a Jew.

The boys had purchased passage on the *Hammonia*, a 2,250-ton, 510-passenger steamer captained by H. F. Schwensen. The tickets had cost about 600 gulden, equal to the salary paid a rabbi, but it meant the boys would get to New York in about two weeks. Steamers, powered by coal, had been in widespread use for only about a decade. Prior to 1850, emigrants had to sail to America on clipper ships, and the trip could take anywhere from six weeks to three months. By the end of the voyage, the food and water were often rancid.

The *Hammonia* had been built by Caird & Company of Greenock, Scotland, for the Hamburg America Line in 1855 but had immediately been chartered by the French to use during the Crimean War. It made its first commercial transatlantic voyage in 1856 and would run the Hamburg–New York City route for eight years before being sold to another company. Isaias and Herman Hellmann would share a cramped room with dozens of other passengers in the steerage compartment of the *Hammonia*, but the discomforts were minor compared to those of earlier travelers.

Most of these Jews were destined for New York, other states on the eastern seaboard, or the Midwest. But for a few, California beckoned. Or, more accurately, it glistened. With gold.

James Marshall's 1848 discovery of a chunk of the bright and malleable metal in the American River near Sacramento touched off a worldwide rush to riches, and the Jews of rural Germany were not deaf to the siren call. Newspapers throughout Europe detailed news of the discovery and reported that miners were excavating gold as fast as they could dig. For impoverished Jews looking to break free of the shackles imposed on them by the government, the notion of living in an unformed and wild society was alluring.

There is no clear count of the number of Jews who came to California in the decades after the discovery of gold. In 1860, the German Jewish traveler Israel Joseph Benjamin estimated that there were ten thousand Jews in the state, with five thousand in San Francisco and the rest scattered in smaller towns. "The lure of gold, which brought people from all lands in 1849, also brought with it a number of Abraham's progeny, who have in the meantime expanded their population to such an extent that there is no town in California where not a few of our brothers are settled, and who are dedicated to the most various occupations," wrote Rabbi Julius Eckman of San Francisco in 1856.[4] By the mid-1870s, sixteen thousand Jews lived in San Francisco, and by the 1880s it had the second-largest Jewish population in the United States after New York.[5]

Most of the Jews who came to California because of the gold rush never made a fortune in the mines. But they found something much more valuable—acceptance. So many nationalities streamed to California and so many towns sprouted overnight that there was little opportunity to discriminate. Unlike states on the East Coast, California did not have one dominant culture, and the tolerant atmosphere permitted people with varying religions and nationalities to flourish. While the legislature passed a short-lived law ordering all stores to be closed on Sunday—the Christian, not Jewish, Sabbath—the general climate was one of acceptance. "The Jews are greatly respected by the non-Jews and it may well be said that nowhere else are they regarded with as much esteem by their non-Jewish brothers, and nowhere else are they so highly valued in social or political circles, as in [San Francisco]," the traveler Benjamin wrote.[6]

California was so lightly populated and so obsessed with creating wealth that the structures of ordinary civilized life—housing, a regular supply of water, a police force, houses of worship—were not yet established. Jews who settled in the East or Midwest had to fit themselves into existing social structures. Those who came to California found a society wide open, teeming with men and women from around the world. Jews, for the first time in their lives, found easy acceptance. While there were episodes of discrimination, they were minor, and the early Jewish settlers had a chance to become the builders of California. "I have yet to speak of the social position of our brethren on the Pacific Coast," Rabbi Max Lilienthal of Cincinnati wrote to his congregation in 1876 on returning

NEW NAMES, NEW LIVES23

from a trip to California. "Here, too, we must exclaim: California is a land of wonders indeed! We, in the Eastern and Middle States, have hardly an idea of the rapid growth of this young State. We do not know what to admire the most: nature, with her bounty and inexhaustible resources, or the energy, daring enterprise and astonishing success of her men. . . . Arriving at Sacramento, my son Philip, the Cashier of the Anglo-California Bank, at once introduced me to a crowd of millionaires . . . and they were a motley crowd of both Jews and Gentiles."[7]

Isaias and Herman were traveling with three friends from Reckendorf—two Fleishman cousins and fifteen-year-old Isaac Walter. The Hellmanns were on their way to Los Angeles, a place so small and remote it barely registered on maps of California. But it was filled with the boys' relatives. Two of their Hellmann cousins had established a dry-goods store in the small town and had written home about their success and the opportunities available in that remote section of the state.

As the Hellmann brothers got ready to board the ship that would carry them across the Atlantic, they must have been worried about the arduous journey ahead. Once they arrived in New York, they would have to buy tickets for a steamer to Panama, where they would cross the isthmus by train. From Panama City, the teenagers would have to take another boat to San Francisco, and yet another south to Los Angeles.

While the hardship of the voyage was daunting, it was insignificant compared to the difficulty of leaving behind everything they held dear. Isaias and Herman knew it might be years—or never—before they saw their mother and father again, or walked up the well-worn steps into their family's small home. But the alternative to leaving was worse—a life constrained by archaic, punishing laws that repressed most attempts to get ahead. Who knew what life in America would bring? Like hundreds of thousands of immigrants before them, the Hellmann brothers must have hoped it would be a better existence than the one they were leaving behind.

COMING TO LOS ANGELES

1859

The side-paddle steamer pulled slowly toward the port of San Pedro, its chimney belching puffs of gray smoke into the warm May air. The ship was still a mile offshore but couldn't pull any closer to land or its hull would scrape the shallow bottom of the bay.

The Hellmann brothers' first glimpse of the region they intended to call home revealed marshes and mudflats stretching for miles along the shore, broken only by an occasional barrack and a spit of sand. The port was a speck on the land, an afterthought with no real moorings, and nothing suggested it would ever be anything more than a twice-monthly stop for the San Francisco–San Diego steamer.

San Pedro was $20 and twenty miles from the Hellmanns' final destination—the small pueblo of Los Angeles. Gathering up the valises they had toted from Reckendorf, the boys boarded a small boat to carry them to shore. As they stepped off the boat, dressed in dark wool coats more suited to the cold spring they had left behind in Germany than the warm weather of southern California, they were—like all travelers—accosted by drivers from two rival stage coach companies, each promising a quick ride to Los Angeles.

The trip to Los Angeles was even more grueling than the fifty-one-hour sea voyage from San Francisco. For two-and-a-half hours passengers sat squeezed together on the rough wooden planks of a Conestoga wagon, and every bounce and jerk over the narrow, rutted roads jarred their backsides and sent them crashing into one another. Drivers on that route were intent on beating the competing stage, so they whipped their broncos into a run, swirling up a dust so thick it became difficult to breathe.

Los Angeles lay east of the port in a broad basin that abutted the San

Gabriel Mountains. The Hellmann brothers' ride took them across a vast plain covered in grass that in May had already turned from green to brown. They passed golden poppies and blue lupine and ocher mustard plants that grew taller than men. Grapevines covered the lowlands next to the Los Angeles River. Cattle and sheep grazed freely on the range, their only sign of ownership an elaborate brand on their flanks.

The competing wagons raced toward their final destinations: the two hotels opposite each other on Main Street. As the Hellmanns descended from their seats into the soft light that was so particular to southern California, they stepped into a world completely different from the one they had left behind. Most of the buildings were one-story adobes with thick whitewashed walls with the most impressive houses clustered around the Plaza, the town's central square. Strings of red chilies and jerked beef decorated the storefronts, and the air was noisy with the grating sounds made by *carretas*, crude Mexican wagons whose ungreased wooden wheels scraped against the ground. People on the street conversed mostly in Spanish, while a few talked in English and the rest spoke in French or German.

It was May 14, 1859. After traveling for six weeks, the Hellmann boys had finally arrived in Los Angeles. They had come halfway across the world in hopes of building a life where they would be judged on their merits rather than their religion. The challenges were daunting. They were just fifteen and sixteen and on their own, away from their parents' home and support, with less than $100 between them. They couldn't speak either Spanish or English. If they were going to make in in this new world, they would have to adapt to it quickly, drawing on strengths they had never tapped before.

L os Angeles in 1859 was a town in transition, a place slowly evolving from Mexican to American rule. While the gold rush had brought thousands of people to northern California, transforming San Francisco almost overnight into a bustling city, southern California was still a frontier on the edge of the continent, difficult to get to and almost completely isolated.

Only 4,400 people lived in the town, with another 11,000 in the surrounding counties. There was no regularly scheduled stage coach from San Francisco or Salt Lake City, and steamers stopped at the port only a few times a month. There was no telegraph connection to San Francisco; news often took two weeks or more to reach the area. Both of the town's newspapers, the *Los Angeles Star* and *El Clamor Publico*, published news in Spanish, although the *Star* also had an English edition. But most people were illiterate. A self-selected volunteer group called the Rangers acted as a police force, and they answered to their own authority.

The isolation had not mattered when California was part of Mexico, as many families lived in self-supporting haciendas and traveled to Los Angeles only for special occasions. Mexico, which took over the region from Spain in 1833, had granted its most respected citizens vast ranchos spreading over thousands of acres. The dons built large sprawling homes to hold their families and the workers who kept the haciendas going: large groups of Native Americans who tilled the land, and dozens of cowboys who cared for the enormous herds of cattle and sheep.

In recent years, the Californios, as those upper-class native Mexicans were known, had grown enormously rich by selling beef to gold rush miners. Cattle that had sold for $3 a head before James Marshall spotted a gold nugget in the American River in 1848 went for $75 each a few years later. Many Californios, swimming in cash for the first time in their lives, treated their newfound wealth as if it would last forever. They adorned their boots with spurs made of pure gold and draped their horses with ornate silver trimmings. They decorated their houses with costly furnishings imported from around the world, and held dances where friends and relatives stayed for days, feasting on one rich meal after another. When they ran out of coin, the Californios borrowed funds from local businessmen, putting up their ranchos as collateral, convinced that gold would flow forever. "The streets were thronged throughout the entire day with splendidly mounted and richly dressed caballeros, most of whom wore suits of clothes that cost all the way from $500 to $1,000," wrote one visitor. "Everyone in Los Angeles seemed rich, everybody was rich, and money was more plentiful at that time, than in any other place of like size, I venture to say, in the world."[1]

But that way of life was not destined to last long. When California became a state in 1850, the United States promised to honor the property rights accorded when the land was part of Mexico. But many of the dons had difficulty producing papers and deeds that proved they owned their ranchos. They were forced to go to court, an expensive and laborious process that soon left many of them in debt—without their land. The cattle market crashed by 1857, never to rise again.

The face of Los Angeles was changing as well. The first significant influx of Yankees came to Los Angeles in 1841 with the Rowland-Workman wagon train. Many of the most ambitious men married the young daughters of the Californio elite, creating a sort of hybrid society that produced its own batch of the wealthy. By 1859, the time the Hellmann brothers arrived, there were three hundred European settlers in Los Angeles, and they had started to transform the quiet town into one that reflected their brand of industriousness. The exchange of gold and silver was replacing the barter of tallow and hides. The new Americans set up hauling and freighting companies, built piers to unload shipping goods, and opened dry-goods stores, drugstores, and blacksmith shops. They constructed brick buildings in place of adobes.

The clash of cultures and underlying racial tension created an almost lawless town, a place where violence ruled. A murder a day was not uncommon. Down-on-their-luck prospectors and criminals who had been run out of San Francisco by that city's vigilante committees found their way to the pueblo, poised to flee to nearby Mexico if anyone came looking for them. They gathered in Calle de los Negros, a narrow block-long alley lined with gambling halls, saloons, and houses of prostitution, all located just a short walk from the Plaza and Roman Catholic church. Crowds in the alley were so thick at times that a man had to push his way through to get to the gambling tables where monte and faro were played with octagonal $50 silver slugs. Disputes over money and cards were handled on the spot by men with Colt pistols or bowie knives. Men also laid bets at the town's numerous cockfights or bullfights. The occasional bear battles were extremely popular. "Human life at this period was about the cheapest thing in Los Angeles, and killings were frequent," one resident noted. "Nigger Alley was as tough a neighborhood, in fact, as could be found anywhere, and a large proportion of the twenty or thirty murders a month was committed there."[2]

No records remain that detail Isaias and Herman's reunion with their older cousins, but it must have been a happy affair full of news about family and friends in Reckendorf. The older cousins, Isaiah M. Hellman, twenty-eight, and Samuel M. Hellman, twenty-one (they had dropped the extra *n* upon arriving in the United States, as would Isaias and Herman), had arrived in Los Angeles five years earlier, in 1854. They had set up a small store in Bell's Row, one of the town's few two-story adobes. It was an ideal location, right near the prime intersection of Aliso and Los Angeles streets along the main route to the San Gabriel Mission. The cousins lived in an apartment in the back with another brother, also named Herman, who would soon return to Reckendorf. Their sister, Jette, twenty-three, lived next door with her new husband, Jacob Weil. Other Jews had also set up shop in Bell's Row, making it a welcoming Jewish enclave for the two brothers.

A crude hand-lettered sign, "Hellman and Bro. Books Stationery & Cigars," rested above the store's doorway. Businesses were so transitory in Los Angeles that few took the time to make proper signs. Brothers joined in business and then split apart just as quickly. Men who traveled overland together or met on the steamer from Panama to San Francisco combined forces, only to dissolve their companies when they couldn't earn enough to support themselves and their families.

The Hellmans' store stocked everything that could make life on the frontier comfortable: Havana cigars, bundles of writing paper, hats, clothes, and books. The brothers, like other merchants in the area, not only supplied settlers in the pueblo, but also sold items across a vast expanse of the West. They traded with the Californios still living in their ranchos outside of town, and with the Mormon settlements in Bakersfield and Salt Lake City, Utah. Trade to the Mormons had become so important that the *Los Angeles Star* reported in February 1859 that in less than a month, sixty wagons laden with $70,000 in goods had left for Salt Lake City. Another one-hundred-ton shipment was set to leave soon.

Isaias had a cot in the back storeroom, a bed so narrow and hard that he frequently woke up with stiff, cramped legs. It was uncomfortable, but sleeping in the storeroom, surrounded by clothes covered in cloth to keep off the dust, stacks of shoes, and bundles of tobacco, thrust Isaias right into the heart of his cousins' business. He had been exposed to accounting and business practices at his school in Marktbreit, and he now applied his knowledge to bettering the store. He spent his days arranging and rearranging the items on display, trying to make them irresistible. "I. W. Hellman immediately showed much ability and greatly improved his cousin's [*sic*] business," wrote

Harris Newmark, a friend who had arrived in Los Angeles only five years before Isaias.[3]

Isaias's salary was $25 a month. Before he could speak English, his cousins sent him to the countryside, where he peddled lace, handkerchiefs, ladies hose, beads, and cheap jewelry to the women of the haciendas.[4] As the clerk, he also was responsible for keeping the store clean, no small task, since Los Angeles was a town of dirt. In the summer, dust would blow through the city, making its way into every crevice and hole, settling on top of all the goods for sale. At times it was ankle deep, stinging eyes and noses with each step. In the winter rains, the dust on the unpaved roads turned into mud, bogging down both horses and men.

While the banks of the Los Angeles River were verdant with grapevines, gardens, and citrus trees, shrubs and vines that could hold down dirt were scarce in outlying areas. Los Angeles had a peculiar water distribution system, one that began during Mexican rule and was continued by the Americans. The main source of water was the Los Angeles River, which meandered from the mountains in the east until it emptied in the Pacific Ocean. Early settlers just scooped up water from the river, but eventually they built a series of ditches to carry water into the fields for irrigation. The ditches were called *zanjas*, and the *zanjero*, the man in charge of the ditches, was paid more than the mayor. The ditches often got clogged with debris and garbage, so private homes and businesses frequently contracted with private water purveyors. In 1859, a man with a long walrus mustache nicknamed Bill the Waterman, delivered it "fresh" from the Los Angeles River.

There were few other amenities in frontier Los Angeles. There was a planked wooden sidewalk outside the Hellmans' store, and the building's second-story veranda formed a canopy over the walk. But there were no sewers and no garbage collection. When Isaias swept, he pushed debris into a street already littered with broken glass, pieces of paper, and garbage.

In the heat, the pueblo smelled acrid, as the garbage and raw sewage baked in the sun. Packs of wild dogs sometimes gnawed at carcasses left to decompose in the street. When spring arrived, the air was filled with the smell of boiling pitch from nearby tar pits. Once a year, when the rains had long passed, the citizens of Los Angeles would whitewash their adobe houses and then cover the roofs with a fresh layer of tar and sand.

Business wasn't exactly brisk in the Los Angeles of 1859. Most people bartered hides or tallow for goods, only occasionally paying with gold dust or coin. Whenever the Hellman brothers amassed gold, they would hide it at night in buckskin bags pushed deep in the folds of their merchandise. Then they would send it to San Francisco by steamer to store in a bank.

The slow pace of business permeated everything. While the Hellmans kept their store open from 8 A.M. to 9 P.M., it wasn't uncommon for hours to pass without any customers. When trade lagged, the shopkeepers on Bell's Row would drag a barrel to an adjacent store, set it up under the wide adobe ledge of the window, and play a few rounds of cards. Isaias took advantage of the slow times to study both English and Spanish. He made friends with a young Catholic priest, Francisco Mora, who agreed to tutor him.[5] Mora nicknamed him "Ysaia," which was Spanish for Isaias.[6]

Isaias adapted to the city's primitiveness. He worked hard, determined to repay his family members for their contribution to his fare from Reckendorf. He also needed to send money back to Bavaria for dowries for his unmarried sisters. "I wanted to get ahead, and I did not count the hours until my work was done and I gave my employer the best service I could, and I expected to be well paid for my efforts," Isaias later recalled.[7]

While he was grateful to his cousins for the job, he regarded his position as temporary. Isaias came from too long a line of Jewish men who had been unable to work in the professions they desired for him to be satisfied with answering to a boss. In this new world, he wanted to succeed by the new rules and leave the restrictions of Germany far behind. He had not been in Los Angeles for very long before he started to look for his opening.

W hile Isaias was laboring in the dusty pueblo, his brother Herman stayed in the crude harbor of San Pedro, a cluster of wood warehouses and small homes on the edge of the Pacific Ocean. There hadn't been room in the cousins' store for two inexperienced workers, so Herman had taken a job with Phineas Banning, the man whose barge had transported the Hellman boys from their steamer to the shores of southern California. Banning, twenty-nine, a barrel-chested, round-faced man with penetrating eyes, personified the new breed of Southern California citizen who rejected the languid life of the Californio for the opportunities available to any ambitious man.

Banning had come from Delaware in 1851 and within a few years had built a transportation network that spanned the entire region. His fleet of fifty stagecoaches and mule wagons hauled passengers and freight from San Pedro to Los Angeles and all the way to Fort Yuma on the Arizona border, as well as to the gold mines on the Kern River. Banning built a steam-driven lumber mill at the port and warehouses to store the hides that were waiting to be shipped to New England. In later years, he would construct the region's first railroad.

Working for Banning gave Herman a chance to see American ingenuity up close. Banning seemed to find opportunities everywhere he looked. He also delighted in training young men in business, and many of his protégés went on to hold prominent positions in Los Angeles.

Banning took a special interest in Herman, even inviting him to live with his wife and three sons. He liked to play tricks, though, and a friendship with Banning required a tolerance for jokes. One time Banning ordered Herman to take his wife to Los Angeles in a two-horse buggy, even though Herman was too inexperienced to drive such a fancy carriage. Banning ignored Herman's concerns, and the young man soon found himself clutching the reins of an out-of-control buggy as the horses raced through the pueblo's streets. Herman somehow managed to get Mrs. Banning to her destination safely. Another time Banning invited Herman to dinner and served pork, which Jews did not eat.

September 1859 brought a heat wave to Los Angeles, and the temperature climbed day after day until it reached 104 degrees in the shade. As the Jewish holidays approached, Isaias was confronted with how different Jewish life was in Los Angeles compared to Reckendorf. For the last sixteen years he had spent Rosh Hashanah, the Jewish New Year, inside the cool stone walls of Reckendorf's ancient synagogue, listening to the primal sound that came from the blowing of the shofar, the ram's horn that signaled a new beginning. But there was no temple in Los Angeles, no formal place to worship, which meant the Jews had to pray either in someone's home or in a public meeting hall.

The first Jews had settled permanently in Los Angeles only during the previous decade. The 1850 census recorded eight men with Jewish surnames, and all of them were bachelors with stores in Bell's Row. Over the next decade, the Jewish population grew to nearly sixty men and their families, and a good proportion of those were Hellmans or their relations from Reckendorf. By the time of Isaias's arrival, there were at least twelve Hellman relatives living in the town, including two of Isaias's maternal uncles.

From Los Angeles's early years, Jews dominated the merchant class. They came to the pueblo and immediately opened dry-goods stores, stationery stores, and blacksmith shops—anything that might flourish in a slow-moving frontier economy. Bachman and Brothers had the biggest wholesale grocery store, in a two-story brick building with a handsome balcony on the second floor. Solomon Lazard ran the most prosperous dry-goods store in a corner of Bell's Row. Fleishman & Sichel, run by Isaias's relatives, was a thriving hardware store.

Since Los Angeles was so isolated, most of these merchants had partners in either San Francisco or New York, men who could select and ship new merchandise for the stores. Frequently, these were family members, for early Jewish settlers relied on extended kinship networks to keep down their costs.

From the start, the Jews had been accepted in Los Angeles. By the time Isaias arrived, two Jews were serving on the city council and one had been elected city treasurer. Jews, including Isaias, were also welcome in the Masonic organizations. Life in America was different than in Germany, where a man was a Jew first, second, and last. "They form an enterprising and intelligent part of the population and have come together from all parts of the globe," a visitor noted in 1862. "They are in trade and business and own a number of vineyards. Indeed, the largest vineyard and the one in the best condition belongs to a Jew—Mr. Morries."[8]

Formal religious life did not begin in the pueblo until 1854, when a group of men bought a plot of land in Chavez Ravine, about one mile northeast of the Plaza, and laid out a burial ground. They called themselves the Hebrew Benevolent Society and charged $5 to join the organization and another $1 a month for dues.[9] In April 1855, the society advertised for bids to build a brick wall with a double wooden gate to enclose the cemetery. The newspapers praised the action, noting it came before the Protestants even had a burial ground.[10] The Jewish community soon planted trees, bushes, and flowers.

The Hebrew Benevolent Society, like similar groups scattered throughout the West, organized informal religious services. While there was no rabbi to officiate over deaths, births, or marriages, there was a man who had helped start two synagogues in the East before coming to Los Angeles, and who was tapped as the pueblo's spiritual leader. Joseph Newmark had come with his wife, Rosa, and six children on a ship around Cape Horn, arriving in Los Angeles in 1854. He joined his nephews Harris and J. P. Newmark, and the family quickly became the backbone of the Jewish community. While his daughter Sarah married her first cousin, Harris Newmark, his other daughters all married French Jews. Matilda, the eldest, married Maurice Kremer, Caroline married Solomon Lazard, and Harriet married Eugene Meyer. All the men would play an important role in the development of Los Angeles.

Joseph Newmark had been trained as a *shochet*, or ritual butcher, and his presence meant the community could eat kosher meat. In 1860, he arranged for a local baker to make matzo, the unleavened cracker, for Passover. "He came to our bakery to see that the matzos, that father agreed to make, conformed strictly to the Jewish ritualistic law," recounted Joseph Mesmer, the baker's son. "Everything within the bake room had to be gone over from floor to ceiling: floors washed, walls and ceilings whitewashed, dough bins, even though they were ever so clean, had to be washed and scrubbed with soap and water and all materials cleaned and polished and nothing could be done, except under his ever-watchful eye and when he absented himself, all work had to cease."[11]

While the Jews mingled freely with other residents of Los Angeles, they also formed a tight social group. They ate at one another's houses, played cards together, and attended one another's marriages and funerals. Holidays like Passover or the end of Yom Kippur had always been important in Europe, and these immigrants continued the tradition. Isaias formed some friendships that would last him the rest of his life. He grew close to Harris and Sarah Newmark and to Eugene Meyer and his brother Constant, who came from France and were clerking in a cousin's dry-goods store. He spent a lot of time with all his cousins as well. "Social life was in very narrow limits, the city being small in population and in size," Isaias wrote years later. "Every man and woman was known to each other and good fellowship was the rule."

So Isaias, who had been born in a town that Jews had inhabited for more than 220 years, found himself spending Rosh Hashanah in a pueblo that had its first significant Jewish settlement only 9 years earlier. Instead of listening to a rabbi during the High Holidays of Rosh Hashanah and Yom Kippur, he prayed with an ordinary man. Instead of chanting Hebrew inside the familiar sandstone walls of the synagogue in Reckendorf, he prayed inside the walls of a new brick building on Main and Spring streets, owned by John Temple, a Catholic Yankee.

The next few years would bring even more daunting challenges.

A SAFE AND A DREAM

1861–1868

The first hint of the string of natural disasters that would completely transform the pueblo of Los Angeles came on the evening of December 24, 1861. Until then, the southern California winter had been normal, with bouts of cold rain followed by stretches of clear weather. But on Christmas Eve it was as if the heavens gave way. Sheets of rain pelted down without mercy, drenching adobes, filling rivers, and turning land into a morass of ankle-sucking mud. "The rain has been the severest for eleven years," one surveyor noted in his journal. "Probably as much as six or seven inches fell in about forty hours. It was very hard on these adobe houses. Several have fallen, one row of stores, among the rest, involving a loss of many thousand dollars."[1]

The rain pushed the Los Angeles River higher and higher until a waist-high wall of water jumped its banks and rushed through downtown, forcing mud and debris into a line of stores on Bell's Row. As the surging waters inundated Hellman and Brother, Isaias and his two cousins rushed inside to salvage any goods they could. The three men started to grab shoes, books, tobacco, and other merchandise, but the roiling, icy waters made maneuvering difficult. They fled when the saturated adobe walls started to crumble.

When the floodwaters receded, Los Angeles had been transformed. The facade of the Church of Our Lady the Queen of Angeles, which had stood sentinel near the Plaza for forty years, had melted away, its straw and mud bricks unable to withstand the water's onslaught. The cascading river ripped out thousands of grapevines by their roots, and their twisted branches became a wall of detritus that tore at whatever lay in its path. Sand lay a foot thick over once-fertile orchards. Thousands of cattle and sheep drowned. Roads became so impassable that Los Angeles went without mail for five straight weeks.

The entire state suffered that year. From early November to the end of January, thirty-seven inches of rain fell in San Francisco. Rain and melting snow turned the Sacramento and San Joaquin valleys into an inland sea, 250 to 300 miles long and 20 to 60 miles wide. When Leland Stanford returned to his Sacramento home after his gubernatorial inauguration, he traveled by rowboat—and climbed into a second-story window. When the rain stopped, it made the news: "On Tuesday last the sun made its appearance," the *Los Angeles Star* noted. "The phenomenon lasted several minutes and was witnessed by a great number of persons."

The heavy rains were followed by two years of drought, years of sun and wind so relentless that the grasses covering the valleys and gentle hills running from Los Angeles to the ocean twenty miles away turned a brittle brown. In the spring of 1863, when residents thought the drought couldn't get any worse, hot winds from the desert carried in millions of grasshoppers that ate the little pasturage that was left.

Most of the cattle and sheep that roamed the hills began to die as, weakened and bony, they desperately searched for food and water. While some of the more resourceful ranchers sent their herds to the mountains or into Mexico, or dumped them at fire sale prices into the glutted northern markets, many cattle owners lacked sufficient capital to move their stock. Soon, voyagers taking the stage from the port of San Pedro to Los Angeles saw hills heaped with decaying carcasses rotting under a merciless sun. In 1860, the census had recorded seventy thousand cattle in Los Angeles County; by 1865 the number dropped to twenty thousand. "Thousands of carcasses strew the plains in all directions, a short distance from this city, and the sight is harrowing in the extreme," wrote the editor of the *Southern News* on April 6, 1864. "Famine has done its work, and nothing can save what few cattle remain on the desert California ranches."

The gods weren't finished yet. More disasters followed. A smallpox epidemic raced through Sonoratown, a small section of Los Angeles north of the Plaza populated by Mexicans from Sonora. The plague also killed hundreds of Native Americans. There were so many deaths that town officials stopped tolling the church bells at each passing. In fear, people stayed in their homes and business came to a standstill.

The series of natural disasters finally wiped out the old leisurely way of life, as many Californios saw their cattle die and their land auctioned off to pay their debts. The delinquent-tax rolls were filled with the names of men who had once been the richest in the region: Pio Pico, the last governor of Mexican California; Jose Sepulveda, who in 1852 commanded more than one hundred thousand acres of land and a vast herd of cattle; and Manuel Dominguez, owner of the Rancho San Pedro. Abel Stearns, a Yankee who had married Arcadia Bandini, the daughter of a rich landowner, had so many back taxes that the newspaper listed two pages of his delinquencies. To survive, many of these men were forced to sell their land for rock-bottom prices to the Yankees and Europeans then settling the region. Some land went for as little as 10¢ an acre.

The breakout of the Civil War in 1861 further decimated the economy. At first, the war seemed far away. Residents didn't see a copy of President Abraham Lincoln's inaugural address for eight days. They didn't hear about the firing on Fort Sumter and the start of the Civil War for twelve days. The town had long been Democratic, with a smattering of Whigs, Know-Nothings, and a few antislavery Republicans. But soon it was bitterly divided between the Union and the Confederacy. Many settlers had come to Los Angeles from the South and were sympathetic to the Confederacy's pleas to secede peacefully from the Union. They made the Bella Union—the city's finest two-story hotel—their headquarters, and hung a huge portrait of General Pierre Beauregard in the saloon, toasting the Southern general every time they sang their favorite anti-Union ditty: "We'll hang Abe Lincoln to a tree. / We'll drive the Bloody Tyrant from our dear native soil." Union supporters who used to dine at the hotel, including Isaias, were barred from entering.[2]

Tension grew when Southern sympathizers plotted to take over Los Angeles by riding into the Plaza and hoisting the Bear Flag to declare southern California independent of the pro-Union north. Governor John Downey quickly dispatched troops, turning Los Angeles into a military town swarming with men in blue uniforms.

The Jews of Los Angeles were caught in the bitter divide. Many Jews had settled in the South before making their way to Los Angeles and felt affinity for their former home. While most opposed slavery, others supported states' rights or felt they couldn't support the Union after General Ulysses S. Grant prohibited Jews from trading with the Union army.

The first Los Angeles election in 1861 after the outbreak of the Civil War put many pro-Confederacy Democrats in power. Newspapers blamed the Jews for the Democratic sweep. "Nearly the whole of the Jewish population of this city voted the secessionist ticket, and we sincerely believe many of them will live to rue the day they did so," wrote the *Southern News* on September 6, 1861. "That a foreigner should come from a land of tyranny and oppression to a free and enlightened republic, from a land where he is no better than a serf, having no choice in the selection of his rulers; should come here and give his vote and influence against our government and in favor of the same state of affairs he left behind in the old world, seems passing strange." The tirade prompted thirty Jews to cancel their subscriptions to the newspaper.

It was under these difficult conditions that Isaias opened his own store on April 15, 1865—the day Abraham Lincoln was assassinated, and six years after he had first arrived in Los Angeles. Isaias was no longer the smooth-faced, sheltered youth who had first come to America. He wore gold-rimmed glasses and had grown a Vandyke—a goatee and mustache named after the seventeenth-century Flemish painter—that made him look almost as old as his twenty-two years. He now spoke English and Spanish fluently and knew most everyone in town.

Isaias had been thinking about opening his own store almost from the moment he landed in Los Angeles, so he had lived frugally. He got his opportunity when the merchant Adolph Portugal returned to Germany and put his store on Main Street near Commercial up for sale for $525. Isaias bought the store and its contents and invested another $1,000. He tried to create an elegant atmosphere where customers would feel pampered as soon as they walked through the door, an environment far from the mud and disorder outside. Isaias painted and plastered the walls, installed five gaslit chandeliers, and placed a scale to measure gold dust and nuggets on the gleaming new counter. Hats, caps, trimmings, bolts of cloth, and boots and shoes lined the shelves. A $160 Tilden & McFarland safe stood sentry in the rear, a symbol of stability and security.[3] Isaias touted his new business in newspaper ads that promised the "finest dress goods" and the "lowest cash prices."

Operating a dry-goods store during this turbulent era posed many risks, and a number of long-established merchants gave up their businesses just as Isaias was starting out. Isaias's cousins Isaiah and Samuel had dissolved their partnership three years earlier after the flood devastated their store. One cousin set up another dry-goods store, and the other opened a stationery store.

The risk came from the fact that most business was done on credit rather than in coin, and any break in a long link of relationships could mean disaster. Isaias could have numerous customers, but if they all bought on credit he would not have the money to pay the wholesaler from whom he bought his goods. If the wholesaler was shorted, he might not be able to pay the businessman running the supply store in San Francisco, and that merchant might not be able to repay the New York bank that extended credit. So a merchant needed to be able to assess a customer's credit risk, often just by gut instinct.

The opening day of Isaias's business was not auspicious. Isaias stood in his store, ready to greet new customers, but only three people made purchases. Isaias dutifully recorded the sales in his new red-and-black Boston ledger book: "J. M. Griffith - $6." "Adolph Portugal - $20." "Meyer and Lowenstein - $175.48."[4]

Determined to keep his prices low, Isaias worked without a middleman whenever possible. He periodically took the steamer to San Francisco so he could wander the wharves and see firsthand the exotic items carried on the great seafaring clipper ships from China. He meandered on Sacramento Street, where stores bulged with goods imported from around the globe. Isaias got to know who sold the freshest tobacco, whose linens were the finest, and whose candy could withstand a trip back to Los Angeles on a boat rocked by the seas.

There were a number of men from Reckendorf living in San Francisco, and Isaias came to rely on them for an informal merchandising network. The mutually beneficial business arrangement would extend throughout the rest of these men's lives. One of the men Isaias depended on was Kalman Haas, who came to the United States in 1854 and settled in Portland, Oregon, where he and his brother Charles opened up Haas Brothers, a dry-goods store. Kalman moved down to San Francisco to establish a buying office and eventually joined H. Levi and Company, a wholesale grocer on California Street. Isaias could trust Kalman to offer him the lowest prices on food and other items.

Isaias could also call upon his old friends the Walters, whose carpet and furnishing store was regarded as the finest in San Francisco. Isaias had emigrated with one of the younger brothers, Isaac, who in 1865 was working in the firm's Portland office. D.N. & E. Walter was on California Street, just a few blocks away from a dry-goods store run by their first cousins from Reckendorf, Herman, Nathan, David, and Leopold Bachman.

In subsequent years, the group would refer to themselves as the "Reckendorf aristocracy," but that was after they had amassed millions. The Haases would go on to open an extremely profitable liquor company, and one of their descendants would eventually take over the Levi Strauss Company. The Walters would marry into some of the most prominent Jewish families in America, including the Contents and the Seligmans, and branch out into real estate and other investments. But in 1865, they were all still small-time merchants struggling to keep their place in San Francisco's highly competitive mercantile industry.

By 1867, business had started to pick up. Silver and lead were discovered in mines on the eastern side of the Sierra Nevada in Inyo County. Miners flocked to the region to work the shafts, and when they returned they infused cash into the economy. Civil War veterans and settlers tired of long winters heard about southern California's temperate climate and ideal growing conditions, and soon long lines of immigrant wagon trains were on their way to Los Angeles. These new residents meant more business in the stores crowded downtown.

Since Isaias had a safe, he offered to store gold and other valuables free of charge for his customers. Merchants and farmers turned to Isaias because there were no banks in Los Angeles. Those with gold could ship their coin via Wells Fargo Express to banks in San Francisco, but the company charged a steep $1 surcharge on every package. So most residents still hid their money under mattresses or floorboards, far away from the safety of a locked vault. Soon, Isaias had more than $200,000 in his safe from men like Miguel Leonis, William Workman, and Jose Mascarel (about $3 million in 2006 dollars).

Isaias didn't feel completely comfortable storing all that gold. "It began to worry me after a while, for I feared they would make some mistake and think they had some more money than was the case, or that some complication would result," Isaias remembered later. "I spoke of this to Leonis or one of them one day but he laughed and said there would be no trouble. Then he suggested that I use the money and let him establish a credit for the amount and draw on me when he wished it, but this did not seem like a proper business."[5]

Banking remained a side business for Isaias—until he had a run-in with a bleary-eyed, irate miner. The Irishman, covered with dust, came into Isaias's dry-goods store and strode past the piles of pants, hats, and shoes displayed on the counter. The Irishman had been in and out of the store a number of times in previous days, gloriously drunk, and always eager to take more money from the worn leather pouch he had stored in Isaias's safe. Now sober, the man decided to withdraw his remaining funds. But when Isaias retrieved the pouch, once bulging with gold, it was nearly empty. The Irishman exploded. "You dirty Jew!" he yelled. "You have stolen my gold." He lunged, reaching for Isaias as if to strike him.

A friend calmed down the Irishman. "Pat, that will not do," said the friend. "It is not true. I have been with you. I told you not to drink and gamble, but you would do it. You took this gold out yourself and you must apologize to Mr. Hellman."

The Irishman backed away from Isaias and fled suddenly into the street. Isaias was shaken from the encounter and felt lucky to be alive. "What is to prevent one of those fellows from cracking me over the head, sticking a knife in my ribs, or shooting me?" he later recalled thinking.[6] Nothing, he realized.

Californians had a deep mistrust of banks. In 1849, when California was still a territory ruled by a military governor, its leading citizens gathered in Monterey for a constitutional convention to create new state laws. The delegates voted to permit private individuals or associations to accept deposits of gold and silver, but prohibited the creation of corporate banks that could mint their own paper money. They also made it illegal for banks to loan money or issue certificates of deposit that circulated like money.

This distrust of bankers had its roots in the 1830s, when "free banking" was introduced in eastern states. Americans viewed the idea of a central federal bank as an excessive concentration of power, so the federal government issued only a small amount of paper money. Instead, states chartered and regulated banks, but not very closely. Almost anyone could set himself up as a banker, with few requirements on how much money he had to keep in reserve. Each bank was permitted to issue its own money, so hundreds of different currencies from different states circulated. These notes were, in theory, exchangeable for gold. Some of the banks were sound and solvent, but others were not, and when the economy soured, thousands of Americans found themselves holding worthless slips of paper.

Most of the delegates to the 1849 convention remembered the havoc of the free-banking era and were determined to set California up as a state run on hard currency based on gold or silver, rather than the paper banknotes so common in the East. And if anyplace could be run on gold, they thought, it was California. There was gold everywhere, to be had by merely leaning down and picking up nuggets from the banks of the rivers that spilled from the Sierra Nevada—at least that was the myth. Gold was so abundant that in California it was valued at $16 an ounce in the early days of the gold rush, while it brought $20 an ounce in the East. The delegates thought there was no need for middlemen such as bankers.

In the early days of the gold rush, everything was paid for in gold. Miners and merchants in San Francisco and Sacramento carried around buckskin bags that were wide enough around the top that they could reach in their hands and easily grab a few pinches of gold dust. But using gold dust as a means of payment soon proved impractical. Gold dust and nuggets were heavy, and varied in purity. A pinch of gold often depended on the size of a man's fingers. As weight began to determine the value of gold, miners had to start carrying around their own scales to measure out gold.

In the early 1850s, private mints sprang up in San Francisco. These operations would take a miner's gold and melt it down, extracting pure ore, which they formed into gold slugs marked with the mint's name and seal of approval. Soon these slugs, as well as coins from Mexico, France, England, Germany, and elsewhere, circulated as currency. There was still a need for U.S. gold coins, as all import duties had to be paid in United States coin— and virtually all goods in California at that time were imported from somewhere else. The federal government finally established a U.S. mint in San Francisco in 1854 and began making U.S. gold coins to alleviate the shortage.

Despite the ban on banks—which lasted until the late 1870s—dozens of men set themselves up as bankers in San Francisco and Sacramento. By the end of 1853, there were nineteen banks in San Francisco alone. These businessmen held miners' gold, sent it back to eastern banks for them, and exchanged it for paper drafts, which were more easily traded. Since these banks were illegal—the state created no oversight for them because they technically didn't exist—many of them went in and out of business quickly. With so much instability, a banker's reputation became extremely important. But these bankers still could not issue their own paper money in California. Distrust of paper was so ingrained that when President Abraham Lincoln introduced federal greenbacks during the Civil War, they were honored in California for only a fraction of their face value.

While there were numerous banks in San Francisco, there were none in Los Angeles. Small farmers and merchants who wanted to borrow money to expand their businesses were forced to turn to bankers hundreds of miles away or to borrow money from private businessmen, who lent funds out at 4 to 5 percent compounded interest each month. Some even charged 15 percent interest. These usurious rates had accelerated the downfall of the Californio elite, who often borrowed small amounts using their land as collateral and watched in astonishment—and fear—as the compounded interest created enormous debt. Despite the difficulties caused by a tight money supply, few in Los Angeles regarded banks with approval.

Isaias's altercation with the Irishman prompted him to reconsider the way he had been handling other people's money. Men had just been leaving their gold with him and taking it out as they pleased, with no record of deposits or withdrawals. Isaias wasn't making interest on the gold, and he could see that it was no longer safe.

Isaias decided to set up formal banking functions. He realized that he should buy the miners' gold outright, offer to keep the funds on hand, and issue a passbook to record all transactions. Customers could write drafts against their deposits. He would use the money to loan funds to others, which would encourage new business and capital growth.

So that Saturday afternoon (he kept his store open on the Jewish Sabbath in recognition of American shopping habits), right after the altercation with the Irishman, Isaias rushed over to the printers and ordered deposit and withdrawal slips labeled "I. W. Hellman, Banker."

With those slips, Isaias become Los Angeles's first banker. His new business would lead southern California into prosperity and stability and turn Isaias into a financier with an international reputation.

Isaias's brother Herman also had to experiment with various jobs before he found one he liked. After clerking for a while, Herman decided he wanted more action and got a job as a driver in Banning's far-flung transportation network, which took goods all around the region. Driving a coach was brutal work. The roads were poor, the dust was merciless, and the bandits were fearless. Yet there was something thrilling in thundering behind sweating horses, lurching from side to side and bouncing up and down as the stage traversed miles of uninhabited country. When Herman sat up high in the driver's seat, exposed to all, he was both a target and the man in command.

The job soured for him when he had a run-in with a bandit. As the Americans squeezed the Californios from positions of power and economic influence, some disgruntled natives turned in retaliation to robbery and violence. Many of them had few options, since their way of life was disappearing and they found most Americans reluctant to share resources. The most famous of these bandits was Tiburcio Vasquez, who robbed and terrorized California until his capture in the mid-1870s.

Herman was driving the stage in the Cahuenga Pass, a steep, winding road that led into the pueblo, when he first sensed something was wrong. The hills jutting above him were barren, covered in short grasses and large rock outcroppings that could easily hide a group of men. There was only one paying passenger on the stage, but $9,000 in gold, money that would not be safe till it was brought to the Wells Fargo Express office.

Herman applied the brakes as the stage headed down the slope of the pass. The loudest noise was the squeal of metal against metal. Suddenly a shot whizzed past Herman's ear. Thinking quickly, he picked up his Winchester rifle and fired it in the direction of the gunshot. Then he loosened the brakes, cracked a whip above the horses, and flew down the hill.

The stage went faster and faster, drawing dangerously close to the horses, but Herman did not slow it down. He could hear hoofbeats behind him, and curses in Spanish, and he knew that bandits were on his tail. He whipped the horses into a frenzy. They galloped over the rutted, narrow trail as if sensing their death lay behind them. Herman held on to the reins with his knees and turned and fired his gun at the men pursuing him. It was not until he neared Los Angeles that he knew his attackers had faded away.[7]

Bringing the bullion back safely thrust Herman into the limelight and made him a local hero. He recounted his story at the dinner table of his cousins, at the bar of the Bella Union, and anywhere else people would listen. With his gregarious personality and ability to set others at ease, he was the toast of the town.

But Herman hadn't come to America to die for someone else's gold, and he decided to try a more sedate line of work. He left Banning's employ in December 1861—despite the offer of a substantial raise—and went to work at his cousin Samuel Hellman's stationery store, which sold paper, envelopes, and other goods. Before long, Herman and Samuel were partners.

The relationship soured in 1866, and the two men agreed to go their separate ways. Before long, however, they were in court, with Herman claiming that Samuel was trying to get him to pay a $1,200 promissory note that Samuel had taken out from his brother-in-law, Jacob Weil. The court dockets of Los Angeles in that period were littered with these kind of lawsuits, fights over dissolution of partnerships, unpaid promissory notes, and defaults on mortgages. The court ruled in Herman's favor, but the fight further deteriorated the relationship between the cousins.

In 1867, Herman opened his own store—even though he had promised Samuel he wouldn't compete with him. The new store was located at 9 Downey's Block, a commercial building on Temple and Main street. Herman stocked the store with toys, gift books, garden seeds, and fancy goods. Samuel was so angry at the competition that he vowed never to talk to Herman again. "You will probably know that Sam and Herman have split partnership," Samuel's wife, Adelaide, wrote a cousin, Max Hellman, on June 7, 1867. "Herman showed himself very mean and dirty towards Sam and I could write plenty about it but it's best not to say anything."[8]

The two cousins weren't speaking, yet their animosity spilled out into the newspapers. Samuel Hellman transformed his store into an auction house, advertising with the slogan "Is Money Your Object? Then come to S. Hellman's Auction Store." This ad would often appear right next to Herman Hellman's in the *Los Angeles Weekly Republican*. Then in December 1867, Herman retaliated with a line written in small type at the bottom of one of his ads: "No connection with any Cheap John Trash Auction House in the City. All Goods sold by me warranted."

Soon, Isaias was earning more money as a banker than as a merchandiser. His income in 1868 reached $3,387—making him one of fewer than thirty people in Los Angeles who earned more than $1,800.[9] He had cordoned off a small corner of his store by erecting a low wooden fence across the back and had hung up a sign on the wall near the safe, large enough to be seen from a distance. Isaias longed to focus on banking, but he needed additional capital to create a strong independent bank. At twenty-six, he found that all his training—the bookkeeping and economics he had studied at his secondary school in Marktbreit coupled with the practical knowledge he had gained as a storekeeper—was coalescing and fueling his instincts as a businessman. And he might have been carrying the hopes of generations of Hellman men before him. For centuries, the Hellmans had been limited in their occupational pursuits because of the restrictions placed on Jews. Now Isaias was unencumbered by anti-Jewish laws. He was free to use his mind and imagination to pursue his dreams.

Isaias wasn't ready to set up a new bank on his own, so he turned to the old landed gentry, the Yankees who had married into the Californio elite, for capital. It was a pattern that Isaias would repeat the rest of his life—forging alliances with men more powerful and prominent than he, and running the business from behind the scenes. Isaias left no writings or letters that discussed his reluctance to be the front man in a business, but it might have been a sense retained from Germany that it was better for Jews to keep a low profile.

Isaias went to see William Workman and his son-in-law F. P F. Temple about forming a partnership for a new bank. It was an astute choice, for Workman was one of the oldest European settlers of Los Angeles, and Temple was an aggressive businessman with flair.

Born in England in 1799, Workman first came to America in 1825 to work in his brother's saddlery shop in Franklin, Missouri. After three years he left to trap furs in Taos, New Mexico, then part of Mexico. He opened a store with John Rowland and became a naturalized Mexican citizen—and a Catholic—in 1828. In 1841, he and Rowland led one of the first wagon trains of white settlers to Los Angeles. The twenty-five-member party included the first Jew to come to Los Angeles, Jacob Frankfort, a German tailor.

Once in California, Workman became aligned with the Mexican governor Pio Pico, who, in gratitude, granted him large tracts of land, including the island of Alcatraz off the town of Yerba Buena (now San Francisco), the missions of San Rafael and San Gabriel, and a forty-eight-thousand acre ranch known as La Puente, located about thirty miles east of Los Angeles. Workman built an adobe on his land and reaped a fortune selling beef to the miners who flooded the northern portion of the state. By the time Isaias approached him, Workman was extremely wealthy.

Francis Pliny Fisk Temple was known as "Templito" or Little Temple because he was just five feet four inches tall. Temple came to California by ship in 1841, when he was nineteen, to join his half brother Jonathan, who had already become wealthy in the eleven years since arriving in southern California. Temple soon married Workman's daughter, Antonia, and launched into the purchase and sale of numerous businesses. He became a large landowner and farmer and surprised local residents when he paid $7,000 in 1860 for the racehorse Black Warrior.

Hellman, Temple & Company opened its doors on September 1, 1868, becoming the second official bank in Los Angeles. In January of that year, former governor John Downey and James A. Hayward, whose father had made his fortune in mining, had opened the town's first formal lending institution. Isaias contributed $25,000 in capital, while Workman and Temple contributed $50,000 each.

The bank moved into an imposing two-story building with a fireproof iron front on Main Street, right next to the Bella Union Hotel. Isaias was the cashier, in charge of day-to-day operations. He also supervised the clerks who accepted deposits and gave out funds.

The papers gushed over the event. "The exterior is beautiful, presenting a specimen of architectural design, creditable to the enterprising proprietors," said one article. "The vault embraces all the modern appliances to ensure safety, is massive and substantial, while the bolts and bars connected with the locking of the door, combine intricacy with simplicity."[10]

It was no coincidence that the new bank building was decorative and lavish. It was meant to convey a sense of solidity and safety, a reassuring advertisement that depositors' gold would be safe. Almost every bank in California sank large sums into its building as a physical symbol of security. In towns where roads were unpaved, violence was common, and the liquor flowed freely, the banks were decorated with marble and brass and ornately carved wood.

Men flocked to Hellman, Temple & Company to borrow funds to buy land, plant crops, and start businesses. Before long, the client list read like a who's who of Los Angeles gentry. Pio Pico was a customer, as was Diego Sepúlveda, a former *alcade*, or mayor, of Los Angeles, and Ozro Childs, a pioneer horticulturist, deposited his funds there.

The ready access to money transformed the small pueblo. Before Hellman, Temple & Company or its competitor, James A. Hayward & Company, opened, men had to borrow money at high rates. Now they could get funds at 1½ to 2 percent interest a month. Merchants who bought their goods in San Francisco previously had to pay Wells Fargo Express a handling fee to ship funds to that city. Now they could open an account with Isaias, who kept funds in San Francisco banks to pay bills. By the end of 1868, in just four months of business, the bank had made 724 loans averaging $1,140 each.

On one cold February day in 1869, Isaias and a partner, the jeweler Charles Ducommun, paid $16,000 for a slope of land rising from the Los Angeles River. The plot was covered by gnarled, twisted grapevines laid out in neat rows, remnants of the vineyards planted in 1789 by the Franciscan priests who had come from Spain to convert the native population to Catholicism. For more than eighty years, the vines, gray in the winter chill, had been flooded by the river and baked by the sun, a magical combination that produced luscious Mission grapes used for wine.

But the Laborie Vineyards, as they were called, now lay directly in the path of the city's development. When Isaias looked at the vineyards, he may have imagined the land dotted by small farms reaching down to the river and a row of offices and stores along Commercial Street. Isaias and Ducommun hired a work crew to pull out the ancient grapevines, ripping out the old to make way for the new.

By 1869, land sales were soaring in Los Angeles, as the dons' control of their ranchos slipped away because of debt or their inability to prove their property claims in an American court. The former Californios watched helplessly as developers eagerly rushed in to subdivide vast tracts of land that once was theirs.

The first large-scale land development, and the one that would set the tone for the rest of the region, came when early pioneer Abel Stearns put up 177,000 acres for sale. Stearns, a pockmarked Yankee with a knife scar running down one side of his face, had at one time been the richest man in the region. He owned an impressive block-long business building in the downtown named after his wife, Arcadia Bandini, huge herds of cattle and sheep, and more property than he could keep track of. His financial empire collapsed with the precipitate drop of cattle prices, but rather than wait for his creditors to come after him, Stearns went on the offensive. He sold his land to a syndicate of financiers in San Francisco in May 1868, negotiated a set kickback for each acre sold, and managed to pay off his debt.

Those selling the Stearns land recognized they had to market the idea of southern California, and they drew up promotional materials lauding the gentle climate and fertile soils. The syndicate printed thousands of brochures, which they sent around the globe. Every time a steamship left San Francisco for Los Angeles, agents came on board to pass out brochures describing the land, which had been broken up into twenty- and fifty-acre plots that sold for $5 to $13 an acre. By 1870, the syndicate had sold more than twenty thousand acres—and had set a precedent for how the future of Los Angeles would be marketed.

Other men got into the land business as well. Isaac Lankersheim formed a partnership with businessmen from San Francisco, including Levi Strauss & Company and L. N. Sachs & Company, to buy a large chunk of the former Mexican general Andres Pico's Rancho San Fernando for $115,000. Dr. John Griffin acquired two thousand acres on the east side of the Los Angeles River for 50¢ an acre in 1863. He had to build a bridge to connect the property to the main part of town, but then proceeded to market the lots.

Isaias bought his first parcel of land in 1863, when he was twenty-one years old. He held on to it until his death. "I was visiting a friend's house one day when the cook came up to me and asked me to buy that Seventh and Hope Street property from her," said Isaias. "She offered it to me for two hundred dollars. It was very far out of the city and I could not take the time to look at it, so I hunted it up on the map and decided it would be worth more some day and bought it."

After that, Isaias began to purchase as much land as he could afford. During one three-month period in 1868, he bought and sold plots worth almost $20,000. He soon accumulated parcels on the northeast corner of Second and Broadway, the northwest corner of Seventh and Grand, along Main Street, and a large swath in the area that eventually became known as Boyle Heights. While Isaias generally paid market rate for the land, he did acquire a few plots at foreclosure sales for only pennies per acre.

In 1869, Isaias tore down an adobe on the northwest corner of Los Angeles and Commercial streets and constructed a new brick building with an ornate, curved, white false facade on top. One of his anchor tenants was the Los Angeles Social Club, a group formed by a cross section of the city's most prominent inhabitants. There were Californios, Frenchmen, Germans, Mexicans, Yankees, and Basques—a diverse membership that reflected the city's early cosmopolitanism.

Isaias also bought land outside of city limits. He and John Downey purchased an eight-hundred-acre track of the Dominguez family's Rancho San Pedro and drilled an artesian well that shot water so high in the air that it became a regular stop on the stage route from San Pedro to Los Angeles. Soon Isaias was advertising forty-acre plots for sale in local newspapers. "Two Thousand Acres of the best agricultural land . . . lying on the line of the Railroad," read an advertisement in the *Los Angeles Daily News*.

Isaias's keen eye for real estate soon made him one of the largest landholders in the region, and he would eventually own tens of thousands of acres throughout the region. Once he bought a piece of property he often was reluctant to sell it, for he recognized that the value would only increase with time. Within a few years, Isaias's net worth would reach $55,000 (about $900,000 in 2006 dollars)—a tremendous amount of money for a twenty-eight-year-old man living in a frontier town.

In March 1870, eighteen months after the opening of Hellman, Temple & Company, the bank installed an ornate new wooden counter, one that the *Los Angeles Daily News* called an "exquisite" piece "which, for beauty and design and elegance of finish is not surpassed, and is probably unequalled by any similar work in the state." The massive wooden counter had a walnut top, three inches thick, which was burnished to a warm glow. Its front was mahogany, paneled with rosewood inlaid with bird's-eye maple. The project had cost the bank close to $1,500, but it projected permanence and authority. It announced that the bank—and by extension, Los Angeles, with its population now reaching six thousand people—was here to stay.

FIVE

MARRIAGE

1870–1872

Isaias stood on the deck of the steamer as it pulled out of San Pedro late in the afternoon of March 18, 1870, and watched the coastline of southern California recede with each chug of the boat's engine.

The view from the ship was very different from the one Isaias had seen upon his arrival eleven years earlier. Wooden warehouses and small homes now covered the mudflats and marshes that lined the coast. A long pier, sturdy enough to bear the weight of the new train that traveled between Los Angeles and the port, jutted into the water. San Pedro Bay was still too shallow for large ships to dock directly, so small lighters picked up passengers and freight and ferried them to the mass of ships anchored just offshore.

Isaias had changed as well. The scrappy, wide-eyed boy was gone, replaced by a successful businessman properly dressed in a dark frock coat and tie. Small round spectacles perched on his nose, further projecting authority, which was exactly the image the twenty-eight-year-old banker hoped to convey.

Isaias was off on the most important trip of his life. He was on his way to New York, via the recently completed transcontinental railroad, to meet nineteen-year-old Esther Newgass, who had emigrated from Bavaria four years earlier. If all went well, if the two liked each other enough upon meeting, they would marry.

As the cold wind of the Pacific Ocean gathered force, Isaias shivered and headed to his cabin. He had a twelve-day trip ahead of him. He was used to the two-day steamer trip to San Francisco—he had completed the journey dozens of times—but he didn't know what to expect on the recently completed transcontinental railroad. The cross-country trains had been running less than a year. Though they were fast, going from twenty-two to thirty-five miles an hour, they were notoriously jerky, starting and stopping dozens of times each day. Isaias must have hoped the arduousness of the trip wouldn't trigger one of his brutal migraines.

Isaias had never taken an extended train trip, but then neither had most Americans. The Central Pacific and Union Pacific railroads had driven in the gold spike linking the rails and uniting the country only the year before. The formidable plains, deserts, and mountains that separated the coasts of the United States were finally conquered, and now men and women could make a transcontinental journey with relative ease. It was a dramatic shift for America—the West, once so distant and exotic, was now just a rail-car ride away.

Isaias was a believer in the railroad. There were some who resented its intrusiveness, its loudness, and its ability to maim and kill dozens in a single accident. But Isaias knew the railroad was the answer to Los Angeles's isolation. The city was on the edge of the continent, so far from the San Francisco economic engine that it remained a backwater. Stage lines and wagon trains and steamers brought a trickle of visitors to southern California, but Isaias believed the railroad would link Los Angeles to the world and open up markets for the town's wheat, barley, grapes, and oranges, crops that now made their way slowly by ship or wagon. He envisioned carloads of new immigrants— and new customers—coming to settle the rangelands of the Los Angeles basin. But a railroad link directly into Los Angeles was still years away, so Isaias had to travel to San Francisco first.

Isaias had paid around $100 for his ticket. The train would travel from Oakland to Sacramento and then wind its way up the western slopes of the Sierra Nevada, gaining elevation through a series of hard-won switchbacks and tunnels blasted out of the mountains by the thousands of Chinese who had come to America to work the rails. The train's trip through the mountains was a massive engineering feat. Snowdrifts could be so deep that the company built thirty miles of snow sheds and attached eleven-foot-high snowplows to the front of each train. When the weather was fine, trains would pause for ten minutes on a promontory above the American River canyon so passengers could see where gold had been discovered in California.

From the slopes of the Sierra Nevada the train would drop into the deserts of Nevada; cross the alkaline flats of Utah and the highlands of Wyoming; traverse the prairies of Nebraska with their dense populations of buffalo, antelope, and prairie dogs; and then make its way to Chicago and its famous stockyards. Finally, after ten to twelve days, depending on whether he took a break, the traveler would reach New York.

Isaias was going to travel in style. While the trip was bumpy and exhausting, the introduction of the luxurious Silver Palace cars on the western section of the trip did a lot to make the time tolerable. Passengers sat in velvet-covered seats surrounded by dark damask coverings and wood-paneled ceilings. There were pianos to play and books and newspapers to read, all free to first-class passengers. The views through the broad plate-glass windows were spectacular, and travelers often hoped to glimpse Native American warriors riding their horses, albeit at a distance. The train also pulled its own dining car; travelers could order anything from Porterhouse steak and lamb to oysters and fried eggs. At night, Isaias retired to a bunk in a sleeping car.

For a young man living in a frontier town with few amenities and just a slight veneer of respectability, Isaias's potential engagement was remarkable. Esther Newgass came from a refined and affluent family. Her forebears in Germany were wealthy and well educated, and her relatives in the United States were among the most prosperous of the new German Jewish elite of New York.

Esther's older sister Babette was married to Meyer Lehman, a Bavarian Jewish cotton merchant who had started a firm called Lehman Brothers, which was quickly becoming one of the most successful commodity houses in the country. The family, with their eight children, lived on West Twentieth Street in New York and counted among their friends the families that had made millions during and after the Civil War—the Seligmans, the Strauses, the Loebs—a German Jewish group that would be dubbed "Our Crowd" a century later. Seventy thousand Jews lived in New York in 1870, making it the country's largest Jewish community.

The Lehmans, like most Bavarian Jews, had come to the United States from Germany with just a small amount of money. Starting with a store in Montgomery, Alabama, the Lehmans soon became some of the South's largest cotton merchants, involved in many aspects of the trade. Lehman Brothers bought cotton from farmers, extended credit, stored cotton bales in its warehouses in New Orleans, and sold it to factories in Liverpool, England. In 1858, Emanuel, the older brother, moved to New York to open a branch of the company's operations.

The Civil War caught the Lehmans divided, with one in the North, the other in the South. Both men supported the Confederacy. Emanuel went to England for a time to try and sell bonds for the rebel states. Toward the end of the war, Meyer, working on behalf of the Confederate government, appealed to General Ulysses S. Grant to be permitted to sell cotton to alleviate the horrendous conditions of Southern soldiers in Northern prisoner-of-war camps. His request was denied.

At the end of the conflict, when the South lay in ruins, the Lehmans realized there was money to be made in other commodities besides cotton. Meyer made plans to move north to join his brother. In 1866, before the family left, Babette's younger sister, fifteen-year-old Esther, moved to the United States. She accompanied the family when it moved to New York two years later.

On April 14, 1870, a warm spring day that prompted tree buds in Central Park to burst forth, Isaias stood under a huppah, or canopy, in the magnificent sanctuary of Temple Emanu-el, the grand Reform synagogue on Fifth Avenue and Forty-third Street and the center of upper-class Jewish life in New York. A series of archways ran from the back of the hall to the bimah, where the wedding was performed, and the lavishly decorated ceiling gave the sanctuary a slightly Moorish feeling. The temple was much more elaborate than the sandstone temple in Reckendorf and stood in even starker relief to the crude buildings where Isaias worshipped in Los Angeles.

At his side stood nineteen-year-old Esther, whose soft brown eyes were enhanced by the cluster of silky brown curls she wore draped on her forehead. Esther was not pretty, as she had a squarish head and prominent nose, but her keen intelligence and zest for life enhanced her plain face. Most important, Esther had a strong sense of adventure. She needed one, since she was preparing to start a new life three thousand miles away in a town most considered barely civilized.

Rabbi James K. Gutheim, an old friend of the Lehmans from Alabama, performed the ceremony before a small group of friends and family, including

Israel Fleishman, Isaias's maternal uncle and the man who had suggested the match. Fleishman had run the Fleishman & Sichel hardware store in Los Angeles with Julius Sichel before moving to New York in the late 1860s to open a branch at 165 Water Street. Two doors away, Sichel's brother Joseph had a tobacco store. His partner was Lewis Newgass, a cousin of Esther's.

Fleishman must have bragged of his nephew's business acumen and of the opportunities available in Los Angeles. The Lehmans would have been impressed by what they heard of the young Jewish banker, and, like many financiers, they knew there were investment opportunities on the far side of the country.

Isaias's marriage provided him with an extended network of relatives who would help him significantly in the decades to come. In addition to Meyer Lehman, Isaias was now related to Esther's older brother, Benjamin Newgass, a brash, charismatic man who had come to Kentucky in the 1850s and made a mark in the tobacco business.[1] Newgass and Lehman were partners in Lehman, Newgass & Company, a cotton brokerage in New Orleans. Two years after Isaias and Esther's wedding, Newgass extended his company's reach by opening a branch office in Liverpool, England, the world's center of cotton manufacturing. The three brothers-in-law soon did extensive business with one another, buying and selling stocks and bonds for various enterprises, extending credit, and investing in one another's ventures in railroads, banks, and commodities. They created their own informal financial syndicate that moved capital from Britain to New York to California and to other parts of the country.

Other German Jewish families had similar ties. Joseph Seligman, the oldest of the eight famous Seligman brothers who turned a peddling business into a string of interlocking investment banks around the globe, married a cousin, Babet Steinhart. His wife's brother, Ignatz, left Bavaria for San Francisco, where he helped set up the Anglo-California Bank in 1873. Seligman's daughter Bella later married Phil Lilienthal, one of the bank's young associates and part of an old German Jewish family with roots in both San Francisco and Cincinnati. Another of Joseph's daughters, Sophie, would marry Moritz Walter, a descendant of the Walters of Reckendorf. Regina Jacobi of New York married the stockbroker William Seligsberg of San Francisco. Her brother Frederick Jacobi would marry Flora Brandenstein, the oldest daughter of the San Francisco tobacco merchant Joseph Brandenstein.

The interlocking marriages greatly increased Jewish ability to raise capital from around the world. Early Jewish immigrants relied on brothers and cousins to man the peddling carts, work at the dry-goods stores, or travel to New York or San Francisco to obtain goods. As the Jews settled into American life, they extended these family business contacts through marriage to others in their social group. In time the business transactions evolved from helping one another get the best price on dry goods to investing in one another's railroads, factories, bond deals, and financial institutions.

After the wedding ceremony, Isaias and Esther celebrated with a party at the Lehmans' home and retired that evening to a $20-a-night suite at the Hoffman House, a luxurious Manhattan hotel on Broadway and Twenty-fifth Street. The Hoffman House, which would become well known in future years as the informal headquarters of the Democratic Party, served sumptuous meals in its dining room on the eleventh floor overlooking Madison Square. The Hellmans could stroll through the park or shop at the nearby fashionable ladies' stores that lined Madison Avenue.

Two days after the wedding Isaias and Esther boarded a transcontinental train for Los Angeles. Isaias couldn't take much time for a honeymoon, as he needed to get back to Hellman, Temple & Company. But the newlyweds stopped for a few days in Chicago to take in the sights, which included the massive stockyards and the new water tower.

The hours Isaias and Esther spent traveling on the train were the first time they really got to know each other and became the basis for a long and loving marriage. Esther's vivaciousness and wit delighted Isaias and made him feel less lonely. He quickly discovered that he loved to indulge her by buying her beautiful things to wear. Soon, he had a hard time telling her no. Esther learned to love Isaias's sober intelligence, his fierce loyalty to friends and family, and his growing sense of obligation to make the world a better place.

Los Angeles was a sharp contrast to Esther's previous homes. She had been raised in Würzburg, a cultivated city in Bavaria along the Main River. The baroque palace in the center of the city, with its spacious sculptured gardens, was so beautiful that it had been dubbed the eighth wonder of the world. Churches, cafés, fountains, and elegant shops lined the city's crooked streets, and rococo buildings surrounded the central market square. The Marienberg fortress on a hill on the opposite side of the river from the city offered sweeping views of the region's famous vineyards.

In coming to Los Angeles, Esther encountered a different life, where even the best efforts at luxury paled compared to the comforts of Würzburg. Los Angeles was still a primitive place with rampant violence, disease, unpaved streets, and no city sewer system. Her first home was the Bella Union Hotel, one of the city's first brick hotels. The hotel's new owners had recently expanded the place and added a decent restaurant, but Isaias didn't intend to let his bride reside there long. By July, the Hellmans had settled into their own house on Main Street and had hired a German woman to cook and clean for them.

Isaias took Esther to meet his close friends, including Eugene and Harriet Meyer. Eugene was a handsome and athletic man who faced challenges with a Frenchman's flair, while his wife was delicate and somewhat sickly. Both Isaias and Herman had served as groomsmen at the couple's 1867 wedding, which took place at their home on Third and Fort streets. One visitor declared the house as "beautifully furnished, good enough for any City." Their house certainly demonstrated that it was possible to live luxuriously on the frontier. It was decorated with horsehair sofas, Belgian carpets, black walnut and rosewood furniture, and soft draperies in the parlor.[2]

On the weekends, the Hellmans went exploring. Esther loved horses, and outings were popular. "Driving was one of the great daily amusements," according to historian John McGroarty. "The well-to-do families all had their own carriages. Those who were not so fortunate patronized the livery stables." The Hellmans would picnic in the Arroyo Seco, a sycamore grove three miles north of Los Angeles, or go to fashionable Santa Monica to walk the beach, bathe in the ocean, look in on the encampment that had sprung up, and stop for a bite at Eugene's, a popular restaurant.

Another attraction was the Garden of Paradise, a pleasure resort on Main Street a short walk from their house. The Hellmans could stroll the verdant gardens, pluck a juicy prickly pear cactus for an unusual yet refreshing snack, pause in front of statues of Adam and Eve in the Garden of Eden, or visit the Round House, a circular building with an octagonal roof that was modeled on houses in Africa. In 1871, a roller-skating rink opened in Teutonia Hall and immediately became "nightly crowded with beaus and belles on the town—billing and cooing as they whirl around the hall on wheels," said the *Los Angeles Express*.

Isaias's close-knit circle of friends and family quickly embraced Esther. They threw a welcome party for her at the Bella Union and invited her into their homes. Herman took an immediate liking to Esther, whom he found agreeable and good-natured. They both shared a love of horses and riding in the outdoors. Herman must have felt that Esther also softened his stern brother. When Isaias was around Esther, he shed some of his authoritarian traits and laughed and joked more easily. But Herman got to spend only a short time getting to know Esther, for he sold his stationery store and left in June 1870 for an extended trip to Reckendorf.

Esther also found friends among the members of the Ladies Hebrew Benevolent Society, which Rosa Newmark had started in January 1870. The society got together for lunches and meetings, but its main mission was to raise funds for the needy. Its first major project came in 1871, after a devastating fire tore through Chicago, leaving thousands without homes. The society raised $100 for the fire's victims, and the Hebrew Benevolent Society brought in another $250. Their contributions to a non-Jewish cause were unremarkable, for the Jewish community of Los Angeles had long supported ecumenical projects. Isaias and others had donated money to support the school and orphanage of the Sisters of Charity, to start St. Vincent's College, and to construct a Catholic cathedral. Their generosity was noted in an editorial in the *Los Angeles Daily Star* on May 22, 1869. "Who [are] so ready as the descendants of Jacob in our midst to respond with heartiness to every charitable appeal."[3]

The Ladies Hebrew Benevolent Society also nursed people who were sick, regardless of religion, and offered critical support in times of trouble. In July 1871, tragedy struck at the core of the organization. Eugene Hellman, the five-year-old son of the society's cofounder Adelaide Hellman and her husband, Samuel, was playing with his older brother, Maurice, around a truck on Main Street. The boys kept crawling on top of the truck, only to be told by the driver to get down. The boys ignored his commands. Eugene Hellman lost his balance and fell to the ground. The horses bolted and Eugene was crushed to death by the truck's wheels. He was the first Hellman to die in Los Angeles.

The creation of a Jewish organization just for women reflected the tremendous growth of the Jewish community since Isaias's arrival in 1859. There were now about 350 Jews in the city. It was no longer a ragtag collection of mostly single men, but a close-knit group of families. The start of the transformation could be traced to 1862, when the community hired its first rabbi.

Finding a leader had not been easy. Even though more than 150,000 Jews had immigrated to the United States by the mid-nineteenth century, rabbis were in short supply. Most of the immigrants came from poorer families; the learned men who studied under Europe's great rabbis remained at home, content to participate in the modernizing of Jewish life in the cities of Europe.

In 1861, a rabbi from San Francisco came south to hold High Holiday services in the Arcadia Block. But the Jews of Los Angeles wanted their own spiritual leader. In 1862, Joseph Newmark and Moritz Morris traveled to San Francisco in search of a permanent rabbi. If there was someone appropriate in the state, he probably would be living there, as the city had two temples and a flourishing Jewish community of more than 5,000. Newmark and Morris turned to Henry A. Henry, the rabbi of Temple Sherith Israel, for help.

Henry did not have to look further than one of his prized students: forty-two-year-old Abraham Edelman, a burly man with penetrating eyes. While not a formally trained rabbi, Edelman had studied in a yeshiva in Warsaw during his youth and had taught Hebrew in New York City, Buffalo, and Paterson, New Jersey. After Edelman moved to San Francisco, he continued his studies with Rabbi Henry. He spoke many languages—and would soon learn Spanish quickly—and Newmark and Morris enticed him to move once again, to the small frontier town of Los Angeles.

Edelman faced a daunting task upon his arrival in southern California. While the Jewish community was growing and settling down, its members had not had the wherewithal to organize regular religious services. A month after Edelman's arrival in June 1862, he and Newmark presided over another organizational meeting—this time to start a brand-new synagogue.

Temple B'nai B'rith would become one of America's success stories, eventually growing into the Wilshire Boulevard Temple, one of the largest Reform synagogues in the country. But its beginnings were hardly auspicious. Jews in America in the 1860s had a background in traditional Judaism, which meant that men and women sat apart in temple, services were conducted in Hebrew, and people were expected to rest and reflect, not work, on the Sabbath. It was an approach ill-suited to a country where commerce and survival consumed the daily energies of most settlers. Edelman had to create a synagogue that would respond to the needs of his congregants, one that balanced the traditions they cherished with the democratic ideals they were coming to honor.

From rented halls in various buildings, including the courtroom of Judge Ygnacio Sepulveda, Edelman constructed a new kind of hybrid community, one branded traditional, but one that acknowledged the changing times. Edelman expected his male congregants to refrain from all activity on Saturday, the Sabbath, and to cover their heads whenever they were at services. "Lighting a match, tearing paper, smoking—these were forbidden on Shabbos, as were innumerable other things," remembered his son David Edelman.[4] Edelman's first sermons were in Hebrew, but with time he added a sermon and a few prayers in English. He allowed men and women to sit together during services—a huge departure from traditional norms—and added an organ and mixed choir.

Esther and Isaias had grown up in traditional communities in Germany, but Isaias, at least, had made accommodations to American realities. He kept his businesses open on Saturday mornings, as was the America custom. The competing demands of religion and commerce were difficult to reconcile, but Isaias clearly felt the pull of business more strongly.

A month after Esther's arrival in 1870, Edelman held Los Angeles's first-ever confirmation ceremony. B'nai B'rith rented space at the Teutonic Hall, bringing a Torah to create a sacred atmosphere. The five young women who would be confirmed all dressed in white and carried flowers; the four young men just dressed in their best. The city's newspapers covered the ceremony as if it were an exotic ritual, despite the almost total integration of Jews into the mainstream. "Here, in this beautiful part of the ceremony, was [sic] exhibited the practices of the high priests of old in the holy temple of Solomon, in offering their sacrifices unto God," reported the Los Angeles Daily News. "Instead of the burnt offerings of those days, they placed upon the holy altar their humble tribute of beautiful flowers, accompanied with sweet and humble supplications to the Almighty to accept their innocent tribute of adoration."

The community's focus increasingly turned toward the need to build a house of worship. For too long the Jews had wandered from hall to rented room to borrowed house. At Passover services in 1872, held at the Odd Fellows Hall, Rabbi Edelman expressed discomfort that the "Israelites are constantly under obligation to their Christian brethren for places in which to worship."

To raise money for a synagogue, the Ladies Hebrew Benevolent Society threw a ball on February 10, 1872. With few opportunities for socializing, the dance became one of the biggest events of the year. Both Jews and non-Jews clamored for tickets, and their desire to attend reflected the egalitarianism of the time. Former governor John Downey, a Catholic, attended, as did Andres Pico, who had fought the American takeover of California so bravely in 1848. Dancing started at 10 P.M. at Stearns Hall and continued through the early morning, breaking only for a midnight supper. "Last night the ball given in aid of the Hebrew Congregation at Stearns Hall, was one of the most fashionable balls that has ever been given in this city," reported the *Los Angeles Star*. "The ball room was well filled. The dresses of the ladies were splendid and in keeping with the most stylish patterns, de la mode de Madame Demorest, and reflected credit, as well as beauty, on their fair owners."[5]

Four months later, on a blazing Sunday in June, a crowd gathered on a vacant lot on Fort Street (now known as Broadway) not far from the Plaza. By 4 P.M., waves of heat shimmered up from the ground and made the cool relief of night seem far off.

A group of men conferred in the center of a field while women wearing the light colors of summer circled them, their overskirts swaying back and forth in the slight breeze. Young children, already bored with the grown-up chatter, ran around the grassy lot, kicking up dust. A newspaper reporter from the *Los Angeles Star* stood at the edge of the gathering and scribbled descriptions into his notebook.

The crowd quieted when Isaias stood up to speak. In recognition of his growing stature and influence, Isaias had recently been elected president of Congregation B'nai B'rith. Now, as the congregation took the historic step of building its first home, Isaias paused to reflect on the enormity of the occasion.

"We are assembled here today to lay the cornerstone of this, our future synagogue," said Isaias. "It is a happy moment for all of us Hebrews to be present and assist on this holy occasion and also to know that the long and seriously felt hardship of not having a place of worship of our own will soon be at an end."[6]

Twenty-two years after California had been admitted to the United States, thirty-one years after the presence of a Jew was first noted in Los Angeles, the community was about to build its first synagogue. It had taken years of fund-raising, years of concerts and fairs and balls, to raise the money, but now the city's Jews would have a place to pray.

The building, designed by Ezra F. Kysor, would be one of the finest in Los Angeles, Gothic in design, with two massive buttresses topped by spires and a five-pointed star sitting on top of a finial. Two flights of stairs, each six feet wide, would lead to an entryway graced by imposing black walnut doors. More than 365 worshippers would fit inside.

The congregation had scraped the money together with a decade of fund-raisers, a call to its members, and a beneficial, unexpected $1,000 donated from two of its San Francisco brethren. As construction on the temple was about to begin, the congregation laid a cornerstone filled with objects that commemorated the city's times and culture. Joseph Newmark, who had struggled for almost twenty years to build a viable community, laid artifacts into the box, which would fit into the building's foundation. The documents included the constitutions of Congregation B'nai B'rith, the Hebrew Benevolent Society and its ladies' auxiliary, and various Masonic orders, and the rules of the Société Française Bienfaisance Mutuelle de Los Angeles. There were copies of various newspapers and examples of popular currency, such as an American half-dollar, a Mexican dollar, a Maximilian dollar, and an old Spanish half-dollar.

As the cornerstone was nestled into its permanent resting place, soon to be covered by stone and plaster, Newmark asked for the crowd's attention. Standing in front of Isaias, who was young enough to be his grandson, Newmark took out a silver trowel that had been specially purchased for the occasion. "Mr. President," began Newmark. "It becomes my pleasing duty to present to you this trowel, which is offered to you by the congregation B'nai B'rith as a slight token of the esteem and respect of your continued devotion to our society."

The bearded young man who had so eloquently spoken a few minutes earlier was at a loss for words. Isaias managed to sputter a few thanks, barely expressing the devotion and gratitude he felt for his Jewish brethren. Rabbi Edelman said another prayer, and the ceremony was over. The Jewish roots of Los Angeles grew a little deeper.

THE FARMERS AND MERCHANTS BANK

1871–1875

The air was crisp and cold on the first night of February 1871, but the group of men gathered in Isaias's banking office right next to the Bella Union Hotel didn't notice the chill of winter. The men were some of the richest, most powerful people in Los Angeles, men who had made their fortunes on grapes, cattle, sheep, water, wine, and land. They had come together to tackle a problem that was constraining their businesses from further growth: lack of capital.

Los Angeles was thriving in 1871. The end of the Civil War had brought many settlers to the region, former soldiers and their families in search of peace after the bloody conflict that had torn apart America. They streamed across the United States in long lines of covered wagons, lured to southern California by reports of fertile soil and good weather. Their demand for small farms spurred a boom and hastened the breakup of the vast ranchos that had once spread for miles.

The skyline of Los Angeles was changing as well. Brick structures now hovered over the adobes, another sign that the Californio way of life was on the decline. The most impressive was the elegant Pico House, the first three-story hotel in the city, with eighty rooms, gas lighting, and an indoor toilet on each floor. The hotel had been constructed by the former Mexican governor Pio Pico, one of the most prominent and influential of the old Californios. Pico, a cattle trader and large landowner, had seen his fortune rise with the American takeover of California, but he would hold on to his wealth for only a few more years. The new hotel faced the Plaza, where the old brick water-storage tank had been recently replaced by a circular park with trees and flowering shrubs. A railroad stub now connected the city to its port at San Pedro, vastly speeding travel and the transportation of goods.

Isaias's bank had made a small but noticeable impact on the usurious interest rates charged by private lenders. By 1870, after two years in business, Hellman, Temple & Company had given out 1,462 loans totaling $851,000. Most of those were small loans of about $1,000, with fewer than ten loans larger than $10,000.[1]

Isaias wanted to do more. The city called for it. He envisioned a bank with many hundreds of thousands of dollars in capital, money that could be used to turn Los Angeles from a town into a city—the leading city of the southland.

His old bank hadn't worked, primarily because Isaias and his partners disagreed on basic banking principles. Temple and Workman had little financial experience and liked to loan money to anyone who seemed agreeable. A man from Kansas could walk in off the street and ask for a loan to buy a farm, only offering up his wagon and oxen as a guarantee, and Temple would agree. He couldn't understand Isaias's insistence on collateral, or some guarantee of repayment, and the difference led Isaias to buy out his partners in February. "Mr. Temple's only qualification for a borrower was that he must be poor," said Isaias. "I saw that doing a banking business on that basis would leave me poor also, and I dissolved the partnership."[2]

Isaias had his sights on a new partner—a man so charismatic, so respected, that no citizen of Los Angeles would hesitate to put money in his bank. The man was John Downey, the former governor of California. Downey had charm and charisma and was welcome at any dinner table in town.

Downey had been born in Ireland in 1827, had come to the United States while a young boy, and had traveled to California in 1849 with the hordes that streamed west in quest of gold. He quickly determined that mining was too messy and difficult, and returned to San Francisco, where he bought a shipment of drugs that had been abandoned by a Philadelphia merchant.

Downey then headed south, arriving in Los Angeles in 1850. He and James McFarland opened a drugstore in an adobe building on Los Angeles Street and cleared $30,000 in just a few years, which Downey invested in cattle and sheep. In 1853, Downey, twenty-six, married the lovely fifteen-year-old Maria Guirado, the daughter of a respected, landed Californio family. The union gave him instant entrée into the ruling class of the region.

Everything Downey touched after that seemed to turn into money. He was a good-looking man, with brown hair, a full beard, and hazel eyes, and he had a way of setting people at ease. From the start, Downey had a vision for southern California, a belief that its mild climate and fertile lands were untapped resources that would soon be discovered. People seemed to trust Downey, and his passion about the future of Los Angeles garnered him a seat on the Los Angeles Common Council in 1856. From there he was elected to the state assembly, and in 1859 he became lieutenant governor. Five days after the election, the newly elected governor of California, Milton Latham, was appointed to complete the term of U.S. senator David Broderick, who had been killed three months earlier in a duel over slavery by state supreme court justice David Terry. Downey took over the governor's office. He was thirty-two.

It was an interesting perch from which to view the Civil War. California was a divided state, with the north supporting the Union and the southern section mostly supporting the Confederacy. Downey was torn; he favored the rebel states, but he set aside his personal feelings to raise the Union troops requested by President Abraham Lincoln. Downey even sent soldiers to Los Angeles to exert control over vocal secessionists. But his political beliefs lost him reelection, and he never held public office again.

Downey returned to Los Angeles in 1862, and nine years later he was regarded as the richest man of the region.[3] Land formed the basis of his fortune—land that many hinted was gained by unscrupulous methods. In 1852, Downey had loaned $5,000 to Lemuel Carpenter, the owner of a soap factory on the banks of the San Gabriel River. Carpenter put up his seventeen-thousand-acre Rancho Santa Gertrudes as collateral. By 1859, the loan and compounded interest had ballooned to more than $100,000—a debt so unwieldy that a despairing Carpenter committed suicide. A few days later, Downey acquired the entire rancho in a sheriff's auction for $60,000. He subdivided it by 1865 and set up a new town named Downey.

By the winter of 1871, Downey lived in a mansion on Main Street and was just finishing construction on the imposing Downey Block at the corner of Main and Temple streets. The two-story brick structure was among the most modern in town and soon became home to the businesses that would shape Los Angeles: the law and real estate offices of Robert Widney and the headquarters of the Los Angeles and San Bernardino Land Company. Doctors and lawyers rented space on the upper floor. The Commercial Restaurant on the ground floor became a favorite lunch spot for local businessmen.

Downey was everything Isaias longed to be, a man who traveled easily and successfully through the old Californio aristocracy and the new American merchant and capitalist class. He seized opportunity wherever he saw it, taking calculated risks for advancement. Isaias knew Downey would project an image of prosperity for a new bank. In a time when banks were still technically illegal, and were almost completely unregulated, the reputation of the owners often made the difference between success and failure.

"Governor Downey was the most prominent political and historical character of the American regime," William Spaulding wrote in his *History of Los Angeles City and County*. "He was paternal and kindly, and everybody was very fond of him. No meeting of public-spirited citizens was complete unless Governor Downey was present and he was generally called on to preside."

But Downey, who had opened a bank with James A. Hayward in 1868, wasn't interested in joining Isaias. His small bank was profitable, making him money without too much work. He turned down the offer. But Isaias wouldn't take no for an answer. For six months Isaias hounded Downey, trying to persuade and cajole him to join forces. Isaias finally promised to do all the work if Downey would just lend his name. Isaias would be cashier, the bank's true manager, and Downey would be president.

"I was induced to leave my own little bank, where I was doing well, in order to go in with Hellman and I had the assurance that I would have nothing to do, that I was taken, as all bank presidents are taken, to be a figurehead, and having a reputation for wealth, whether true or not, and that was about the position I occupied in the bank," Downey recalled later.[4]

While Isaias's reputation had been growing, the partnership with Downey elevated it to new heights. The association unquestionably put him in the top tier of men in Los Angeles, and that is whom the pair turned to for a large infusion of capital. On that cold February night, most of the twenty-three businessmen that Isaias and Downey had selected to help start the new bank crowded into Isaias's office. They needed little convincing to put up money for the financial institution. Most of the men were already in business with either Downey or Hellman, flourishing capitalists who spread out their investment interests in the subdivision of ranchos, in the creation of utilities, or in new construction.

The group included Dr. John S. Griffin, a leading physician and major landowner who had founded the Los Angeles Water Company in 1868, of which both Downey and Isaias were major stockholders; Ozro W. Childs, a pioneer horticulturist and former member of the city council, with whom Isaias and Downey would invest heavily in land development; Matthew Keller, an Irishman who was one of the first to produce wine in southern California and the owner of the vast rancho containing Santa Monica; Domingo Amestoy, a Frenchman who grew up in Argentina and now had one of the area's largest flocks of sheep; William H. Workman, a saddle-maker and the nephew of Isaias's former banking partner; John F. Burns, the county sheriff; Cameron E. Thom, the county's district attorney; John M. Griffith, who owned a lumber firm; William H. Perry, a lumber merchant; Isaias's cousin Isaiah M. Hellman, who had been elected city treasurer in 1876; his brother Herman, who was traveling in Europe; and more.

These were the men who considered themselves the problem solvers of Los Angeles. They had left their homes on the East Coast or in Europe to make new lives and were determined to transform Los Angeles into an economically vibrant city—regardless of the cost. They didn't wait for the city council to innovate or build; when they had an idea they did the work themselves. It was men from this group who built the city's water and gas lines, subdivided the land, and laid out town plots. They socialized together in the city's Masonic lodges and the Los Angeles Social Club. But never before had such a concentration of Los Angeles's capitalists come together for a single purpose. The gathering in Isaias's banking office showed them their collective power, and the group would soon learn to use their strength to better the town—and themselves by extension.

The group of businessmen was as interesting for what it didn't represent as for what it did. There were no men of the old guard in the group, no Californios who had dominated the region for the past ninety years. It was a stark reminder of how the ruling elite of Los Angeles had turned over completely in just the twelve years since Isaias's arrival. Most of the Californios did not successfully make the transition to American rule and an American economy.

By the time Isaias and Downey had finished lobbying the group, they had $500,000 pledged in capital for the bank—five times more than had ever been raised before for a Los Angeles bank (and the equivalent of about $8.5 million in 2006 dollars). Isaias and Downey contributed $100,000 each, with others donating between $5,000 and $25,000. Downey became president at an annual salary of $2,400, and Isaias became cashier, earning $3,380. They named the new bank the Farmers and Merchants Bank.

A local paper made note of the February 1871 meeting:

"New Bank—At an informal meeting of capitalists held on the evening of the 1st, it was resolved to organize a new banking institution to be known as the Bank of Los Angeles. [The name was later changed.] It is understood that the respective banks of Governor Downey and Mr. Hellman will be consolidated to form the nucleus of the new concern, which is to commence operations with a paid up cash capital of $500,000. . . . The establishment of such a bank would not only enable financial operations to be carried on upon a larger and more metropolitan scale than heretofore, but would tend to foster manufactures and new enterprises of every kind in our midst and to the lasting advantage of our people."

Isaias spent the weekend of April 8 and 9 combining funds from the two old banks into new accounts at the Farmers and Merchants Bank. Downey's bank contributed $35,500 and Isaias's bank put in $189,500. When the doors opened at 8 A.M. that Monday, the temperature was fifty-six degrees and Hellman was waiting with his two tellers for new customers. The new bank was in the same location as Isaias's last bank—in a two-story brick building built by Pio Pico, right across the street from Solomon Lazard's dry-goods and clothing store, which advertised that "spring and summer goods" would go on sale two days later. By the end of the first day, new customers had deposited more than $20,000.

To lure customers accustomed to sending their gold and coins to better-established banks in San Francisco, Isaias initiated a new product: he offered time deposits, or savings accounts, the first time interest had ever been paid in Los Angeles. The innovation persuaded many merchants and farmers to switch accounts to the Farmers and Merchants Bank. Within six months, more than six hundred people had deposits on account.

Mortgages made up the bulk of the bank's transactions. New settlers streamed into the area and went to Isaias to request loans to buy farmland. Isaias was conservative and rarely offered to loan more than half the value of an unimproved piece of land. Isaias also got requests for loans for new businesses, and he often took a personal stake when he thought a company looked especially promising. His investment was considered a coveted stamp of approval. It meant that Isaias considered the owner's prospects good.

The early 1870s was a time of experimentation in Los Angeles, when farmers and merchants were still trying to figure out the crops and businesses that would flourish in the region. In the late 1860s, California and its temperate climate seemed an ideal place to raise silkworms. Aspiring farmers planted thousands of mulberry trees and imported silkworms from China, in part to capture subsidies offered by the state legislature. The fad faded as quickly as it started. Farmers then turned their attention to growing wheat, barley, walnuts, and Mission grapes, which were used to make wine. A number of growers tried raising oranges, and the number of fruit and nut trees planted in the region tripled in just a few years. One inventive farmer even managed to raise pineapples.

Two brothers, Otto J. and Oswald F. Zahn, capitalized on the growing travel between Los Angeles and Catalina Island, located twenty-two miles offshore. The construction of the railroad to the Pacific Coast made getting to Catalina Island much easier, and hearty adventurers would camp out and swim in the blue waters. But once on the island, they were cut off. The Zahns filled a void with the Catalina Pigeon Messengers, a flock of homing pigeons that carried news between the island and the towns on the mainland. It was cause for celebration when the Zahns' prized pigeon, Blue Jim, flew the channel in only fifty minutes.[5]

Isaias's former partners, F. P. F. Temple and William Workman, were unhappy about the Farmers and Merchants Bank. Temple, in particular, had no intention of abandoning the banking business and the profits it promised. He was one of Los Angeles's boldest innovators, a visionary whom many admired for his efforts to develop Santa Monica and the waterworks at Cerro Gordo mines. Temple had just spent $150,000 on a brick addition to the Temple Block. He envisioned a bank anchoring the bottom floor along Spring Street.

Temple was determined to open his own bank, one that would compete with the Farmers and Merchants Bank for capital and prestige. On November 23, 1871, eight months after Isaias and Downey opened the doors of their new bank, Temple founded the Temple and Workman Bank. Temple still had a proclivity to lend money on unsecured investments, but now that Isaias was no longer his partner, he had no one to stop him from lending unwisely. Workman was a partner in name only. "It soon became evident that anybody could borrow money with or without proper security, and unscrupulous people hastened to take advantage of the situation," said Harris Newmark.[6]

That attitude would prove cataclysmic for the struggling city.

Any notion that Los Angeles was becoming civilized, a place that honored decorum, elegance, and wealth, was shattered on October 24, 1871, when hordes of men, some white and some of Mexican descent, attacked and massacred some of the town's small Chinese population.

About 235 Chinese people lived in Los Angeles, with most of them crowded into old adobe houses that lined Calle de los Negros. Just a short stroll from the Plaza, the alley was still the city's underbelly. Among the brothels and gambling dens, however, was a thriving Chinese community. There were stores that sold food for Chinese cuisine, Chinese laundries, Chinese herbalists, and families eking out a living.

The Chinese had moved to America to work on the transcontinental railroad, and were paid $1 a day for backbreaking, dangerous work. When the railroad was completed in 1869, many of them moved south to Los Angeles to work on other construction projects. Many people in California did not understand the Chinese, since they looked and dressed differently than Westerners. The men wore their hair in long pigtails called queues and wore padded silk jackets rather than frock coats. They worshipped different gods and ate food that seemed peculiar. Many of the Chinese settlers were single, which led some Americans to think they they did not value family and thus were morally inferior. Americans were also afraid the Chinese would steal jobs that they considered rightly belonged to Americans.

Many referred to the Chinese as "Celestials," derogatory shorthand for the Chinese Celestial Empire. Newspapers didn't think twice before casually insulting the Chinese. "The antipathy inherent in persons of the white race against the hideous and repulsive Mongolians . . . was well illustrated on Main Street yesterday," the *Los Angeles Daily News* reported on July 19, 1871. "Two boys of the respective ages of about six and eight years were observed shaking their little fists at a passing Chinaman."

Chinese society in California was controlled by tongs, or large groups with a strong leader. Many whites thought the Chinese disregarded American law and instead had their own code of conduct, which some believed included using torture to exert control. "There is in the rear of one of the dens of Negro Alley an apparatus regularly arranged for whipping informers and others who may be thought to need it, in the most approved Chinese fashion," reported one newspaper. "Is not this carrying things a little too far?"[7]

The massacre was sparked by a fight between two rival tongs over a prostitute. On the evening of October 24, members of the competing tongs exchanged a short burst of pistol fire in the alley. A police officer named Jesus Bilderrain went to investigate and soon found himself fleeing from a fusillade of bullets. He called for help, and a few people, including a man named Robert Thompson, rushed to his side. Someone from inside one of the Chinese stores fired at Thompson, striking him in the chest. He was taken to Wollweber's drugstore on Main Street, where he died an hour later.

As news of Thompson's death spread, angry men gathered around the Coronel Block, one of the more crowded adobes in the alley. The Chinese had barricaded themselves inside, closing the shutters and locking the doors. As many as a thousand armed whites and Mexicans stood in front of the adobe, holding guns and shouting threats to those inside. When a shot rang out, the mob attacked, rushing to open the doors and windows and even knocking holes in the roof to take aim at the Chinese inside.

The mob then started to seize random Chinese men—men who had nothing to do with the tong war—off the street and proceeded to drag them, beat them, kick them, shoot them, and then hang them. When one Chinese man escaped from the alley, he was followed by the mob. A group of police officers intervened and captured the Chinese man with the intent of placing him in jail, where he would be protected from the violence. But the infuriated mob grabbed the man and hung him on a makeshift gallows at a corral on New High Street.

The sheriff and police department were unable to stop the mob and were later criticized for not intervening more forcefully. By the time the mob finished, at least nineteen Chinese men were dead, with most murdered by hanging. The dead included two young boys and Gene Tung, a well-respected Chinese doctor who pleaded with his captors and offered them $3,000 to let him go. They ignored his cries, hung him, and cut off his fingers to get the rings he wore.[8]

The leaders of Los Angeles condemned the violence, which they blamed on the lower classes of the city, particularly those of Mexican descent. A grand jury indicted more than 150 men for their involvement in the massacre, but when the time came to identify the attackers in court, few stepped forward as witnesses. California law prohibited the Chinese from testifying in court, making the case that much more difficult to prosecute. A few perpetrators were sentenced to San Quentin prison, but they stayed in jail for only a few weeks. Of the nineteen murdered Chinese men, only one was found to have had anything to do with the shooting of Robert Thompson.

In late 1871, Herman returned to Los Angeles. He had spent the previous year in Reckendorf with his family, where he had gotten trapped by the Franco-Prussian War. But it had been a triumphal visit, as Herman had returned to Germany with sizable savings. His sisters wrote glowingly to Isaias about the new silk frocks and other presents Herman had bought them. His parents were grateful for his contrbutions toward his sisters' dowries.

Herman had also gone back to look for a wife. He wanted to find someone who could provide him with a comfortable home yet adapt to the rigors of California. He didn't become engaged on this trip, but it is likely that he renewed his acquaintance with his nineteen-year-old cousin, Ida Heimann, a heavyset woman with soulful brown eyes. Ida's family lived in Treviso, Italy, but had originally come from Reckendorf, and they visited regularly.

When Herman returned, he had no interest in running another stationery store. As he cast about for a new project, he noted the brisk trade between Los Angeles and the Arizona Territory. Herman decided to start a wholesale grocery company, one that could sell both locally and throughout the Southwest. It was a business that would take a fair amount of money to start, and Herman asked Bernard Cohn to be a partner. Cohn understood the rigors of frontier merchandising because he had once owned a store in the gold-mining town of La Paz on the eastern shore of the Colorado River.

The third partner was Jacob Haas, a Reckendorf native who had run the dry-goods store, Haas Brothers, in Portland. Haas was now living in San Francisco, where his cousin Kalman was partner in Loupe and Haas, a dry-goods store on California Street. Haas would run the San Francisco division of the company, selecting and ordering goods from the hundreds of wholesalers clustered around the bay. Haas's younger brother, Abraham, would join Hellman, Haas & Company in 1873, later becoming a partner.

Hellman, Haas & Company opened in a two-story brick building on the east side of Los Angeles Street between Aliso and Requena, right across the street from another wholesale grocery run by Harris Newmark. The store was stocked with virtually everything a person needed from cradle to grave, including liquor, cigars, farming implements, doors, blinds, candy, and bluepoint oysters. The store also bought products to resell, such as fruit, wool, hides, corn, barley, and other produce. "The mammoth wholesale house of Hellman, Haas & Co. is now ready for the transaction of business," noted the *Evening Express* on December 21, 1871. "This firm has the largest and most complete stock of goods of any wholesale house on the southern Coast and everything in their line can be purchased at this house on terms as reasonable as at any house in San Francisco."

Less than six months after opening, Hellman, Haas & Company advertised itself as the largest wholesale grocer on the southern coast. In August 1872, the assessor calculated that the company owned $35,590 in property, which included real estate and merchandise. That earned Herman a spot in the *Los Angeles Star*'s annual report "Rich Men of Los Angeles County."

Herman certainly enjoyed living well. On August 17, the newspaper reported that Herman had raced his horse, Hector, against George Butler's horse, Brown Dick, in a "long expected contest." The two horses raced before a large crowd at Agricultural Park. Hector had been injured during training, though, and he lost the three heats to Brown Dick, costing his owner $100.

For Isaias and Esther, 1871 was a very good year. In addition to the opening of the Farmers and Merchants Bank, the couple had their first child. Isaias Hellman Jr. was born on March 31. He was nicknamed Marco.

SEVEN

THE RAILROAD

1871–1876

A tightly packed horde of men and women streamed down Main Street toward the courthouse, torches held aloft. Electricity hadn't come to Los Angeles yet, but there were so many flames leaping upward that the sky sparkled with light. Rockets shot into the air, and forty gas burners lit up a huge platform that had been assembled as a stage. A brass band played whimsical tunes.

It was November 2, 1872, and the people of Los Angeles had come out in droves to express support for one of the most important proposals in the town's history. In three days, voters would decide whether to offer a subsidy to lure the railroad to town. The men marking their ballots would have to figure out not only if they wanted to pay $600,000 for the privilege, but which railroad to offer it to. Both the Southern Pacific, controlled by Collis Huntington and former governor Leland Stanford, and the Texas Pacific, owned by Thomas A. Scott, were interested in constructing a line to the region.

The choice had split the town in two, pitting friend against friend, business partner against business partner. Debates about the merits of each proposal raged in bars and stores. Which railroad would help the city the most? Was the city getting suckered by fast-talking millionaires or sold for cheap by unscrupulous politicians and businessmen? Newspapers detailed the behind-the-scenes maneuvers, lobbying, and arm-twisting by backers of the various deals.

Los Angeles was caught up in railroad frenzy, an affliction that had recently affected much of the United States. Ever since the transcontinental railroad had been completed with the hammering of a gold spike in 1869, cities and towns around the country had fought hard to link up to railroad spurs. Hundreds of small railroad lines had sprung up, linking isolated hamlets to the iron tracks. When the lines went in, the towns flourished. When the lines bypassed towns, they withered.

For California, the railroad was an economic necessity. The state was isolated geographically from the rest of the country, retarding growth in trade. Its roads were poorly developed, making it difficult to travel easily among the state's cities. It still took two days to travel by steamer from San Francisco to Los Angeles, and even longer by stage. Moving goods was expensive and laborious.

Isaias and other businessmen saw a new railroad link from Los Angeles to the rest of the country as an economic lifeline, a vein surging with trade and money. They wanted a locomotive to pull into a station in downtown Los Angeles and discharge freight and passengers. In 1872, the city was still an economic backwater compared to San Francisco to the north.

A year earlier, it had looked as if the Southern Pacific Railroad might bypass Los Angeles entirely and leave it stranded. The Southern Pacific had just started building lines south from San Francisco, and the company proposed to lay tracks down the center of California, through the flat and fertile valleys of the state and on to dusty Bakersfield, ninety miles northeast of Los Angeles, where it would veer east on its way St. Louis. For Isaias and other businessmen, the route was unacceptable. It was miles from Los Angeles, too far away to be of any benefit.

Benjamin Wilson, a pioneer rancher and former Los Angeles mayor, county supervisor, and state senator, recognized that the only way to ensure that Los Angeles would be on the main railroad line was to travel to the town that handed out favors to railroad magnates: Washington, D.C. In 1871, he went there at his own expense and became a one-man lobbying machine, hounding California congressmen, arguing to them the importance of remembering Los Angeles. He spoke eloquently on the matter before a House subcommittee. All he asked for was that six words, "by the way of Los Angeles," be inserted into an upcoming bill authorizing a new southern transcontinental route. Those words would guarantee that Leland Stanford, the president of the Southern Pacific, would lay his new line through Los Angeles, not just lay tracks through Bakersfield.

The congressional vote came in late February 1871. No one on the West Coast knew of the results for days, and anxiety mounted in town. A telegram announcing the results finally arrived from San Francisco on March 3, directly into the offices of the *Los Angeles Star*: "The Southern Pacific Railroad Bill has passed—all right!"

The *Star* rushed two extra editions onto the street. Men were frenzied with happiness. They rushed through the business district, cheering and clapping and making noise. Some climbed to the balcony of the Bella Union Hotel and gave impromptu speeches. Others lit celebratory bonfires throughout the city. Los Angeles would flourish!

The battle for a railroad was really just beginning. After the initial euphoria, Isaias and other businessmen realized that the Southern Pacific didn't have the funds to build into Los Angeles. It needed enticement—and capital—to come in a hurry.

Isaias and his partner, John Downey, gathered with a small group of other local leaders. On May 6, 1872, the group published an open letter to the community in the newspapers. It was an invitation to a meeting to discuss the railroad and its subsidy. The letter, beginning with the salutation "Dear Sir," was signed by "your obd't sv'ts" (your obedient servants), nine prominent businessmen, including Isaias; Downey; Judge H. K. S. O'Melveny, the president of the city council; F. P. F. Temple; and other notables such as John M. Griffith and Robert Widney.

The decision of a small group of businessmen to lobby the Southern Pacific was a pivotal moment in Los Angeles's history. The town had been growing steadily, but it remained a backwater, a city without consequence. The "obedient servants" realized that the city, without a natural harbor, navigable river, or precious metals, was going to need to fight to grow. There was no organized city operation to lure the railroad; leading businessmen were the ones to lead the campaign.

The meeting drew four hundred people, many knowing of Leland Stanford's ability to circumvent federal law or get out of deals that looked airtight. They expressed concern that the Southern Pacific would figure out a way to bypass Los Angeles and argued that the city needed to sweeten the offer to the railroad.

"A railroad has been settled to be built from San Francisco to St. Louis, and if that railroad should not pass through here the people will remove from this valley," said O'Melveny. "I predict that in less than 25 years hence this city will have few inhabitants if the railroad passes it forty or fifty miles away. If we can get a railroad to connect with us without any outlay on our part, then let us take it; if, however, we must pay something for it, let us make the effort to get it as cheap as possible."[1]

The group elected a "Committee of Thirty" to negotiate directly with Leland Stanford and the Southern Pacific, although voters would have to approve any deal. After numerous trips to San Francisco, where they would lay out maps of southern California and debate the best routes with Huntington and Stanford, the committee offered the Southern Pacific more than $600,000 in enticements (about $140 million in 2007 dollars) to build to Los Angeles. The county would float about half the amount in bonds and deed to the Southern Pacific the county and city's stock in the Los Angeles and San Pedro Railroad.

The high price tag turned many men's stomachs and spurred an antirailroad group. Its leader was Colonel Benjamin L. Peel, a hulking, powerful six-foot-two merchant originally from Texas. He was wary of granting the Southern Pacific control of the existing rail line to the port because he was convinced the railroad would use its new monopoly to raise freighting prices to exorbitant levels.

Around this time, Los Angeles was presented with another offer of a link to a transcontinental railroad—and the proposal ignited the warring parties. The owner of the Texas Pacific, Thomas A. Scott, who controlled more railroad track than any other man in the United States, offered to build a branch line from San Diego to Los Angeles, to hook up with a transcontinental line he was planning to build along the thirty-second parallel. That would also provide Los Angeles with a transcontinental link. Scott asked for a subsidy but said he did not want control of the existing railroad to the port.

The offer gave men like Peel something to rally around. Los Angeles became divided into two camps, and each side tried to promote its position with parades, rallies, bonfires, bands, and speeches.

Isaias was not tempted by the San Diego offer. "Governor Stanford's road is the only one that will ever be built," declared Isaias. "The Los Angeles and San Diego road is a great humbug, and is only put up as a blind."

But other influential businessmen, including Isaias's partner, John Downey, were not so sure. Downey, originally a supporter of the Southern Pacific deal—he was one of the men to convene the first meeting and he was on the Committee of Thirty—switched sides. He had been turned off by the railroad's bullying tactics; it had supposedly threatened to build another town and make it the terminus if Los Angeles did not provide a generous subsidy. Downey later reverted to his original position, but not before he had persuaded many other men to back the San Diego offer.

Half-truths, innuendos, and outright lies swirled through the region, and each side claimed to offer Los Angeles a more secure future. Judge Robert Widney, a Southern Pacific supporter, wrote a fourteen-page pamphlet examining the issues. The booklet, mailed to every voter in the county, was so logically and clearly presented that it turned public opinion against the San Diego offer.

But neither side wanted to take any chances. In a time-honored, though illegal, Los Angeles tradition, backers of the San Diego railroad decided to bribe some non-native residents to vote for their side. Many of the city's citizens had been born in Mexico and were not particularly interested in issues at the ballot box. They often sold their votes.

On the night before the election, leaders of the Mexicans herded three hundred men into a corral. They were supposed to remain there until morning, when they would be led to the polls to cast a vote. But in the middle of the night, backers of the Southern Pacific line met with the captain of the corralled men and offered to pay more for their votes. The Mexicans immediately switched sides.

Around 9:30 A.M. on election day, Isaias was standing outside a polling place when he ran into Dr. John Griffin. The two men had known and worked with each other for years. Griffin was Isaias's doctor and a founding investor in the Farmers and Merchants bank. They both served on the boards of the local Democratic county committee and the Los Angeles and San Pedro Railroad.

This time their meeting was not amicable. The medical man glared at Isaias, his eyes conveying anger and contempt. Griffin hated the Southern Pacific and wanted to forge a deal with the Texas Pacific. He started to shout at Isaias about dirty "vote buying." Isaias yelled back, and soon the two men's screams attracted a crowd.

Griffin became so incensed at Isaias that he lifted his walking stick and thumped it on Isaias's head. Isaias fell to the ground, dazed, as blood seeped out of a wound on his scalp.

Friends circled around the wounded Isaias. They picked him up and rushed him back to his house, where Esther was at home with baby Marco. Shocked to see the blood running out of the wound on her husband's head, she frantically asked him which doctor they should call. As if it were nothing more than a scratch, Isaias said, "Oh, call for old Doc Griffin."

The fight reflected the intense emotions swirling around that day. Friends and companions had turned on one another, each convinced that his position was the only sensible one. The vote wasn't even close, though. The Southern Pacific won easily, garnering almost three times as many votes as the Texas Pacific.

I n 1873, Isaias found himself embroiled in another election and the hits he received were much worse than those he got during the railroad fight. The election that September became about him, in opposition to him, a judgment on his honesty and social standing. But he wasn't running for any office.

"Smash the Hellman Ring Today and a Future Prosperity Dawns," read one headline in the September 3, 1873, edition of the *Star*. "Let All Good Citizens Array Themselves Against the Man Who Says He Carries Los Angeles County in His Vest Pocket," read another headline a few inches down the page. "We must form a phalanx of opposition to these jobbers and pawnbrokers and put down the Hellman democracy and its accompaniments in the ugly shape of high taxation and rates of interest that would have made the revengeful old Shylock himself shudder," said another editorial that day.

Isaias's fall from respect to disdain had been swift and unexpected. The cause was money, and the question was whether some of the richest men in town were manipulating the government in order to pay lower taxes.

The problem started, according to the florid accounts of the newspapers, in June, when the deputy assessor, L. Seebold, went to see Isaias at the Farmers and Merchants Bank. There was no federal income tax then, and each person paid a tax according to his or her wealth. The county assessors would assign a value to real property and also ask individuals how much money they had.

The deputy assessor asked Isaias to describe the property of the Farmers and Merchants Bank. Isaias did so, listing the bank's furniture as worth $1,000. When the deputy assessor asked him to list the bank's cash, Isaias said the bank had no funds of its own. The assessor than asked for a listing of all the bank's clients and the amount of the bank accounts because he wanted to use the bank's overall deposits to determine the amount of tax it should pay. Isaias declined to provide the information because he felt the deposits belonged to the individual account holders, not the bank itself. "He refused compliance, saying that it would be a breach of trust or confidence to publish the names of the depositors," said the assessor Seebold in a testimonial printed in the *Star*.

Isaias's reluctance to pay what he considered outlandish taxes was an attitude he would carry throughout his life. Like many businessmen of his time, Isaias looked down on politicians because he regarded most government as incompetent, even corrupt. Isaias thought that private businesses did a better job than government of providing services to citizens.

But Isaias quickly realized he would probably not win this battle. Several days later, Isaias asked the assessor to return to the bank, where he filled out an amended assessment and listed the bank's cash assets at $30,000.

The flap over the bank's assessment might have gone unnoticed, but the city's common council, acting as the city's board of equalization, reviewed all of the assessments in the city. The board raised some people's assessments and left others intact, infuriating residents who thought the decisions smacked of cronyism. They charged that city politicians had left their friends' assessments alone.

The angry residents formed a new political party called the People's Reform Party and put up a new candidate for treasurer—F. P. F. Temple, Isaias's former banking partner. Many members of the People's Reform Party were people who had opposed offering a subsidy to the Southern Pacific the year before. Temple challenged Thomas E. Rowan, the incumbent treasurer and a former teller at the Farmers and Merchants Bank. Rowan was widely seen as Hellman's man.

While anger against the established government was at the root of dissension in the city, it became personalized against Isaias. His rise to prominence had been steady ever since he started banking in 1868, and his financial acumen seemed a lightning rod. Isaias was now one of the wealthier men in the city and a major player in the local Democratic Party. He could also be arrogant and would dismiss those he considered beneath him. Newspapers suggested that he was the city's true power broker and represented the interests of the monied class of the Democratic Party, not workingmen and farmers. "The people have come to look upon the little financier who declares that he carries the county in his vest pocket as a dangerous medium," reported the *Star*.

The election also became a battle between banks, the Farmers and Merchants and the Temple and Workman. As treasurer, Rowan had discretion where to deposit the city's money, and he had selected the Farmers and Merchants Bank. Since Rowan was a bank employee, some residents thought he might be improperly profiting from the arrangement. If Temple won the election, he promised, the funds would go into his bank.

Isaias tried to explain his actions, but his words were derided. "In the madness of political excitement men appear to ignore veracity in order to injure an opponent or benefit a friend," Isaias wrote in a letter to the *Express*.

Despite the hyperbole and the thinly disguised anti-Jewish nature of the attacks against Isaias ("jobbers" and "Shylock" being just two of the references used in association with him), Isaias's candidate, Rowan, won reelection, handily defeating Temple. But several other candidates associated with Hellman's wing of the Democratic Party were thrown out of office.

In 1874, Herman Hellman once again returned to Germany, where he married his cousin Ida Heimann on July 26. They traveled back to Los Angeles and moved into a gingerbread-style house with a bay window and front porch on Fourth and Spring streets. In 1875, they had their first daughter, Clothilde.

Herman may already have had a child, one conceived out of wedlock with Louisa Wattell, a former housekeeper for Isaiah M. and Caroline Hellman. Wattell had been born in Rochester, New York, in 1855, and moved with her parents to Los Angeles around 1864. In 1874, when she was nineteen, she gave birth to a son whom she named Junot Wattell. Though Herman never formally acknowledged the boy, he gave Louisa money to live on and set up an account for her at the Lapprovich grocery store on First and Main streets. In 1880, Louisa moved to Iowa, where she married Louis Jungst.[2]

Frieda was born in 1876, followed by Marco, Irving, Waldo, and Amy.

The first four years of the Farmers and Merchants Bank were good years, in which business boomed throughout the state. California's flourishing economy started with the gold rush in 1848, but it continued with a silver rush. In 1859, huge veins of silver were found in Nevada, and soon hordes of men were streaming eastward over the Sierra Nevada toward Virginia City. The Comstock Lode made megamillionaires out of a small group of mine owners, but speculation on silver stocks made thousands of others wealthy as well. Crowds would gather hourly at the stock exchange in San Francisco to watch the rise and fall of mining stocks. The city was full of stories of overnight success, of how someone traded a few shares of stock for a new pair of boots, enabling a cobbler to become a man of affluence a few weeks later. "For most of the public, the giddy pace could never end," wrote one historian. "Millionaires and sand-shovelers, businessmen and gamblers, waiters, bankers, Chinese laundrymen, butcher boys, cab-drivers, all were caught up in the speculative whirl."[3]

The fluctuations were immense: On January 8, 1868, a single share of stock from the Hale & Norcross Mine in Virginia City sold for $300. Two days later, after news spread of an especially good strike, the stock sold for $1,475. By February 15, a share sold for $7,100.[4] A man who spent $800 to buy one hundred shares of Consolidated Virginia stock in 1870 would see those shares soar in value (through stock splits and consolidation) to $680,000 by December 1874.[5]

One of the best-known tycoons of the era, a man with a mythical stature, was William Ralston, whose fortune was inextricably tied up in the Comstock Lode. Ralston came to California during the gold rush and in 1862 started the Bank of California, which evolved into the dominant bank in California, Oregon, and other western states. The bank invested in woolen mills and cigar factories, hotels and theaters, the Alaska fur trade—and in the silver mines of Nevada. Ralston believed in doing everything on a grand scale. His one-hundred-room villa in Belmont, south of San Francisco, was modeled after the Palace of Versailles and featured a mirrored ballroom, crystal chandeliers, and more than three hundred gaslights. Ralston's dinners were famous for their ostentation, and his guests included President Rutherford B. Hayes, Ulysses S. Grant, Mark Hopkins, Leland Stanford, and Mark Twain.

While the silver stocks retained their value, Ralston rode high. When they dropped, his bank felt the bite. The silver boom came to an abrupt end in early January 1875. On the seventh, the market value of the major silver mines totaled almost $194 million on the San Francisco Stock Exchange.[6] The next day the stock prices dropped precipitately. They continued their slide through the end of February. The worst hit was the Ophir Mine, owned by Ralston and his partner William Sharon. Its stock went from $315 a share down to $65 a share.[7]

The sudden decline in silver stocks was a long-delayed reaction to rampant speculation as well as a financial downturn on the East Coast in 1873. In the years after the Civil War, the United States enjoyed one of its greatest periods of economic expansion, one driven largely by the enormous growth of the railroads. Between 1865 and 1873, railroad men laid down sixty-five thousand miles of track, with much of the expansion financed through the sale of stock. In the fall of 1873, the investment banking house of Jay Cooke failed because of its heavy investment in the stock of the faltering Northern Pacific Railroad, setting off a chain reaction throughout the East. The New York Stock Exchange closed for ten days, banks failed, people lost their homes and businesses, and credit dried up. By 1875, 25 percent of the workers in New York City were unemployed.

California was so far away from New York that it took two years for its economy to feel the repercussions from the failures. Many West Coast businessmen had blithely predicted that bad times could never hit them. But when the ripple effects of the failure eventually made their way westward to California, the results were calamitous.

The summer of 1875 found Isaias in Europe, his first trip back to Germany since he left in 1859. After visiting family in Reckendorf and Würzburg, Isaias and Esther spent time at two separate spas. Isaias went to Bad Kissengen with Esther's brother and his wife to seek treatment for his recurring headaches. Esther and four-year-old Marco stayed at Bad Schwalbach. Isaias didn't enjoy the separation from his family, and his depression was only deepened by the economic news from the United States.

When Isaias had left Los Angeles, he had been convinced that the Panic of 1873 that had devastated the East Coast would not travel westward. But by late August, California had been hit hard. On Thursday, August 26, nervous depositors swarmed Ralston's Bank of California in San Francisco, long considered the state's biggest and soundest bank. Thousands of panicked people rushed into the marble lobby and demanded their money. By late afternoon they had withdrawn almost $1.5 million, and Ralston was forced to shut the bank's doors.

People in Los Angeles heard about the run on the Bank of California, and it spurred worries about funds in the city's two banks. If the state's largest financial institution could close its doors, what guarantee was there that other banks wouldn't do the same? The thought scared them, and a rush of customers crowded into the main room of the Farmers and Merchants Bank. They demanded their money and wouldn't listen to suggestions that it was safe. By the end of the day, customers had withdrawn about $36,000, almost half the bank's cash reserves. The Temple and Workman Bank paid out large sums as well.[8]

The next day came the shocking news that Ralston was dead. The burly millionaire had drowned during his customary daily swim in San Francisco Bay. Initial reports declared Ralston's death a suicide, but it was later ruled accidental. The thought that one of the state's richest, most successful men was so threatened by business misfortunes that he chose to end his life sent customers surging into the banking rooms of the Farmers and Merchants Bank demanding their money. It was a Saturday, and the bank closed at noon, so withdrawals only came to $5,700. Downey, the bank's president, sent a telegram from San Francisco: "Keep a stiff upper lip and your doors open, all your credits are secured."

The situation at Temple and Workman was even more dire. F. P. F. Temple had never been one to worry about security, and he was lax about keeping large amounts of cash on hand. As customers insisted on their money, he watched his bank's deposits dwindle dangerously low.

Los Angeles was in the midst of its first full-scale bank run. With Isaias in Europe and Downey in San Francisco, the directors of the Farmers and Merchants Bank held an emergency meeting, one of nine they would hold over the next few days. None of them was an experienced banker; they were just frontier businessmen who had gone into banking as a sideline business. Scared by the notion that the bank would soon run out of money, they voted to close. The officers of the Temple and Workman Bank made the same decision.

The doors of the Farmers and Merchants Bank remained shut the next Monday, August 30. It was the first time in the bank's four-year history that it was shuttered for business on a workday.

Isaias was in Venice when he heard that the Farmers and Merchants Bank had suspended operations. The news infuriated him. The sterling reputation that had taken him ten years to build was wiped out in that one decision. Isaias had always been a conservative banker, one acutely aware of the need to give customers their money when they demanded it. He had made it a habit to keep large cash reserves on hand, often as much as 50 percent of total deposits—a practice that Downey clearly had not followed in his absence. Isaias would never have agreed to the bank closure.

Now all Isaias could think of was returning to Los Angeles. His vacation was supposed to last for another few months, but there was no possibility he could enjoy himself while his business floundered. He made plans to return without his family. Esther, Marco, and Isaias's fifteen-year-old brother James, who was moving to Los Angeles, would follow later.

Isaias took a train from Venice to Liverpool, where he found an ocean liner leaving almost immediately for Boston. Once he got to the United States, he wired his brother-in-law Meyer Lehman and asked for a $20,000 loan. He then boarded a westbound transcontinental train, where he had ample time to mull over the financial disaster awaiting. "I did not hear about Los Angeles until now, the whole story was 'mismanaged,' " Isaias wrote to Esther on September 20, 1875. "Our losses were pretty high. I received dozens of letters and dispatches here, each of them saying, 'Come, come, raise all the money you can and come.' I will have a lot of hard work. I will prove to the people that Farmers and Merchants is ready for an emergency and has honorable intentions."[9]

The time Isaias spent alone on the train must have been excruciating. He longed to be back in Los Angeles, where he could take action, yet he was stranded in transit. "The more I think of the mismanagement of our own Bank, the worse I feel," he wrote his wife. "If I had been at home, Temple would have had to close, but we would have stood firm."[10]

Isaias stopped in San Francisco, but only long enough to arrange a loan from the banking firm Lazard Freres. Then he boarded the Telegraph Stage

Line for Los Angeles, arriving there on September 29, the eve of Rosh Hashanah, the beginning of the Jewish New Year. Isaias had traveled more than six thousand miles in twenty-three days, an astonishing feat. But would there be anything left to come back for?

T he papers in Los Angeles reacted blithely to the news of the two banks' decision to close: "The banks of Los Angeles very sensibly closed their doors today, to await the latest development from San Francisco. Our Los Angeles banks are on excellent footing and their action in this matter meets with the general approbation of the business community."

It soon became clear that the banks would not open anytime soon. Downey rushed down from San Francisco and had an emergency meeting with Temple, who asked that the two banks coordinate a thirty-day cooling-down period. The harsh fact was that gold coin was in short supply. Ralston had put much of the Bank of California's currency into the state's wheat crop, depleting coin reserves. The Farmers and Merchants Bank, while solvent, had lent heavily in support of the city's recent growth, money that would make the institution future profits, but not money that was easily liquidated.

The banks announced their decision in the *Los Angeles Star* on Thursday, September 2. "Owing to the difficulty of obtaining Gold coin for immediate demands in our home market, and the impossibility of that en route from the East to reach us—this, coupled with a reluctance to press our customers and bring upon our community unnecessary disaster—we are compelled to close our respective banks for thirty days from this date. . . . Every dollar will be paid to our depositors in gold coin and with all possible dispatch. We will allow to all depositors, without distinction, interest at the rate of one percent per month for the time they are thus involuntarily deprived of the use of their money."

Ironically, the day before, voters had elected Temple the county treasurer—putting into office a man who had only a tenuous hold over his own bank. Temple had finally defeated three-term incumbent Rowan, Isaias's neighbor, friend, and former employee.

Downey and the directors believed the Farmers and Merchants Bank was ultimately sound, and they arranged for depositors to withdraw up to $250 by cashing a draft at Hellman, Haas & Company. Temple and Workman made a similar arrangement with H. Newmark and Company. The town's other bank, the Los Angeles County Savings Bank, was a bank that required a six-month advance notice to withdraw funds, so it was not affected by the bank run.

The closure gave the Farmers and Merchants Bank some breathing room while its directors frantically searched for coin, agreeing to pay high rates of interest just so the doors of the Farmers and Merchants Bank could reopen. The federal government did not guarantee any accounts in 1875, so individual bankers had to weather the vicissitudes of calamity themselves. Many banks never recovered from bank runs, and many people saw their life savings disappear without a trace.

Downey immediately borrowed money from his brother-in-law, Peter Donahue, a director of the First National Gold Bank in San Francisco. Donahue agreed to lend $20,000 at 1 percent interest a month, and he followed that a few days later with a similar loan at 1½ percent interest. In the meantime, Isaiah M. Hellman, Isaias's older cousin and a bank investor, secured a $15,000 loan from Haas Brothers of San Francisco.[11]

Still, those loans were not enough. To raise more money, Downey boarded a steamer for San Francisco on September 13, 1875. He carried with him the bank's most precious commodity, $175,000 of mortgage loans, which he planned to offer to the First National Gold Bank in exchange for a line of credit of at least $200,000. The credit would provide liquidity for the Farmers and Merchants Bank, but strip it of the interest income paid on the notes.

Downey trolled for funds wherever he could. He ran into his friend James Flood, who had made a fortune in the Nevada silver mines, and who was unaffected by the crisis. Downey explained the bank's financial situation. Flood, who was planning to open his own bank, the Nevada Bank, in San Francisco in a matter of weeks, clapped Downey on the shoulder and pledged to lend him $70,000.

The directors waiting back in Los Angeles grew increasingly nervous about the bank's future prospects. John S. Griffin, Ozro W. Childs, Matthew Keller, and Cameron E. Thom sent a desperate telegram to Downey: "You thoroughly understand our absolute necessity for coin. We must have it cost what it may. If it does not come the alternative is financial dishonor, to us that idea is too abhorrent to be entertained for a moment: we pin our faith in you. For if your success is commensurate with our wants, the honor will be all yours; if we go under, curses, both loud and deep, will especially attach to your financial name. We must have $100,000 over and above whatever may now be on hand, here or in San Francisco."[12]

This panic led the directors to overpay for money. They arranged a ruinous loan with Alexander Weil, who agreed to lend $40,000 at 1¾ percent interest a month. Since the bank only lent funds for 1¼ percent interest a month, the loan was a guaranteed money loser.

Isaias returned to this chaotic environment hours before the thirty-day cooling-off period ended on October 1. As the sun rose over the dusty streets of Los Angeles that morning, residents wondered whether the city's banks would reopen, or if the fledgling financial system that had brought tangible growth to the area had collapsed on itself, never to rise again.

The doors to the Temple and Workman Bank remained ominously closed. But the Farmers and Merchants Bank opened for business, and when customers went inside, they immediately felt reassured. Isaias, the bank's cashier, had returned and had stacked up on the counter the money the bank had borrowed. Customers coming in saw towers and towers of gold, concrete proof of the bank's solvency. "Persons who dropped into the Farmers and Merchants Bank yesterday afternoon could not well avoid seeing a rather pretty sight," the Los Angeles Daily Herald reported on October 2. "The tables were covered with trays filled with twenty-dollar pieces, piles of gold notes were lying about, on the floor were a score or more of boxes filled with silver, and a peep into the vault disclosed a number of large bags puffed out with coin."

This trick of displaying towers of gold to reassure nervous customers was one that Isaias would use throughout his banking career.

The Temple and Workman Bank did not open its doors for another two months. When Temple went out to borrow funds, he found that very few people were willing to lend his institution any money. His reputation as a lax manager preceded him, and no bank was willing to take the risk.

Desperate to avoid bankruptcy, Temple turned to E. J. "Lucky" Baldwin, one of the most successful—and calculating—businessmen in the state.

Baldwin had made millions in Comstock's Hale & Norcross Mine and had sold his shares in the Ophir Mine for $5.5 million right before the bust. He was the owner of the opulent Baldwin Hotel in San Francisco, and in March 1875 he had purchased from Harris Newmark and his partners the Santa Anita Rancho, which he would later develop as a horse track. He was a notorious womanizer—two women would shoot at him during his life, and he would later go on trial in Los Angeles for seducing a young and innocent girl.

Baldwin agreed to lend Temple $310,000 but insisted on hard terms. In addition to paying interest on the money, he demanded that Temple, Workman, and their friend Juan Matias Sanchez back the loan with mortgages on all their personal property, including the Temple Block on Main Street and Workman's beloved Rancho La Puente.

The arrival of Baldwin's money became a community affair, with all eyes watching its journey from San Francisco to Los Angeles. Men armed with Henry rifles and Colt revolvers guarded the stagecoach as it made its way from Caliente near the Tehachapi Pass. "Yesterday morning at an early hour an immense crowd besieged Temple & Workman's doors, all in good humor and jubilant at the termination of the financial embargo," the *Daily Herald* reported on Tuesday, December 7, 1875. "At ten o'clock the doors opened and when the crowd saw Mr. Temple standing behind his counter, smiling pleasantly as he stood flanked by piles of gold, a hearty cheer went up which meant encouragement to the bank and confidence in Los Angeles."

The jubilation lasted a month. While people in Los Angeles publicly expressed faith in Temple, they privately had concerns. Withdrawals continued, and the bank abruptly shut its doors on January 5, 1876, this time for good. Trapped inside the vaults was $23,000 of the city's funds (put there once Temple became county treasurer) as well as the hopes and dreams of hundreds of people.

Baldwin was merciless. He demanded the personal property of the banks' owners. Sanchez had to hand over the deeds to almost 5,500 acres, leaving him with only a small 200-acre parcel he had deeded to his wife. On Wednesday, May 17, William Workman was in bed in his home, which was no longer just a modest adobe. Four years earlier the architect Ezra Kysor, who designed Temple B'nai B'rith, had transformed the modest structure into an English manor house with a gabled slate roof. Workman was so delighted with the change that he spent more time than ever at Rancho La Puente. That morning, though, the seventy-six-year-old man was resting in an attempt to recover from a bug that had sidelined him the past few days. But he forced himself out of bed when he was told there was someone to see him. The visitor, a stranger, handed Workman a paper that declared his property was to be sold at sheriff's auction.

The news sent a deep shock through Workman. How could this be? There was no place Workman loved more than Rancho La Puente, no place which fed his soul so deeply. He had spent years building his dream home, planting the grounds and raising stock, adding a mill and a cemetery. Now it would be stripped from him.

Bereft over the loss of his home, Workman went into the living room. Still wearing only his undergarments, he shot a bullet through his head.

The collapse of Temple and Workman badly hurt the local economy. Scores of people lost everything they owned, and the city feared it would never get its money back. The bank went into receivership, but Temple's assets and Workman's fortune were barely enough to pay fifty cents on the dollar at the bank.

The collapse, along with a general weakening around the state, contributed to a slowdown in the economy. Los Angeles was still a small town with a mere seven thousand inhabitants, and the downturn reverberated strongly. Land sales slumped. A parcel that might have gone for $100 in early 1874 went for $30 to $55 in 1876. So many people were unemployed that a third of the male population went temporarily to Arizona to find work.[13]

The depression made people angry, and they looked around to ascribe blame. Soon rumors swirled that the Jews were responsible for the closure of the Temple and Workman Bank. The Jews had supposedly stormed the bank and withdrawn so much money that they promoted its collapse. Jackson Graves, then an attorney for both banks, refuted the accusation in his 1927 memoir, pointing out that the depositors at Temple and Workman were almost 100 percent Protestant or Catholic. The Jews tended to bank at Farmers and Merchants.

Isaias clearly felt the sting of occasional anti-Semitism, because he told Graves, "Graves, I have to be a better man than you are, because I am a Jew.

You can do things I cannot do. If I did them I would be criticized, while you will not be. I have to keep that steadily in mind, in all my dealings."

Isaias never fully trusted Downey after the bank's closure. Like in his previous partnership with Temple and Workman, Hellman realized that his approach to banking was different from Downey's. He regarded the customer, not himself, as his primary responsibility. In the coming years, Isaias would learn just how self-centered Downey had been when Isaias was vacationing in Europe.

As Isaias set about repaying all the loans the bank had taken out, a sixteen-month process, he started to reconsider his position at the bank. Isaias had urged Downey to become his partner to offer the Farmers and Merchants Bank visibility and prestige. But the 1875 bank closure had changed the dynamic. Now it was Isaias, not Downey, who was credited with saving the bank and putting it once again on a sound footing. The bank had resumed paying dividends in December, after having suspended them in September after the closure. Isaias was the hero, and his actions enhanced his reputation in financial circles.

Downey was forty-eight years old and Isaias was just thirty-three, but he regarded himself as the more competent of the two. He decided it was time to come out of Downey's shadow, to take command of the institution he had worked so hard for. Isaias decided he wanted to replace Downey as president of the bank.

Isaias began to lobby various directors of the Farmers and Merchants Bank. Any change in leadership would have to come at the bank's annual stockholders' meeting, which was set for Monday, July 10, 1876.

The day of the meeting came, and Isaias waited in his office, but he soon discovered Downey wasn't stepping aside easily. The elder banker had plenty of friends on the bank's board, and he convinced them to boycott the meeting. Without a quorum, the meeting was canceled.

The next day, Isaias tried again. He called a meeting of the stockholders. Once again, not enough directors showed up to form a quorum.

The next day the same thing happened. The meeting was canceled.

The standoff continued for nine days. On the surface, it didn't look like anything was happening. Behind the scenes, Isaias and Downey wrestled for control of the bank. After days of negotiations, the two struck a deal. Isaias agreed to buy seventy-two shares of stock from Downey for $64,000, which came to about $889 a share. That, along with his wife Esther's stock, would give Isaias majority ownership of the bank's five hundred shares.

The board of directors finally met on July 19, when they voted to install Isaias as president of the bank. It was a position he would hold for the next forty-four years, until his death in 1920. Downey stepped aside, although he remained on the board.

The two men who had founded Los Angeles's first successful bank, an institution intimately involved with the city's growth, now found that the power balance between them had shifted. They had to seek a new kind of business alliance. It would not be easy.

The excitement on the platform was palpable. Hundreds of people crowded into the newly constructed station, impatient to board the train that would carry them to a ceremony ending decades of isolation. Los Angeles was about to be linked by rail to the rest of the nation. For three years, the Southern Pacific Railroad had been building tracks to Los Angeles. Thousands of Chinese workers had labored twelve-hour days building north from Los Angeles and south from San Francisco to complete the line. On Tuesday, September 5, 1876, it was completed.

Isaias was among the hundreds who crammed onto the platform, eager to get on the train that would take the group to the ceremonial laying of the gold spike. At 9:30 A.M. he boarded, along with 352 other passengers, all invited to celebrate the completion because each had played some role in bringing a rail line to Los Angeles. The train pulled out of the station and slowly made its way through the pueblo. American flags streamed from the front of the train. Thousands of people lined the streets to see the locomotive off.

At 10:30 A.M. the train passed through the seven-thousand-foot-long San Fernando Tunnel, the longest tunnel west of the Appalachian Mountains. The tunnel was an engineering marvel, hewn from wet, oil-saturated sandstone that was prone to collapse. It took 330 Chinese laborers, overseen by Southern Pacific engineer Frank Fates, months of work to conquer the mountain. It took ten minutes for the train to travel through the dark passageway.

Close to noon, the train pulled into Soledad Canyon, an inhospitable, windy plot of land fit only, Benjamin Wilson noted at the time, "for the production of horned toads and scorpions." Bare mountains rose up in the distance, and prickly pear cactus plants and greasewood bushes dotted the ground.

An amazing sight greeted the revelers. Three thousand Chinese workers, all wearing triangular grass basket hats and blue denim jackets and trousers, stood lined up along the tracks to greet them. The Chinese were almost in a military formation with their long-handled shovels held front of them "like an army at rest after a well-fought battle." Dozens of construction wagons, rails, and carts were clustered nearby. Hundreds of white canvas tents had been set up as temporary homes for the workers. The Atlantic and Pacific Telegraph Company had erected two white tents with batteries and operators standing by to flash details about the ceremony around the country.

About an hour later, after the revelers had been fed by Native Americans who came from the hills to sell grapes and other fruit, a train from the north arrived. It stopped a short distance from the group from Los Angeles. A brass band started to play as dignitaries from the south went over to greet those coming from the north. Leland Stanford, one of the owners of the railroad, came to the ceremony, as did the mayor of San Francisco; six county supervisors; Darius Ogden Mills, one of the richest bankers on the coast; and Michael De Young, the owner of the *San Francisco Chronicle*. Jacob Haas, Herman's business partner, also made the trip down from San Francisco.

"Far to!" called Charles Crocker, one of the owners of the rail line, and with that the thousands of Chinese workers jumped to life and started to lay line as fast as they could. In just eight minutes the workers dragged rails from flatcars and affixed them down, followed quickly by dozens of men who pounded in spikes to secure the rails.

When the Chinese workers had finished connecting the rails coming from the north to the rails coming from the south, Crocker took a specially inscribed gold spike and nailed it in with a few quick hits from a silver hammer. The track linking the northern and southern parts of the state was completed. "It has been deemed best on this occasion that the last spike to be driven should be of gold, [to indicate] the great wealth which should flow into the coffers of San Francisco and Los Angeles when this connection is made," said Crocker.[14]

The crowd roared and the telegraph operators got to work, sending out the news. When it reached Los Angeles, a cannon went off, announcing to residents of the pueblo that Los Angeles was isolated no more.

Bringing the Southern Pacific Railroad to Los Angeles was the single most important decision ever made by the town's citizens. It connected the city to the rest of the country and set the stage for the region's huge population explosion. The advent of the railroad also greatly expanded southern California's ability to sell its crops. In 1877 William Wolfskill, one of the region's largest purveyors of fruit, shipped a train car of oranges to St. Louis, the first large-scale shipment of fruit. By 1880, there would be more than 1.25 million citrus trees in southern California. Many of those would be navel oranges, which got their start in 1873 when the Department of Agriculture shipped a cutting of the fruit to Mrs. L. C. Tibbetts of Riverside. In 1886, trains carried five hundred carloads of citrus out of the state.

But the men who worked so hard to bring Southern Pacific to the region soon had reason to regret their actions. By 1876, the rail line had seized control of most of the transportation routes out of Los Angeles, including the steamers that traveled up and down the coast. The Southern Pacific proceeded to increase its freighting rates dramatically, in some cases bumping the cost of shipping from $8 to $30 a ton.

Merchants tried to fight back. Herman Hellman and Harris Newmark chartered a steamer and offered to ship goods for only $3 a ton. The Southern Pacific retaliated. Since it owned most of the warehouses at the port and at the depot in Los Angeles, it declared that it would charge storage costs for any goods connected with Hellman and Newmark's competing steamer.

Charles Crocker, then president of the Central Pacific Railroad, which owned the Southern Pacific, came down to a city council meeting called to address freighting rates. Men smoking and chewing tobacco packed into the meeting room and refused to treat Crocker with the respect to which he had become accustomed. When one city council member suggested that Crocker be permitted to speak first, another legislator insisted he would be heard when his time came. After listening to disparaging remark after disparaging remark, Crocker could no longer contain his fury. He threatened to squash his opponents: "If this be the spirit in which Los Angeles proposes to deal with the railroad upon which the town's very vitality must depend, I will make grass to grow in the streets of your city!"[15]

In an effort to kill the competition, the Southern Pacific then lowered shipping costs by $3 a ton and offered to carry some crops, like potatoes, for free between Los Angeles and San Francisco. There was no way Hellman and Newmark's upstart freighter could beat that offer. "The mask was now discarded, and it became evident that we were engaged in a life-and-death struggle," wrote Newmark.

After a ten-month battle, most of the competing shippers except Hellman, Haas & Company and H. Newmark and Company abandoned the fight. Those companies finally conceded after Phineas Banning brokered a deal whereby the railroad would take over the lease of Hellman and Newmark's freighter.

The Southern Pacific had won.

PROSPERITY

1877–1880

By 1877, the lower part of Main Street had become a Millionaires' Row of sorts, shaded by towering glossy pepper trees dangling with red berries. These houses were not grandiose like the sandstone palaces on New York's Fifth Avenue or the turreted Italianate homes that sat on San Francisco's Nob Hill, but they were big and imposing for Los Angeles. Most important, the mansions announced that Los Angeles had arrived; the dusty pueblo was gone, replaced by a more modern, more civilized city.

Former governor John Downey had been the first to build a mansion on Main Street. In 1865, flush with funds from selling twenty-acre plots from the vast Rancho Santa Gertrudes he had gotten at a sheriff's sale, Downey and his wife, Maria, built a brick house, the most elegant the town had ever seen. It had large windows to capture the southern California sun, a recessed porch that overlooked expansive tropical gardens, an orange grove, a billiard table, and the town's first ballroom. Mrs. Downey came from an old Californio family, one steeped in the tradition of friendship, and she often opened the doors of her home for elaborate dinners and dances.

In 1876, Isaias started to build a new home on a parcel of land on Main Street that he had bought thirteen years earlier. It was near Downey's house at Fourth and Main, and was still such a long way from the business center— about three-quarters of a mile—that Isaias worried his wife and five-year-old son would feel isolated. "We found it so far out of town that it was unbearably lonesome," Isaias later recalled. "So I gave Tom Rowan a 40-foot lot next door, made him a present of it on condition that he would build and make his home near to me so that I could have a neighbor."[1]

Isaias was ready for a grand house, one that would announce to the world that he, the president of Los Angeles's biggest bank, was a success. Although Isaias didn't believe in bragging and held up modesty as a virtue, he had no trouble living lavishly. For the rest of his life he would live in large, ornate houses that couldn't help but draw attention—and even notices in the newspaper.

The Hellmans built a thirteen-room Italianate home, two stories tall with a mansard roof. Large bay windows jutted out on both floors, and a graceful staircase led to a wraparound veranda, a perfect place to pass balmy evenings and watch children play in the large yard. The dining room was frescoed with painted scenes from the Hellmans' lives, including landscapes of rural life in Germany, a view of the Mississippi River, and the shaded sycamore groves of their favorite picnic spot in the Arroyo Seco. Esther may have gotten the idea to fresco her walls from her uncle Lewis Goldsmith, whose home in New Orleans was decorated with frescos that were widely regarded as the most elaborate in the South. With a library, billiard room, and conservatory, the Hellmans' house cost $12,000.[2] "Taken altogether, outside and inside, this is the most stately, elaborately furnished and magnificent mansion in Southern California," the *Los Angeles Star* reported.[3]

Shortly after they moved into their new home, the Hellmans had their second child, Clara, born on September 13, 1877. She was followed by Florence on August 18, 1881. The family gained a new member when Isaias's seventeen-year-old cousin, Henry Fleishman, moved in. Henry's father, Israel, was the brother of Isaias's mother, Sara. His hardware store in New York was on the verge of bankruptcy. He wrote Isaias a desperate letter asking if he could serve as his "confidential man," or business associate in New York. Short of that, he asked if Isaias would take in Henry. Isaias had always had a fond spot for Henry—a feeling that would grow in the coming years—and he set him up as a clerk in the bank, paying him $95 a month.

The creation of a Millionaires' Row was symbolic of the new culture of city building that now gripped Los Angeles. Bringing the Southern Pacific Railroad to town had been a huge success for the small group of about 170 businessmen who formed the core of the city's elite.[4] The group, mostly Americans and Europeans who had come to the region before 1859, knew the city's growth was not guaranteed; Los Angeles had no natural port, no navigable river, and few mineral resources, and the development of its fertile lands was hampered by the lack of an extensive irrigation system.

Men like Isaias, his brother Herman, John Downey, Eugene Meyer, Robert Widney, John Griffin, Harris Newmark, and others knew that they had to equip Los Angeles with the infrastructure needed to make a town grow—and only then would the city develop. They couldn't rely on elected officials, for it was an era when people looked suspiciously on government ownership of utilities. Instead, the city council handed out franchises for water, gas, and transportation lines to the highest bidders—who invariably came from this small set of businessmen. By the mid-1870s, these men controlled the city's utilities and sat on one another's boards. Isaias helped start the Los Angeles Water Company and later became its largest stockholder; he also sat on the board of the gas company and of the Los Angeles and San Pedro Railroad before it was folded into the Southern Pacific.

Transportation was one of the industries pushed by these men. In the previous decade, Americans had watched in fascination as inexperienced businessmen around the country had thrown up railroads and grown enormously rich. There was the hope that local rail lines would also offer enormous profits.

As Los Angeles grew, people built houses farther from the Plaza and the businesses along Main, Los Angeles, and Commercial streets, and they needed a way to get around. The first to see this problem was Robert Widney, a real estate salesman who had moved to Spring Street and found his walk to work inconvenient. In 1873, he built a mile-and-a-half-long trolley line from Main Street at the Plaza down to Sixth and Pearl. The line was primitive. One horse pulled a single trolley car down a track. Passengers would board the car and were expected to hold the reins while the conductor collected the 10¢ fare. When the tracks got muddy or filled with the ubiquitous summer dust, the trolley sometimes derailed. Passengers would disembark and help set it back in place. The trolley ran round-trip each hour from 6:30 A.M. to 10 P.M. On Sundays, service was more limited.[5]

Despite these inconveniences and the long wait between trolleys, Widney soon noticed that plots of land near the terminus of the line were selling briskly. Others noted his profits as well as their link to escalating real estate prices. A quartet of bankers built the next trolley line in 1875 and started the stampede into the transportation industry.

This second line, called the Main Street and Agricultural Park Railway, was only marginally more modern than Widney's original trolley. It had more turnouts where two cars could pass and an innovative fare box that let passengers put in their slugs from anywhere on the car. All of the town's bankers—Isaias and Downey from the Farmers and Merchants Bank and Temple and Workman from the bank bearing their names—had invested in the line. The group capitalized the project at $50,000 and set out to recoup its expenses through the sale of bonds.

The new route traveled south from the Plaza past Temple Block and down Main Street, and eventually made its way to the Agricultural Park, the newly built and wildly popular oval horse-racing park. On warm summer days the trolleys would be jammed with men, women, and celebrating children, all a 10¢ fare away from watching the horses or betting on the greyhounds. The line eventually extended more than five miles through town.

Three of those bankers would soon sell their shares of the Main Street and Agricultural Park line, leaving Isaias as the only original investor. It was a role he would embrace, and over the next fifteen years, as more and more trolley lines crisscrossed the region, he would emerge as the city's most powerful trolley magnate.

When the storied 13,000 acre Rancho Cucamonga in San Bernardino County fell onto hard times, Isaias viewed it as an unbeatable business opportunity. He could subdivide and sell a portion of the rancho and generate income by planting the rest with grapes, barley, and wheat. It was becoming increasingly clear that agriculture would soon replace mining as California's most important industry, and Isaias wanted to capitalize on the emerging market.

The Mexican government had granted the rancho, located thirty-five miles east of Los Angeles, to Tiburcio Tapia in 1839. Tapia had planted grapes on the land in the 1840s, producing some of California's earliest wines. His family sold the rancho after his death in 1859 to John and Merced Maria Rains, who brought in herds of sheep and cattle and horses and planted 150,000 grape vines. They built a brick house on the property and installed an ingenious cooling system. Summer temperatures could easily reach 100 degrees, and Rains ran flumes from a nearby stream through the kitchen, into the patio and under the house, cooling the air temperature.

In November 1862, Rains and his wife took out a $12,000 mortgage on the house. Five days later, Rains set out on a trip to Los Angeles. He never made it. His bruised and beaten body was discovered eleven days later in a clump of bushes. He had been lassoed and shot, but the murderer was never found.

His widow, Merced, eventually signed away control of her properties to an unscrupulous brother-in-law, who neglected to make mortgage payments. Rancho Cucamonga was sold in a sheriff's auction in 1870.

Isaias purchased the land for $49,819 and within a few weeks sold 5,480 of the acres to a San Francisco syndicate for $53,000, bringing him a quick profit of $4,000. Isaias held on to the other eight thousand acres and formed a partnership with Downey, Childs, and his cousin Isaiah M. Hellman to subdivide some of the land and plant other parcels with wheat, walnuts, oranges, and other crops. Isaias also retained the services of one of southern California's best winemakers, Jean Louis Sainsevain, who emigrated from France in 1839 with his brother Pierre. He restored the vineyards to their previous glory and started producing port, brandy, and Angelica, a sweet white wine. For a time, Rancho Cucamonga was the biggest winemaking estate in California.[6]

Benjamin Cumming Truman, a traveler in the 1870s, wrote glowingly about the ranch. "In my somewhat extensive tour through this region, I have nowhere seen a vineyard which presented a finer appearance than Cucamonga. The foliage of the vines was just sufficiently advanced in growth to present an even surface of delicate green over the whole extensive area. Not a weed disfigured the ground, which careful cultivation had rendered almost as smooth and level as a ball-room floor. That the new proprietors intend to make their valuable estate one of the finest properties in California, must be evident from the fact that they last year planted 40,000 foreign grape vines. There are 160,000 bearing vines on the place at present."[7]

Isaias parlayed his new experience in making wine to help one of his oldest friends out of a tough financial situation, an act that enhanced his reputation as a financial wizard. He was close friends with Matthew Keller, an Irishman who had come to Los Angeles in 1850 and set up a general merchandising store. Shortly after his arrival, Keller bought a fifty-year-old twenty-acre vineyard at Alameda and Aliso streets. In 1858, Keller—then known as Don Mateo—set up the Rising Sun Vineyard on one hundred acres on the west side of the Los Angeles River. He produced wine, port, and brandy. (He also bought—for 10¢ an acre—the Rancho Topanga Malibu, a thirteen-thousand-acre parcel that included twenty-one miles of seacoast.)

Don Mateo soon became one of the leading vintners of the state. He constantly tinkered to improve his product, substituting European grape stock for the ubiquitous Mission grape brought to California by the Spaniards, and employing Louis Pasteur's new machine to aerate wine. At the 1865 State Agricultural Fair, he won prizes for his white, red, and sweet Angelica wines.[8] His November, 29, 1875, party celebrating the Rising Sun Vineyard was one of the social events of the season. The *Los Angeles Times* described it as "the merriest gathering ever seen in Los Angeles." The guests dined on mock turtle soup, blanquette of chicken, and apricot pie, and drank many different types of wine. They danced to an orchestra until 5 A.M.[9]

But by 1876, Keller was struggling. There was an oversupply of grapes, and markets had not recovered from the eastern bank panic that finally arrived in Los Angeles in 1875. Keller fought back by opening wine storage depots in New York and Philadelphia. He soon traveled there to rescue his business.

While away, Keller left much of his business in the hands of Isaias. The men were close friends, and Keller had been one of the original twenty-three founders of the Farmers and Merchants Bank. Keller had a knack of ascribing humorous nicknames to people. He named Isaias "Valiente," or valiant one, in a show of high regard.[10]

Isaias immediately set out to reduce Keller's debt. He lent him funds for his East Coast operations and renegotiated a $6,000 mortgage held by the San Francisco banker Antoine Borel. Isaias even advised Keller to sell his vast Malibu land holdings for $220,000. "Properties of all kinds have greatly depreciated in value here and I do not believe another such offer will be made soon," Isaias wrote Keller. "Do not be influenced by my opinion in the matter, I might simply take the view of a banker who looks at the dark side."[11] Keller did not sell, but his son sold the rancho a few years later for $300,000.

Keller was extremely grateful for Isaias's help. "Your letter of July 30 has filled me with gratitude," Keller wrote. "It has given me new life & renewed vigor. Since you have promised to counsel and help me, now I can joyfully work in peace."[12]

Isaias seemed genuinely glad to help a man he liked and admired. "I feel gratified to know that I have a chance to do my friends some good, once in a while, and I know of no other friend whom I would rather do a kindness than my amigo Don Mateo."[13]

Keller returned to Los Angeles in 1879 and was soon out of debt. When he died in 1881, Isaias became the executor of his estate, guardian to his young son, and financial adviser to his three daughters.

A year after Isaias wrested control of the Farmers and Merchants Bank from Downey, he sued his former partner, the first in a series of lawsuits that weakened the bonds of the men's relationship. All the lawsuits centered on profits from various business deals, some done through the Farmers and Merchants Bank and some done outside. While the details differed, the lawsuits publicly illuminated the men's deteriorating friendship and must have made for some good gossip in the back rooms and offices of the city's merchants and businessmen.

In one lawsuit, the Farmers and Merchants Bank sued Downey for taking a cut of the profits of a land deal. While Isaias was in Europe in May 1875, Downey had authorized the bank to lend $15,000 to a land development company in exchange for giving Downey one-third of the land company's profits. The bank successfully argued in Judge Ygnacio Sepulveda's courtroom in the Temple Block that a bank officer had no right to benefit personally from a bank loan. When Isaias was called to testify, he used his time on the witness stand to criticize the way Downey handled the 1875 bank crisis. Isaias said his former partner borrowed funds at ruinous interest rates and undermined the bank's once-sterling reputation. "The Farmers and Merchants Bank became in bad repute, our best customers left us," Isaias testified. "Our business has declined and kept on declining for six or eight months."[14]

In another lawsuit, this one over proceeds from the sales of land at Rancho Cucamonga, Isaias offered that he no longer had "unlimited confidence" in the man he had once regarded as a mentor. In fact, Isaias intimated, maybe he had become the better businessman.

"You have considerable confidence in yourself as a financier?" asked one of Downey's attorneys.

"I don't know as I have confidence in myself," Isaias responded. "Other people have."

"Do you think you are as sound a financier as Governor Downey?" continued Downey's lawyer.

"That is for somebody else [to say]" said Isaias. "A man should never brag on himself."[15]

But the subtext was clear. Isaias felt the torch had been passed and he now held it tightly. It was an important moment, for it indicated Isaias's willingness finally to stand front and center in the community, rather than hide behind the reputation of another man.

September 4, 1880, dawned warm and clear in Los Angeles. By the early afternoon, hundreds of carriages were massed on Wesley Avenue, a new major thoroughfare in West Los Angeles. Women dressed in silks and cottons and men in dark frock coats made their way over the rough dirt road to gather on a barren patch of ground. This land, everyone hoped, would soon become the home of the University of Southern California.

As the region had grown, the need for better educational facilities had became clear. The best college in the state was the University of California, but it was located more than four hundred miles north in Berkeley. The Jesuits had started St. Vincent's College in 1865, but it was still quite small and appealed to only a particular segment of Los Angeles's population. In 1879, Robert Widney announced that he and a group of Methodists intended to start a new institution of higher learning, a place that could provide an excellent education to men and women in the southern part of the state. Widney put out a call for land to be donated for the university, enough land to sustain future growth.

The needs of the fledgling university coincided with the needs of Isaias and his partners, John Downey and Ozro Childs. In 1876, the trio had bought thousands of acres southwest of the outskirts of Los Angeles, in an area covered with grassy fields and little else. Intending to subdivide the land, they took out an ad that ran an entire column length in the September 17, 1877, edition of *Los Angeles Daily Herald*, dwarfing other real estate notices.

"Lots for sale!" read the ad. "Offers the best opportunity for delightful homesteads of any that has ever been offered for sale to the public. The whole tract is level. The soil is excellent. This is really the West end of our beautiful city, with the benefit of FRESH, PURE BREEZES FROM THE OCEAN, uncontaminated by gas or sewer effluvia."

Despite the hyperbole, the land was not easy to sell, as it was about three miles from the Plaza. There was a trolley line (started by the partners) running through the property, and Agricultural Park, the racetrack, was nearby, but the $300 parcels were not selling briskly. Part of the problem was oversupply; almost every businessman in Los Angeles, it seemed, was in the real estate business. John Griffin, for example, was advertising heavily in the papers to create a new community in East Los Angeles.

When Widney announced in May 1879 that the Methodists were looking for land on which to put a new university, Isaias and his partners jumped. They knew that having a school nearby would make West Los Angeles an attractive place to settle, and that it would spawn new houses and farms. Other large landowners felt similarly, and soon Widney had multiple offers of land.

To make their offer more attractive, Isaias, Downey, and Childs offered to extend the trolley line, the Main Street and Agricultural Park Railway, directly onto the new campus. That enticement may have done the trick— Widney accepted their offer of 308 lots of land, about 110 acres, in July 1879. The bulk would be sold off to form an endowment for the University of Southern California, and the rest would be used for the school.

On the day of the dedication, Isaias, Downey, and Childs were the guests of honor, and some of the land they had donated would soon bear their names: Hellman Street, Downey Way, and Childs Way. At 2:30 P.M., a church choir raised its voice in a hymn and the Reverend Marion Bovard read a short scripture, followed by a prayer read by university president Elder C. Shelling. Bishop I. W. Wiley then introduced Downey, who said a few words, and a shovel went into the earth, turning over dirt to lay the cornerstone.

"The dedication of the University of Southern California yesterday . . . is one of the most pleasing evidences of the new era into which we are entering," read an editorial in the *Los Angeles Daily Herald* the next day. "Los Angeles ought really to be the educational center of the Pacific Coast. Nowhere else are there so many advantages for colleges and academies as here. With an unsurpassed climate, the requisite seclusion for scholastic pursuit is found at the same time that the student is within an hour's walk of the rail and water highways of the world."

The University of Southern California opened its doors to fifty-three students and ten teachers in 1880. The names Hellman, Downey, and Childs would forever be associated with the school. Within a few years, parcels in the West Los Angeles tract owned by the trio had tripled in value, up to $1,000 each.

Isaias's donation to the University of Southern California caught the attention of Governor George C. Perkins. In July 1881, Perkins surprised Isaias by asking him to be a regent of the University of California, a member of the board that oversaw the university. It was a prestigious appointment, as the board was filled with some of the state's top politicians and businessmen, like Andrew Hallidie, the Scottish engineer who invented the cable car, and Darius Ogden Mills, the president of the Bank of California, the state's biggest financial institution. In fact, Isaias was appointed to fill the two years left on Mills's term. Perkins apparently had been lobbied to appoint someone from southern California—even then the northern and southern halves of the state were competing for resources—and had first considered John Downey before settling on Isaias. "The appointment will be accepted as quite a compliment to Southern California, which has been too much neglected in the past in all lines," said an editorial in the Daily Herald. ". . . Mr. Hellman, in addition to his sterling and sagacious business aptitudes, which will be found of great service to his colleagues in the management of the University, has many notable qualifications for the trust."[16]

The University of California had been created by the legislature thirteen years earlier and was still struggling to define itself. Most colleges in the United States had religious underpinnings and offered a rigid curriculum, but from the start the University of California strove to offer a broad education that pursued knowledge and truth, not dogma, in the arts and sciences. Classes for the two hundred students included Latin, Greek, European languages, chemistry, engineering, and mechanical arts, as well as practical training in farming. The university sat on a hill in Berkeley and offered a commanding view of San Francisco and the bay.

The regents' biggest challenge was financial. Berkeley had a reputation as a "poor man's university," since more than half of the students did manual labor to make ends meet. The school needed affluent students not only to increase enrollment, but also to attract private money, since the legislature offered only minimal financial support. But most of the state's rich men sent their sons east for college, unconvinced that their children would benefit from this western type of education.

In addition, while the state paid to support elementary schools, it did not fund high schools. Of the state's fifty-two counties, only seven funded a public high school. As a consequence, many students stopped their schooling after the eighth grade, greatly reducing the pool of applicants qualified to enter a university.[17]

Isaias served as regent for two years without incident, but his reappointment thrust him into the center of a political controversy. In Governor Perkins's last days in power, when the legislature was in recess, he appointed Isaias to a full sixteen-year term as regent. In the same proclamation, Perkins appointed former state senator Nathaniel Greene Curtis and former governor Leland Stanford to the board, in part because he hoped Stanford would leave his vast riches to the fledgling university. These lame-duck appointments angered members of the legislature, and when the Democratic caucus reconvened, it rejected the appointments and refused to bring them up for a vote. Isaias and Stanford were forced to withdraw their names from consideration. Stanford was so insulted that he went on in 1891 to start his own university, the Leland Stanford Jr. University, named after his son who died of typhoid at fifteen. The University of California never saw a penny of Stanford's estate. The next governor, George Stoneman, reappointed Isaias, and his nomination was approved. He would serve as a regent for thirty-seven years.

Rancho Los Alamitos sprawled from the Pacific Ocean eastward, its outermost boundaries reaching well into the hills gently edging from the coastal plain. At 26,000 acres, it was one of the larger remaining land grants in southern California, and its history reflected the turbulence of the last fifty years.

Los Alamitos had originally been part of a 167,000-acre tract given to the Spanish foot soldier Manuel Nieto, who had marched north from Mexico in the 1760s. When his commission finished, he remained, first living near San Diego and then moving north to be near the small pueblo of Los Angeles. Nieto asked his former commander, who was then the Spanish governor ruling California, for land, and was granted such a vast parcel that he could not possibly traverse it in a day.

When Mexico took over control of California, Nieto's heirs were still living on the land, making a good income by selling beef, tallow, and hides. Problems of inheritance ultimately troubled the family, which decided in 1834 to partition the sprawling rancho into six smaller pieces. One of these became Rancho Santa Gertrudes, which would eventually be sold to John Downey. Another was Rancho Los Cerritos, which would one day belong to the Temple family, and then to the Bixbys. Yet another was named Rancho Los Alamitos, or Little Cottonwoods, for the trees that lined its creeks.

Over the next thirty years, the rancho went through a number of owners, including the Mexican governor of California, Jose Figueroa, and Abel Stearns, the successful Yankee who married into the prominent Bandini family. In 1866, after Stearns was beset by financial problems, the mortgage holder, San Francisco financier Michael Reese, foreclosed on the ranch.

Reese never lived on Rancho Los Alamitos but rented it out to tenants, who continued to raise sheep and cattle. In 1878, John W. Bixby, a recent transplant from Maine, rented 1,000 acres of the rancho, and he moved his young family to the decaying adobe that stood on the hill overlooking the Pacific Ocean. Reese died in an accident later that year: Although he was a millionaire, he decided he didn't want to pay a small sum to enter a German graveyard to view his parents' graves. Instead, Reese vaulted the fence, fell, and broke his neck. His death made Rancho Los Alamitos available once again.

Bixby wanted to buy the entire rancho but did not have the funds. He approached Isaias for a loan, and in 1881 the Farmers and Merchants Bank financed the $125,000 acquisition. The purchase launched a partnership, with Isaias owning one-third of the rancho, John W. Bixby owning one-third, and a Bixby family company, J. Bixby & Company, owning one-third.

For the next six years, Bixby managed the rancho, turning it into one of the biggest and best stock farms in the region. Marshland near the ocean was pumped and drained and more than 500 acres of corn were planted by renters, soon to be followed by the planting of sugar beets. Bixby planted 150 acres of alfalfa in a western section with slightly alkaline soil, and he had plans to increase the alfalfa to 1,000 acres—enough to fatten the herds of livestock. "There are on the rancho at the present time 1000 head of cattle and 8000 head of sheep," reported one newspaper article. "The latter are in excellent condition and are nearly thoroughbred Spanish merino. There are about 300 milk cows, of which 140 are being milked to supply the Alamitos cheese factory. The products of the factory have gained such a reputation that it is simply impossible to keep the market supplied. Two hundred and thirty pounds of cheese per day are now being made, and three times that quantity could easily be disposed of."[18]

John W. Bixby died from appendicitis in 1887. His heirs and remaining partners agreed to subdivide Rancho Los Alamitos. They spun off close to 5,000 acres to the Alamitos Land Company, a jointly owned partnership between Isaias and the Bixbys. They planned to develop that property, which hugged the ocean and extended up onto Signal Hill, into home sites and towns. The rest was divided into thirds, with each partner getting 7,000 acres. John W. Bixby's widow, Susan, got the central portion of the ranch, which included the old adobe homestead as well as the name Rancho Los Alamitos. Isaias got the southern section hugging the Pacific Ocean, which included the modern city of Seal Beach. Other Bixbys got the rest.

Isaias had never owned such a large parcel of land. He could stand on the marshes on the westernmost edge of his property and not see its end. He could ride horses up into the hills, traveling for hours along deserted trails that led northward toward Los Angeles. The land struck a chord in Isaias, perhaps filling an unacknowledged need. The rolling hills covered with grazing cows and sheep, the fields of barley and sugar beets, reminded him of the bucolic early days of southern California, days he did not even know he missed until they were gone. He built a small ranch house on his land, and he used to take Esther and the children there for part of the summer. "When you visit Alamitos Ranch stay at least one night; you have likely never seen California ranch life before; it will give you an idea of the mode of living when I first arrived here," Isaias wrote to his brother-in-law.[19]

Esther loved the land too. She had always liked horses, and the Bixbys, who lived full-time on the ranch, raised horses. Esther and the girls "will go to our ranch and stay a fortnight," Isaias wrote Benjamin Newgass. "Marco has been there for some time, he has plenty of outside exercise—horseback riding, fishing, some hunting although his mother objects to the last part, he is getting to be a big boy. Our daughters are both doing well, Clara somewhat delicate, Florence a regular rowdy—but a very smart child."[20]

The property earned money. By 1890, Isaias stocked 1,890 head of cattle,

12,400 sheep, and a large assortment of mares, stallions, two-year-old colts, saddle horses, and racing colts. Soon the Bixbys started to call him "Shire," a nickname that reflected his heavy investment in horses. An inventory prepared for the ranch estimated that Isaias owned about $87,000 worth of livestock and equipment.[21]

As president of the Farmers and Merchants Bank, Isaias was in a perfect position to learn about business deals. While the bank mostly carried mortgages, in the 1880s it directed an increasing amount of money into promising businesses. Before lending funds, Isaias tried to determine whether a business would help the region's economy grow. If it could, he was more inclined to fund it, for he thought the positive effects of the loan would have a ripple effect. He also put money into a few risky ventures—but only when he decided that the men behind the enterprises were trustworthy. This decision to fund emerging companies would play a pivotal role in the growth of California.

In the mid-1880s, Los Angeles, like much of America, was oil crazy. America had been obsessed by oil since 1859, when Colonel Edwin Drake discovered rock oil while drilling a well in Titusville, Pennsylvania. The automobile hadn't been invented yet, but an increasingly industrialized America still needed oil for lamps and heating, and its by-product, gas, for illumination.

Residents of the Los Angeles region had been using oil products from the time of the earliest settlers. The region was dotted with brea, a sticky tarlike substance that Native Americans had used to waterproof baskets and Californios had used to tar their roofs. In 1855, Andres Pico started to excavate the asphaltum that lay in pools of oil on his large Rancho San Fernando. His discovey prompted other businessmen to start exploring, and within a few years there was a mini–oil boom. John Downey, Phineas Banning, and Benjamin Wilson formed the Pioneer Oil Company, one of the earliest companies formed to explore for oil. Despite spending hundreds of thousands of dollars to drill wells, the Pioneer Oil Company never found a rich strike and went out of business.

By 1887, there were only four companies exploring for oil in southern

California.[22] One was the Hardison & Stewart Oil Company, founded in 1883 by Lyman Stewart and Wallace Hardison, who had worked together successfully in Pennsylvania. They had moved their operations to Los Angeles and spent four years traipsing around the region, digging hole after hole in a fruitless search for oil. They borrowed all they could and soon found themselves broke and $183,000 in debt, with no gushers in sight.

The men went to see Isaias. "We didn't know what to do or where to turn," said Stewart. "We owed IWH all that we dared to owe him. But we saw him and told him that the Hardison & Stewart Co. needed $20,000. Mr. Hellman was in ill health and was preparing for a six-month trip abroad. He was calling in all loans. I told him how we were situated and how badly we needed the money. He replied, 'There are millionaires in this town that I won't lend another dollar to because they are doing nothing to benefit the community, but you are doing something to develop the resources of the county. Let me see your statement.' That made us tremble. We were then at the high water mark of our liabilities and our statement showed we owed one hundred and eighty-three thousand dollars. Mr. Hellman looked at the statement and said, 'Draw your checks for ten thousand more, and I will order them paid.' He did not ask for any collateral."[23]

The men eventually discovered oil. Their company today is known as Unocal.

On a spring evening in 1886, Harrison Gray Otis, a forty-nine-year-old Civil War veteran who now was one of the co-owners of the *Los Angeles Times*, visited Isaias at home. As the two men settled in Isaias's parlor, Otis talked about his troubles with the newspaper. Otis had come to California in 1876 and worked for a few years as the editor and publisher of the *Santa Barbara Press*. He had moved to Los Angeles to work for the *Times* in 1882, when the paper was eight months old, and within four years had gained control of half of the paper's assets. But Otis and his main partner, Henry H. Boyce, did not get along, and each man wanted to buy the other out. The trouble, Otis told Isaias, was that the purchase would cost $18,000, money that Otis did not have.

Los Angeles was crowded with newspapers in the early 1880s, each competing for a small segment of the city's twelve thousand residents. In addition to the *Times,* there was the *Daily Herald,* the *Evening Express,* and a smattering of smaller papers—a crowded market in which to make a profit.

Boyce was threatening to seize control of the paper unless Otis came up with the money. Otis was desperate to remain associated with the paper, which he was convinced would one day become very successful. After hearing his story, Isaias promised to lend Otis the funds to gain control of the *Times.* Otis would remember the gesture of faith the rest of his life.

"I have never forgotten the pregnant interview which I had with you, in your own parlor, about March 1886, when the problem to be resolved was how to get full control of the paper and rescue it from impending ruin by a pretender and a scoundrel," Otis wrote Isaias in 1894. "Then it was that you said that wise thing, that it would be of no avail, in the long run, for you to help me unless that help was made sufficient to enable me to get control and tread the deck of the ship as its sure enough commander. That aid you rendered and then and there was the problem solved, the battle won. For all of which, believe me, I am your friend."[24]

The loan turned out to be a propitious one. As Otis's paper grew and his power increased, Isaias could turn to him and ask that the pages of the newspaper report his side of the story.

While Isaias used the Farmers and Merchants Bank to lend money, he made many direct investments with his own money. As Los Angeles grew, Isaias invested more heavily in the city's trolley lines. In 1882, he and two partners, William J. Brodrick and John O. Wheeler, proposed installing a line from the Southern Pacific depot on North Spring Street southeast to Washington and Pearl streets. The men wanted to build the city's most modern streetcar line, one that could carry passengers three miles in thirty minutes. Lines that fast then existed only in large cities like San Francisco and Chicago.

From the start, Isaias faced opposition. While it had been easy to get a franchise from the Los Angeles City Council when he built his first trolley line in 1874, the political climate had changed significantly in the ensuing years. The city council had virtually given away its franchises as the pueblo developed into a metropolis, but now grappled with the sentiment that perhaps the city had not gotten enough in return. Some citizens felt that Isaias had too many trolley lines and wasn't paying enough for them. They also thought the city, not the private operators, should set the fares.

Bernard Cohn, a former business partner with Herman in Hellman, Haas & Company and the city's chairman of the Board of Public Works, was the most vocal in his opposition. "I desire, simply, when the city gives out another franchise, that the rights of the people are not given away with the franchise, as has been done in all previous matters," he told a newspaper.

Isaias was furious that his reputation was impugned, and defended his actions in letters to the editor. He even ghostwrote an editorial that may have been intended for the *Los Angeles Daily Herald,* where he held a minority interest. "Mr. Hellman proposes to build this road first as a safe investment and second to benefit the people," Isaias wrote about himself. "Look all over the city and see the amount of money expended by this gentleman in improvements. It proves his faith in Los Angeles more than any other individual and company."[25]

Cohn was unsuccessful in his efforts to squeeze more money out of Isaias. The franchise was approved, and the company, called the City Railroad of Los Angeles, incorporated in July 1883.

Isaias never forgave Cohn for his public attacks. When Cohn's name was put forward a few years later for the state banking commission, Isaias wrote to the governor and successfully killed his nomination.

Hellman and Brodrick soon launched an ambitious building campaign. Dozens of workmen graded the streets and laid down tracks. The company installed double cars pulled by two horses to increase the line's carrying capacity. The *Los Angeles Times* described the cars as "unquestionably the most substantial, comfortable and durable cars ever brought to Los Angeles." Heads turned even more a few months later when the City Railroad started to use eye-grabbing steel blue excursion cars with nickel-plated hardware. The company's lines extended four and a half miles through Los Angeles. Its trolley cars could indeed cover three miles in thirty minutes.

In 1886, the City Railroad merged with the Central Railroad, owned by the banker E. F. Spence and operated by J. F. Crank, who would soon emerge as Los Angeles's most savvy railroad builder. The two rail lines competed fiercely with each other, had numerous duplicate routes, and were poised to build extensions that went virtually to the same places in East Los Angeles. The merger had the benefit of eliminating this costly competition and creating a company with nearly fifteen miles of track.[26] It didn't necessarily make the riding experience any better, though, since the two companies used different-size rail gauges, making their trolleys incompatible.

Part of the plan for the new merged company was to convert parts of it to cable propulsion. In recent years, railroad entrepreneurs had been struggling to determine the best technology to run trolley lines. Driving them with steam was not practical, as the coal was dirty and the noise of the engines frightened horses pulling other vehicles on the street. The Scotsman Andrew Hallidie had invented a cable system that was powerful enough to pull cars up the steep hills of San Francisco, and many thought that technology was the answer. Cables could run from a central powerhouse, eliminating the need to put a source of propulsion on individual trolley cars. Its biggest liability, however, was expense. It required a large capital outlay to get started. (Electricity, which would become the favored means of propulsion in coming years, was not economically viable then.)

Isaias appeared again before the city council, this time asking for a franchise to convert a portion of the City Railroad to cable propulsion. He promised the politicians that he could raise the $750,000 needed to construct a large and impressive rail line. But once again, Isaias ran into opposition. One of the councilmen suggested that the city require Isaias to pay 5 percent of the new line's earnings to acquire the franchise. The proposal infuriated Isaias, who pointed out that others petitioning for franchises had not been asked to give a 5 percent payback. Isaias also pointed out that he and his partners "were not strangers here who came to gamble, but old residents."[27] In the end, the council did not require the rebate, but the discussion augured a change in the way business would be done in the future. But the council approved the conversion of a part of Isaias's rail line.

A little more than a year later, Isaias, J. F. Crank, and Charles Forman formed a new company, one that would be the largest transportation enterprise attempted in Los Angeles. The founders intended to capitalize the project with $2.5 million. Crank would own half of the stock of the Los Angeles Cable Railway, Isaias would own a quarter, and other investors would divide the rest. The plan called for the company to lay ten miles of new double-track cable for about $1.5 million, eventually expanding service to cover sixty-five miles around Los Angeles. Existing horse-drawn trolley cars would feed into the new cable lines, creating an expansive network. Three power stations would propel the cables. Three elevated viaducts would be built to carry the cable cars over the yards of the Southern Pacific Railroad Company.

While Isaias and Crank started the project with great enthusiasm, they soon realized the capital outlay was too great. The project was conceived during the heady days of a boom, and when inflated land values collapsed in 1888, buyers became wary of the Los Angeles Cable Railway bonds. Isaias ended up selling most of his shares to a Chicago syndicate. He would not return to active involvement with the Los Angeles transit system for almost a decade.[28]

The coming of the railroad and the growth of regional trolleys had propelled Los Angeles's economy forward, but progress had its price. On January 29, 1883, John and Maria Downey and a hundred other passengers were on an express train southbound from San Francisco to Los Angeles. It was a cold and wintry morning when the locomotive steamed and chugged its way through the Tehachapi Mountains, the series of sharp, stark mountains separating California's Central Valley from the state's southern sector. The conductor stopped at a small station on a mountain summit to refuel, and as he got out to make his report, an engineer and a fireman also disembarked. Then a young woman asked to enter the station. Since it was so dark and cold, the brakeman offered to escort her inside. In his moment of gallantry, he forgot to set the brake.

The train, perched on the summit, was suddenly pushed by a strong gale. It started to move down the tracks, slowly at first, but then faster and faster as the hill got steeper and steeper. Too late the conductor and other railroad workers realized that there was a runaway train. They rushed outside, only to see the locomotive out of their reach.

There was no one to temper the speed of the train rushing down the steep mountain grade. As it rounded a curve, the locomotive derailed and plunged into a ravine, where it rolled over and over. When the train finally came to rest, it burst into flames, burning those who had not been crushed. Dozens of people were killed.

When news of the accident reached Los Angeles, the baker Louis Mesmer rushed to the United States Hotel and lowered the flag to half-staff to alert people that something serious had happened. Rumors began to swirl that Downey and his wife had been killed. Horace Bell ran an editorial in his paper, the *Porcupine:* "On the reception of the news of the Tehachapi horror, and of the probable death of our most honored fellow citizen, Gov. Downey, and the wearing monotonous uncertainty of his fate, caused the utmost public concern among our people and proved that the Governor has a firm hold and large place in the affection of our people."[29]

News soon came that Downey's wife had been burned to death. Her remains were never found. Downey, however, had survived. A rescuer had rushed to the burning train and dragged the former governor from a sleeper car. He suffered only a few broken ribs. Downey was transported to his house on Main Street, where hundreds of people gathered outside his home to hear news about his health.

Downey eventually recovered physically, but he suffered from nervous shock the rest of his life. Faced with living without Maria, he set out on a three-year journey around the world. He wanted to put as much distance between himself and Los Angeles as possible.[30]

The demand for capital had transformed the financial profile of Los Angeles. While the Farmers and Merchants Bank was still the dominant institution, it was no longer the only one. There were now six banks in the city, and five more would open between 1885 and 1887.[31]

Many of the men who opened these banks had come to Isaias for advice and assistance. Isaias had helped organize the Los Angeles Savings Bank in 1884, and would play a major role in the creation of the Security Trust and Savings Bank. In 1888, J. F. Satori borrowed $20,000 from the Farmers and Merchants Bank to start the Los Angeles Loan and Trust Company. A year later it became the Security Trust and Savings Bank with Satori serving as cashier and F. N. Meyers serving as president. Isaias sat on the board of directors. In 1890, Maurice Hellman, the son of Isaias's first cousin Samuel M. Hellman, was elected to the board, and in 1895 he became vice president of the bank.[32]

Isaias would join the boards of other institutions, and would become president of the Pasadena National Bank in 1886. Isaias was considered the king of finances, a sober statesman who linked Los Angeles to its rowdy past.

E sther Hellman looked at the crowd meandering through the house. Some lingered at the dinner table, talking and laughing, while others made their way to the ballroom to dance to the waltz of the orchestra. Teenage girls in silk frocks made up with tight bodices clustered along the walls of the dance floor, giggling and whispering about whether anyone would approach them to dance.

The formally dressed orchestra paused after one dance, and then suddenly started to play the light ditty "The Irish Washerwoman." As the notes floated through the air, a five-year-old girl with blond ringlets walked onto the dance floor and began to jig. The sight of her graceful feet brought smiles to the faces of the partygoers, but no smile was larger than that of the girl's surprised father, Isaias Hellman.

The evening of March 28, 1884, was a celebration for Isaias and Esther's son, Marco, who had become a bar mitzvah earlier that evening at the B'nai B'rith synagogue. Marco, thirteen, had stood at the front of the synagogue with Rabbi Abraham Edelman and chanted portions of the Torah, the sacred book of Judaism. After the ceremony, hundreds of the Hellmans' friends had come to their spacious home on Main Street to one of the fanciest parties in recent memory. The dancing lasted for hours, and guests mingled in the library, the billiard room, and the conservatory, which looked out onto the gardens surrounding the house. The party was so elaborate, the gifts so lavish, that people talked about the event long afterward.

"I will tell you what presents he got," Louise Lazard wrote her friend Rosalie Meyer in San Francisco. "He got a hundred dollars from his mother to buy a horse, four lots from his father, a handsome writing desk from his two sisters, diamond cuff buttons from Henry Fleishman, a gold watch and gold chain from Mrs. Goodwin, a gold locket with an immense diamond from Mr. and Mrs. H. Hellman, a diamond scarf pin. . . . and an index dictionary stand. . . . He also received any number of flowers. . . . I forgot to say he received a silver-mounted saddle from Mr. Fred Bixby. We spent a delightful evening in dancing."[33]

Giving parties was one of Esther's specialties. Growing up in Germany, she had been raised to be a proper lady, one who created an inviting home. Esther often entertained Isaias's business acquaintances and opened her house to visiting relatives and friends. Every New Year's Day she threw an open house and invited dozens of people to stop by.

In many ways, Los Angeles was still primitive. The streets were unpaved, and dust still made its way into every nook and cranny when the hot Santa Ana winds blew in the fall. There was no citywide sewer system, and foul odors were not uncommon. Diseases like smallpox or fever took hold of children without warning, often killing them in a day or two.

Despite this—or perhaps because of it—the affluent women of Los Angeles did their best to re-create the elegance of New York, San Francisco, or Boston. They had their evening clothes made by French dressmakers, like Madame Delpach on Main Street. They worked hard to create a "civilized" home, one that would provide a refuge from the crudeness of the streets. Homes were decorated in the latest Victorian styles, with horsehair sofas, rosewood cabinets, glass-fronted display cases, and Brussels carpets.

The women held visiting days, when they would present embossed calling cards imprinted with their names at the front door. The visitor would scribble a short note if no one was home, or fold down the right corner to show she had come in person rather than having sent a servant. Esther received guests on Mondays in the late afternoon, as did Mrs. Harrison Gray Otis. Mrs. William H. Workman's visiting day was Tuesday, and Mrs. Henry O'Melveny opened her home on Thursdays.[34] Since there was not much outside entertainment, the women frequently hosted parties for one another.

Eda Kremer, a granddaughter of Los Angeles's pioneering Jewish couple, Joseph and Rosa Newmark (and who would one day marry Isaias's youngest bother, James Hellman), described a typical evening's entertainment to a friend, a dance that involved an elaborate arrangement of couples: "The Germain did pass off very nicely. We had about thirty couples and this is the way we arranged the partners. As every person entered the room they were handed an envelope not to be opened until the signal was given. When they were all assembled in the room word was given and all envelopes opened. Inside was a flag of some nation, of course a pair of every nation and whatever gentleman and lady had flags alike were partners. We danced until about twelve when we went over to dear Rosalie's house and had refreshments and after that we danced anything we cared to. I think everyone had a nice time or seemed to."[35]

In the summer, society moved to the beaches. Santa Monica, eighteen miles from downtown, was a favorite vacation spot, with its shimmering ocean and comfortable temperatures. At first, people camped in tents along the shore, but by the late-1880s, the town had a number of comfortable boardinghouses and hotels, including the Arcadia Hotel and the Santa Monica Hotel, where the old and infirm basked in the sun in glass-walled patios. Mothers and young children and their white-capped nurses strolled the streets, jostling for space with young ladies and their chaperones. On Fridays, the businessmen arrived for the weekend, a horde of dark-suited men pouring off the Los Angeles and Independence Railroad. So many people moved to Santa Monica for the summer that Congregation B'nai B'rith began holding Friday-night services there instead of at the synagogue in town.

But this small world of society women began to change in the early 1880s as Los Angeles boosters began to promote the region heavily as a health spot, a place with air so soft and clean it could cure ailments overnight. The new Santa Fe transcontinental railroad connection made it much easier to reach Los Angeles, and the population soared with arriving midwesterners and easterners. The city was unprepared, and the scarcity of housing and jobs became an issue. The transformation of Los Angeles also coincided with a societal reexamination of women's roles. Whereas upper-class women once were confined to overseeing their households and the moral education of their children, they now were regarded as "mothers to all," and were expected to try and help needier women and children.

Esther had always been involved with charity work. When she arrived in Los Angeles in 1870, she joined the Ladies Hebrew Benevolent Society and helped nurse the sick and poor, Jews and non-Jews alike. But she now plunged into helping others in a much more dedicated fashion.

The world of women's organizations in Los Angeles had been transformed in 1875, when one of the nation's most famous women's reformers moved to Los Angeles. Caroline Severance was a radical social thinker, a woman who fought to bring women out of their homes and into society. She had fought for women's suffrage alongside Elizabeth Cady Stanton and Susan B. Anthony and was close friends with the abolitionist William Lloyd Garrison and the poet Ralph Waldo Emerson. In 1868, Severance had started something in Boston called the New England Women's Club, devoted to bringing women together to talk about—and act on—social issues.

Severance moved to Los Angeles so her husband could recover from bronchial problems. When she arrived she immediately tried to organize the town's women into clubs, but was not particularly successful. Most of the women in Los Angeles were not ready to challenge social norms. In 1876, Severance and Mrs. Robert Widney did start a private kindergarten by luring the well-known German educator Emma Marwedel to town. Marwedel was a disciple of Frederich Froebel, who introduced the notion that children would benefit from free-form schooling and outdoor play starting at the age of three, a precursor to today's preschools and kindergartens. Marwedel's California Model Kindergarten opened in a private home on Hill Street in September 1876, but lasted only two years. It was the first kindergarten in California.

But the influx of people and the city's growing social problems convinced many women that they could no longer just sit by and let poor women and children suffer. Starting in the early 1880s, Severance organized a number of new women's clubs that would change the landscape of the city. She organized groups to help orphans, to offer free kindergarten to the poor, and to tackle local municipal issues. This time the women of Los Angeles responded.[36]

Esther was a charter member of the Kindergarten Association, established in 1884. The group opened a free kindergarten on October 1, 1885, and added a second site the next year. Within a few years, the Los Angeles school system had adopted the kindergarten model.

Soon Esther was a member of seven charitable groups and spent a good portion of her free time organizing balls, recitals, readings, and outdoor fetes to raise money. In addition to being a member of the Kindergarten Association, the Ladies Benevolent Society, and Ladies Hebrew Benevolent Society, she was a member of the German Ladies' Benevolent Society, the Orphans' Home Society, the Boy's Home Society, and the Flower Festival Society.

The women's groups provided cradle-to-grave help for poor women and children. The Flower Festival Society started a boardinghouse for young, unattached, and elderly working women. To raise money, the society inaugurated a ten-day festival of flowers that drew crowds from around the region. The women dressed Hazard's Pavilion with hundreds of thousands of colorful blossoms. Hundreds of people would visit the fragrant bowers to admire and smell the flowers, buy ice cream, and listen to music.

The various benevolent societies raised money for the poor and offered housing for poor orphans.

By the mid-1880s, the company that Herman Hellman ran with Jacob and Abraham Haas was one of the largest wholesale grocers in the Southwest. From its store and warehouse on Los Angeles Street, Hellman, Haas & Company distributed goods throughout California, Arizona, New Mexico, and northwest and central Texas. The company employed forty people and did $2 million in business a year.

Herman was one of Los Angeles's most prosperous businessmen. He had started to buy and sell property too. He and his wife, Ida, had four children, and had constructed a large Queen Anne–style home framed by palm trees on South Hill Street. The family also purchased a twenty-acre country home in Alhambra, where Herman and his son raised horses. "Herman W. Hellman loved horses and was a good judge of horses," wrote Herman Frank in *Scrapbook of a Western Pioneer.* ". . . Many pioneers like myself will remember that big mare named Queen, of which he was so proud. He drove Queen first single, then matched her with a fine gelding, making a fine stepping team."[37]

In 1884, tragedy struck the Hellman household. Nine-year-old Clothilde went to school on Tuesday and was sent home after lunch because her throat was so hoarse she could not recite her lessons. Ida Hellman summoned the doctor, who first diagnosed her with a cold, then attributed her labored breathing to asthma. Her teacher, E. Bengough, visited her on Wednesday and took tea with her. Then, unexpectedly, the little girl died.

"On Friday morning, Clara Milaure rushed into the house [the elementary school] calling out to the children that Clothilde was dead!" Bengough wrote on November 20, 1884, to Rosalie Meyer in San Francisco. "You can imagine the shock I received. It made me quite ill. I dismissed school and went at once to the house and found the poor parents in a sad, sad state. Too much stunned to believe almost that they were bereaved. When the father awoke around six in the morning, he found the child dead by the mother's side. Was it not dreadful! The poor parents have borne their trouble better than we thought they would. . . . It will take a long time to lift the shadow from them all."[38]

The family buried Clothilde in the Jewish cemetery in Chavez Ravine. Just days later, Herman and Isaias's sixty-nine-year-old father would die as well. "My brother Herman lost his eldest child a beautiful girl of 10 years," Isaias wrote his brother-in-law. "She was only ill 3 or 4 days—and then my good father was taken away very suddenly. . . . I hope the Lord will keep in the future all misfortune away from our whole family."[39]

Herman and Ida would soon have another son, Waldo, born in 1885. But he too would die prematurely. They buried him next to his older sister in 1887.

TRANSFORMATION

1886–1887

In 1886, Senator John F. Miller of California died in office, opening the way for the appointment of a new senator. Southern California saw its chance. There had never been a senator from the southern region, a fact that irritated businessmen, who felt Los Angeles was being shortchanged. The region had grown enormously in the last few years, and while it couldn't rival San Francisco's population, it was clearly the economic powerhouse of the southern part of the state. "Southern California with all its vast interests has never had representation in the US Senate," Isaias wrote Governor George Stoneman in March 1886. "San Francisco and the whole northern part of the state feels [sic] jealous towards Los Angeles and consequently are not aiding us, but on the contrary are opposing any and all just demands hailing from this country."[1]

In the late nineteenth century, U.S. senators were not elected directly by the people but instead were appointed by whichever political party was in power. When a vacancy occurred while the legislature was in recess, however, a governor could make an interim appointment.

That's what happened at Miller's death. Governor Stoneman ignored southern California's pleas and instead appointed George Hearst, the multimillionaire mining tycoon from San Francisco, to fill out the remainder of Miller's term. Hearst would join the railroad tycoon and former governor Leland Stanford in Washington.

Hearst, a poorly educated man who preferred work clothes and muddy boots over black frock coats and silk hats, was a brilliant miner whose business savvy and bravado had earned him tremendous respect. He had come to California during the gold rush but didn't hit it big until he was forty, when he acquired control of the Ophir silver mine in Nevada. By 1886, he had reaped an even more enormous fortune from the Homestake gold mine in South Dakota and the Anaconda copper mine in Montana. Just as important, he had purchased the *San Francisco Examiner* in 1880 and turned it into a crusading voice for California Democrats.

Hearst, who had served in the state assembly from 1865 to 1866 and had run unsuccessfully for governor in 1882, was also a generous contributor to Democratic candidates, a factor that surely played a big role in his appointment. "Reports have been rife here for a long time that a deal had been made between Stoneman and Hearst so that the former in the event of Miller's death was to make Hearst Senator, and Hearst would use his influence to again secure the nomination of Stoneman for governor," reported a Washington, D.C., newspaper. "It is said Hearst's appointment means a very large contribution to the Democratic campaign fund next fall when Hearst will be a candidate for the Senate for the full term."[2]

Stoneman, a Democrat, had appointed Hearst while the Republican-controlled legislature was in recess. As soon as it reconvened in August, the Republican members called Hearst back from Washington, D.C., where he had served less than five months. The legislature appointed a Republican, Abram P. Williams, instead.

In the meantime, Isaias had thrown himself into the political whirlpool of Los Angeles politics. For years he had been a prominent member of the Democratic Party, but always as a behind-the-scenes player. Isaias felt more comfortable lining up votes, writing letters to win appointments, or even donating money than standing up before a crowd stumping for a platform. Party politics interested him tremendously, but he was too naturally reserved to serve as a spokesman.

Los Angeles, once a Democratic stronghold, had turned increasingly Republican in the previous five years as more and more settlers arrived from the East and Midwest. The Democrats of the area were worried that they would not be able to send members to the legislature or even muster up a significant number of votes to return a Democrat to the governor's office. As the Democrats huddled at their county convention in September, they struggled to come up with strong candidates for mayor, sheriff, assessor, and other positions. The delegates eventually nominated Stephen Mallory White, a former Los Angeles district attorney, and L. J. Rose, a large landowner, as candidates for the state senate. Isaias was appointed the head of White's campaign.

It was a bitter battle. White was an affable and well-spoken man who had come to Los Angeles in 1874 and who was already being touted for higher office. But his opponent was Henry Hazard, the incredibly popular former mayor.

The Southern Pacific Railroad took a keen interest in the Los Angeles campaigns, just as it did in most political contests around the state. The railroad poured money and support into an array of candidacies, making it that much harder for the Democrats to succeed. White was an outspoken opponent of the railroads and had written numerous letters urging the state to tax the system more heavily. Isaias helped get his message out and also lobbied for votes for Washington Bartlett, the mayor of San Francisco and the Democratic nominee for governor. Isaias "is working like a bear," White wrote to William D. English, the chair of the Democratic State Committee.[3]

The November election was a partial success for the Democrats in Los Angeles. While three Los Angeles Republicans won the assembly seats, Democrats White and Rose were sent to the state senate. White won by a slim margin of 184 votes out of 6,507 votes cast.[4] The victory was enough to return control of the state senate to the Democrats. Bartlett won as well.

As soon as the Democrats sensed their triumph, they started to deliberate about whom they would choose for U.S. Senate, since Williams's brief four-month term was set to expire. White immediately put forward Isaias's name, since Hellman had played such an important role garnering critical Democratic votes in southern California. It was not an outlandish choice, because previous political office was not considered necessary for election to the Senate.

But would a Democratic legislaure choose Isaias over Hearst? From the time his name was put forth, there were doubts. "The county will vote for Hellman," White wrote to the state Democratic Party chairman. "He made a very effective campaign and would like the compliment, and states openly that he is a candidate for the purposes of staying. Of course, I have no idea if he has any chance of election. This, however, I say to you *privately* because he probably thinks he has a chance and would not enjoy having cold water thrown on his aspirations but as long as he wishes us to vote for him we will feel under obligation to do so."[5]

Isaias too had concerns, but they focused less on his ability to outmaneuver Hearst and more on his religious affiliation. "I have been foolish enough lately to take a hand in state and national politics and with some success—now southern California demands for me as a reward the United States Senatorship at Washington from the state of California," Isaias wrote to his brother-in-law in England. "I do not know whether it is possible for me or any other Jehuda [Jew] to attain this high and exalted position being next in honor to the President of the United States and the highest obtainable by a foreigner."[6]

Isaias's concerns were not just paranoia. In September he had received a letter full of misspellings and grammatical errors from an E. McDonell, who had overheard people at a cricket match disparaging Isaias. It was a hint of the anti-Jewish sentiment that would soon pervade Los Angeles. "Do you know a man named Perkins and his son?" wrote McDonell. "They know all about you and your family. [They said] [y]our wife is the meanest woman in this town. If young Perkins tells the truth he says she would go all the way back to Russia to save five cents. You got your money selling suede and bogus rings, shirt buttons, and neckties and begging at every house. . . . The men laughed to think you wanted to be a senator an old Jew peddler wanted to be the same as an English lord."[7]

Stephen White traveled to Sacramento in early January for the opening of the legislative session. White hoped to capitalize on the distaste many felt for the coarse, semiliterate Hearst and swing votes to Isaias as a compromise candidate. He thought the best way to accomplish this was by delaying the Senate vote for as long as possible, thereby giving those pledged but not devoted to Hearst ample time to regret their promises and switch their votes. By January 2, White had lined up at least eighteen senators who he thought would vote for a postponement. He wrote to Isaias about his plans. "The fight is getting warm. . . . The enemy are getting excited which is a good sign. The opposition . . . must finally come our way. No one else has any show to beat Hearst—my plan is delay because the more our fight is understood the better for us."[8]

Three days later, White was still convinced of the efficacy of his plan, but he worried about whether Isaias would be effective if he was elected by a pack of legislative renegades. "If we organized a band of bolters we might possibly beat Hearst but his people would be so mad at us that we would never get a proposition through," White told Isaias.[9]

Meanwhile, Hearst was not sitting idly by. His handlers swarmed around the new Democratic caucus, armed with packets of cash to sway the legislators' votes. There was no subtlety to Hearst's get-out-the-vote campaign. One paper reported that the San Francisco contingent refused to show up and vote unless Hearst guaranteed them $25,000. When Hearst delayed and offered to pay after the vote, the legislators said they wouldn't work COD.

Isaias was rich enough to play the same game. He could easily have passed out $25,000 in "boodle," as it was commonly called, to make his candidacy more attractive, but the thought repelled him. He honored the position of senator highly enough to think it should be above bribery and games, but it was becoming increasingly clear that Hearst would do whatever was necessary to win the nomination. "I shall go into it only on strict high moral and Democratic principles," Isaias told a San Francisco newspaper. "I shall have no corruption. No matter how highly I value the honor of being the coming Senator of this great State, I will have nothing to do with it if it is procured by a lavish expenditure of money. I would not accept a great trust from the State under such circumstances."

White knew at once that this stance meant defeat. "I admire your determination not to make this a mere exhibition of money," he wrote Isaias. "While other people may have the desire to purchase the place, you at once took the high . . . and gentlemanly course. If any opportunity is offered to get you in on the square basis you have indicated, one thing is certain—that I will be on hand for you."[10]

The vote came on the cold, clear evening of January 12 in the state senate's ornate red chambers, decorated with 1869 Bruener desks and set up to resemble England's House of Lords. As the legislators gathered, White and his fellow state senator from Los Angeles, Rose, still hoped to adjourn the meeting. Delay might swing sentiment toward Isaias. But they were outmaneuvered. Senator Thomas J. Clunie put Hearst's name in nomination. White decided right then not to formally nominate Isaias, since he had no chance of winning, and a failed nomination would look bad.

The roll call was taken. White, Rose, and just one other senator cast their votes for Isaias, bringing his total to three. A few other candidates got three or four votes, but Hearst won in a landslide, garnering fifty-four votes.

The moment for a senator from southern California passed, and it would be another six years before people in Los Angeles saw one of their own—

White, as it turned out—elected. The defeat was a blow to those from Los Angeles. "When we came north we discovered that Hearst's friends had an immense advantage and that the whole power of the state central committee was enacted in his aid," White wrote. "It was therefore an uphill fight. Yet at one time it seemed that Hellman might win and it is the opinion of those best informed that he could have made the fight successfully provided he resorted to financial methods—this he would not do."[11]

Isaias had never before suffered such a major defeat. He was not used to losing, and he didn't like it. "The boys will find out before long that they killed the goose who laid the golden egg when they robbed and cheated me at the last election and forced me out of politics," he wrote White. "I will *never reenter it.*"[12]

By 1887 the Los Angeles area had grown tremendously, and homes and new towns dotted the region. The city had burst out of its pueblo-era boundaries, with homes going up on the hills, and new settlements, like Pasadena, going in. "You would be astonished to see the great changes in Los Angeles; houses being torn down, gardens destroyed; blocks going up, real estate going up, . . . everything going up," one young Los Angeles native wrote to her friend in San Francisco. "Ring out the old, ring in the new is our proverb."[13]

The image of southern California had been enhanced considerably with the publication of the novel *Ramona* by Helen Hunt Jackson. The book told the story of a doomed Indian girl, set against the idealized backdrop of southern California's mission past. The novel portrayed Los Angeles as Edenic, balmy, verdant, with sweet air and almost constant sunshine. It quickly became a bestseller around the country, imprinting a romantic image of California on readers.

Land sales continued steadily in Los Angeles until around 1887, when a rate war between the Southern Pacific and Santa Fe railroads brought fares from the East to incredibly low levels, luring tens of thousands of tourists. Los Angeles had always gotten a large number of winter visitors who settled in the city briefly to escape the snows of the East. But they usually returned home in spring.

The Santa Fe Railroad arrived in Los Angeles in March 1887 despite a

series of man-made and natural obstacles. At first, the Santa Fe tried to coordinate rates with the Southern Pacific, offering the established railroad 50
percent of the business in southern California and 27 percent in the north.
The Southern Pacific rebuffed the offer, and the two rail lines made a grab
for passengers by lowering prices.

For years, the Southern Pacific had charged $125 for a ticket from Los
Angeles to Kansas City, but in 1885 it dropped the price to $100, and later
lowered it to $95. In March 1887, after the Santa Fe was finished, a ticket from
New York to Los Angeles was $45 and one from Chicago was $32. A ticket
from Kansas City the morning of March 6 was $12, which dropped later in
the day to $10, then to $8, then to $4. In the early afternoon, the Southern Pa-
cific sold tickets from Kansas City for $1. The rates quickly rebounded, but
they didn't rise above $25 for nearly a year.

Everyone who had been thinking of visiting southern California now
tossed aside their hesitation and got on a train. They were lured by the low
fares, the myth of Ramona, and railroad advertisements that heavily promoted the region's mild climate and fertile soil. The railroads induced poorer
visitors to come by offering seats on the "emigrant car," with chairs that converted to beds and a stove on which to cook meals. Settlers could also buy land
directly from the railroads, fold in the price of a ticket, and pay off the debt
slowly. Among the people who came were Adolph and Isidore Fleishman, the
sons of Isaias's sister Bertha, who still lived in Germany.

Four trainloads of people were dumped in Los Angeles each day. The population of the city went from 11,000 in 1880 up to an estimated 80,000 at the
boom's peak in 1887 and down to 50,000 by 1890—which was still a 350 percent increase in a decade. As many as 120,000 people came just to visit in 1887.

Suddenly, everyone wanted to live in southern California. "Los Angeles
city and county are now having the biggest boom in their history," Isaias
wrote. "Thousands of Eastern people of wealth and culture have settled here
this spring and more are coming daily."[14]

Land that previously couldn't find a taker became irresistible. Promoters
lured prospective buyers with promises of free trips and elaborate lunches.
They would send brass bands to meet the incoming trains and immediately direct the new arrivals to wagons waiting to take them to view property—land,
the promoters promised, that would soon be rich with houses, elegant hotels,
promenades, and schools. Never mind that the "town," as described, was just

a few structures set among barren hills. It was still extolled as a miniparadise on earth.

"Selling and bartering were carried on at all hours of the day and night, and in every conceivable place; agents, eager to keep every appointment possible, enlisted the service of hackmen, hotel employees and waiters to put them in touch with prospective buyers; and the same properties would change hands several times a day, sales being made on the curbstone, at bars or restaurant tables, each succeeding transfer representing an enhanced value," Harris Newmark wrote in his memoirs.[15]

The spiraling prices set off more spiraling prices. Twenty-five acres on Seventh Street near Figueroa in Los Angles were offered for sale—and went unsold—for $11,000 in 1886. A year later, the plot sold for $80,000. Acreage along Main Street that once sold for $20 a foot jumped to $800 a foot in 1887. Isaias saw the value of his bank property on the southeast corner of Main and Commerical streets go from an assessment of $28,000 in 1887 to $54,250 in 1889—a 93 percent increase.[16]

By 1887, twenty-five new towns were laid out along the thirty-six-mile stretch from Los Angeles to the San Bernardino County line.[17] The planned towns followed the line of the Santa Fe Railroad. This run on land started Los Angeles's steady march toward urbanization, a transformation its builders had longed for but had never before achieved.

Former sheriff George E. Gard was one of the speculators who made a fortune almost overnight. In January 1886 he bought 161 acres of land in San Bernardino County, about twenty-seven miles east of Los Angeles, for $12,000, or $75 an acre. In March 1887 he sold half of the land to a development company for $16,000. Then the Los Angeles and San Gabriel Valley Railroad put a depot on Gard's land. No sooner had the railroad company started erecting a prefabricated building than real estate developers came and started to lay out the brand-new town of Alosta. Buyers soon arrived.

"They came in buggies from all along the foothills and the ready-made house was the focus of a considerable assemblage from an early hour in the morning," read an article from the March 24, 1887, *Los Angeles Times.* "Lots were sold as rapidly as they could be checked off the map and receipts given for the advance payment. This continued while daylight lasted and was then discontinued for lack of candle power. Tuesday morning the rush was renewed, and, by noon all the available lots had been disposed of."

The paper estimated that the aggregate sales came to $75,000—before the town survey was completed and before a single advertisement or notice was published. "This record is hard to beat," the *Times* noted. In a little more than a year, Gard made $91,000 on his $12,000 investment.

Henry Fleishman, who had been working as a clerk in Isaias's bank, caught the real estate fever too. He had never been content with the regular world of a banker, preferring thrills to steady progress. He loved horses and fast riding and spent much of his salary on them, which drew Isaias's ire. Fleishman had lived with the Hellmans until 1884, when he could no longer abide Isaias's paternalistic admonitions to save money rather than spend it. When it became possible to earn huge amounts of money by buying and selling real estate, Fleishman took the chance. He quit his job at the Farmers and Merchants Bank in 1887 and joined the ranks of the speculators.

Isaias did not feverishly buy and sell lots during the frenzy. He was a conservative businessman who distrusted the huge increase in land prices and did not want the bank associated with get-rich schemes. He could have sold his land holdings for enormous profits, but he held on to them because he thought they would probably be worth more in the long run. "Business is quite fair with us," Isaias wrote Benjamin Newgass. "If I had the disposition of being a little speculative I could have made a great deal of money—as it is I have done fairly well and that is all."[18]

Still, Isaias found himself indirectly involved in the boom as many of his real estate partnerships tried to cash in on the frenzy by setting up townships. Isaias held shares in the Azusa Land and Water Company, which was controlled by J. S. Slauson. Azusa was an undeveloped town on a barren patch of alkaline soil east of Los Angeles near the San Gabriel Mountains. That didn't prevent Slauson from carving it into lots and advertising their sale in the newspapers.

Isaias, Harris Newmark, and Kaspare Cohn purchased the 5,000-acre Repetto Ranch in the Monterey Hills south of Alhambra in 1887. Newmark carved out the town of Newmark from his portion of the land and promoted it as a delightful place to live. (It was eventually renamed Montebello.) Isaias kept his share for farming and ranching.

In 1888, just as the boom was slowing, Isaias and the Bixby family spun off 4,700 acres from Rancho Los Alamitos into the Alamitos Land Company. They planned to build a fashionable resort on the ocean at Alamitos Bay, not far from the new city of Long Beach, but the ambitious project never got very far. Intent on turning their unsettled ranch land into a city, Isaias and the Bixbys next tried to lure Quaker and Baptist colonies to the area by offering a small chunk of free land for a meeting or community house. In exchange, the religious groups would have to buy a few hundred acres in a designated period of time. Neither organization took up the offer, and the Alamitos Land Company failed to capitalize on the boom. The land would eventually be developed, but it would take years.[19]

Isaias did offer his real estate expertise to outsiders looking to make some quick money. "I got it from reliable authority that Mr. I. W. Hellman of Los Angeles has made four million dollars during the last six months, without investing a cent, acting merely as the treasurer and adviser of the syndicates," wrote Isidor N. Choynski, a leading Jewish journalist, in the *American Israelite* on September 9, 1887. "His countrymen in this city, the Reckendorfers, tell me he is the wealthiest Jew in America today, and I believe it."

In 1887, Isaias prepared a spreadsheet of his real estate holdings that included land he held separately and jointly in partnerships. He calculated that the properties were worth $1,477,980 (about $32 million in 2006 dollars).[20] The *Los Angeles Express* reported December 29, 1886, that Isaias paid the most taxes of any man in Los Angeles—more than $14,000.

Promoters predicted that the boom would continue indefinitely, and land sales were vigorous in the first part of 1888—$20 million worth in the region. But then prices collapsed, mostly ruining the professional speculators. One of those was Henry Fleishman, whose dreams of real estate glory were dashed completely. He lost virtually all his savings in speculation and came back, chastened, to ask Isaias for his old job at the bank.

The end of the boom was due in part to the Farmers and Merchants Bank. Isaias believed that the run-up in land prices could not be sustained. While deposits at the bank grew steadily during the boom, increasing from $5.5 million in 1886 to $8 million in January 1887 to $12 million by the end of the year, Isaias took a cautious view of the growth and ordered the bank to cut back on its rate of lending. So while in 1885 loans amounted to 80 percent of deposits, the rate dropped to 50 percent by July 1887 and to 25 percent by December. In October 1887, Isaias announced that the Farmers and Merchants

Bank would no longer lend funds for any real estate purchases. Other banks immediately adopted similar policies. When the boom collapsed in the second half of 1888, the city's banks were in a strong enough financial position to weather the downturn. While hundreds of individuals lost huge paper fortunes, the economy of the region was not mortally wounded.[21]

"It is very certain that the refusal of the Farmers and Merchants Bank to loan freely on real estate during the fall of 1887—at the critical period when the speculative boom was at its height—is one of the chief reasons why no disastrous collapse has followed the crazy buying of those feverish days," read a *Los Angeles Times* editorial on January 5, 1889. "Banking and gambling are two separate branches of finance which the management of the Farmers and Merchants Bank rightly believes should not be combined under one roof."

The boom was over, but Los Angeles had been transformed from a sleepy insular town to a modern American city.

THE NEVADA BANK

1890–1895

By late 1889, Isaias was starting to feel restless in Los Angeles. The boom had brought huge profits to the region, funds that made their way into the Farmers and Merchants Bank and the other financial institutions with which Isaias was associated. After living in southern California for thirty years, Isaias itched to expand, to become a bigger player in the world of finance.

Restlessness took hold of him even more strongly after he and Esther accompanied Meyer and Babette Lehman to Europe in the spring and summer of 1889. After visiting Würzburg, where Babette and Esther's mother, Fredericka Newgass, lived, Isaias couldn't help contrasting his situation with those of his brothers-in-law. Meyer, as head of Lehman Brothers in New York, was now one of the country's most successful private bankers, trading commodities like cotton, coffee, and oil and buying and selling stocks and bonds.

Isaias's other brother-in-law, Benjamin Newgass, had moved to Liverpool in 1872 to head up Lehman Brothers' British interests, but he soon abandoned the cotton trade to speculate in stocks and railroads. Newgass would earn and lose many millions in his lifetime and would frequently turn to his relatives to bail him out of tight times. But he seemed to enjoy thoroughly the high-stakes game of investing, and at the time of Isaias's visit he owned the controlling interest in the International Bank of London, an accepting house that traded bills of exchange. Newgass lived in an enormous country home called Shernfold Park in Sussex.

Though he may have been the president of Los Angeles's most successful bank and involved in most of the city's utilities, Isaias saw that Los Angeles was a backwater compared to New York, London, and even San Francisco. The boom had swelled Los Angeles's population to fifty thousand, but the city was small compared to San Francisco's three hundred thousand residents. Its economy was still lagging, too, from the collapse of real estate prices.

"Dear Sigmund," Isaias wrote to a nephew in November 1889. "We are home again, all well, but not as contented with our lot as we were before our European trip. Business is bad; people are loaded down with real estate. Thank God I have kept out of speculation and am not hurt. I wish that I could realize and move on to New York."[1]

Isaias had been looking to buy or start another bank in a larger market for more than a year, and his chance came in early 1890. For the previous three years, the once-mighty Nevada Bank, headquartered in San Francisco, had been struggling. One of its owners, John Mackay, was now quietly shopping it around.

The Nevada Bank was an institution, a symbol of the sudden wealth and power the West could bestow on people with poor beginnings and limited education. Its origins were rooted in the Nevada silver boom, when an unlikely quartet of Irishmen, two saloon keepers, James C. Flood and William O'Brien, and two mining engineers, John Mackay and James G. Fair, pooled their money and struck it rich in the Consolidated Virginia silver mine in Nevada. In 1872 the owners found a silver vein 1,200 feet below the surface of Virginia City. Seven feet across at its widest, the vein was the largest single pocket of silver ever discovered in North America, yielding $400 million of ore over five years.

Its owners were soon nicknamed "the Silver Kings," and the world watched in fascination at how these new millionaires spent their money. Flood, the former proprietor of the Auction Lunch saloon on Washington Street in San Francisco, went on a building spree. He imported brownstone from Connecticut to build a magnificent $1.5 million, forty-two-room mansion on Nob Hill, right across the street from the mansions of the railroad barons Mark Hopkins, Leland Stanford, Collis Huntington, and Charles Crocker. The brownstone mansion, which would not have been out of place on Fifth Avenue, was surrounded by a $30,000 fence of pure bronze, and Flood supposedly kept one man in his employ just to polish the metal. He spent just as lavishly on his country home in Menlo Park on the Peninsula, erecting a three-story, forty-three-room home.

Mackay, a gold rush miner whose first job in the Comstock Lode was as a

$6-a-day timber man, was less interested in spending his money, but his wife, Louise, had no qualms about transforming herself into a worldly woman. The family built homes first in Virginia City and then in San Francisco. They then moved to New York and Paris to try and break into the ranks of high society.

In 1876 Mackay sent half a ton of his mine's silver to Tiffany in New York, and ordered the most elaborate silver service possible. Two hundred silversmiths worked for more than two years on the 1,350-piece set, which was so heavily ornamented that there were no smooth spaces on the handles. The newspapers followed the manufacture of the silver set as if it were a young woman making her debut.

In 1875, in another grand gesture, the Silver Kings opened the Nevada Bank on the corner of Pine and Montgomery in the heart of San Francisco's financial district. With a capitalization of $10 million, it was one of the richest banks in the nation. The walls of its main banking room were covered in pristine white marble, and its ceilings were adorned in mahogany. In the rooms above the bank, rented out to doctors, lawyers, and other professionals, the fireplaces had mantels of quartz inlaid with gold. One tenant supposedly paid a few months' rent in advance and then chiseled the gold out piece by piece, making a tidy profit.

By 1890, however, the bank's glamour had been stripped away. O'Brien and Flood were dead, and Fair, once a U.S. senator from Nevada, had retreated to Sausalito on the northern side of San Francisco Bay, one son dead by suicide, another married to a former prostitute. His two daughters were estranged from him. Flood's son, James L. Flood, was the bank president, and Mackay served on the board of directors, but both men left day-to-day control of the Nevada Bank to others.

While the men were focusing on other investments—Mackay was building a private telegraphic line across the Atlantic—a newly appointed cashier named George L. Brander decided on his own to corner California's vast wheat market. He drained the bank of funds and borrowed even more to buy wheat crops, betting that his monopoly would drive prices even higher. Brander's attempt to corner the wheat market failed, and the price of wheat dropped precipitately. The Nevada Bank lost millions in the ill-conceived venture.

"We have had some considerable excitement in financial circles—the Nevada Bank of San Francisco, at one time the wealthiest bank in America, has met with heavy losses in a wheat deal," Isaias wrote Newgass in 1887. "Some estimate their loss at $13 million—they have been selling most of their securities in New York and San Francisco."[2]

Flood and Mackay were forced to pour more of their personal fortunes into the bank to keep it afloat. The wheat catastrophe made them realize that they were no longer equipped to run a bank. In December 1889, Mackay traveled to London, where his wife lived, and began to talk to British investors about buying the bank. Isaias's brother-in-law Benjamin Newgass learned of these quiet conversations and immediately wrote to Isaias, "I just wish hurriedly to inform you that Mr. Mackay is here, and has been in communication with the Exploration Corporation here. . . . And it is probable that he may dispose of his interest in the Nevada Bank. Now this may be an excellent chance of acquiring the whole thing—anyway I shall see, if any progress is made, that I obtain certain advantage for you: but I wish you to cable me immediately what you think of the matter."[3]

Newgass arranged to meet Mackay, and he conveyed that Isaias was interested in buying the Nevada Bank. Mackay appeared intrigued. "I think it is very desirable for you to arrange a meeting with M. who expresses himself very highly of you, and would be most pleased to come to an arrangement with you. I mentioned you and your friends as being disposed to invest not less than $1 to $2 million and probably, if it becomes known that you take an interest in it, all the capital can be placed there [the United States] without making an issue here. If you think, however, that it would be desirable to have a London connection and quotation as it might later enhance the value of the shares by having a larger market, this can be done."[4]

Mackay returned to San Francisco in early February, and Isaias traveled from Los Angeles to meet him. They quickly hammered out a deal: Isaias would raise $2.5 million in new capital and become the president of the Nevada Bank, and Mackay and the others would retain a minority interest with $500,000 of the new stock. Isaias telegraphed Newgass on February 14, 1890: "Arranged Mackay satisfactory terms 60 days option—Cable amount desired place San Francisco."

The opportunity to move to San Francisco and head a new banking concern immediately thrust Isaias into the top echelon of Pacific Coast financiers. San Francisco was the hub of the West Coast, the center of shipping, manufacturing, and finance. Isaias could see evidence of that just in his brief walks from the Nevada Bank Building on Pine and Montgomery to his hotel on Market Street a few blocks away. He had to pass dozens of tall office buildings, as well as small shops and restaurants. Crossing Market Street meant dodging clanging streetcars and wagons laden with goods for sale. Cable cars climbed the steep hills.

The amount of wealth in San Francisco was staggering. Some said the city had the most millionaires per capita in the nation. Its twenty-six banks, which included the Bank of California, the Anglo-London Bank, and the Crocker-Woolworth Bank, controlled $114 million in assets, almost twice as much as all the other California counties combined. Manufacturing was a big source of funds. San Francisco's factories cranked out 110 million cigars and 40 million cigarettes a year and $10 million worth of boots, shoes, and other leather goods. The city was full of small merchants, too. Thousands of Chinese families ran their own laundries.

Isaias still had to raise the $2.5 million needed to buy control of the Nevada Bank. He moved into San Francisco's most luxurious hotel, the Palace, where rooms boasted plush carpets, marble mantels, private bathrooms, and even call buttons. The centerpiece of the hotel, and San Francisco's premier gathering place, was the spectacular Garden Court, a six-story-high glassed-in atrium graced by ferns, trees, and other plants.

Word that Isaias would take over the Nevada Bank soon leaked out, and businessmen clamored to buy its stock. "While I regret that Los Angeles is to lose its ablest financier I can not help but congratulate you for having gained such universal confidence and been called to the responsible position you are about to assume," Los Angeles pioneer fruit grower Eugene Germain wrote Isaias. "Having been an old customer of yours for years past . . . I would much like to be interested with you in your new [venture]. Could you favor me by reserving say 10, 20, or 25 shares of stock in the Nevada Bank?"[5]

Isaias saw this as an opportunity to reward all the men who had supported his financial endeavors through the years. He had long discussions about his vision to turn the institution into a commercial bank with merchants like Levi Strauss, the jeans and clothes manufacturer, and William Haas, who ran Haas Brothers. Within a few weeks it became clear that the demand for stock was higher than the supply. "My idea was to get as many holders of stock in the bank as possible, and not a few very rich men only,"

Isaias explained to a newspaper. "The matter had barely been presented here when I was almost flooded with applications. I took the names, with the amounts applied for, but saying that the latter would undoubtedly be cut down."[6]

Meyer Lehman was one who expressed disappointment that he could not get as many shares as he wanted. "I am sorry to notice . . . that you intimate the likelihood of cutting down our recent subscription to the Nevada Bank stock, which will be a great disappointment to our young people, for when we asked for the additional $30,000 to $40,000 and received your liberal reply we were equally so to the family, and had distributed to every one of our sons and nephews a fair amount, and thus I shall be obligated to again withdraw the same from them."[7]

The stock went on sale for $100 a share the morning of March 24. Within hours Isaias had orders for $15 million worth, but he could sell only a fraction of that amount. Lehman Brothers in New York bought $150,000 worth of stock, and B. Newgass & Company of London took $100,000 worth. Levi Strauss took $120,000 worth and a seat on the board of directors. D.N. & E. Walter & Company, the home-furnishings store run by Isaias's compatriots from Reckendorf, bought $100,000 in stock and took over a directorship. Other investors originally from Reckendorf included the Haas cousins, Kalman, Abraham, and William, who bought $200,000 in stock, as well as the Bachman Brothers. Other major investors included the tobacco merchant Joseph Brandenstein; Louis Sloss and Lewis Gerstle, the founders of the immensely successful Alaska Commercial Company; Herman Hellman; Isaac Van Nuys from Los Angeles; and William Perry, who ran the privately held Los Angeles Water Company.

Two men who invested in the bank would soon become Isaias's closest business partners. One was Antoine Borel, a Swiss capitalist and private banker with an office in the Nevada Bank Building. The other was Christian de Guigne, investing for the estate of his late father-in-law, the banker John Parrott. De Guigne was French and would soon start the Stauffer Chemical Company, which would grow to be one of the largest companies of its kind.

"Millionaires stood in rows for hours waiting their chance to subscribe to the stock and men feeble from age were represented among them," the *Los Angeles Herald* reported in 1890. "One of the best known businessmen, not only of San Francisco, but of the state, told the writer that he was recently present at a discussion concerning Mr. Hellman's financial status in which he was held up as the wealthiest Hebrew in America with the total being placed at $40,000,000. One thing is certain, however, and that is that his brief connection with the Nevada Bank has been signalized by the most remarkable occurrence ever noted in the financial annals of California."[8]

Isaias was delighted by the show of support for his financial acumen, but he was careful to balance the religious makeup of his stockholders. Isaias wanted to enter into the lucrative business of marketing bonds, and to do that, the Nevada Bank had to serve a broad constituency. While the majority of the stockholders were Jewish, there were also Catholics and Protestants. "I am vain enough to believe that the reputation I enjoy in America has caused capitalists to come in here who would not have purchased stock before," Isaias wrote to Newgass. "I have selected an excellent board of directors all strong men, privately speaking seven Christians and including myself four Jews. I have done this to avoid the idea which exists with other banks here of making a Jewish bank or Catholic or any other institution. I want it to be a popular institution—I think it is so considered, if not I will endeavor my best to make it so."[9]

The news that Isaias was taking over the bank filled the pages of the papers around the state. Editors in Los Angeles wrote pieces questioning how Isaias's move would affect the city. They soon suggested it would expand the flow of capital between Los Angeles and San Francisco. "No deleterious effect can come to Los Angeles from the proposed change," said an editorial in the February 24, 1890, edition of the *Los Angeles Herald*. "Mr. Hellman, whose interests here are immense, will be at the head of a bank that will be from the moment he enters it the controlling influence on the finances of the Coast. It will be his pleasure and his interest both to aid in every legitimate enterprise thought of in Los Angeles. He will have control of unlimited funds, and if any industry can show him it is one of merit, it may safely count on his encouragement."

Isaias moved up to San Francisco, leaving Esther, Clara, and Florence temporarily behind in Los Angeles. While Isaias told the papers he would spend half his time in Los Angeles, Esther soon started to look for someone to rent the family home on Fourth and Main streets. "The children hate to leave their pleasant home and you know your sister, she does not want her house to be left without a good person to take care of it," Isaias wrote to

Newgass.[10] Moving meant saying good-bye to close family and friends, like Henry Fleishman, his wife, and new baby son; Herman Hellman and his family; and the Newmarks, among many others. But it also meant an exciting new venture.

"On my arrival here last Thursday I went at once to the Bank, did some work and had a two-hour business talk with Mr. Mackay," Isaias wrote Esther from the Palace Hotel on March 20, 1890. "He is as friendly and kind as ever and predicts great success for the *new* Nevada Bank. I am quite satisfied with the bank's prospects, as is every one of my subscribers to the stock. This morning I shall start in good at the Bank."

Isaias's departure for San Francisco left a leadership void at the Farmers and Merchants Bank. Isaias was reluctant to give up control of the bank, so he asked his brother Herman to resign from his wholesale grocery company and take over as the bank's vice president. Isaias intended to continue actively managing the Farmers and Merchants Bank and thought he and his brother could share power. Isaias installed a direct telegraph line between the two banks to ease communication and devised a cipher, an encrypted list of words, with which to communicate. Isaias asked that Herman consult him on all major loans.

Isaias thought that the banking community would have confidence in Herman and would continue to look to the Farmers and Merchants Bank as the city's leading financial institution. Herman owned large quantities of real estate around the city and was one of the founding members of the chamber of commerce. He also had served as president of Congregation B'nai B'rith since 1886. "I am glad that my brother has taken such good hold of the bank," Isaias wrote in a March 31, 1890 letter. "I have never doubted his ability, nor his enthusiasm to succeed in anything he undertakes."

But Isaias would soon find it more difficult than he had imagined sharing control with his brother.

Isaias and Esther rented a house on Sutter Street in the Western Addition, which was fast becoming a popular place for San Francisco's new upper class. The area, which in later years would be renamed Pacific Heights to sound more upscale, was bordered on the east by Van Ness Avenue, a broad boulevard lined with a double row of trees. Imposing Victorian and Queen Anne homes flanked the street, houses with turrets and towers, marble stairs and numerous windows to catch the California sun. Louis Sloss and Lewis Gerstle of the Alaska Commercial Company both had mansions on the street, as did David Walter and Claus Spreckels, who dominated the Hawaiian sugar industry.

The Hellmans enrolled their daughters, Clara, twelve, and Florence, eight, down the block at Miss Lake's School for Girls, one of the many private schools in San Francisco aimed at turning rambunctious young girls into ladies.

Marco had already been living in the Bay Area for three years. He had graduated in 1887 from Los Angeles High School, where he delivered a valedictorian speech titled "The March of Civilization." He then enrolled in the Belmont School, an all-male boarding school ten miles south of San Francisco, to prepare for the grueling three-day entrance exam to the University of California. William T. Reid, a former president of the university, ran the school and advertised it in an 1895 issue of the *University* of *California* magazine as intending "to give such attention to moral, mental, and physical culture as well as meet the reasonable demands of the most earnest and thoughtful people."

While Marco had done well in Los Angeles, he didn't take the Belmont School seriously, preferring instead to visit friends in San Francisco. He spent money without consideration of his budget and had to write home for an additional allowance. "We are much pleased with Marco's conduct and with the spirit in which he enters his work," the headmaster William Reid wrote Isaias. "He is gentlemanly and courteous, and ready to do anything that he is asked to do in his studies. I am therefore sorry to have to add that his work theretofore has not been well-done, and that he will find some difficulty entering the University next spring."[11]

In September 1888, Marco stayed so long with friends at the Cliff House, the pleasure resort on San Francisco's westernmost edge, that he had to rush to Berkeley to take the university's entrance exams. Isaias was furious at Marco's choices, particularly since he was a regent of the university and he expected his son to set a good example. "I cannot express (nor do I desire to) my feelings," Isaias wrote Marco. "My son, for whom I would sacrifice almost life, should have so little principle & what is worse embitter his parents' life—change & change you must—Even if you enter the university it is by a scratch."[12]

Marco surprised his parents by passing the university exams. Before taking the ferry to Berkeley to enroll and look for a place to live, he asked his father if he might use the name I. W. Hellman Jr. rather than Marco. "You have my permission to enter your name in the registry of the University as I.W. Hellman, Jr., and I hope, and pray that you will never tarnish nor soil that name which I have carried so far through life without a blemish," Isaias wrote his son on June 16, 1888.[13]

San Francisco society in 1890 was dominated by an alliance between an unlikely pair of social arbiters: the liquor distributor Ned Greenaway and his patron, the gem-clad, proper Eleanor Martin. The pair despaired at the crudeness of the city's social life; anyone with a pretense to fortune considered himself good enough to grace the ballrooms of the mansions that now dotted the city. The social world was not as exclusive as New York's, where Mrs. William Astor and her social sidekick, Ward McAllister, had drawn up a list of four hundred names—the number that could fit in Mrs. Astor's ballroom—and declared that these—and only these—were the best people of the city.

San Francisco society still reflected its coarse frontier roots, as much as people tried to hide them. While there was an opera house and an appreciation for classical music, theaters and dance halls were the secret pleasures of many of the well-to-do. Men of means openly met their mistresses in the boudoirs of the city's "French restaurants," which offered respectable meals on the bottom floors and places of assignation on the upper stories. "The general opinion of the most liberal-minded men of the East and the South, who spoke from actual experience, was that San Francisco's alleged society was in such a sorry state that it would require many generations to purify it," the social climber William H. Chambliss wrote in his popular book *Chambliss' Diary, or Society as It Really Is*. "They said there were more divorces in San Francisco in a given time than in any city in the world of its size. . . . And in addition to this, they could name many prominent men of wealth who posed as leading members of the alleged best society and kept secret establishments and raised second families at the same time."

Eleanor Martin and Ned Greenway decided to transform San Francisco society using the same strategy as Mrs. Astor, though both of them were first-generation Americans and could not claim her social pedigree. Mrs. Martin had been married to Edward Martin, the founder of the Hibernia Bank but had spent her childhood years living in poverty in Ireland. (Her brother was John Downey.) Ned Greenway was from Baltimore and came to San Francisco in the 1870s to sell Mumm's Champagne. He was charismatic, courtly, and enormously large, and he reportedly showed few signs of inebriation as he made his way through his daily diet of twenty-five bottles of champagne.

Greenway and Mrs. Martin organized a series of five dances that began with dinner at the Martin mansion on Broadway and ended with a ball and light supper at the Odd Fellows Hall. They called the dance series the Cotillion, and it remains one of San Francisco's most coveted invitations.

While the papers covered the dances in detail, there was an even more exclusive society in San Francisco than the one created by Ned Greenway and Eleanor Martin. That was the world of the Jewish elite. Birthplace, not wealth, was the most important criterion for membership in this society. Those who were born in Bavaria or Hesse or Bohemia—former independent states that became part of Germany in 1871—were admitted, as were French Jews from Alsace-Lorraine. But Jews from Poland and other eastern European countries were excluded from this group, presumably because they were considered less refined.

Most of the men in this German Jewish and French Jewish group had come to northern California during the latter part of the gold rush. They had parlayed their peddler's packs into stores, which eventually led to larger enterprises, such as factories to manufacture clothes and tobacco.

One of the best-known was Levi Strauss, who emigrated from Buttenheim, Bavaria, and arrived in San Francisco in 1853 to start a dry goods business. In 1873, he started manufacturing denim pants with pockets reinforced by copper rivets. These "blue jeans" became immensely popular, and made Levi Strauss & Co. extremely successful.

There were many other success stories: the Fleishhackers made a fortune selling paper boxes; the Zellerbachs transformed a small box company into a successful paper company; the Brandensteins sold tobacco, rice, tea, and coffee; the Dinkelspiels established a chain of wholesale dry-goods stores up and down the Pacific Coast. Eugene Meyer, who had moved from Los Angeles to San Francisco, now worked for the international banking house of his cousins, Lazard Freres. Daniel Meyer (no relation to Eugene) moved from selling cigars in a store with his brother Jonas to selling stock on the San Francisco Stock Exchange to handling large securities in his own bank.

All of these families belonged to the city's most exclusive synagogue, Temple Emanu-el, which started in a tent on a dirt street in the early 1850s but in 1890 occupied an imposing Gothic edifice on Sutter Street between Stockton and Powell. The building dominated the city skyline with its two octagonal towers topped by bronze-covered orbs. A huge stained-glass window with the six-sided Star of David stood above stairs leading into an enormous vaulted sanctuary that could seat more than one thousand worshippers.

Temple Emanu-el guaranteed that its members would be the wealthiest in the city by charging $100 in annual dues. The other prominent Reform synagogue, and a friendly competitor, Sherith Israel, asked its members to pay on a sliding scale. Some paid as little as $36 a year.

This group of German and French Jews who had made their fortunes in the heady years after the gold rush didn't seem to question the assumption that they were better than those who came from countries farther east, like Poland; nor did these eastern Jews. "That the Baiern [Bavarians] were superior to us, we knew," Harriet Lane Levy, a Polish Jew, wrote in her memoir of the period, *920 O'Farrell Street*. "We took our position as the denominator takes its stand under the horizontal line. On the social counter the price tag 'Polack' confessed second class. Why Poles lacked the virtues of Bavarians I did not understand, though I observed that to others the inferiority was as obvious as it was to us that our ash man and butcher were of poorer grade than we, because they were ash man and butcher. . . . Upon this basis of discrimination everybody agreed and acted."

Isaias and Esther were afforded immediate entrée into the upper crust because they were friends with the group that had started to refer to itself as the "Reckendorf aristocracy." It is not clear whether this name was a joke or whether its members took their status seriously. But the Hellmans, Haases, and Walters, who had grown up together in the tiny village in Bavaria, clearly held one another in high regard and endeavored to help one another as much as possible. When Esther and Clara went to Germany, their companion Hannah Walter wrote letters back home to Isaias, reassuring him that his family was not subject to hardship. "Just to settle your mind upon a subject that seems to have caused you a little annoyance," she wrote. "Let me try to convince you that we are living a No.1 in style and comfort and convenience. Being fully aware that as members of the 'Reckendorf aristocracy,' and may justly lay claim to the best that this and other countries afford we chose our quarters accordingly. Members of such less illustrious families than ours, Prince Reuss, occupied the rooms that [Esther and Clara] occupy and [as] they are nearly related to the royal family we concluded to try it."[14]

These families had lived in San Francisco for decades, and they opened their homes to the Hellmans and offered them entrée into their elite German Jewish circle. The Hellmans soon joined Temple Emanu-el, buying three seats in August from Abraham Weil. Isaias also joined the city's German Jewish clubs, both male only, the Concordia and the Verein. When the latter was established in 1853, it was a club for Germans of all religions to gather, dine, and play cards in a civilized atmosphere, one distinct from the bawdy Barbary Coast bars. By 1890 its Gentile membership had dwindled, a reflection of the increasingly separate lives Jews and Gentiles in San Francisco were starting to live.

Isaias was happy to be included in what he regarded as high society. "When you are up here, you will also be pleased with my Jewish friends; they are the best and first men in San Francisco and one and all are apparently pleased to have me come up here," Isaias wrote to Meyer Lehman.[15]

Shortly after their arrival, the Hellmans started to look for a summer place. San Francisco in June, July, and August is usually frigid, for the heat of the outlying valleys sucks in fog from the ocean, which then settles over the city like a lid on a pot. San Francisco's wealthy usually escaped to their country houses to avoid the dreary weather, and in 1890 the location of choice for the German Jewish set was San Rafael, a city across the bay in Marin County. The Gerstle, Sloss, and Lilienthal clans had adjoining compounds there and the social swirl they created attracted other Jewish families to the bucolic town.

The Hellmans rented a bungalow on the grounds of the Hotel San Rafael, an ornate white building that was just a one-hour ferry ride away from Isaias's office on Pine and Montgomery streets. It was a delightful place to relax, as lawns and gardens dense with flowers surrounded the rooms, and vacationers played croquet on the lawns. Most of the men, including Isaias, left the hotel around eight each morning to catch the ferry to San Francisco for work and returned from the foggy city at six each night. Men and women dressed in formal summer attire for supper, then retreated to the hotel's public rooms for after-dinner conversation and (for the men) a cigar. A month's stay for a family could cost as much as $500.

This world of this Jewish elite had such well-defined rules and such limited entry that the *Wasp*, a satirical San Francisco magazine, parodied its social strictures. "In no society circle are the caste lines more closely drawn than among the Jewish residents of American cities. The inner circle keeps the gates closely shut against intruders, only when one of the outer circle marries into the inner are there any friendly telephonic connections. For many years the dominating set in San Francisco has consisted of the Sloss, Greenbaum, Gerstle, Hecht, Walter, Greenwald, Meyer, Sutro, Sachs, Koshland, Lowenberg, Lilienthal, Hellman, and a very few other families the Sloss clan with its intermarrying members, being, perhaps, the ultra. . . . In Gentile society they are not so severely cold against climbers as are the real Jewish social leaders."

Resurrecting the Nevada Bank proved to be more difficult than Isaias had expected. Just a few days after he took over the bank's management, Isaias came down with a severe case of pleurisy, a painful inflammation of the lungs. He spent five weeks sick in his bed at the Palace Hotel and was nursed back to health by Esther, who rarely left his side. The sickness meant that Isaias could not spend time with the Lehmans, who were finally visiting California.

After he recovered, Isaias set out to capture new business for the bank, which had lost many of its more prestigious clients in the years after the wheat debacle. Merchants did not keep large balances and tended to overdraw their accounts. Isaias called on all his friends and asked them to open accounts in the Nevada Bank, and he asked them to talk to their business acquaintances.

"The Nevada Bank is growing somewhat, but slow," Isaias wrote to Benjamin Newgass. "It is hard work to build up a business that has been under a cloud and which had been down so much, but I feel convinced that in the course of a year or two we will do a large and profitable business."[16] Despite this measured outlook, the Nevada Bank earned more than $225,000 in net profits during Isaias's first year of management.[17] The bank went from clearing the least amount of money through the San Francisco Clearing House to clearing the third most.[18] The next year profits would increase to almost $245,000 and the bank would start paying a 6 percent dividend.[19]

As Isaias worked at bringing in business for the bank, Marco was across the bay, studying philosophy at the University of California. The school had grown tenfold since Isaias was appointed regent in 1881 and now had 2,550 students. Marco took most of his classes in North Hall, which served as the informal center of the school. Students gathered daily on the building's dual staircases to eat lunch, talk, and pass time between classes. North Hall was only a brief stroll from the flagpole where professors, students, and the university president often gathered to make speeches, and the Bacon Library and Art Gallery.

Marco was enrolled in the College of Letters and had to take a demanding course load that included Greek and Latin. In June 1892 he graduated with a bachelor's degree in philosophy. Commencement was held June 29 in Berkeley, and Isaias had the honor of sitting on a platform next to Governor Henry Markham during the ceremony. "Your son has graduated with honors from college and feels proud and happy," Isaias wrote Esther, who was traveling in Europe.[20]

Marco soon joined his father at the bank. At twenty-one, Marco was a handsome young man with warm brown eyes, thick brown hair, and a handlebar mustache that curled above round cheeks. He had matured during his years at the university and appeared more focused. For his birthday, Isaias presented him with an enormously generous gift: $50,000 in stocks and property ($1 million in 2006 dollars). Marco didn't get much time to enjoy his new freedom, for Isaias was determined to teach him about the banking business. "I have made up my mind to put Marco to work, idleness is the worst thing for a young man," Isaias wrote to Esther. "As soon as we come back in July from Los Angeles, he will start in the Nevada Bank."[21]

Marco spent time in various departments of the Nevada Bank to get an overall picture of the way the institution functioned. Most transactions were conducted by draft or coin, since paper money was still sold at a discount. The best tellers used gold shovels to scoop up $20 gold pieces, which they then counted, not one by one, but by grabbing a handful and stacking them in a tray. With practice, a teller could tell a stack of twenty gold pieces with his eyes closed.

Isaias sent Marco to Stockton, a city on the Sacramento–San Joaquin Delta, to learn about oil exploration. Isaias also expected Marco to learn the details of his personal investments, and Marco spent time on the ranch in Cucamonga in southern California to investigate the state of his father's grapes, oranges, wheat, and barley.

Though Isaias was well respected, he lacked the flash and glamour of the Nevada Bank's original owners or other capitalists of the Gilded Age. He had earned his wealth slowly, through long-term investments. He never took on debt. He lived sumptuously but did not trumpet his wealth. Though the profits of the Nevada Bank increased regularly, the press bemoaned the fact that he was not a colorful, charismatic figure. He represented the future of banking—secure, steady investments rather than the glorious, crazed past where men made and lost fortunes with regularity. "Mr. Hellman is mainly from Los Angeles and is more interesting than his colleagues, because less is known about him," read an April 3, 1892, article from the *Wave*. "He is fond of work, is amusingly conservative and has novel banking ideas which accompanied him from LA. So far, Mr. Hellman is a bit of a disappointment. There has not been the increase in the deposits and paying accounts that was looked for from his reputation. But there is time. He is accused, with some reason, of having ability."[22]

The notion that Isaias was not a man to make dramatic gestures would change within a year when his name was plastered across every newspaper in the state.

While Isaias was busy building up his San Francisco bank, Esther was busy setting up a new household. She had definite standards on how to keep a proper home and she quickly hired a butler, a housekeeper, a cook, a lady's maid for herself, and a valet for Isaias. She shopped at Bibo, Newman & Ikenberg, the grocery and delicacy store on nearby Polk Street that advertised its wares in handwritten ads in the newspaper. Isaias had installed a phone in the house, and the cook could call in her orders. The livery that housed their horses and carriages was just up the street.

Visiting day at the Hellmans' was Friday. Esther would rise early, bathe, get dressed, and then wait in the parlor for friends to stop by. On other days,

Esther would make her own excursions into the homes of her society friends, like Matilda Esberg, Rosa Walter, and Bella Lilienthal.

By December 1891, the Hellmans were looking for a house to buy. They found a Queen Anne Victorian house four blocks away on Franklin and Sacramento owned by Nathaniel Cole, a former sea captain. Isaias had tried to buy an empty lot on that block nine years earlier but had been outbid by Phil and Bella Lilienthal, who constructed a stately Victorian mansion on the corner of Franklin and Clay. Isaac Walter, Isaias's boyhood friend from Reckendorf, lived between the two ends of the block. William and Bertha Haas lived two blocks down, and the Swiss banker Antoine Borel also had a house in the neighborhood.

Although the new house was already imposing, with curved marble steps leading to the entry, bay windows, and a tower with a widow's walk, the Hellmans hired the German-born architect Julius E. Krafft to remodel it. When the house was finished in 1893, its living- and dining-room walls were covered with carved black walnut. A large stained-glass window with a center pane twenty-two feet high dominated the stairwell leading to an upstairs ballroom. When the sun shone through, rays of red, yellow, green, and blue light danced on the stairs.

Esther loved to shop and spent months picking out new furniture. The style of the day was still Victorian, which favored dark wood furniture, brocaded drapes, plush carpets, and many knickknacks. Esther decided to decorate her bedroom with a set she bought for $1,000 from Herz Brothers. She put in a white carpet along with a carved mahogany Louis XV bedstead, bureau, chiffonier, and mantel. She put a deep library-table type desk in Isaias's study, which was trimmed in gold rococo appliqué.

Shortly after the Hellmans bought their new house, Esther and her daughters left on a lengthy trip to Europe. Clara had been suffering from severe stomach pains, and since no American doctor seemed able to cure her, Isaias and Esther decided that they needed to seek the advice of a specialist in Berlin. "Our daughter Clara is not yet feeling any better," wrote Isaias. "While the doctors here make little of it, she is nevertheless in continuous pain and more so after every meal. She is now living mostly on milk and gruel."[23]

Isaias couldn't leave the bank for an extended period, so he moved into the Richelieu Hotel on Geary Street and sent Esther and the girls off alone, although they would be accompanied across the Atlantic by the Walters and another Reckendorf family, the Greenbaums. The separation proved difficult. "If your son were not here with me, I do not know what I would do," Isaias wrote Esther on July 28, 1892. "I often feel lonesome & forlorn, working hard all day and when coming home in the evening no one there. To say I miss my good wife is not expressing my feelings, for I miss you awfully much but we must have patience and with the help of God you will soon come back and bring my daughters in good health here with you."[24]

Isaias also felt isolated because he and Meyer Lehman were no longer speaking. For twenty-two years Isaias had poured his heart out to Lehman in lengthy letters that touched on family matters and business. He could no longer confide in his brother-in-law, and the separation made him bitter.

The disagreement started as a misunderstanding about money. Isaias used Lehman Brothers as a correspondent bank in New York, leaving large amounts of cash on deposit to cover customers' drafts and other withdrawals. Lehman Brothers paid interest on the funds ranging from 2½ to 4 percent per annum, which did not always match the highest rates paid by other banks.

In 1889, the United States economy went through a brief recession. It hit New York first and then rippled across the country. When the dip hit California in January 1891, Isaias found that his cash reserves at the Nevada Bank were lower than he liked. He had always been a conservative banker who kept at least 45 percent of deposits in cash, so he could meet any demand. Isaias decided he needed to redirect the funds he had stored in New York to California. He called a loan held by Lehman Brothers, assuming there was an ample money supply in New York, as Lehman Brothers was paying only 3 percent interest on Isaias's deposits. In contrast, there was such a shortage of coin in California that banks were lending at 8 percent interest. He wired Lehman Brothers to send the money immediately.

What Isaias didn't realize was that Lehman Brothers was also short of cash. When the banking house got Isaias's telegram, Meyer Lehman got angry and wrote what Isaias later characterized as a "contemptible" letter. The fight escalated until the two men severed communication. Isaias felt he was in the right, and he lobbied for his version of events by writing to Lehman family members. "My standing here was not yet assured; a misstep might have ruined me forever," Isaias wrote to Abraham Stern in Liverpool, who was married to Esther's sister Bettie. "But what cared the Lehmans for that as long as they were making 'sefeinkel' [money] for a long time and they had about made up their minds they owned me body and soul."[25] In their "venom and anxiety," Isaias told Stern, the Lehmans sold their Nevada Bank stock.

He put it in even stronger terms for his other brother-in-law, Benjamin Newgass. "The truth of the matter is the Lehmans have had for years past many favors from me. They have had hundreds of thousands of my money, without even the acknowledgement of a promissory note or an acceptance and without collateral they have allowed me whatever rate of interest they saw fit (never any too much) & they had about made up their minds, come what will, even if I had to sacrifice my name & my credit they could retain my funds. I have *never* received a favor from their hands, they always found an excuse when I even intimated that I *might* want something, but I have, on the contrary, never tired to be of service to them."[26]

For more than two years Isaias refused to acknowledge he might have contributed to the disagreement and instead tried to persuade others that Lehman was in the wrong. "I am sorry that you are still under the impression that I am the aggressor, that I am all wrong and Lehmans are in the right and that I should make the first advance to make reconciliation," he wrote to Newgass.[27]

Isaias even insisted that Esther keep her distance from her sister and brother-in-law. Although he said she could speak to them when they saw one another in Europe over the summer, he ordered her to take no favors from them. "You ought to try and prove to them that even if they are small and mean that our ideas are more elevated & less vindictive, nor as selfish as theirs."[28] "Will you do me a favor? If so, please do not accept any favors from the Lehmans. I do not want to be under any obligations to them."[29]

The standoff continued until the end of December 1892, when the Lehmans sent a dispatch announcing the engagement of their daughter Clara to Richard Limburg. This may have been just the gesture Isaias was waiting for, and he used it as an excuse to make amends. He couldn't help himself, though, from restating his side of the story. "As this happy event paves the way to reconciliation and good feeling between us, an explanation from me may be in order," Isaias wrote to Meyer. "In all candor I will say that this misunderstanding has been of much grief to me, especially as I know that I am innocent from any wrong done you. You were angry dear Meyer that I withdrew the bank funds, but had you known the circumstances connected with it, you would not have been half as harsh in expressing your opinion. Months after all danger had passed in New York, we in California on the eve of an impending monetary stringency, I took it for granted that you were all posted, which apparently was not the case. My 2 banks were absolutely in need of their funds—no other reason existed for the withdrawal of the money. I know it will be hard for me to prove it to you, but such is the case and here I will let it rest."[30]

While Esther was in Europe, Isaias found himself spending time with Marco. They frequently went to see plays at the Baldwin and California theaters or played hands of a card game called 66. Marco usually won. Isaias also found himself swept up by San Francisco's German Jewish society and his remarks about it showed that he could be shy despite his financial position. "Yesterday noon I met Phil Lilienthal and amongst other nice things and statements he remarked, I wish Hellman when your wife returns and especially when you move into your new house you *feel* and become neighborly," Isaias wrote to Esther. "I told him we have never been in the habit of forcing our company on *anybody* but have no doubt that when you come home again you will be pleased to become better acquainted with his wife."[31]

Soon, Isaias was able to share some gossip with his wife, and he appeared to be pleased to have an inside view. The news concerned the daughter of his old friend Eugene Meyer who was now a banker with Lazard Freres in San Francisco. Rosalie Meyer was a petite, pretty woman of twenty-two who had become engaged in 1891 to Sig Greenbaum, the son of a well-established family. When the betrothal fell apart, the Meyers whisked Rosalie and her younger sister Elise to Paris to recover. The news upon their return was that Rosalie had become engaged to Sigmund Stern, the middle-aged nephew and heir apparent of the Levi Strauss & Company. At five feet four inches tall, Stern was shorter than his fiancée. "We visited Eugene Meyer last night, met the whole Stern family. All seem to be very happy. Sig Stern is a head smaller than Rosalie Meyer, but has lots of gold to make up the height," Isaias wrote Esther.[32]

He continued the saga a few days later: "Rosalie Meyer is going to be married in a fortnite, the Strausses and Stern family are all crazy about her & are making even more of her than Greenbaum & Co. did. I heard Leopold Bachman speak yesterday of her as if she was the most perfect beauty to be found.—I almost wanted to ask whether he intended to cut his brother-in-law out. I have no doubt the 2nd and third one[s] [daughters] will now make good matches."[33]

Despite Isaias's pointed remarks about Rosalie Meyer, he was considered a good family friend—close enough to be one of the few non–family members invited to the marriage ceremony itself, which took place October 3, 1892, at the Meyer home on Pine and Gough. More than two hundred guests came to the reception and danced to the Ballenberg band in a room decorated with palms and evergreens. The papers commented on the newlyweds' gifts and finances. "The presents were really magnificent. From the Lazards . . . there came a solid silver tea set, royal size . . . Levy [sic] Strauss's gift was very handsome. Indeed, such splendid presents are rarely seen but it must be remembered that Mr. Stern's relative are all millionaires, and that Miss Meyer's friends are all rich beyond dream of avarice."[34]

In early 1893, Isaias opened a second financial institution in San Francisco, one that would grow enormously in the coming years. It was the Union Trust Company, and it was incorporated on February 6 with a capital of $1.25 million.

While the Nevada and Farmers and Merchants banks were geared toward business customers, the Union Trust Company served individuals. When someone died, the trust company could act as an executor for the estate and distribute assets. It could also offer mortgages, collect rents, and offer investment services for people.

In April 1893, gold reserves in the U.S. mint dropped below $100 million, an ominous indication of the shakiness of the economy. Europe was suffering from an economic slowdown, and overseas investors started to sell their holdings in American companies. In early May, the stock market plunged, prompting a financial meltdown. Bank after bank shut its doors, including two in San Bernardino County on June 17.

Isaias, like other financiers, grew concerned as bank deposits in both San Francisco and Los Angeles declined steadily. Loan payments slowed, bringing less cash into his banks. "I do not expect any monetary stringency in San Francisco but cannot foresee what may come," Isaias wrote Lehman. "It usually strikes Wall Street first and several weeks or months after follows and reaches the West. I am preparing for it."[35]

Ever since John Downey had decided to close the Farmers and Merchants Bank during the 1875 bank run, Isaias had advocated keeping as much as 45 percent of a bank's deposits on hand. As the U.S. economy faltered, Isaias started to amass extra coin by selling some of his own assets and borrowing funds to shore up his banks' money supplies. He instructed his brother Herman at the Farmers and Merchants Bank to cut back on making loans and to collect as much money as possible. By mid-June, the vaults of the Nevada Bank were bulging with Isaias's private coin. The Farmers and Merchants Bank had $442,000—enough money, Isaias believed, to stave off any bank run.

But on June 20 the financial uncertainty that had swept the country made its way to Los Angeles. Rumors of a gold shortage prompted workingmen and workingwomen to rush to their various banks in an attempt to secure their savings. By morning, the City Bank had posted a sign that it would "temporarily suspend" paying depositors. An hour later, the University Bank had drawn curtains across its windows and posted a notice: "Bank closed. Depositors will be paid in full." Worried depositors besieged other banks as well.

The crowds came to the Farmers and Merchants Bank, too, even though it was the oldest institution in the city and everyone knew that Isaias Hellman insisted on keeping large cash balances. "It is, I suppose, acknowledged by everybody that the Farmers and Merchants Bank is as solid as the Rock of Gibraltar," Isaias had written Herman just a few days earlier. "A great deal of money that will likely be withdrawn from our weaker sisters will be placed with our bank."[36]

But there was no reassuring the crowd. Panicked depositors streamed into the Farmers and Merchants Bank and insisted on their money.

The situation was so dire that Herman sent Isaias telegrams throughout the day.

At 9:54 A.M. he wired, "City Bank failed university bank has cash on hand 12000."

At 12:10 P.M. he wired, "LA Savings Bank sharp run."

At 2:23 P.M. Herman's message was: "Ship this evening 100,000 additional big run on 1rst National Bank. We are in fine shape. Come down this evening without fail."

Then twelve minutes later, at 2:35, Herman wrote: "Except assistance comes tonight First National will have to close."

At 2:58: "Am completely worn out with work. Considerable money drawn out. . . . Come down sure."

At 3:37: First Nat'l Bank will not open tomorrow you must come down. Get special train and bring lingering ($350,000) without fail. Herman.

At first, Isaias did not understand the urgency of his brother's request. "You do not need me, will send some coin as fast as needed," he telegraphed. Within a few hours, when the scope of the Los Angeles bank run became clear, Isaias sent another message: "I leave this afternoon train."[37]

Isaias immediately ordered that $500,000 in gold be withdrawn from his personal accounts at the Nevada Bank and loaded onto an armored express train headed for Los Angeles. Isaias boarded the train as well. It made its way through California's Central Valley and the Tehachapi Pass but then got delayed. The train sat on the tracks in tantalizing reach of Los Angeles, with its cargo of precious gold, money that could stop the bank run. But the train didn't move.

Herman got on the phone to the Southern Pacific. The mayor of Los Angeles got on the phone to the Southern Pacific. Isaias told the train's conductor that he had urgent business in Los Angeles; every minute of delay increased the chance that the Farmers and Merchants Bank would run out of coin and have to shut its doors—the action Isaias most feared in the world.

Finally, the train began to move. On the afternoon of Wednesday, June 21, after a lengthy journey, Isaias arrived at the San Fernando Depot in downtown Los Angeles. Armed guards met the train and loaded sacks of gold into a Wells Fargo Express wagon. The wagon wound its way to the Farmers and Merchants Bank on Main Street.

Isaias went directly to the bank, where he ordered gold coin to be heaped on the counter. Like towers of gold, the money dazzled the bank's customers, reassuring them that the Farmers and Merchants Bank was sound and solid.

The panic, which stretched to other cities in California, forced dozens of banks to suspend operations. A few never reopened, including the Pacific Bank in San Francisco, the first commercial bank of the West. The panic revealed glaring weaknesses in the oversight of banks. The federal government did not offer any insurance on deposits—that innovation would not come until 1933 with the passage of the Banking Act.

California had made very few changes to its bank laws since 1878. The state had set up a banking commission that required banks to file regular balance statements, but too often the commission was nothing but a rubber stamp. It had no authority to deny a bank permission to operate even if that bank was more of a shell than a viable business. In 1890 and 1891 the banking commission had sent reports to Sacramento urging the "enactment of a law fixing the minimum amount of cash capital required of a banking company." The reports described one bank that was able to open with only $1,000 in capital.

The bankers of the state had taken it upon themselves to cooperate to improve the financial climate of California. In 1868, San Francisco bankers formed a clearinghouse association to facilitate their debts. Prior to this, if the Bank of California had a draft drawn on the Anglo-California Bank, another draft drawn on the Bank of British Columbia, and yet a third on a separate bank, a messenger had to go to each bank and collect the gold the draft represented. With a clearinghouse, there was a central place that banks could go to calculate their debts and credits.

The banks in Los Angeles did not form a clearinghouse until after the real estate boom in 1887. Isaias pushed to form the organization and was elected its first president.

California bankers still operated as if the state's northern and southern halves were separate. It was not until 1891, after members of the Los Angeles Clearing House organized a meeting, that the bankers formed a statewide organization. And the first gathering reflected the north's opinion of the south: only six banks from San Francisco sent representatives. The other seventy-one attendees came from banks in the southern portion of the state. Isaias attended the conference and was elected vice president of the California

Bankers Association with the expectation that he would become president in 1892.

The association struggled along and made its presence felt most strongly after its 1894 convention in San Francisco. There, the bankers heard a scathing report from a committee about the lax laws regulating banks. They agreed to work with the banking commission to get the legislature to order more stringent capital requirements.

In 1895, the state enacted many changes. It made it illegal for anyone to use the word "bank" in a company name unless the business was actually regulated by the banking commission. This meant that pawnshops and other moneylenders could no longer represent themselves as banks. The legislature set minimum capital requirements according to population for savings banks. If an institution was located in a town of five thousand people, it had to have at least $25,000 in capital. If the place was in a city of one hundred thousand people, it needed $200,000 in paid-up funds. This closed a long-existing and dangerous loophole that had allowed almost anyone to set up a banking institution.

Isaias took the opportunity of the 1893 panic to push through a reform. When he came to the Nevada Bank he was surprised to find that business owners were allowed unlimited credit on their accounts. They routinely withdrew more money than they had and paid interest on the overdraft. It made bookkeeping complicated, and increased the probability of defauting on the credit lines. Isaias and other banks stopped the practice in 1893.

Isaias returned from Los Angeles chastened, but pleased that the Farmers and Merchants Bank had been able to meet its depositors' demands during the panic. "I am still so nervous over the excitement which existed here in all the banks the past week that I hardly know what to say," he wrote Lehman. "The crisis reached California like a whirlwind. It took every weak institution and crippled even strong ones."[38]

Within days ugly rumors began to circulate, reports that Isaias had created the gold shortage to knock out competition and bolster the Farmers and Merchants Bank. Instead of being a savior, he was really a Shylock, a Jewish merchant interested only in his own reward. The rumors were similar to the scurrilous accusations leveled against Isaias after the 1875 bank panic in Los

Angeles. "Ever since the financial flurry last month, certain busybodies have been industriously circulating reports derogatory to the management of the Farmers and Merchants Bank," said an article in the *Los Angeles Times* on July 9, 1893. "They have charged, in fact, that I. W. Hellman played the part of wrecker with the object of crowding out some of the smaller banks and gobbling up their business."

Isaias objected strenuously to these charges. He pointed out that it would be crazy to foment a run on a rival institution, for it would inevitably hurt his own bank. He also said that he was the largest taxpayer in Los Angeles, and doing anything to hurt the region's economy would deflate the value of his own property. "Would I do anything to bring about a reaction that would hurt the business of the place, depress real estate values and rents and destroy my own property with the rest? Those miserable fellows who are circulating such reports do not know what they are talking about. If I could close every bank in Los Angeles except the Farmers and Merchants Bank, it would be financial suicide for me to do it. I would simply be destroying my own property."[39]

Privately, he told his brother that he thought religion was behind the attacks. "You must not for a moment forget that as we have weathered the storm there is naturally a good deal of jealous and envious feeling, more so especially since we are Jewish."[40]

By 1890, the widespread acceptance of Jews in Los Angeles had begun to ebb. The boom of the eighties had brought in large numbers of people from the East and Midwest. The newcomers were overwhelmingly white and Christian, and their presence diluted the multicultural population that had been the hallmark of the city's early days. Ethnic groups that had once mingled socially now preferred to gather with their own kind.

Just a few years earlier, in 1887, a group of Jews and Christians had started the California Club, a men's social club. At first the club had a rough-and-tumble feel to it; its headquarters were situated above a livery station, the Tally-Ho, on First and Broadway streets. But it soon became one of the most prestigious clubs in the city, with Isaias, Henry Fleishman, Ozro Childs, Hancock Banning, John Bixby, and Kaspare Cohn among its founding members. In its second site in the Wilcox Building on Second and Spring streets, members could relax in a plush reading room furnished with Turkish smoking chairs, play billiards, or eat in a dining hall that could seat hundreds of people.[41]

But as white Protestants became an overwhelming majority, groups that had once mingled freely started to go their separate ways. In 1891, the sons of Los Angeles's pioneer Jews started the Concordia Club, which was geared toward Jewish fraternal cheer. In 1897, Joseph Satori, the founder of the Security Trust and Savings Bank, who had asked Isaias to invest in his institution and had brought in Maurice Hellman, one of Isaias's cousins, as a partner, created the Los Angeles Golf and County Club. No Jews were allowed.

Isaias began to feel the strain of running major financial institutions in two cities that were four hundred miles apart. "I have been foolish in loading so much responsibility on my shoulders," he wrote to Meyer Lehman on July 7, 1893. "Had I only one institution to look out for, it would not be so much trouble, but two in San Francisco and two in Los Angeles in such times as we are having is too much. I often have these miserable headaches."[42] (He also ran the Southern Trust Company.)

The 1893 panic thrust much of the country into a depression that would last for three years. But the seeds of recovery, in fact the beginnings of a huge economic boom, were started in April 1893 in a field near the center of Los Angeles. There, two men made a discovery that would change the face of the region forever. Using a drill attached to a makeshift twenty-foot-tall derrick constructed out of four-by-fours, Edward Doheny and Charles Canfield penetrated a hard outcropping of rock two hundred feet into the ground. When the metal bit broke through the strata, it uncovered a pool of dark, viscous oil, the biggest strike ever uncovered in Los Angeles.

During the next few months, Doheny and Canfield pumped out barrel after barrel of oil and sold it to eager businessmen and factory owners for $2 a barrel.[43] Their success led others to scout the rock outcroppings and dips of southern California, looking for telltale signs of brea. The sticky black substance didn't guarantee that oil lurked below the surface, but it was a strong indication.

Isaias played a fundamental role in Doheny and Canfield's success. The two men were veteran miners and explorers when they first met in New Mexico. Canfield moved to Los Angeles in the mid-1880s and made an enormous fortune buying and selling real estate. He built a beautiful mansion in Westlake Park and bought the renowned O.K. Stables, where he raised Thoroughbreds.[44]

Doheny followed his friend to Los Angeles in hopes of getting rich, but soon found himself living in a run-down boardinghouse on Sixth and Figueroa streets with his wife and sickly seven-year-old daughter, out of funds and out of ideas. Then one day he noticed a wagon rolling past his boardinghouse, its back heaped with black pitch. Doheny asked the driver what it was and where it came from and soon was rushing toward Westlake Park. He found a hole oozing with a tarry substance. He picked it up. He smelled it and noticed it had a sweet odor. He asked a nearby worker what the brea could be used for, and learned that it could be burned for fuel.

Doheny had been a miner and prospector for twenty years at that point, and he realized there might be a business in collecting and selling the brea. Los Angeles was fueled by coal, which was expensive at $20 a ton. Doheny thought there might be a market for a lower-priced heating and light source.

But where would he get the money to acquire land? Canfield was broke, his last fortune having evaporated in a downturn in the real estate market. Nonetheless, Doheny managed to convince him to set up a partnership. Canfield went to see Isaias and asked to borrow $500. He had no money, no prospects, just the idea that there must be reserves of oil lurking below the city. No bank would lend to him, but Isaias saw something he liked in Canfield, a determination that would not quit. Isaias lent Canfield the money, setting the stage for the creation of one of the state's largest and most lucrative oil companies.[45]

Isaias was rapidly becoming a man of distinction. One of the clearest signs of his prestige came in late March 1894 when former president Benjamin Harrison came to San Francisco with his daughter. Adolph Sutro, the Comstock Lode millionaire who owned about 12 percent of the land in San Francisco, held a small reception at his estate. Only the mayor of San Francisco, his wife, Isaias, and Esther were invited. The party gathered at Sutro's mansion overlooking the Pacific Ocean and spent time wandering the forty-acre grounds. When Sutro first acquired the property it was nothing but sand dunes, but the indefatigable engineer (he spent more than ten years fighting to build a tunnel in the Nevada silver mines) brought in enough dirt and foliage to convert his property into a lush garden dotted with classical statues, including two life-sized lions.

The exclusive invitation delighted Isaias, and he wrote to his family about the day. "I had the pleasure of spending last Saturday with President Harrison, that is to say Adolph Sutro invited President Harrison and Mrs. McKee, his daughter, Mayor Ellert and his wife, Esther and me to take lunch and spend the balance of the day with him, which we did and had a quite delightful time," Isaias wrote his brother. "This evening I am invited by Mr. C. P. Huntington for a stag dinner, so you can see in addition to my bank duties which are quite arduous I have social ones as well."[46]

Isaias had grown close in recent years to Collis Huntington, the president of the Southern Pacific Railroad and one of the most powerful men in the country. The two men had first met in 1876, when Isaias was part of a group of businessmen lobbying to bring the rail line to Los Angeles. In the past eighteen years, the power of the Southern Pacific had grown enormously as it expanded its routes and control of freight rates throughout the state. Its political arm extended into numerous races, and a growing chorus of critics had started to denounce the influence of the Southern Pacific. In June, the nationwide Pullman strike paralyzed the rail line for three weeks, and the company's violent response to the strikers—it fired all who desired to remain in the union—brought it much criticism. Sutro, for example, made a successful run for mayor of San Francisco in 1894 largely by running an anti–Southern Pacific campaign.

Isaias had mixed feelings about the Southern Pacific. Though he was not prounion, he thought that workingmen deserved a decent wage. He regarded the Pullman strike as unfortunate and feared that the working classes might revolt outright if they continued to receive the kind of treatment they had gotten from the railroads. He blamed the country's obsession with speculative railroad investments for part of the problem. "It behooves one who is not mixed up with these various corporations to ask himself the questions, 'Is there no cause for the trouble? Is labor entirely responsible for these disturbances?' I for one say 'No,' " Isaias wrote to his brother-in-law after the Pullman strike. "When in London four years ago in discussion with Ben who at the time was buying and selling large blocks of stocks I then prophesized that the time will be coming when the people in the US would rise either through their legislature or their Congress or through rebellion and demand that this over-issuing of stock and overbonding railroads will have to stop. You living in New York and not coming into contact with the producing classes have no conception in what desperate condition that class of citizens is today."[47]

Isaias remained cognizant, however, that the Southern Pacific held significant power in California. It was also one of the Nevada Bank's biggest customers, and Isaias was careful to maintain cordial relations with Collis Huntington and the Crocker family. Leland Stanford, one of the founders of the rail line, had died the year before, and Isaias and his widow, Jane Stanford, kept in regular contact. Stanford University would soon move much of its funds to the Union Trust Company.

Huntington apparently enjoyed discussing business matters with Isaias. He told John Mackay that Isaias was "one of the ablest bankers" he knew. When Huntington came to San Francisco, he made a point of talking to Isaias. "I have been coming to see you almost every day since I came out, but every day seems to bring business that holds me very closely to the corner of Fourth and Townsend Streets; not that I have any special business, only I wanted to come in and talk matters over generally with you," Huntington wrote Isaias.[48]

The issue of expanding the port of Los Angeles tested Isaias's ability to navigate sticky political matters and not offend any of his friends. The waters off the coast of San Pedro had never been deep enough to permit oceangoing vessels to dock near the shore, and Los Angeles's business community looked to the federal government to build a massive breakwater. After two federal committees recommended that San Pedro be developed, Huntington threw a wrench into the process by proclaiming that Santa Monica would be the better port and should get the federal appropriation. By 1894, the Southern Pacific had constructed a 4,300-foot wharf extending into the ocean at Santa Monica, and Huntington wanted to capitalize on his $1 million investment.

The battle over the port would rage for years, pitting Huntington against a determined group of businessmen from Los Angeles, including the chamber of commerce and Harrison Gray Otis, who turned the pages of his *Los Angeles Times* into a forum for the Free Harbor Association. The business-

men favored San Pedro over Santa Monica because it was the city's traditional port, but also because they feared that the Southern Pacific was too
firmly entrenched in Santa Monica and would use its position to jack up shipping rates. They didn't want "Uncle Collis," as the newspapers called him, to
become even more dominant.

Isaias tried to tread a middle ground by endorsing the development of
both ports, thereby not antagonizing either Huntington or Otis. It was relatively easy to maintain neutrality, since he now lived in San Francisco. "If
possible, why not have appropriations for both harbors?" Isaias wrote to
Otis.[49] After Congress finally concluded that San Pedro was superior to
Santa Monica, the Farmers and Merchants Bank would lend $50,000 to help
build a breakwater.[50]

It was around 1894 that Isaias became acquainted with another Huntington, one who would ultimately play a large role in Isaias's business life and
have a profound impact on the development of southern California. That
man was Huntington's nephew, Henry Edwards Huntington, who had come
to San Francisco in 1892 to represent his family's interests in the Southern
Pacific. One of his early tasks was to secure rights of way for expansion, and
he and Isaias met during negotiations over property near Pasadena.

While Henry Huntington had been named assistant to the president of the
Southern Pacific, the Crockers, the Stanfords, and the Hopkins heirs were
too nervous about his ambitions to permit him to play a major role in the
railroad line. Instead, Henry Huntington was put in charge of the company's
streetcar lines. This mutual interest in trolley lines would soon bring him and
Isaias together.

The streetcar system in San Francisco was a mess; dozens of different
lines owned by dozens of different companies ran through the city, each using a different technology. A horsecar line fed into a system propelled by a
cable line, which then met up with a line that was powered by overhead electric wires. The result was slow service and spotty coverage.

The Southern Pacific owned the largest rail line in the city, the Market
Street Cable Railway, which in 1892 had fourteen miles of double track,
twelve miles of single track, eighty-four horses, and 232 cable cars. Its cars
ran down San Francisco's main street—Market Street—and along other
busy corridors, such as Mission Street and Valencia Street.

Huntington dived into an acquisition and modernization plan for the

Market Street Cable Railway, one that would take advantage of new electric technology and offer San Francisco a comprehensive system of electric lines that were fast, efficient, and cheap to run. But Huntington's vision required money—a commodity hard to come by in the years after the Panic of 1893. He would soon turn to Isaias for help.

While Isaias's social life in San Francisco was going well, his relationship with his brother Herman was not. Isaias had at first been pleased with his brother's handling of the Farmers and Merchants Bank, but he quickly decided that Herman was not a good banker and began to disparage his efforts in daily letters and missives. Isaias would write and question a loan Herman had approved or tell him he had lent out money to someone who didn't have sufficient collateral. Herman was perplexed at his brother's disdain because he attributed the bank's growth to his own business acumen. "I must say that I am really surprised and disgusted with this continual uncalled for remarks," Herman wrote to Isaias on June 15, 1891. "I am trying to do well for the Farmers & Merchants Bank. . . . I have had since I am in this bank more sleepless nights and more headaches than I have ever had before, only thinking over matters so I would not make any mistakes and so that you should not have any complaints to make, and instead of pleasing I am only receiving scolding words, grumbling and growling in return!"[51] "In your estimation everyone is a fool and you know it all," he wrote on November 17, 1891.[52]

The two brothers had set up an arrangement that clearly was unworkable: Isaias needed someone to run the Farmers and Merchants Bank, yet he was unwilling to give up control. If Herman had not been his younger brother, but merely a hired manager, Isaias may have offered criticisms in a more diplomatic manner. He clearly didn't feel the need to be gentle with Herman. Isaias's growing reputation in San Francisco may have also made him more judgmental and arrogant. The tension that had always existed between the two brothers now came out into the open.

Two years later, Isaias's annoyance had only grown more pronounced. "Can you change matters by worrying or complaining?" Isaias wrote his brother on August 24, 1893. "Don't you think I have *ten times* more annoyances in these times than you have? I keep everything unpleasant from you and beg of you to do likewise. Your position and responsibility is play work in comparison to what I have. If business would always run smooth, anybody could succeed, just now it means ultimate success for the fittest and failure for the weak ones."[53]

In mid-1894, Herman and his wife, Ida, planned a six-month vacation in Europe. Herman had not been feeling well for months, and he attributed his bad health to stress from running the bank. He intended to recuperate from the tension at a spa in Wiesbaden, Germany, while Ida planned to go to Bad Kissengen to lose weight.

Marco had been spending chunks of time at the Farmers and Merchants Bank the previous two years, and Isaias decided he should serve as acting president in Herman's absence. Marco traveled down to Los Angeles in mid-April, arriving in town on the day of the annual Fiesta, a large parade that celebrated the city's historical ties to Mexico. When Marco arrived at the bank, he "found the whole force from Uncle down . . . standing on top of the counter, looking at the procession. The sight was very funny but not very businesslike."[54]

After Herman departed for Europe, Marco settled in as the bank's acting president and began to investigate the bank's loans. He soon began to question some of Herman's decisions. It appeared that Herman had a habit of lending money to friends and tenants. "The question of paying uncle $10,000 per year has often come up to me since I came here and I cannot see where he was worth it (this in strictest confidence)," Marco wrote to his father. "I like the loans he made less every time I go over them. . . . He placed lots of loans to tenants of his and other friends with whom we have the greatest difficulty in collecting interest and in some cases the principal is not over safe."[55]

Marco's observations reinforced some of Isaias's bad feelings. For years he had second-guessed the loans Herman made. Even though Herman was the head of the bank in Isaias's absence, Isaias requested that Herman check all large loans with him. It was clear that his brother had not followed those instructions.

Herman returned to Los Angeles in the fall of 1894 and expected to resume running the bank. But Isaias did not recall Marco to San Francisco. Even worse, he let Marco keep his title of acting president, which meant that Herman, who only held the title of vice president, would be reporting to his nephew. Herman was insulted by the challenge to his authority. "I cannot go in and have a boy of 24 years of age be my superior and therefore kindly ask of you to accept my resignation by November the 5th," Herman wrote his brother on October 29, 1894.[56]

Marco was also having difficulty with the arrangement. "My dear Papa," he wrote on October 30, 1894. "Well one more unpleasant day has passed since I last wrote you, and I sincerely hope that there will not be many more like it. Uncle Herman has taken a new tack he just interferes enough in the management to make it unpleasant. He sits in the office and naturally when people want anything they go there and then he rings the bell the boy calls me in and he says right before the person that he has as yet nothing to do with the bank but that the loan is good and I should approve it. In this way he puts all the responsibility on me and he acts the fine fellow who gives favors to everyone. Now, dear Papa, I am going to stand this only until I get an answer to this letter from you and then he must either take full charge or get out. I am positively getting so nervous and worried that I don't sleep one hour all night."[57]

Isaias didn't believe Herman's threat to resign. On November 9, he wrote to Marco, "If he wants to leave the bank nobody will prevent him from doing so, he can pack up his traps and go. I have told you from the beginning that he never intended to resign, he simply tried a little of his bulldozing on me. Tell him I do not want to take notice of his resignation, but he is at liberty to do as he thinks best."[58]

Isaias may have felt that his son would one day be a better banker than his uncle, but that day had not yet arrived. On November 16, the board of directors of the Farmers and Merchants Bank held a special meeting to act on Herman's offer of resignation. It was rejected.[59]

To avoid a confrontation, Isaias finally pulled Marco out of active management of the Farmers and Merchants Bank. But the truce with Herman would be only temporary.

ELEVEN

A DEATH THREAT

1895–1898

On a cold Saturday morning in February 1895, Isaias kissed his wife good-bye, donned his top hat, and headed out of his Franklin Street home for his customary thirty-minute walk downtown to his office at the Nevada Bank. He normally walked with his neighbors and boyhood friends, Isaac Walter and William Haas, but on that day he set out alone.

As Isaias took a left onto California Street, one of the city's busiest thoroughfares, he could see a city coming to life. Streetcars clanged by, thronged with dark-suited men on their way to work. Liverymen at Nolan's stables hitched up horses to buggies. Smoke belched from the towering chimney of a cable car barn. As he crossed Van Ness Avenue on his way to Polk Street, he passed a group of carpenters constructing a new home, the sound of their hammers ringing in the cool air.

Suddenly a fashionably dressed man in a gray frock coat and top hat stepped in front of the banker. "Mr. Hellman?" inquired the man, who had a red beard and mustache flecked with gray.

Isaias looked up—the stranger was taller than he—and peered through his spectacles. "Yes," he replied.

The man stared at Isaias with a strange expression on his face. "I want you to repay me for the injury you have done me," said the man, the words tumbling from his mouth. Suddenly, he pulled a black-handled pistol from his pocket and raised it toward Isaias. For a moment the two men looked at each other, as if time had stopped around them.

"I'll kill you," said the assailant, his eyes blazing.

"Here. Here. Don't," said a frightened Isaias as he whipped his cane into the air to deflect the gun. The man grabbed the cane and flung it aside.

At that, Isaias fled. He ran down California Street as fast as he could, his top hat flying off his head and coming to rest on the sidewalk. He had the presence of mind to zig and zag as he ran so he would be less of a target. The gunman fired two shots at Isaias. They missed.

The third shot found its target: in the center of the man's own forehead.

The police found a note in William Holland's pocket as he lay dying at the Receiving Hospital. "I feel very bitter towards Hellman. Hellman is too much for me. A scoundrel of the deepest dye. Why should a man holding a position as President of such a corporation try and do me out of my rights? It is monstrous and I can scarcely keep myself from that man. . . . I have come to the conclusion to take the law in my own hands and I cannot say what the end will be. But I will have satisfaction."[1]

Police found other notes on the assailant, and grouped together they explained his grievances. Holland, a German who had lived in South Africa before coming to San Francisco eleven years earlier, had once been rich, with an estimated fortune of $30,000. He gambled his money away, forcing him and his wife to move to a boardinghouse on Grove Street. Ten days before the shooting, Holland had walked into the Nevada Bank, where a teller thought he recognized Holland as someone who earlier had passed a forged check. The police came and Holland was hauled to headquarters, where he was grilled for seven hours and then released, apparently a victim of mistaken identity.

Though Holland was not charged with a crime, he became convinced that Isaias had ordered his arrest. He asked for an apology, and the teller who had mistakenly identified him sent a letter outlining how the mistake had been made. But Holland still blamed Isaias and was enraged enough to try to shoot him.

The assassination attempt made the front pages of the newspapers in San Francisco and Los Angeles. "Extra! Shot At," read the *San Francisco Daily Report.* "Crazy Forger Tries to Kill Banker I. W. Hellman," said the *Los Angeles Times.* The *Los Angeles Express* put out an extra edition, and newsboys roamed the downtown streets yelling, "Express, full account of the shooting of I. W. Hellman."

Shooting at capitalists had become somewhat of a sport in the last years of the nineteenth century as conflicts erupted between the rich and those who toiled in factories and mines. The anarchist Alexander Berkman had attempted to murder industrialist Henry Clay Frick in July 1892 in retaliation for Frick's role in a steel strike that resulted in the death of ten steelworkers. A man named Wesley C. Rippey had shot John Mackay in the back in February 1893, seriously wounding the Silver King, which Mackay reminded Isaias in a telegram. "Glad to hear you had such a lucky escape you had better luck than I did," Mackay wrote.[2]

Immediately after the assassination attempt, Isaias spoke calmly with reporters. He even made it to work an hour later. But the attempt on his life unnerved him deeply. His sense of omnipotence, of being a man at the top of his profession, slipped away. His migraine headaches intensified. From that time on, Isaias felt most secure when he was surrounded by his family. The bullets had never penetrated his body, but they had shattered his well-being.

B y 1895, Isaias had grown much closer to Henry Huntington, who was in the midst of his modernization plan for the Market Street Cable Railway. Huntington had converted numerous horse-pulled trolley lines to electricity. He wanted to convert the entire system and expand it into fast-growing residential neighborhoods of San Francisco. To get the money to do this, Huntington tapped Isaias to sell $5 million of bonds through his Union Trust Company.

All visionary railroad men in the late nineteenth century needed a close relationship with a banker to make their dreams viable. Edward H. Harriman had Jacob Schiff. Collis Huntington had James Speyer. And Henry Huntington picked Isaias Hellman. It was a relationship that would mutually serve the men for more than a decade and expand beyond the confines of transportation into land development, electric power, steel, and other industries.

Isaias was an inspired choice, for he was ambitious, well connected, and already enamored of the financial possibilities of the transportation industry. Isaias had owned or been involved with the street railways of Los Angeles for almost twenty years prior to meeting Henry Huntington, and he was familiar with the arguments of cable propulsion versus electric power, consolidation versus competition, and with the details of transportation financing.

But selling $5 million worth of bonds in the depressed financial climate after the 1893 panic was not easy, particularly since there were some concerns about the legality of the consolidation of the Market Street Cable Railway. Isaias didn't want to take the bonds to market only to have their sale held up during a legal challenge. So Isaias decided on an unusual strategy—he would challenge the legality of the bonds before they went on sale.

The board of directors of the Market Street Cable Railway voted to issue the bonds and then had a book of blank bond forms delivered to its banker—Isaias Hellman. Isaias refused to accept the booklet and stated that he was worried the bonds were not issued legally. The railway filed suit to compel Isaias to accept the bonds.

The case went all the way to the California Supreme Court, which ruled on October 20, 1895, that the bonds had been legally issued. "This settles the whole question and we will take the bonds and pay for them," Isaias told the *San Francisco Call* on October 21. "It has been my opinion from the start that the bonds were legal, but we wanted the very highest authority in the State to decide the question once and for all before placing our money."

Isaias immediately put together a syndicate made up of the bankers Antoine Borel and Daniel Meyer and the estate of the former banker John Parrott to buy $2 million of the bonds. Within a few years, Isaias sold $5 million of Market Street Cable Railway bonds and became one of the company's major stockholders. Henry Huntington took over as president of the company in 1897 and appointed Isaias a company director.

The sale of the Market Street Cable Railway bonds thrust Isaias into a new business, one that had traditionally been outside his role as banker. As a market maker of bonds, he made a commission on their sale. He also attracted rich and powerful men who were looking for investments and who believed that Isaias Hellman's stamp of approval of a security was almost a guarantee of its success. In the coming years, Isaias would become one of the West Coast's leading bond dealers, executing sales for the Southern Pacific Railroad, the Spring Valley Water Company, and the region's various electric utilites.

When Meyer and Babette Lehman decided to throw a coming-out party for their two nieces, they reserved the gold and red ballroom on the second floor of Delmonico's Madison Square restaurant at Fifth Avenue and Twenty-sixth-Street in New York City. For sixty-five years Delmonico's had been the most fashionable restaurant in New York, the place that invented à la carte dining, and had kept the public intrigued by constantly reinventing itself. The restaurant regularly moved locales to keep up with the northward growth of the city and put new items on the menu that immediately became much-imitated signature dishes, such as lobster à la Newberg.

The Lehmans' own daughters were grown and married, and the ball was in honor of Esther Hellman's daughter and Benjamin Newgass's daughter. While each young woman had a social presence in her respective city, a debut in New York offered a caché not available elsewhere.

Clara Hellman, nineteen, and Cecile Newgass, twenty-six, of London, would be making their entrance into society on Saturday, December 12, two nights after the First Assembly Ball at the Waldorf-Astoria, the unofficial kickoff of the winter debutante season. The evening would begin at 9 P.M. with a series of waltzes, followed by a supper prepared by Delmonico's internationally known chef, Charles Ranhofer.

Marco Hellman decided to attend the festivities. In mid-November he boarded a train for New York. Isaias, Esther, and their younger daughter Florence had recently returned from a long trip to Europe, and they stayed behind.

It may have been at this dance that Marco looked at Frances Jacobi with new interest. When he had first met her six years earlier, she was just the thirteen-year-old daughter of his parents' neighbors on Sutter Street. Her family now lived in New York—her father was a partner in a prominent wine-distribution firm—and Frances had turned into a beautiful nineteen-year-old with dark brown eyes and hair and a slender waist. Marco, twenty-five, was slim and athletic and sported a dashing mustache.

Marco and Frances spent time together at the ball at Delmonico's, which lasted into the early hours of the morning. They got to know each other even better the following week during a set of activities put together to honor the young debutantes, including a holiday pageant at the Lyceum Theater, where they saw *The Wife of Willoughby* and *The Late Mr. Castello*.

When Marco returned to San Francisco and his duties at the Nevada Bank, he continued to think about the lovely Frances Jacobi. Thirteen months later, in February 1898, Marco asked Frances to marry him and presented her with an engagement ring studded with three diamonds, along with a diamond pin.

"I am pleased to give you some pleasant news at least for me & mine," Isaias wrote a cousin in St. Louis. "My son engaged himself last week to Miss Jacobi. Her parents formerly lived in San Francisco but are now residents of New York. Both my wife and I are happy as we wanted Marco to settle down. He is a splendid young fellow, not spoiled, and quite popular in this city."[3] In another letter, Isaias called Frances "a lovely girl."[4]

In June 1897, Esther, Clara, and Florence departed on a trip to Alaska. Isaias's work was too pressing to permit him to accompany them. No sooner had they left than Isaias received the devastating news from New York that Meyer Lehman was dead.

Lehman had experienced stomach pains on a Friday that at first were diagnosed as colic. By Sunday, the pains were worse. A surgeon arrived at the Fifty-seventh Street house to operate and announced two hours later that there was no hope. Lehman had an obstruction in his intestine that had turned gangrenous. He died at 3:30 P.M. the next day.[5]

Isaias felt unmoored. Esther was sailing in the north and could not be reached for two weeks. "The demise of our much beloved Meyer Lehman, your worthy brother, has so shocked me, that for some days I could hardly realize it," Isaias wrote Emanuel Lehman, Meyer's older brother.[6]

Ever since they had met in 1870, Meyer Lehman had been Isaias's touchstone. Isaias looked up to him, admired him, and emulated him. If Isaias needed a life to model his on, Lehman provided it. Like Isaias, he had come from Germany, started out by peddling dry goods, and used his smarts and savvy to develop a nationally important business. For twenty-seven years—except during the eighteen-month period in 1891and 1892 when they quarreled over money—the two men had been close friends. Isaias wrote detailed letters to Lehman about his business challenges and successes. The two families had traveled in Europe together numerous times. "I know of no other man whom I more loved and respected," Isaias wrote.[7]

When Esther returned from her two-month excursion to Alaska, she and Isaias left almost immediately to spend time together and to grieve Lehman's death. The Hellmans retreated to their favorite summering place, Tallac House at Lake Tahoe. The three-story white wooden hotel stood nestled among the sugar pines at the southwestern edge of the lake and offered sweeping views of the snowcapped Sierra Nevada mountains and the ever-changing blue waters. E. J. "Lucky" Baldwin, the Comstock millionaire who had forced the closure of the Temple and Workman Bank in Los Angeles after the 1875 depression, owned the hotel and had turned it into the grandest resort on the lake.

Before 1883, anyone could visit Tallac and stroll the manicured paths or take a dip in the frigid waters. As Tahoe's tourist trade grew, Baldwin remodeled the hotel to make it more dramatic, adding a steeple spire that would not have been out of place in San Francisco. He imported the chef from the Palace Hotel to cook multicourse meals for breakfast, lunch, and dinner.

Baldwin also decided to limit guests to those with a particular social pedigree, despite the fact that he owned a horse track, had been tried in court for sex with a minor, and had been shot by two women. Baldwin insisted that the visitors be wealthy and accomplished. Soon, the Tallac House was filled with "tony people," according to the *Truckee Republican*, a place where women changed their outfits five or six times a day: for breakfast, a morning stroll, lunch, boating, tea, and dinner.

It was ironic that vacationing at Lake Tahoe took on a decidedly eastern air, with societal connections and the size of one's pocketbook replacing outdoor adventure. For most of the previous fifty years, Lake Tahoe had been a place of little consequence, revered more for its timber than for its natural beauty and healing properties.

For hundreds of years, the only humans along the lake's shores were the Washoe, a nomadic Native American tribe that fled the sun-parched Nevada desert each summer for the cooling climate of the mountains. The first white men to spot the lake were John C. Frémont and Kit Carson, who sighted it in February 1844 while scouting for a route across across the Sierra Nevada to Sutter's Fort in the Sacramento Valley. "With Mr. Preuss, I ascended today the highest peak to the right, from which we had a beautiful view of a mountain and a lake at our feet, about 15 miles in length so entirely surrounded by mountains that we could not discover an outlet," Frémont wrote in his diary. He named the lake Bonpland, after a French botanist, but Frémont's topographer, Charles Preuss, marked it "Mountain Lake" on the map.[8]

The lake's name was later changed to Bigler Lake, in honor of California's third governor. But the name Bigler never caught on, perhaps because it was too prosaic for a place as majestic as Lake Tahoe, which was twenty-two miles long, twelve miles wide, and almost incalculably deep. Even Mark Twain was captivated by the area's beauty. "The air up there in the clouds is very pure and fine, bracing and delicious," Twain wrote in *Roughing It,* an account of his time as a newspaperman in the West. "And why shouldn't it be—it is the same air the angels breathe." In 1945, the name was officially changed to Lake Tahoe, which according to legend, means either "big water" or "big blue" in local Indian dialect.

In 1859, silver was discovered in nearby Virginia City, Nevada, and thousands of miners saw Lake Tahoe for the first time as they traversed the Bonanza Road, which cut by the southern end of the lake. They stopped only long enough to eat or sleep at one of the many wooden lodging houses and cheap hotels that sprang up to accommodate the miners, and then moved on to try their luck in the Comstock.

The owners of the silver mines soon returned, not to recreate, but to plunder the pine forests that covered the mountains. They needed wood to prop up the mine shafts in the watery and unstable ground, to power the steam generators that processed the silver, and to rebuild Virginia City after it burned down in 1875. When construction on the transcontinental Central Pacific Railroad began in the late 1860s, the demand for timber skyrocketed.

California was still a frontier, and its natural resources—water, land, and wood—seemed unlimited. It was the land of opportunity, a place whose minerals made men rich, and there was no thought of slowing down that capitalistic fever.

The slopes of the mountains were steep and difficult to log, but by 1867, lumbermen had developed an ingenious method to extract wood. They constructed V-shaped flumes that ran down the hillsides and dumped the logs into the lake or holding ponds created by damming the Truckee River. Sometimes the flumes were greased with tallow and sometimes with water. By 1881, there were thirty log chutes in the mountains. The loggers would cut and trim the massive trees and feed them into the flumes, where they would plummet toward the lake at tremendous speed. Parts of the V-flumes were erected on trestles, and every once in a while a log would careen off and pinwheel down the mountain with a thundering crash. "Tons of sugar pine move faster and faster, forty—fifty—sixty—then seventy miles an hour, now leaving a rocket's trail as sparks and clouds of smoke fan out behind the hurtling missiles, caused by the frictional heat generated as they run down the greased runway," C. F. McGlashan, the editor of the *Truckee Republican*, wrote in 1876.[9]

One of the longest V-flumes was a fifteen-mile-long trough built by the Pacific Wood, Lumber, and Flume Company. The flume, which carried wood from Mount Rose, one of the highest peaks on the northeast shores of Lake Tahoe, to the Washoe Valley in Nevada, was built in ten weeks with more than 2 million feet of lumber and twenty-eight tons of nails at a cost of $300,000. It dropped 1,750 feet along the way and was held up in places by trestles that rose 70 feet into the air.[10] More than a half million board feet of lumber was sent on the route each day.

In 1875, two of the flume's owners, James G. Fair and James Flood—who had made millions in the Comstock Lode—invited *New York Tribune* reporter H. J. Ramsdell to take a ride down the trough. It was a crazy and dangerous proposition, but Ramsdell reckoned that if two multimillionaires were willing to risk their lives for fun, then he could as well.

Strong men held two sixteen-foot boats aloft while Fair, Flood, Ramsdell, and two others got in. As soon as the boats were lowered into the flume, they shot off like rockets, careening rapidly down the narrow trough, bouncing from side to side. Water splashed all over the men and at one point the third man in the lead boat was thrown directly into the V-flume. James Fair reached down and lifted him back into the boat, badly lacerating his hand in the process. "How our boat kept in the track is more than I know," Ramsdell wrote. "The wind, the steamboat, the railroad train never went so fast. I have been where the wind blew at the rate of 80 miles per hour, and yet, my breath was not taken away. . . . If the truth must be spoken, I was really scared almost out of reason; but if I was on my way to eternity, I wanted to know exactly how fast I went; so I huddled close to Fair, and turned my eyes toward the hills. Every object I placed my eye on was gone before I could see clearly what it was. Mountains passed like visions and shadows. It was with difficulty that I could get my breath. I felt that I did not weigh a hundred pounds, although I knew that the scales turned at two hundred."[11]

The five men reached the Washoe Valley battered, bruised, and scared out of their minds. Flood told Ramsdell he would never make the trip again, even in exchange for the millions he had earned from the Consolidated Virginia Mine. Fair expressed increased respect for timber and wood, and vowed never to regard himself as highly as those commodities.

The clear-cutting of Tahoe's forests intensified in 1873, and within twenty-five years most of the hills were denuded.[12] One company, the Carson Tahoe Lumber and Fluming Company, cut 750 million board feet and five hundred thousand cords of wood by 1898. When the Comstock Lode finally ran out of silver, hundreds of thousands of mighty sugar pine trees were entombed underground as buttresses for the abandoned mines.

But the slowdown in logging opened up the area as a tourist attraction. It was an arduous nine-hour train ride from the Oakland terminal to Truckee, the major town in the northern sierra. Visitors then had to take a stage another sixteen hair-raising miles until they reached the shores of the lake, where they boarded a steamer to reach their final destinations. While Tallac House was the most magnificent establishment on the lake, there were dozens of other, more rustic hotels, like McKinney's on the west shore.

By the mid-1890s, Isaias and Esther were making Lake Tahoe part of their annual circuit to escape the fog. They continued to spend parts of the summer at Hotel San Rafael in Marin, where the family could live while Isaias took the ferry to work each day. They also spent time at the Del Monte Hotel in Monterey or the White Sulfur Springs Resort in Napa. They also enjoyed traveling to Catalina Island near Los Angeles, where the adventurous could stay in tent cabins. But Lake Tahoe increasingly became their favorite spot. Isaias loved to fish and could spend hours on the lake bobbing in a boat. Trout was so abundant that it was common to catch more than one hundred pounds of fish in just a few hours.

Isaias found the fresh mountain air invigorating, and he and Esther enjoyed strolling the many miles of paths that the Tallac House had carved through the woods. On those walks, they began to plan how they could spend even more time at Lake Tahoe.

In December 1897, sixteen-year-old Florence decided to give a party on Christmas Eve. She sent out invitations to her friends to join her in a celebration of Santa Claus at her parents' home on the corner of Sacramento and Franklin.

The party was announced in the social column of the *Emanu-el*, the weekly newspaper of the San Francisco Jewish community. The notice was so unremarkable that it appeared alongside an announcement that Mr. and Mrs. Simon Bachman and their daughter Norma had given an "enjoyable reception" at their home where the rooms were "filled with a fashionable company." Another notice announced that "the Misses Simon of 2315 Van Ness Avenue had issued cards for a tea from 4 until 7 o'clock on Sunday afternoon."

The Hellmans, along with many other Jews, did not regard Christmas as a religious holiday. To them it was more of a winter festival, a time of good cheer, not a commemoration of the birth of Jesus. The Hellmans celebrated the occasion with family gatherings, present exchanges, and the decoration of a Christmas tree. Parents told their small children that if they were good, Santa Claus would come down the chimney laden with presents, but for naughty children he would leave a lump of coal.

The Hellmans were not alone in celebrating Christmas. The Haas family up the block on Franklin Street threw such lavish Christmas parties that the planning started months before the event. Their cousins, the Lilienthals, would always join them in decorating the large Victorian house with candles and lights.

Christmas in California in the 1890s was not seen solely as a Christian celebration, but one with remnants of its pagan roots. While the Catholic Church in the fourth century had designated December 25 the official day to celebrate Jesus' birth, for centuries the occasion was more often marked by alcoholic revelry and overindulgence than by spiritual contemplation. Few went to church. Instead, they knocked on the doors of the rich and demanded food and libations. The Puritans were so offended by the bacchanalian excesses of Christmas that they banned the holiday. Massachusetts would not make Christmas a legal holiday until 1856.

The rituals of Christmas—Santa Claus, a Christmas tree, and Christmas cards—only gained widespread acceptance in the middle of the nineteenth century. Saint Nick was regarded as a rather stern Norse god until Clement Clarke Moore transformed him in 1822 into a round, red-cheeked, benevolent man in the poem "'Twas the Night Before Christmas." Even then, it took eighteen more years for the poem to become popular. Christmas trees came into vogue only in the 1830s, after the queen of Bavaria introduced the concept to Munich society. Their use then spread around the world.

The Jews of San Francisco were comfortable celebrating a winter holiday with Christmas trees and images of Santa Claus. "The Christmas tree represents winter season, is of Norse origin and not distinctly a Christian invention or monopoly," read an article from a Jewish paper.[13]

The December pages of the *Emanu-el* were filled with ads touting stores' Christmas gift offerings. One ad for the Emporium and Golden Rule Bazaar in 1898 showed Santa Claus carrying a bag filled with toys while reading from a newspaper. There was a silhouette of reindeer pulling his sleigh at the bottom of the notice. "One of the grandest displays of holiday merchandising in America," the ad promised.

Even the city's Reform rabbis seemed to bless Christmas. They were so sure of their congregants' devotion to Judaism that they weren't afraid that the embrace of Santa Claus would lead to a Christian conversion. "Christmas never supplanted Hannuka in the old Jewish home," wrote Rabbi Jacob Voorsanger in one of his editorials in the *Emanu-el*. "Candies and cake and presents and Santa Claus and all the cheerfulness of the social winter feast was borrowed, but not the heathen spirit of forgetting the obligations at home. The Jewish boy who was intoxicated with the thought of Santa's advent had a distinct knowledge of the claims of is own religion. He knew all about the Maccabees. . . . He knew the story of that mysterious crucible that miraculously supplied the oil for eight days and gave the suggestion, traditionally, for the joys of the Hannuka lamp."[14]

But this impulse toward assimilation would be called into question as another wave of Jewsh immigrants crowded onto America's shores.

The compostion of the Jewish American population changed drastically starting in the 1880s. The czar's army in Russia had swept down on the Jews living in the Pale of Settlement, looting villages, killing thousands, and prompting hundreds of thousands to flee. About 470,000 Russian and eastern European Jews immigrated to America from 1880 to 1900, and another 1.5 million would follow over the next two decades.[15] While most of the refugees settled in New York, a few thousand made their way to San Francisco. They crowded into tenements in a six-block area south of Market, bordered by First and Third streets and Folsom Street.

This new group of immigrants differed vastly from the Hellmans and their friends. These eastern European Jews were Orthodox rather than Reform, spoke Yiddish, were not educated, and were overwhelmingly poor. These Jews would never dream of celebrating Christmas, since it was not a holiday on the Jewish calendar.

From the start, German Jews around the country had ambivalent feelings about their co-religionists. They were concerned that the newcomers would never blend into American society, but would insist on standing apart. They worried that their poor education and distinctive dress would attract attention and perhaps stir up anti-Jewish sentiment. One midwestern Jewish newspaper described the Russian immigrants as "uncouth Asiatics." The *Jewish Messenger* suggested that missionaries go to Russia "to civilize the Russian Jews rather than have their backwardness ruin the American Jewish community."[16] Leaders in San Francisco were as fearful as their eastern and midwestern counterparts. "We are confronted by an invasion from the East that threatens to undo the work of two generations of American Jews," Rabbi Voorsanger declared.[17]

Why were the German Jews so opposed to the immigration of people who were facing slaughter by the czar's army? Some historians believe they were more afraid than anything else. "Doubtless the reaction of America's German-Jewish community was one less of snobbery than of plain and simple culture shock," wrote the historian Howard Sachar.[18]

With time, empathy accompanied disdain. Numerous groups set up programs to help the new immigrants find work and housing and ease the transition to a new country. In 1894, Rabbi Voorsanger suggested that the women of the temple form the Emanu-el Sisterhood for Personal Service, modeled after the sisterhood set up by the women of Temple Emanu-el in New York. The group formed a settlement house south of Market, sewed for the immigrants, taught English, offered vocational classes, and helped them find jobs. In the first year, the sisterhood helped more than 1,350 immigrants and secured jobs for 234 people.[19]

Within a few years, womanhood for wealthy ladies no longer meant lunches and visiting days, but charity work. Many of the richest women in San Francisco turned their attention to the poor. They were led by Esther's neighbor, Bella Seligman Lilienthal, the daughter of the New York financier Joseph Seligman and the wife of Philip N. Lilienthal, the head of the Anglo-California Bank. Other members of the sisterhood included Bertha Haas,

married to the grocer William Haas; Mrs. Max C. Sloss, wife of the future
California Supreme Court justice; Rosa Walter; Sophie Bachman, married to
the tobacco merchant Simon Bachman; and Bertha Brandenstein, whose husband was one of the region's largest importers of rice and coffee. The presence of these women turned the sisterhood into a social club with a purpose,
expanding the role of women in the process.

Esther joined the sisterhood shortly after its founding and soon found
that she most enjoyed working with children. Esther had supported Caroline
Severance's model kindergartens in Los Angeles. One of Severance's first
teachers, Kate Douglas Wiggin, had set up her own kindergarten in San
Francisco in 1878. By the late 1890s, there were two women's organizations
in San Francisco dedicated to free kindergartens.

Yet there was no kindergarten dedicated to teaching Jewish children, so
in 1897 the sisterhood organized one. Its members went out into the streets
of the city to find children who spent their days unsupervised. They
walked through the South of Market area, stopping women with toddlers
to talk to them about the virtues of early-childhood education. They visited synagogues and settlement houses. It wasn't easy to convince the immigrant mothers to part with their children, but members of the sisterhood
persisted.

Esther was elected president of the kindergarten in 1898, a position she
would hold for ten years. The women tried to create a place that would be
fun for children but would also teach them manners, hygiene, and citizenship
skills. The kindergarten opened February 28, 1898, in a building on Folsom
Street in the South of Market area. At first, only seventeen children enrolled;
by the end of the first year it had grown to fifty-five students.[20] A Miss Licht-
enstein was the teacher, and a Miss Meyer soon joined as her assistant.

"The ages of the children range from three to six years, and it is with us
they first are taught the principles of truthfulness, honesty, obedience, and a
very important matter, cleanliness," Esther wrote in the kindergarten's first
annual report. "The good work that has been accomplished in this short
space of time is almost remarkable. The improvement in the appearance of
the children since the founding of the kindergarten is most gratifying: Then,
with few exceptions, they looked neglected in every way."[21]

Many women of the upper classes seemed to confuse poverty with moral
turpitude. Those running the Emanu-el Sisterhood and its spin-off organiza-

tions often viewed their clients as inferior. "We must get hold of the little waifs that grow up to form the criminal element," wrote one kindergarten advocate. "We must hunt up the children of poverty, of crime and of brutality, just as soon as they can be reached; the children that flock in the tenement houses in the narrow dirty streets; the children who have no one to call them by dear names; children who are buffeted hither and thither; the 'flotsam and jetsam on the wild mad sea of life.' This is the element out of which criminals are made."[22]

Many eastern Europeans resented this patronizing attitude. "Only later did I realize that there were Yehudim [German Jews] who fervently wished to help us stand on our own two feet," wrote one immigrant. "The reports of pogroms had stirred them deeply. . . . But agreement between us was practically impossible. . . . With the best intentions in the world and with gentle hearts, they unknowingly insulted us."[23]

There is no indication that Esther or any of the other women in the sisterhood sensed hostility from the families they were trying to help. They thought their efforts were appreciated. For example, here is how the sisterhood's annual report described a time the mothers of the kindergarten students came to a meeting: "The mothers enjoy listening to the songs and games of their children and the vocal and instrumental music played for their benefit. It is evident that by these meetings some of the parents who were at first reluctant to send their children, now consider the kindergarten a benefit, and become gradually more attached and interested in the institution."

The kindergarten became so successful that the sisterhood spun it off into its own organization in 1903. Esther and her colleagues raised funds to build a new structure on Harrison Street.

The kindergarten was not the only charity Esther joined. She was involved with the Ladies Auxiliary of Mount Zion Hospital, serving as president of that group for a number of years. She was on the Ladies' Visiting Committee of the Pacific Hebrew Orphan Asylum and Home Society (Isaias was its treasurer), and she spent time visiting the orphans and sewing for them.

On September 7, 1898, Marco Hellman and Frances Jacobi were married in the home of her grandparents, Joseph and Jane Brandenstein, in their house on Gough and California streets in San Francisco. More than one hundred guests crowded into a ballroom for the 6 P.M. ceremony. Frances, dressed in a gown of white satin and point lace, and wearing a tulle veil decorated with orange blossoms, descended down the stairs to a bower studded with pink orchids. A Sabbath lamp that had been in her family for generations illuminated the altar. Her bridesmaids enhanced the pink theme with their pink silk frocks and bouquets of pink carnations.

After the ceremony, the guests dined on a sumptuous wedding banquet. In a gesture of goodwill, the Hellmans and the Jacobis provided breakfast for those assisted by the Emanu-el Sisterhood.

The marriage brought together two distinguished German Jewish families and would offer a new business alliance for Isaias within a few years. Frances's grandfather, Joseph Brandenstein, was an old friend who had served on the board of the Pacific Hebrew Orphan Asylum and Home Society with Isaias. His oldest daughter, Flora, had married Frederick Jacobi of the prominent wine house of Lachman & Jacobi. Within three years, Isaias would acquire the concern once he took over control of the California wine industry.

When California was admitted into the United States in 1850, Los Angeles was a Spanish-speaking pueblo dotted with one-story adobe houses. Many of the dons who lived on massive ranchos grew rich selling beef to gold rush miners. The first U.S. census showed eight Jewish men in the city. *Courtesy of the Bancroft Library, University of California, Berkeley*

By 1871, the era of the don had waned and Los Angeles had become an American city. Its growth was retarded, however, by a lack of capital. The opening of Isaias's Farmers and Merchants Bank in 1871 was instrumental in spurring the city's development. *Courtesy of the Bancroft Library, University of California, Berkeley*

In 1873, the population of Los Angeles had grown to 5,800 residents as Civil War veterans and farmers from the East were lured by the region's fertile soil and agreeable weather. Los Angeles was still isolated and difficult to get to. There was no railroad connection and the quickest way to reach the city was by a two-day steamer trip from San Francisco. *Courtesy of the Bancroft Library, University of California, Berkeley*

Isaias Hellman as a young man. Isaias arrived in Los Angeles in 1859 when he was just sixteen years old. He went to work for his cousins before opening his own dry goods store in 1865. *Photo courtesy of the author*

The infamous Calle de los Negros. The fifty-foot-long alley was home to many of Los Angeles's brothels, gambling dens, and Chinese businesses. In the late 1850s, when there was a murder a day in the city, much of the violence occurred in this area. It was also the location of the 1871 riots against the town's small Chinese community. *Security Pacific Collection, Los Angeles Public Library*

Herman Hellman opened his stationery store in the Downey Block, shown here in 1870. John Downey came to Los Angeles in 1850 and made $30,000 operating the only pharmacy between San Francisco and Mexico. He purchased large swaths of land and eventually owned tens of thousands of acres. Downey served as California governor during the Civil War. *Security Pacific Collection, Los Angeles Public Library*

Commercial Street was one of the main business streets of Los Angeles. When Isaias opened his dry goods store on Main and Commercial in 1865, most of the buildings were one-story adobes. In 1870, he erected one of the city's first two-story brick buildings at the intersection of Commercial and Los Angeles streets (at left). The construction of larger brick buildings accelerated in the 1870s. *Security Pacific Collection, Los Angeles Public Library*

Isaias opened his first bank, Hellman, Temple & Company, in 1868 in the small building to the left of the Bella Union Hotel. The site became the home of the Farmers and Merchants Bank in 1871. Banks were often the most opulent buildings in frontier towns as they tried to convey a sense of permanence in an era of financial instability. *Courtesy of Seaver Center for Western History Research, Los Angeles County Museum of Natural History*

F. P. F. Temple erected the three-story brick Temple Block in the mid-1870s and it was widely considered the most modern building in town. It stood at the intersection of Main, Spring, and Commercial streets, the center of the business district. After Isaias severed his banking partnership with Temple in 1871, Temple opened his own bank here. Despite the impressive building, Temple's bank would go out of business in 1876 with disastrous results for the Los Angeles economy. *Security Pacific Collection, Los Angeles Public Library*

This is the view down Main Street from Temple Block in 1878. The arrival of the Southern Pacific Railroad in 1876 connected Los Angeles to the rest of the country, giving farmers a means to send navel oranges, lemons, wine, and other agricultural goods to distant markets. *Security Pacific Collection, Los Angeles Public Library*

In 1871, Herman Hellman opened Hellman, Haas & Company, a wholesale grocery store that sold goods throughout the southwest. Two of his partners in the business, the brothers Jacob and Abraham Haas, had grown up with the Hellman brothers in the Bavarian town of Reckendorf. Herman sold his share of the store in 1890 to become vice president of the Farmers and Merchants Bank and the company became known as Haas, Baruch & Company. It was eventually purchased by the grocery chain Smart & Final. *Courtesy of Seaver Center for Western History Research, Los Angeles County Museum of Natural History*

In 1877, Isaias and his wife, Esther, built a new home on Main and Fourth streets in Los Angeles. At the time, the house was so far out of town that Isaias gave an adjacent plot to a friend just so his family would have company. The Italianate house was considered one of the nicest in town. It had frescoes with scenes from Germany, Mississippi, and Los Angeles painted on the walls of the living and dining rooms. *Security Pacific Collection, Los Angeles Public Library*

In 1883, Isaias moved the Farmers and Merchants Bank into a new building on Main and Commercial streets, where it would remain for twenty-two years. Note the advertisement painted on the window: "Oldest and Largest Bank in Southern California." *Security Pacific Collection, Los Angeles Public Library*

Isaias was fifty-seven years old and the president of the powerful Nevada Bank of San Francisco when the German Jewish artist Toby Rosenthal painted this picture in 1899. *Courtesy of the Huntington Library*

Esther Hellman. Esther and Isaias were extremely close even though theirs was an arranged marriage. Esther loved to shop and wear beautiful clothes, and she spent thousands of dollars each year on jewelry, dresses, and furniture, but she was also an astute observer of places and people and helped her socially shy husband navigate through Los Angeles and San Francisco society. Esther's sister, Babette, was married to Meyer Lehman, one of the founders of Lehman Brothers in New York, and Isaias and Lehman entered into many business deals together. *Photo courtesy of the author*

(Below) In 1892, Isaias and his family moved into a house on the corner of Sacramento and Franklin in San Francisco's up-and-coming Western Addition. It was a popular neighborhood for wealthy German Jews. Isaias's boyhood friend from Reckendorf, Isaac Walter, lived next door on Franklin, and the president of the Anglo-California Bank, Phil Lilienthal and his wife, Bella Seligman Lilienthal, lived two doors away. *Courtesy of the Bancroft Library, University of California, Berkeley*

The Hellmans decorated their home in the ornate Victorian style that was popular at the end of the nineteenth century. The walls and ceiling of the dining room were covered in black walnut and much of the furniture was imported from France. *Courtesy of the Bancroft Library, University of California, Berkeley*

The library in the Hellmans' Franklin Street home. *Courtesy of the Bancroft Library, University of California, Berkeley*

In 1903, the Hellmans built a home on the shores of Lake Tahoe, which they named Pine Lodge. The house, designed by architect Walter Bliss, was rustic in style and ushered in a new era of millionaires building mansions on the lake. The home and its two miles of lakeshore are now a California State Park. *Photo courtesy of the author*

Isaias and Esther and their family gathered on the front steps of Pine Lodge in Lake Tahoe in 1903. Back row, left to right: Charles Bransten, Joe Lilienthal, Esther Hellman. Second row: Warren Hellman, Isaias Hellman, Edward Hellman Heller, Frederick Hellman. Third row: Marco Hellman, Frances Jacobi Hellman, Florence Hellman, Clara Hellman Heller, and Emanuel Heller. Front row, bottom two steps: On the bottom two steps are Anis Van Nuys and Elsie Ehrman. *Photo courtesy of the author*

Herman Hellman and family in Los Angeles. From left to right: Frieda Hellman, Herman Hellman, Amy Hellman, Marco H. Hellman, Irving Hellman, and Ida Hellman. *Photo courtesy of the author*

The 1906 San Francisco earthquake and fire devastated the city's financial district, including the Wells Fargo Nevada National Bank on Pine and Montgomery streets. The building was dynamited during the conflagration, but the contents of the bank's safe remained virtually intact. The bank reopened for business a month after the earthquake in new headquarters on Market Street. *Courtesy of the Wells Fargo Archives*

After the 1906 earthquake, the Hellmans and various relatives retreated to Oakvale, the summer home of Marco and Frances Hellman in Oakland. Wealthy San Franciscans often had second homes on the Peninsula, Marin County, or the East Bay to escape the summer fog. *Photo courtesy of the author*

Isaias's childhood home in Reckendorf, Germany. The Bavarian town is about ten miles from Bamberg. *Photo courtesy of the author*

In 1911, Isaias returned to his home in Reckendorf, Germany, which looked much like it had during his childhood. Most of the town's Jews had immigrated to other countries or moved to bigger cities by then. Isaias visited Europe almost every year until the outbreak of World War I. He enjoyed taking the waters at the Bad Kissingen spa. *Photo courtesy of the author*

Marco Hellman and his family in front of the Sphinx and the Great Pyramid in Egypt in 1911. *Photo courtesy of the author*

After Esther Hellman died in 1908, Isaias donated $100,000 in her memory to Mount Zion Hospital in San Francisco. In 1912, her daughter-in-law, Frances Hellman, and son-in-law Emanuel Heller spoke at the dedication of the cornerstone. The hospital, one of the most modern in the city, treated people of all religions. *Courtesy of the Western Jewish History Center of the Judah L. Magnes Museum*

In 1905, Isaias erected an imposing new building for the Farmers and Merchants Bank on the site of his old home at Fourth and Main streets. It served as the bank's headquarters until 1956. The L-shaped office building Isaias constructed around the bank has been converted into lofts and now forms the core of Los Angeles's up-and-coming Old Bank District.
Security Pacific Collection, Los Angeles Public Library

TWELVE

TROLLEYS AND WATER

1898–1901

The Los Angeles trolley system in 1898 was a hodgepodge of devices. Horses pulled cars down tracks on some streets, while cable lines pushed cars up other streets. One company built three viaducts to carry trolleys over the Los Angeles River, but they were so poorly constructed that they blew down in the massive winter storms of 1887 and 1888. Other companies had spent thousands of dollars to electrify their lines, hoping that this time the latest new technology would stick.

Man after man and company after company had tried to tame the system. Financiers from Chicago came, but admitted defeat after a few years and went home broke. An outfit from South Africa considered buying a line. But no one company had yet turned the mishmash of lines into a coherent transportation system.

Imagine the surprise, then, of Los Angeles residents when they plunked down their 3¢ for the September 14, 1898, edition of the *Los Angeles Times*. When they opened the paper to local news on page 4, their eyes were drawn to an article outlined in black. "Gobbled by the S.P.," the headline read breathlessly. "Huntington & Co. Take in the Los Angeles Railway."

The details were sketchy, as the article was only a few paragraphs long. But the gist of the article suggested that the Southern Pacific Railroad had purchased the bulk of the rail lines in Los Angeles. The Huntington family, led by Collis and his nephew Henry, had quietly been negotiating throughout the summer for the trolley company that ran cars throughout the downtown business district.

Throughout the day, reporters from the *Times* and other newspapers raced around town trying to collect more information. When word got out that Isaias might have something to do with the purchase, reporters rushed to the Farmers and Merchants Bank to interview his brother Herman. "That is a matter on which I cannot give definite information," Herman told the papers. "Although I am interested with my brother, Isaias W. Hellman, in the banking business, he is the one who is interested in the Los Angeles Railway system."

Details soon emerged, and it turned out that the *Los Angeles Times* had gotten some important facts right—and some other critical facts wrong. Henry Huntington, his uncle Collis, and his son Howard had made an offer for five of Los Angeles's six rail lines. The buyers paid $3.9 million for the companies and planned to issue $5 million in bonds to pay off the debt and make improvements. But the Huntingtons were not the only buyers. Isaias and a syndicate including Antoine Borel and Christian de Guigne had purchased a 45 percent interest in the deal. This was a private transaction, not one masterminded by the Southern Pacific.

Still, the fact that there were three Huntingtons involved was great fodder for the newspapers, as Collis Huntington and his strong-arm tactics were widely feared. On Friday, September 16, the *Times* ran a large cartoon on its front page picturing a sweating, bearded Huntington holding the entire earth in his arms, with a Los Angeles Railway trolley car gripped in one hand. The cartoon had a caption: "The Earth. This Property Is Owned by the Southern Pacific Railway." In the cartoon, Huntington is thinking to himself: "I wonder if there is anything else I have forgotten?"

"The Huntington methods are so well known on the Pacific Coast that a mere reference to them is all that is necessary to an understanding of the possible dangers which may threaten this community by reason of the transfer of the consolidated street railway property to a corporation under direct control of the men who manage the Southern Pacific Company . . . ," read an article in the *Times*. "If the usual Huntington methods are pursued—and when have they not been pursued in the management of Huntington's properties—the foothold which the octopus managers have secured in the street-railway business of Los Angeles will prove to be one of the worst calamities that has ever befallen his community."

The *Times* seems to have played up the Huntington angle as a circulation ploy and as a means to get back at their rival newspaper, the *Express*, which the *Times* ridiculed as "the Distress," and was partly owned by some of the most influential men in town. The *Times* reporters soon understood that the Huntingtons, as individuals, and not as representatives of the Southern Pacific, had bought the rail line. But the paper ignored the facts and stroked the anti–Southern Pacific flames.

"The Los Angeles Times is continually attacking the street railway system, claiming it is a Huntington corporation," Isaias wrote his brother. "You were present at a conversation I had with the manager, and when I made him the proper explanation he stated that nothing further should appear in the Times against the company. Please see him about this and recall our conversation. I am trying to have a good deal of capital from here [San Francisco] invested in Los Angeles but these continual newspaper attacks may drive it away."[1]

In fact, while Henry Huntington was the front man for the purchase and would take charge of the new railway, to be known as the Los Angeles Railway, or LARY, the deal was Isaias's idea. Huntington had been living in California for six years at that point and had only a cursory knowledge of the Los Angeles transportation landscape, while Isaias had been intimately involved with the city's rails for twenty-four years. Isaias also had financial ties to most of the rail lines that were purchased.

No records remain that reveal how Huntington decided to invest in the rail lines in Los Angeles, but it is not farfetched to think that he and Isaias discussed the state of southern California's trolley system during their time working on the financing of the expansion of the Market Street Cable Railway in San Francisco.

The new owners wasted little time before making plans to modernize and improve their new system, which covered 168 miles of tracks around Los Angeles, including heavily traveled lines downtown along Main, Spring, and Commercial streets.[2] On October 4, a little more than two weeks after the purchase became public, Huntington, Borel, and de Guigne boarded Huntington's private rail car in San Francisco for a trip to Los Angeles. Isaias engaged a drawing-room car to follow, and the four men met at the depot. They then set out on another tour, this time of all the rail lines that would soon be subsumed under the new corporate entity. They looked at the size and stability of the trolley embankments, the wear of the railway ties, the size of the rail gauge, the circulation pattern, and the traffic density on Main and Broadway.

The men had ambitious plans for Los Angeles. Huntington had seen riders flock to San Francisco's streetcars after they were converted to electricity. He watched in glee as new houses sprang up around trolley lines and neighborhoods clamored for service. Huntington was confident that the combination of his knowledge of rail lines and Isaias's access to funds would result in a modern, efficient rail system.

Huntington immediately launched a program to upgrade, modernize, and integrate the various systems. He ripped out light rails and replaced them with more durable ones. He rerouted some trolleys from the congested Spring Street onto the less busy Main and Broadway. (This had the effect of boosting property values on Main Street, where Isaias owned numerous lots.) He planned new extensions. By December, the LARY had purchased two more rail lines, including the Los Angeles and Pasadena Electric Railway, which traveled outside the borders of the city. At the end of 1898, the company controlled more than 200 miles of lines.

One audacious move followed another. The trolleys needed electricity to run, so Huntington, Isaias, Borel, and de Guigne agreed in late November to buy $500,000 in bonds of the newly incorporated San Gabriel Electric Company of Los Angeles. William Kerckhoff, a former lumber dealer and ice manufacturer who had tapped the San Gabriel River to provide electricity for the basin, organized the new concern with a promise to provide all the electricity the LARY would need. It was the beginning of a symbiotic relationship that would only grow stronger.

As Los Angeles grew, with its population edging toward one hundred thousand at the turn of the century, its citizens grew impatient with the notion that private businesses, rather than municipal government, controlled many of the major utilities. This was true around the country, as newspapers and politicians began to attack "trusts" or large corporations that had monopolies on railroads, waterworks, gas lines, and other companies. Congress passed the Sherman Antitrust Act in 1890, which aimed to break up monopolies. Even President McKinley, who was widely regarded as a friend of business, appointed the U.S. Industrial Commission on Trusts to look at capitalists such as Andrew Carnegie and John D. Rockefeller.

In Los Angeles, the privately held water company was considered the biggest villain and was even nicknamed "the Grand Monopoly" by Horace Bell, the gnarly and irascible old soldier who ran the newspaper the *Porcupine*. The Los Angeles City Council in 1868 had granted Prudent Beaudry the exclusive franchise for thirty years to provide drinking water to the four thousand residents of the city. The City Water Company at first agreed to pay Los Angeles $1,200 a year for the right to tap the Los Angeles River, although the owners quickly renegotiated the fee down to $400. The company promised to install twelve miles of iron pipe with capacity sufficient to provide enough water for domestic use, erect a fire hydrant at the corner of each intersection, and provide free water to public schools, jails, and other public buildings. Each year, the city council could set the water rates charged by the company. The city retained control of irrigation water, digging ditches, or *zanjas*, from the Los Angeles River to the fields.

For the next twenty-two years, relations between the city, the company, and the citizens were fairly smooth. There were occasional complaints about the quality of the water, which silted up as the town grew and more people moved close to the banks of the Los Angeles River. The water could even smell foul. But the water company generally addressed the problems. It continued to install more pipes and build more reservoirs as the city expanded.

Relations between the company and the city were harmonious in part because many water company officials served in city leadership posts. For a time, in fact, William H. Perry, the president of the water company, served on the city water commission that set the rates for the water company. That ensured that the water company's requests for rate hikes were approved. The directors also spent liberally to elect city officials friendly to the company. "From 1868 to 1884 the gentlemen constituting the board of directors of the City Water Company were the political bosses of Los Angeles city and county," read a report prepared in 1892 for the *Los Angeles Times* by J. H. Woodard, also known as "Jayhawker." "During that period it was not reasonable to suppose that any council would be elected which would be antagonistic to what was considered the interests of the water company."[3]

While Isaias was not one of the original founders of the water company, within a few years he became its major stockholder with 1,200 shares. There were fifty-eight other owners, most of them early settlers or the heirs of settlers, including Herman Hellman, Harris and Marco Newmark, Solomon Lazard, Andrew Glassell, Charles Ducommun, and the descendants of Ozro

Childs and John Downey. The water company was a good investment for shareholders, as it earned a $30,000 monthly profit and generally returned a 6 percent annual dividend.

The city and the company got into their first fierce fight in 1882, when the company unsuccessfully sued the city over who would pay the cost of sprinkling the streets to keep down dust. Relations were never harmonious after that.

By the mid-1880s, when it became clear that the public wanted the city, not a private enterprise, to control Los Angeles's water, both sides maneuvered to better their positions. Fearful of losing the franchise, the water company had purchased a boggy fourteen-acre tract called Crystal Springs, which hydrologists had identified as the probable source of the Los Angeles River. The water company set up a shell company to purchase the headwaters for $1, then installed pipes to capture the runoff.

The city filed suit in 1891 to stop the diversion, arguing that this water was really part of the Los Angeles River and not some other, separate, source of water as the company claimed. It would take seven years and a long court trial for the city to win its suit, only one of thirty water cases it was battling in court. One of the cases was so complex that its file was more than ten thousand pages long.

Even the private water company's own employees grew disillusioned with its management. William Mulholland, who would later come to personify the water company, first went to work for the company in 1878, rising to superintendent by 1886. He loved his job but later complained that the owners of the water company were mostly businessmen with many investments. They were often too preoccupied to put the needs of the water company first and also balked at large expenditures to upgrade the system.

In 1891, after numerous complaints of irregular water service and even shortages, the city offered to buy the waterworks for $1.8 million. The company said the works were worth $2.5 million. No deal was struck. The anti–water company rhetoric grew louder each year, as more and more people clamored for municipal ownership of the city's water.

By the fall of 1898 the water company's lease had expired, and the issue of municipal ownership became a central theme in the mayoral election between the Democratic incumbent, Meredith Snyder, and his Republican challenger, Fred Eaton, who had worked for the water company for many years. Eaton had grown impatient with the company's emphasis on profits and ran a campaign calling for its conversion to community control. "On the water question I am a municipal ownership man," Eaton told a large crowd of supporters who gathered the Turner Hall Annex at an event organized by Republican supporters. "I am with the city and for the city and will keep this position until the end," Eaton said amid loud cheers and the playing of "The Star-Spangled Banner" by an orchestra of African Americans.

Water company officials worked hard to prevent Eaton's election, meddling as they had done in many previous elections. "I want no Stone left unturned to accomplish the Desired result—we must make no mistakes in Braking [sic] the Slate of our Enemies if Possible," Perry, the water company president, wrote to Isaias the month before the election. "And as you are the largest stockholder with so much at stake—I hope you can come down about Thursday to overlook our work and assist and advise us and remain until after election if possible. You command much that we cannot reach without you and success is of such vital importance to us all."[4]

Eaton handily won the December 6 election, effectively sending out notice that the days of the private water monopoly were coming to an end. Isaias and the other stockholders shifted their attention from renewing the water company's lease to getting a fair price for their system. The water company now supplied more than 14 million gallons of drinking water each day to the city.

The question of the worth of the waterworks was sent to a hearing before a board of three arbiters. For six weeks, engineer William Mulholland testified by memory about the location and layout of the company's pipes. It was an amazing demonstration of his mental acuity and an expression of his deep interest in and sense of obligation to the water company—a commitment he would keep, in various forms, for the rest of his life. Former senator Stephen White, not yet ruined by the ravages of alcohol, argued before the panel on behalf of the water company and insisted that the waterworks were worth more than $2 million. City Attorney William Dunn argued otherwise. The hearings, which explored pipe location, water volume, and cost in numbing detail, stretched on for months, finally collapsing in the spring of 1899 when the arbiters could not agree on the value for the company's waterworks.

The city and the water company were more primed than ever to battle over control.

I n early spring 1899, Isaias was confronted with another important issue: leadership of the University of California. The university's president wanted to retire, and the board of regents needed to find a president to bring the institution into the twentieth century.

Just a year earlier, on January 24, 1898, the university had celebrated its thirtieth anniversary with a grand parade down Market Street. In San Fran-. cisco, carriages picked up Isaias and other regents from the Palace Hotel. They sat in the open air in their top hats and dark coats waving to the crowds.

But the university was suffering from uncertain finances and a lack of leadership. For much of its history, the presidents of the university had been weak managers, content to leave even day-to-day decisions to the regents. In the university's early years, the regents voted on whom to hire and fire. This meant that regents meetings were often taken up with minutiae, arguably not the best use of time for some of the state's busiest businessmen. "I hope . . . a strong native active energetic man will take the place of the present incumbent," Isaias wrote to fellow regent Andrew Hallidie. "I do not know why so much detail work of small importance is continually brought up before the board, while such matters in other corporations are invariably decided by the head of the institution." Isaias went on to suggest that the university pay its next president $10,000 a year—a salary high enough to secure a top candidate.[5]

Isaias had his eye on Benjamin Ide Wheeler, a Cornell University professor of Greek and comparative philology who had come to interview for the job. Isaias had been impressed with Wheeler when they dined together at a banquet in the candidate's honor at the University Club on Sutter Street in San Francisco. But there was a faction from the legislature opposing Wheeler; they wanted someone from California, not the East Coast, to take over the university. Isaias thought this was a ridiculous distinction and an unnecessary qualification for a university president. But as his use of the word native suggests, Isaias thought the university should hire someone born in the United States rather than from abroad.

The regents voted in April to offer Wheeler the position as university president. His appointment was the beginning of a long renaissance for the university.

In April 1899 a thirty-seven-year-old man with a brown mustache and a high collar stepped off a train in San Francisco. He had not set foot on the West Coast for more than six years and was vitally interested in seeing how it had changed. It was clear that the city's skyline had grown upward. Claus Spreckels's new twelve-story building dominated Market Street and was widely regarded as the tallest building west of the Mississippi.

But the man was more interested in changes that couldn't be seen on the skyline. He was James Speyer, the American-born son of a German Jewish banking family, and he had come to San Francisco to help reorganize the Southern Pacific Railroad. The four men who built the western half of the transcontinental railway in the 1860s no longer controlled their creation. Mark Hopkins had died in 1878, Charles Crocker had died in 1888, and Leland Stanford had died in June 1893, leaving his shares to his wife, Jane. Their heirs no longer had the spirit to battle with Collis Huntington, the remaining founder. Speyer and Huntington were negotiating to buy out the other parties for more than $28 million.

Meanwhile, the railroad was planning to reorganize itself, folding the original parent company, the Central Union Pacific, into what had started as a subsidiary, the Southern Pacific. To finance the change, Speyer intended to issue $125 million in bonds.

Huntington had placed Isaias on the board of the Southern Pacific Company of California in the spring of 1899. Isaias had become a valued market maker for Southern Pacific bonds, buying and selling from $10 million to $15 million in bonds in recent years.

Huntington, who spent most of his time in New York, arrived in San Francisco in mid-April. He was in high demand, even after living on and off in California for more than fifty years. On April 22, 1899, D. O. Mills held a dinner for Huntington at the Pacific Union Club in San Francisco. It was a small affair with just fifty of the city's leading businessmen, including Isaias. But Huntington spoke frankly at that banquet, telling the group that he believed "in snatching everything in sight."[6] His words made their way into the newspaper, where they shocked people for their brazen ambition.

Just six days later, the Southern Pacific hosted its own banquet at the Palace Hotel on Market Street. More than 150 men dressed in tuxedos dined on oyster cocktails, frogs Colbert style, saddle of spring lamb, and champagne punch surprise as they listened to Huntington extol the new reorganization plan and the role of the railroad.

The banquet provided a revealing glimpse of the relationship between the railroad and the merchant and professional class in the city. The editorial columns of the newspapers consistently vilified Huntington for his control over the state's political machinery and zeal for profit above everything else. The *Call* referred to his "dictatorship" and opined that Huntington "has strenuously obstructed public justice and aimed to dominate the legislative and executive branches of the State and Federal governments."[7] Yet the bulk of San Francisco's elite came to the Palace Hotel to, in effect, pay homage to Collis Huntington. While many of these men may have abhorred the political and economic tactics of the railroad, they clearly felt they had to maintain cordial relations for the good of the economy. They probably also thought much of the newspaper blather was hyperbole.

Huntington, with his bushy white beard and mustache, was a dignified figure at the head of a huge U-shaped table that was covered with a white tablecloth, adorned with vases of roses, and set with crystal. He sat next to George Crocker, the son of the late Charles Crocker, and near Thomas Hubbard, a Southern Pacific executive who was the evening's other honoree. Speyer sat near three religious men at the head table: Rabbi Jacob Voorsanger of Temple Emanu-el, Dr. Reverend Horatio Stebbins, a former regent of the University of California, and Dr. Reverend MacKenzie. At the tip of the U sat William Herrin, the legendary Southern Pacific attorney who oversaw the railroad's legal and political divisions. Isaias was there too, as was Marco.

In 1899, America had recovered from the panic of six years earlier and was enjoying the largest business expansion in its history. Factories had replaced homes; shops and machinery had replaced farmhands. The country produced more food with fewer people, and more goods and services, than ever before. The old rural way of life, an America of small farms and tiny hamlets, was fading, to be replaced by an urban industrial world of middle-size cities linked by railroads, telephone, and telegraph wires.

The railroads were still the dominant force behind the economy. Their stocks and bonds were traded heavily by Wall Street, and their competitive battles and mergers funneled the nation's capital.

Just a few days before the banquet at the Palace Hotel, Isaias and Esther's oldest daughter, Clara, twenty-one, had gotten married. Her groom was Emanuel Heller, a San Francisco native, a veteran of the recent Spanish-American War, and a promising attorney.

Heller had opened his law practice in San Francisco in 1890, around the time Isaias took over the presidency of the Nevada Bank. He was friends with Marco—and served as his best man at his wedding in 1898—and before long began representing Isaias, the Nevada Bank, and the Union Trust Company. It was a relationship that would solidify Heller's standing in the legal community and serve as the start of one of the state's most successful and long-lasting law firms.

Clara came to the marriage a rich woman, as her father had purchased stocks in her name since her birth. She was worth at least $151,936, which included ten shares of Farmers and Merchants stock valued at $3,000 a share, two hundred shares of Nevada Bank stock valued at $1,800 a share, and eight shares of Union Trust Company stock valued at $1,600 a share, among other investments.

Two weeks after Clara's wedding and the banquets—it was such a busy month that Isaias's livery bill for the rental of thirteen brougham Victoria four-in-hands came to $91—Isaias and Esther departed for Europe. Isaias was exhausted and desperately needed to get away. His migraine headaches had been so bad that he had missed days of work. "I have had a great strain on my mental faculties the past two and a half years and I am advised by my physicians that it is imperatively necessary for me to have a vacation for three or four months and a complete rest," Isaias wrote to the board of directors of what was now the Nevada National Bank.[8] He didn't need to remind the directors just how successful he had made the bank. It had the largest amount of capital of any bank west of the Mississippi and a year earlier had become a national bank, which streamlined it with the way eastern banks conducted business. It also put the bank under government inspection, which helped increase confidence in the institution. The Nevada

National Bank board elevated Marco to second vice president to assist in his father's absence.

Isaias and Esther left from New York on the *Kaiser Wilhelm Der Grosse* ocean liner, one of the fastest and most luxurious ships on the Atlantic, on May 9. The ship had been launched just two years earlier and had handily beat both the eastbound and westbound transatlantic speed records, shocking the British, whose ships had long dominated the sea. Its baroque gilded interiors were designed by Johannes Poppe, the first time a ship had been designed by just one man.

The Hellmans were on their way to take a cure in St. Moritz. Isaias also used this opportunity to have his portrait painted by Toby Rosenthal, an accomplished Jewish artist with a studio in Berlin. Isaias sat for many happy hours among Rosenthal's paint, canvases, and brushes. Rosenthal painted a portrait that speaks banker in every stroke. Isaias is seated on an ornate carved wooden chair, holding a sheath of papers in his left hand, while his right hand rests on the arm of the chair. He is dressed in a black suit with lapels that appear to be satin. His face is supremely confident and composed, half covered by his full beard and mustache and oval glasses. At the time of the painting, Isaias was fifty-seven, but either his face showed no lines or Rosenthal painted out any wrinkles.

The Hellmans returned to New York in late August, and after spending time in New York, they rented their own railroad car and dining car for the trip to San Francisco, a luxury that cost them $471. They may have rushed across the country because on September 11 their first grandchild, Warren, was born to Marco and Frances. It was an auspicious birth, coming just before Yom Kippur, the holiest day of the Jewish year.

The first year of the new century saw Los Angeles boom, and never again would the growth of San Francisco or the northern part of the state outpace the south's. The city was gripped in an oil frenzy, spurred on by the discovery of a huge amount of oil in a nondescript field in 1893 by the two men Isaias had bankrolled, Edward Doheny and Charles Canfield.

The discovery led dozens of other men to hunt for oil. Soon there were more than 250 companies searching for the black gold, up from 4 just thirteen years earlier. Los Angeles was covered with oil derricks, their black latticed towers dotting backyards and empty fields, almost as numerous as the city's fabled peppertrees. The search for oil was so fervent that the city appointed an oil czar to check on the progress of the drilling. When it rained hard in Los Angeles, residents complained because oil overflow rushed into the pond at Westlake Park, turning it into a brown and viscous pit.

Isaias was not immune from the oil fever. He authorized William Mulholland to drill for oil on his Repetto Ranch, and Mulholland found a flammable gas that could be used for light and fuel. Gold and oil were discovered at Anaheim Landing near Long Beach, where Isaias had numerous holdings, launching a "mini rush," according to Isaias's real estate manager, P. A. Stanton. He invested in the Rodeo Oil Company, which wanted to drill on a parcel northwest of the new Evergreen Cemetery in East Los Angeles. He became the major stockholder in the North Whittier Oil Company, which was managed by his cousin Maurice Hellman and his partner in the Security Trust and Savings bank, J. F. Satori. Isaias owned land in Boyle Heights with William H. Workman, who wrote in August that he had started to drill on one of their vacant lots.

The Farmers and Merchants Bank also lent funds to build up the region's oil infrastructure. Doheny and Canfield's Producers Oil Company of Los Angeles borrowed $10,000 to build steel oil tanks, and Puente Oil used $40,000 in loans to construct an oil refinery. California was producing 2,677,000 barrels of good-quality oil each year at that point. "As to the refinery, some tests show as good oil as ever was made here or the state of Pennsylvania," wrote William Lacy, the president of Puente Oil. "I have seen the wick of a lamp in which oil has burned twenty-one hours, which hardly showed a shade of the usual black incrustations that lamp wicks take on."[9]

Herman was also investing heavily in various oil companies, and the Farmers and Merchants Bank became a hub of speculation. Herman had joined forces with his former grocery partner, Abe Haas; William Perry, the water company president; William Kerckhoff, the president of the San Gabriel Electric Company; and others to take over the Reid Oil Company of Bakersfield, where a humongous cache of oil had been discovered a year earlier. "The tone of the Farmers and Merchants Bank has changed completely and instead of being the essence of conservatism it is the rallying place for all the wildcat oil speculators in the country," Marco wrote his father in October. "It simply makes me sick. All I hear is oil, oil, oil, and your brother Herman is continually attending oil meetings."[10] In another letter Marco said, "In plain English, [Herman] thinks himself *the* great mogul and that all he does is right and is so much wrapped up in his oil speculations that his mind will hold nothing else."[11]

Herman was not the only executive at the bank caught in speculation fever. Isaias's cousin Henry Fleishman, who had been appointed the bank's cashier in 1895, was one of the main backers of the Velodrome Cycle and Skating Company, which had constructed a huge indoor cycling rink in the city. The company regularly hosted races, and Isaias grew perturbed that Fleishman's name was linked to such an improper business. Isaias didn't know it, but Fleishman was dabbling in even more speculative stocks, and those investments would soon have a direct—and disastrous—impact on the Farmers and Merchants Bank.

I n 1901 Isaias seized an opportunity to dominate another California industry. He and two other San Francisco bankers, Daniel Meyer and Antoine Borel, purchased controlling interest in the California Wine Association for $1 million. "Banker Hellman and his financial associates have obtained control of the California Wine Association and with it the control of the viticultural industry of California," read an article in the *San Francisco Examiner* of March 3, 1901.

The purchase furthered Isaias's long-standing interest in the wine industry, which had begun in 1871 when he acquired part of Rancho Cucamonga and hired Jean Louis Sansevain, the famed French winemaker, to make port and Angelica for him. Over the years, his vineyards produced thousands of gallons of wines, which he often sent to his St. Louis cousins, the liquor merchants Abe and Louis Hellman, to sell. He had also made other wine-related investments.

The California Wine Association had been started less than seven years earlier, in 1894, by a British accountant named Percy Morgan, but had come in that short time to control the sale of most of the state's wine. Morgan, who came west in 1881, took advantage of spiraling wine prices and overproduction to consolidate the industry.

Wine growing had started in southern California with the Spanish missionaries, who produced a sweet sacramental wine from Mission grapes they brought from Europe. Early Los Angeles settlers pioneered the planting of European varietals, and by 1874 wine production had grown to 1.3 million gallons. By 1880, California was the nation's leading wine-producing state, fermenting 10 million gallons annually. Six years later, California produced 18 million gallons.

The wines, however, suffered an image problem. East Coast merchants complained that it was wildly uneven—sometimes excellent and sometimes undrinkable—and they accused California winemakers of adulterating the product. Though winemakers sometimes did put in additives—cherry juice, in particular, seemed to give a delightful punch to the sweet wine Angelica— transportation difficulties accounted for most of the problems. Winemakers shipped wine in large wooden caskets that loaded easily onto ships and later onto rail. The sellers at the other end put the liquid into bottles or flagons. The wine often spoiled as it was transported through hot climates on its way east.

By 1894 more than two hundred thousand acres were planted in grapes, and California was producing more wine than its customers could drink. The large San Francisco export firm of Lachman & Jacobi reported that its California wine fetched only 10¢ a gallon in New Orleans—less than the cost of producing and shipping it. That news made some of the state's grape growers wonder if they should pull out their vines and replace them with more lucrative crops, like oranges or lemons.

Morgan, an accountant whose clients included the wine dealer S. Lachman & Company, took advantage of the glut. He decided to form a "community of interests"—a palatable euphemism for monopoly—modeled after the ones started by the financier J. P. Morgan. He proposed that the state's leading wine merchants join forces and stabilize the wine business through sheer size. In August of that year, seven wineries merged legally and financially, although each retained its brand name. They called the new company the California Wine Association (CWA). There were results within a year. In its 1895 report, the wine association told its stockholders that it had raised the selling price of wine to 12.5¢ a gallon.[12]

The CWA aimed to put out a uniform product, something that East Coast customers could depend on. It bought grapes from various wineries and blended them, making wine that wasn't excellent, but wasn't awful either. In a major step, the CWA bottled the wine before shipment, which greatly controlled the quality. California's wine reputation started to improve.

Not all winemakers were pleased, however, with the monopolistic practices of the CWA. A small group of growers decided to form their own group, which they thought could negotiate more successfully with the CWA. They called it the California Wine Makers' Corporation. Isaias had a connection with the second group: he was an investor in the Lac-Jac Vineyard near Fresno, put together by Lachman & Jacobi, the firm owned by Frederick Jacobi, his son's father-in-law.

In the first year the CWA bought 4 million gallons of wine from the competing corporation and promised to buy 5 million gallons a year over the next five years. But the accord was not to last. The next year the CWA refused to buy the full 5 million gallons it had subscribed to, and the year after that it completely abrogated the agreement. The corporation sued, and the CWA, led by Morgan, reverted to ruthless tactics, in a series of steps that became known as the wine war.

In May 1897 the CWA reduced the price of the wine it shipped to New Orleans, undercutting the prices of virtually every other wine exporter. It did the same for wines sent to New York. The price gouging drove the competing corporation out of business within two years, leaving the CWA to consolidate its hold on the state wine market. By 1900, all the houses that had tried to resist the CWA had capitulated. Lachman & Jacobi, C. Shilling & Company, and the Italian-Swiss Agricultural Colony joined the CWA.

It was after this consolidation that Isaias stepped in with the $1 million purchase of stock. While he never assumed day-to-day oversight, his financial acumen buttressed the organization. He oversaw the sale of two bond issues, one for $2 million in 1905 and one for $3 million in 1913, money that helped the CWA maintain its grip on the California wine industry. By 1901, the CWA produced two-thirds of the wine made in the state.[13]

Isaias also made sure that his various businesses profited from one another. In 1903 the CWA built a large winery on Hellman's property in Cucamonga. The organization borrowed $100,000 from Isaias's Farmers and Merchants Bank to complete construction. Isaias wrote to the bank's managers, telling them that he approved the loan.[14]

Isaias's close associates soon controlled the board of directors. Over the years his son, Marco, Antoine Borel, Henry Huntington, Daniel Meyer, Mortimer Fleishhacker, and Frederick Jacobi would all sit on the board. Percy Morgan retired in 1911 and went on to build a sumptuous house in Los Altos

Hills near San Jose and to sit on the board of trustees of Stanford University. He also became a director of the Wells Fargo Nevada National Bank and the Union Trust Company. Despite his success, he committed suicide on April 16, 1920.

By 1902 the California Wine Association controlled the output of more than fifty wineries, including Cucamonga, Stag's Leap, and Greystone Cellars. The organization produced 30 million of the 44 million gallons made each year. It was soon the biggest wine concern in the world. Its seal, a young Bacchus standing next to a California bear on top of a ship bearing the California seal, was soon known the world over. That's not to say its wines were universally admired, for the CWA still blended most products to a uniform blandness. The CWA continued to dominate the state's wine industry, controlling 80 percent of the output, until Prohibition in 1920.

In August 1900, Collis Huntington was vacationing at his home near Raquette Lake in the Adirondacks. The seventy-nine-year-old man had spent the day traipsing through the woods, seemingly hale and hearty. But while getting ready for bed he dropped to the floor and efforts by his valet to revive him were not effective. He succumbed to a heart attack.

The death of "Uncle Collis" signaled the passing of the frontier era, and newspapers across the country bannered his demise on their front pages. It also created a power vacuum in the Southern Pacific, and men of means scrambled to fill it.

Henry Huntington, Collis's nephew, was his heir apparent as the closest relative immersed in the railroad business. Henry Huntington had spent more than a decade at his uncle's side, acting in his stead and making decisions to further his uncle's interests. But now that the elder Huntington was gone, James Speyer intended to use Speyer & Company's majority interest in the Southern Pacific to put its own man in charge. The capitalists didn't want profits from the rail line reinvested in the company, as Henry advocated. They preferred the profits be spun into dividends, which would increase the value of the stock. The Speyer interests engineered the election of Charles M. Hays, the general manager of the Grand Trunk Railway of Canada, to the presidency.

Huntington's death was a blow to Isaias. Collis Huntington "was a warm, generous and good friend of mine," Isaias wrote to the officers of the Farmers and Merchants Bank on August 15, 1900. "I much deplore his loss." Isaias also feared losing Huntington's business. The Southern Pacific was one of the Nevada Bank's largest clients, keeping millions on deposit at the bank on Montgomery and Pine streets in San Francisco. Isaias also earned lucrative commissions from the sale of its numerous bonds, and he grew concerned that Speyer & Company would not look as favorably on him as Huntington had.

Isaias sent a letter to James Speyer detailing his critical role in converting California businessmen into Southern Pacific supporters rather than detractors. "As most of the Southern Pacific Company bonds were formerly placed in New York and the stock of the Southern Pacific Company was then owned by the four principal owners, considerable antagonistic feeling existed in the community against the corporation, but since our people have become somewhat interested, through the purchase of the mentioned securities, a much better feeling exists here and the Company has made a great many friends among our best people. I have also given the proper support to these securities at our stock exchange and hardly any are on the market now, except at considerable advance."[15] Isaias even asked John Mackay, one of the former owners of the Nevada Bank, to put in a good word. Isaias needn't have worried. Speyer recognized friendship. In January 1901 he made the Nevada Bank the West Coast broker for the railroad's latest $10 million bond sale.[16]

Collis Huntington's death also had the consequence of turning his nephew's attention south, a move that would forever change the landscape of Los Angeles. Denied the presidency of the Southern Pacific, Henry Huntington and Arabella Duval Huntington, Collis's widow—who would marry Henry in a few years—decided to sell their stock in the company. They found a buyer in Edward H. Harriman, one of the country's savviest railroad men and the owner of the Union Pacific, who bought the block of stock in February 1901. In November of that year, Henry Huntington and Isaias sold the Market Street Cable Railway to a group of businessmen from Baltimore. Isaias earned a large commission on the sale.

In the three years since Henry Huntington, Isaias, and his syndicate had purchased the LARY, the rail company had undergone a radical transformation. Using part of the $5 million bond deal floated by Isaias, Huntington had refurbished and buffed the various different lines, aligning them whenever possible to form an integrated system. Ridership in the company's trademark yellow cars was up and customer satisfaction was high.

The region was growing rapidly as well. Isaias and Esther spent part of April and May in Los Angeles so Isaias could organize a new real estate division for the Farmers and Merchants Bank. He soon recognized that the city's growth pattern was changing. Isaias was preparing to construct a brick building for Chinese merchants along the Plaza, once the center of town, but he could see that the heart of the business district was moving in a southwesterly direction. His own bank on Main and Commercial streets had been centrally located when it opened in 1883, but now stood on the edge of the commercial district. And while Los Angeles was still the biggest city in the region, it had competition. Pasadena was growing in population and popularity, as was Santa Monica and other cities just a short distance from the city's downtown.

Isaias realized that to remain competitive, his trolley network needed to plan for an expanded system that would travel outside of the city's boundaries. He envisioned a system that could carry workers from outlying suburbs into downtown Los Angeles on weekdays and carry pleasure seekers on the weekend to local leisure spots like Santa Monica or Long Beach. He urged Huntington to think bigger—and act quickly before rising prices made the rights-of-way too expensive.

Most historical accounts of Henry Huntington's time in southern California give him almost full credit for the creation of the rail systems that so radically influenced the development of the Los Angeles basin. But Isaias's letters on the subject show that he, too, played a critically important role in the creation of the rail lines. "I have spent a month in Los Angeles and found that city very much improved," Isaias wrote Huntington in May 1901. "I think the time is on hand when we should commence building suburban roads out of the city. If we do not do so soon, others will. There is a great deal of idle capital and men with energy and brains waiting for good business openings in Los Angeles."[17] Isaias had even gone as far as asking W. H. Holabird, a LARY employee, to look at a map and sketch out possible rail routes to Long Beach, San Pedro, Redondo, and elsewhere.[18]

"As for building suburban roads out of Los Angeles, I agree with you that the time has come when we should begin doing it," Huntington responded a week later.

In November 1901, Huntington and the Hellman syndicate incorporated the Pacific Electric Railway, an interurban railroad that would soon become famous for its bright red trolley cars and the lines that crisscrossed the entire region. Huntington held the largest number of shares. He held 22 percent, or 986 shares, while Isaias, Borel, de Guigne, and the Parrott family took 678 shares each. Other investors included two former land partners of Isaias's, John Bicknell, now Huntington's attorney, and Jonathan Slauson, the developer of the town of Azusa.[19]

To finance the system, the shareholders of the Pacific Electric authorized the sale of $10 million in bonds. Isaias's Nevada Bank handled the deal.

Huntington immediately embarked on a building campaign, one more extensive and expensive than the one he had initiated for the LARY. Using the Los Angeles and Pasadena Electric Railway as a core, the company built extensions to Pasadena and Long Beach in 1902, lines to Monrovia and Whittier in 1903, and lines to Glendale, Newport, and San Pedro by 1904. By 1906, the Pacific Electric had almost 449 miles of track.

Huntington developed a method of quickly laying down tracks. One newspaper described an orange orchard in Monrovia that was untouched in the morning but by 3 P.M. had been transformed into a Pacific Electric spur. Huntington sent three hundred men to the orchard at noon, where they quickly cut down two rows of orange trees. Plows leveled the ground, and then the army of men laid down railroad ties and covered them with bands of steel. By midafternoon the crew had set up poles to string trolley wire.[20]

The Pacific Electric had a galvanizing effect on Los Angeles, uniting disparate points of the region and expanding population farther from downtown. Where the Pacific Electric went, crowds followed, and soon cities were clamoring for Huntington to connect them to the bright red cars. One of the first PE lines to open up was to Long Beach on July 4, 1902. It was a boon to Isaias, who held large tracts of land nearby with the Bixby family, the remnants of the vast Rancho Los Alamitos they had purchased in 1881. More than thirty thousand people turned out to celebrate the opening of the PE line.

"Huntington is in a hurry," reported the *Los Angeles Times* on April 8, 1902. "Property along the line of the road has advanced enormously in value. Land that could be bought a few years ago for a very small figure is now bringing $500 an acre. Several men have made fortunes out of it."

The towns linked to the Pacific Electric would soon see enormous growth. Long Beach's population went from about 2,500 in 1900 to 17,800 in 1910. Pasadena grew from 9,000 people to 30,000 in the same period. Monrovia went from a town of 1,205 in 1900 to 3,500. Los Angeles's population took the biggest leap of all, tripling from 102,500 residents in 1900 to about 319,000 residents in 1910.[21]

It turned out that Huntington was in too much of a hurry—for his partners. For a conservative banker like Isaias, all that building and all that spending, with nothing coming back to shareholders in the form of dividends, was not the right business model. He looked for a regular return on his money, while Huntington, the consummate railroad man, looked continually to expand. It wouldn't be long before Huntington's and Hellman's attitudes toward business proved incompatible.

BETRAYAL

1901–1903

In 1901, Esther and Isaias finally started on the project they had been planning and talking about for the past four years: building a summer home on the shores of Lake Tahoe. Since 1897, Isaias had quietly been accumulating land around Sugar Pine Point, a promontory on the western shore of the lake. He knew that land prices would go up once prospective sellers heard that the president of the Nevada National Bank was buying, so he hired a local resident, Joe Savage, to act as his representative. The subterfuge was effective, and by the end of Isaias's buying spree he had amassed more than two thousand acres and almost two miles of lakefront. Land at Lake Tahoe was not particularly valued at that time, and Isaias got good deals from the Central Pacific Railroad, Wells Fargo Bank, the owner of the *San Francisco Chronicle*, and a number of small landowners.

Sugar Pine Point had been only sparsely settled. The Washoe Indians summered there and continued to visit the point throughout Hellman's lifetime. In the 1860s, the trapper General William Phipps, an idiosyncratic veteran of the Indian wars, built a cabin out of the sugar pines on a 160-acre claim around the outlet of a creek on the point. He made his living by trapping the trout that bred at the mouth of the creek, until 1883 when the California Fish Commission cited him for illegally catching spawning fish.

Another pioneer, Captain W. W. "Billy" Lapham, bought a portion of land that jutted into the lake. He built a family hotel, which he named the Bellevue, or beautiful view, and ran it as a popular destination resort until it burned down in 1893.

Isaias had a vision of a summer home that would be comfortable but not ostentatious. He found an architect uniquely suited to designing a mountain home with a splash of East Coast luxury. Walter Danforth Bliss was a local boy, the son of D. L. Bliss, the region's largest lumber merchant. At one point, the Bliss family owned or controlled one-fifth of the land in the Lake Tahoe region. Their lumber mill in Glenbrook at the southern end of the lake churned out wood at a rapid rate.

The younger Bliss had worked in New York with the renowned architectural firm of McKim, Mead, and White. He returned to California with a partner, William B. Faville, and the two won the commission to design the St. Francis Hotel on Union Square. They also drew up plans for Lake Tahoe's newest luxury resort, Tahoe Tavern, near Tahoe City, a three-story shingled hotel with covered porches, gables, and rustic elements throughout. The Bliss family had constructed a narrow-gauge railway from Truckee to Tahoe City in 1901, greatly easing the trip to the lake. So as soon as the Tahoe Tavern opened in 1901, it became *the* place to vacation on the lake.

The Tahoe Tavern served as an inspiration for Isaias's home, for they both drew heavily on the shingle style so popular on the eastern seaboard in the 1880s. Unlike Isaias's fussy and ornate Victorian home in San Francisco, the Tahoe house was simple and designed to blend in with the woods. Its exterior was a mix of locally quarried granite and brown shingles, made interesting by an irregular roofline, squat half towers, leaded windows, and deep eaves.

In early August 1901, Isaias and Esther moved up to the Tallac House to be closer to construction. They stayed there ten days but soon decided the hotel was too far from their home site. Isaias had by then purchased a boat, which the Hellmans used daily, but they were still a considerable distance from Sugar Pine Point. In late August they moved to McKinney's, a rustic cluster of wooded shacks on Lake Tahoe's western shore. It did not offer the amenities of Tallac House—gourmet meals, card playing at night, genteel company—but had the advantage of being just a few miles from the new house.

While at Tahoe, Isaias got a visit from William Mulholland, the superintendent of the Los Angeles Water Company. He was in Tahoe to design water and electric systems for the new house, but he also came bearing a revised offer from Los Angeles city officials. Three years after the water company's lease had expired, the two sides had not yet come to an agreement on the sale price of the waterworks.

The new offer was much higher than the city had previously suggested, but one still considerably less than the privately held water company wanted.

The city now was willing to pay $2 million for the waterworks and rights to the headwaters of the Los Angeles River. Mulholland, who was acting as an intermediary even though he was employed by the private water company, urged Isaias to approve the offer. Mulholland no longer believed that businessmen with a multitude of interests were the best stewards of a growing city's water, and he tried to convey the roots of his dissatisfaction with the company to Isaias.[1] Since Isaias was the biggest shareholder and an adviser to many of the other owners, his opinion was crucial.

One can only imagine Isaias and Mulholland talking about the water situation as they sat by the clear blue waters of Lake Tahoe, the largest lake in the West. Isaias at that point was keenly aware that the public favored municipal ownership. He knew that the standoff would have to end sometime, so he finally agreed to sell his shares for the offered price. Los Angeles city officials didn't want to give him a chance to change his mind, so they set an election for August 28. While some people objected that the price of the waterworks was too high, residents voted for the bonds, thereby finally ending a bitter and divisive struggle.

The city of Los Angeles now controlled its own water supply.

On November 20, 1901, Herman was tallying the cash in the vault at the Farmers and Merchants Bank. It was a job usually done by the cashier, Henry Fleishman, but Herman had recently returned from a lengthy trip to Europe with his wife, Ida, and was reacquainting himself with the bank's business. Herman's health had deteriorated in recent months as diabetes gripped his system. One of his feet had started to hurt so much that the doctor had insisted on an operation. Herman had tried the healing spa waters in Carlsbad and had returned to Los Angeles feeling much better.

That mood soon changed. As Herman counted the day's gold receipts, he noticed something was amiss. There was a discrepancy between the amount tabulated in the ledger and the amount in the safe. And the difference was not small: it was $5,000.

Herman immediately sent a wire to Isaias in San Francisco. It wasn't long before he got a reply: "In reply to yours of yesterday, I think the mentioned shortage will be found," wrote Isaias. "It cannot be otherwise. In the meantime do nothing and say *nothing*."[2]

As a precaution, though, Isaias immediately ordered a change in the bank's accounting system. Previously, the cashier collected the day's cash, stuck it in the vault, and took it out to count the next morning. Isaias instructed Herman to convert to standard banking practices, which required cash to be counted by two bank officers at all times, as well as some other checks and balances.

Still, Isaias assumed the discrepancy was an accounting error. "You have not yet written me whether the shortage has been found, if not, what steps are being taken to discover the error," Isaias wrote Herman two weeks after the shortage was first discovered.

The board of directors of the bank met the next day, December 5. Isaias was not in Los Angeles for the meeting, but he sent Marco bearing a letter that asked the board to authorize the purchase of a new burglarproof safe to be installed in the vault. He also told the board that the officers of the bank planned to count the funds thoroughly and to figure out the source of the discrepancy on Saturday, December 7, after the bank closed.

The forty-three-year-old man hurried through the Los Angeles train station, pushing his black derby hat down low as if to conceal his face. He gripped his tan valise tightly as he made his way onto the platform. It was shortly after eight o'clock on a Saturday morning, and the depot in the heart of the city's downtown was crowded with dark-suited businessmen on their way to work. Two trains were waiting to depart: the 8:20 A.M. for Pasadena and the 8:30 Sunset Limited, which was headed south toward San Diego, Texas, and New Orleans.

The train agent master would later comment that Henry Fleishman's face seemed strained and that he was haggard, not his normally dapper self. It was almost as if the man had spent a whole night drinking.

"Good morning, Mr. Fleishman," the train agent said to the man he had known for more than twenty years. "Where are you off to today?"

"To Pasadena to spend the day," Fleishman replied.

"That's a great place to have a good time," said the depot man.

"Yes, I can get plenty of it there," said Fleishman, his sweaty palms gripping the valise more tightly. With a slight nod as a sign of farewell, he hurried farther down the platform.

A few minutes later, Fleishman climbed onto a train, but not the local heading to Pasadena. Instead, he boarded the Sunset Limited, which was headed south. Somewhere on that route, a man intent on becoming invisible could find a connecting train to Mexico, and freedom.

I saias was at his desk at the Nevada Bank in San Francisco when he got the call from Herman around noon on Saturday. At first the news was sketchy: Fleishman hadn't shown up for work, and a quick check of the vault showed that more money was missing.

Isaias ignored the "I told you so" tone in his brother's voice. For years now Herman had been telling Isaias that Fleishman was no good. He was too flamboyant, too undisciplined, and too cavalier.

Isaias had ignored Herman's warnings, dismissing them as more of his brother's constant complaining. Over the past eleven years, ever since Isaias had moved to San Francisco and left Herman in charge of the Farmers and Merchants Bank, the two brothers had constantly found fault with each other. They fired letters back and forth accusing each other of bad faith, of laziness, of stupidity. Herman had threatened to resign the vice presidency of the bank so many times that Isaias couldn't keep count. The two men were locked in a bitter battle, one from which they couldn't seem to extricate themselves.

Now it looked as if Herman had been right. There had been clues that Fleishman was not forthright, but Isaias had ignored them. He was fond of Fleishman, the son of Isaias's maternal uncle, because he was handsome, athletic, and charismatic. Though Isaias was frustrated by the man's refusal to live frugally, he had been charmed by his vitality.

After Herman's call, Isaias immediately wired Charles Elton, the chief of police in Los Angeles. "I hereby authorize you to offer a reward of twenty-five hundred ($2500) dollars for the capture and return to Los Angeles of HJ Fleishman or $5000 for his capture and return to Los Angeles with the money embezzled."[3] He then contacted the Pinkerton Detective Agency and asked it to assist in tracking down the errant cashier.

The police sent bulletins out to train stations across the country with a description of the culprit: five feet nine inches tall, weight 160 pounds, a dark brown mustache, brown hair thinning on top, good teeth, prominent ears, and a straight nose. The suspect often wore a button of the Mystic Shriners on his lapel, the police noted.

By Monday, December 9, 1901, the bank revealed that Fleishman had stolen between $100,000 and $150,000, but stated that the bank could easily absorb the loss. Fleishman had been bonded for $30,000 by the American Surety Company of New York, the world's largest surety company, whose twenty-three-story headquarters on Broadway was one of the nation's first skyscrapers. The bank would receive that money and could liquidate many of Fleishman's other assets, which totaled around $50,000. Isaias pledged personally to make up the difference.

The theft made headlines around the state. "Los Angeles Bank Cashier Steals a Hundred Thousand," reported the *San Francisco Chronicle*, which said nothing so exciting had happened in banking circles since robbers dug a tunnel under the First National Bank four years earlier.

But Isaias had not been truthful. Fleishman, it turned out, had been stealing money for months, and the amount totaled around $300,000 (about $6 million in 2006 dollars), making it one of the largest—if not the largest—embezzlements in California history. Isaias knew that if the true amount came out, it would forever sully the reputation of the bank and might even prompt a bank run.

"There never was such a case known or known of in the banking business," Herman Hellman wrote to Fleishman's brother Marco in New York. "He speculated with the Funds of our Bank & carried away with him at least 125,000 dollars in large currency & gold bills and gold certificates. The total amount of his defalcation is fully 3 times as much as the paper stated, had we not the showing all over the U.S. it certainly would have busted our institution."[4]

The newspapers speculated daily on Fleishman's whereabouts: he was in Mexico; he had headed north; he had committed suicide. The Pinkerton detectives had staked out two of Fleishman's known haunts in New York, but did not catch sight of him. One man claimed to have talked to Fleishman in El Paso, Texas. Judge Ygnaciao Sepulveda, a longtime Los Angeles judge who had moved to Mexico City, wired Harrison Gray Otis of the *Los Angeles Times* and urged that Isaias arrange for the State Department to issue a warrant for Fleishman's arrest. Shortly thereafter, a man named Herman Fleishman was picked up in Mexico, but he proved not to be the embezzler. Fleishman continued to elude police capture.

While Isaias was angry about the missing money and the harm to the bank's reputation, he was more upset by Fleishman's betrayal. Isaias had loved Fleishman, had regarded him as family. The cashier often traveled to San Francisco to have Thanksgiving dinner with Isaias, his wife, and their children. Now the man had stained the family name.

"This is the greatest disappointment of my life," Isaias told reporters. "I took Henry into my home; my wife was a mother to him and I treated him as if he were my own son. I gave him a position in the bank at a good salary, advancing him from time to time as he was exceptionally bright, and I always trusted him implicitly. He remained a member of my household for seven years. That he should have betrayed my confidence is something that I cannot understand."

For many years, Fleishman had lived a charmed life. He had been born in Los Angeles to Israel Fleishman, who was the brother of Isaias's mother, Sara. His father had run a successful hardware store called Fleishman & Sichel and in the late 1860s had moved his family to New York to open a branch on Water Street. Israel Fleishman met with financial reversals and in 1877 had sent his seventeen-year-old son to live with Isaias in Los Angeles.

Fleishman lived with the Hellmans in their mansion on Fourth and Main streets for seven years. He was like an older brother to their three children. Isaias regarded Henry as a son and put him to work in 1878 at the Farmers and Merchants Bank, where his salary and position improved each year. Fleishman had left the bank for four months during the boom of 1887 to try his hand at real estate, but had soon returned. In 1895, he had been appointed cashier, one of the most important positions at the bank.

Over time, Fleishman had developed a high profile in Los Angeles. He was a good athlete, a handsome man, and a snappy dresser, and he had been one of the founding members of the California Club. His 1889 marriage to Virginia Harrell, the beautiful daughter of a noted capitalist, Jasper Harrell of Visalia, was a social highlight, and the couple was showered with elaborate gifts. His mother and Isaias had not approved of the union, for Fleishman was Jewish and his bride was Christian, but they had eventually become reconciled to the idea. The two had a son, whom they named Harrell.

But Henry and Virginia soon began to quarrel. Their marriage broke apart after five years, and Virginia filed for divorce on the grounds of cruelty.

Henry saw his son less after that, but there was nothing he loved more than taking the boy out on Sundays. The two would often board a train for one of Los Angeles's pleasure spots: Santa Monica, Pasadena, Arroyo Seco. They would spend the day swimming or strolling on the pier, just enjoying each other's company.

Fleishman's divorce let him indulge in another passion: the company of a certain type of woman. He was often seen dining or dancing with women like Marie Cunningham, a "beauty doctor," whom the newspapers rushed to interview as soon as Fleishman's disappearance became known. "It is admitted that his choice of female associates was not always of the highest order," declared the Los Angeles Times.

Fleishman made a number of bad investments and his increasing debt must have worried him. While some of his investments were sound, like his stock in the Los Angeles Times and Canfield Oil, he had lost $20,000 by investing in a bicycle track that failed. Something called the Maxwell patent directory cost him another $25,000. In a bid to recoup his losses, Fleishman invested heavily in the famous Amalgamated copper mines.

Nobody noticed when Fleishman took a few thousand dollars from the Farmers and Merchants Bank. Since Fleishman was the bank's cashier, he was the one who carried the gold and silver into the bank's massive vault. He was the one who tallied the bank's receipts at the end of the day, and his work was only sporadically audited. Stealing soon became a habit, and before long Fleishman had invested thousands and thousands in the copper stocks.

As the stocks had gone down, not up, Fleishman increasingly felt cheated out of the riches he so earnestly desired. His resentment toward Isaias began to grow. "Did you, in all the investments you made, and the engagements and operations large and small, which you fostered and engineered the past years, ever invite me or give me the chance to invest my savings with you, or did you even, when in need of John Does to fill out your different Directorates, ever honor or consider me eligible or worth your attention?" Fleishman once wrote to Isaias. "Or did you always throw such baubles and emolument in the laps of strangers, who through fawning upon you and flattering you, won your delighted notice. Can you mention one opportunity you ever gave me whereby to better my fortune or line my pocket through your assistance or even advice. I foolishly continued, year after year, clinging to the Hellman skirts, hoping some few crumbs might someday be shaken in my direction."[5]

What particularly galled Fleishman was the feeling that his father had set Isaias up to succeed in America, and then had never been rewarded. It was Israel Fleishman who wrote Isaias's parents and convinced them to let their sons immigrate to the United States, according to his son. It was Israel Fleishman who sent the money for Isaias and Herman to come. And it was Israel Fleishman who introduced Isaias to his future wife, Esther Newgass, thereby securing an advantageous alliance with the Lehman family.

"Your brilliant future and accumulated fortune largely dates from the time my Father wrote you to come East and meet Miss Newgass of Liverpool, then sojourning in New York with her sister, Mrs. Lehman, the wife of E. [really Meyer] Lehman of Messrs. Lehman Brothers, then and now one of the prominent Cotton Commission and Banking houses of New York. How you came East and through mutual attraction and indirect family influence eventually married and what thorough domestic happiness has been your lot ever since and likewise with the loving and clever help and assistance of your dear wife, a devoted helpmate and mother with a heart too large for her body, how you have successfully climbed the finance and social ladder until today you stand preeminent on the Pacific Coast."[6]

Despite everything the Fleishmans had done, Isaias had refused in 1889 to lend $10,000 to the family so that the fiancé of a daughter, Rosetta, could start a new business. As Fleishman sank deeper and deeper into debt, he felt justified stealing from Isaias. On December 3, Fleishman shipped $25,000 to a New York bank. He did it again on December 5. And then on the night of December 9, as he was supposed to be reconciling the bank's books, Fleishman stuffed another $125,000 into a valise. He retired to his apartment at the California Club and tried to act as normal as possible. He ran into a friend in the evening and made a plan for dinner the next night. The next morning, a Saturday, Fleishman telephoned the bank to say he was sick and wouldn't be in for work. Then he hurried to the train station. The depot man was the last person in Los Angeles to talk to Henry Fleishman.

The atmosphere at the Farmers and Merchants Bank was poisoned after Fleishman's theft. The brothers seemed to blame each other. Herman thought Isaias should have realized Fleishman's true nature; Isaias thought Herman, as manager of the bank, should have kept a closer eye on Fleishman.

Outwardly, business returned to normal. The Farmers and Merchants Bank still opened its doors at 8 A.M. Monday through Saturday. Customers walking in still saw the bank's advertisement, "Oldest and Largest Bank in Southern California," painted on one of the bank's front windows. They deposited or withdrew their gold and silver from tellers who stood behind gilded bars. But inside the bank, tensions grew.

The two brothers had feuded all their lives, alternately loving and loathing each other. They were only eleven months apart and had competed for attention since childhood. One hint that they fought even as young men comes from a letter their sister Flora wrote Isaias in 1868, on the eve of her wedding. "My only wish is that you reconcile with Herman. I would step into holy matrimony with more pleasure if I knew you could grant me my greatest wish. Your sister, Flora Hellman."[7]

Almost thirty-five years later, the brothers still aggravated each other. It may have been that their personalities were too different. Isaias, as the firstborn who had been selected by his parents to attend secondary school, saw himself as smarter than Herman. He was sober and hardworking and was frequently convinced he was right. While both men were financially successful, Isaias had made a vast fortune compared to his brother's more modest one. Herman, an extrovert who enjoyed the company of others, must have wearied at his brother's stern countenance and dogged pursuit of business.

Isaias's criticism was unrelenting. Just days before the embezzlement, he had written another scathing letter to his brother, the last in a long line of indictments. "Had I met with the losses here, which the Farmers and Merchants Bank has made the past 2–3 years, *which are not excusable* and caused only by bad management, my directors would not have stood it. I have to my knowledge never belittled you, but if you expect that I will tell an untruth or keep from our directors losses which is my solemn duty to report, you will be making a mistake."[8]

Henry Fleishman's embezzlement became one more thing for the brothers to fight over. The situation would soon prove untenable.

In November 1902, Isaias had an unpleasant surprise: an extortion letter from Fleishman from an unidentified country threatening to go public with tales of Isaias's alleged illegal doings. Fleishman's escape had not gone according to plan. He had spent much of his money to get to Central America and had to pay off local officials to stay, he wrote Isaias. Now he was being tracked by Pinkerton detectives hired by the American Surety Company, which was determined to recover the $30,000 it had paid in bonds because of Fleishman's defalcation.

"Nearly a year has elapsed since [the embezzlement] and while temporarily safely located beyond the pale of the law, I have no intention of remaining isolated from the civilized World, but need and want a clear field in order to try and build up my shattered past, make some financial headway, and when possible, repay, gradually, all I may owe and thereby somewhat clear my family name from the disgrace and dishonor in which I have plunged it," Fleishman wrote to Isaias. "That I am a most miserable and unhappy man broken in health and spirit, with all I held dear to me separated from me, goes without saying, but of all this I would prefer not to write, as I am not entitled to anyone's sympathy and it is not of that I am now addressing you."[9]

Fleishman wanted Isaias to pay the insurance company the money it was owed. It would be a small gesture, Fleishman noted, in light of Isaias's fortune and all the Fleishman family had done for him. If Isaias didn't repay the note, Fleishman threatened to go to William Randolph Hearst, the publisher of the *San Francisco Examiner* and a string of other newspapers, to tell him how Isaias had lied and bribed his way to success. He accused Isaias in the letter of stashing away cash each spring so the Farmers and Merchants Bank could report a lower dollar amount of the bank's holdings to the local assessor, and of charging Los Angeles $50 a month to rent a safe stored in the bank's vaults and then kicking back $25 each month to the deputy county assessor for the right to hold the county's funds.

He also alluded to greater malfeasance: "One affair in particular, which being of record on your files, can be easily proven, which, if ever published by me to the World at large, would cause a scandal and sensation almost national, involving, as it does, people high up in the social and political firmament of the State, bringing down, besides other, the name of Hellman, as low as I, unfortunately, have brought my own family name, to my everlasting disgrace and sorrow."

Fleishman apparently was referring to an episode that took place in the president's office of the Farmers and Merchants Bank in early June 1900. According to Fleishman, Isaias helped bribe a federal judge to issue a ruling that would be favorable to local oil companies with which Isaias did business. Fleishman suggested that the deal involved many other prominent men, incuding Ninth District Court judge Erskine Ross, Charles Canfield, and Edward Doheny. Fleishman apparently told the story to a federal investigator, but nothing ever came of the accusation. Its veracity is difficult to assess.[10]

There is no record of whether Isaias responded to Fleishman. Six months later, an even more desperate Fleishman sent another letter in which he said the Pinkerton detectives were pursuing him closely and he expected to be captured at any moment. Once he was arrested, Fleishman promised, he would squeal. He begged Isaias to pay off the American Surety Company bond, and let him live free.

"I am not, Mr. Hellman, saying all this to you, in a spirit of spite or revenge, for I am sick at heart & have no desire to air myself or my knowledge of events and affairs of the Bank to the public gaze, for all the spirit and life I had in me has been crushed through the weight of suffering I've undergone the past eighteen months," Fleishman wrote to Isaias on June 3, 1903. "What I do want and ask of you is the settlement of the Surety Company's claim against me, at the best price you can purchase same or negotiate the settlement thereof, so that I can be left alone, untrammeled and free to go to some civilized country where I can try and earn an honest living and pull myself up again."[11]

Again, there was silence from Isaias.

While Isaias's personal life was in turmoil, his businesses were more profitable than ever. Los Angeles was expanding so fast that the deposits at the Farmers and Merchants Bank were growing more quickly than those up north. Henry Huntington had ordered that all the money for the Los Angeles Railway and the Pacific Electric be kept at the bank, and those deposits helped swell the level of assets.

Huntington had continued his rapid expansion projects and had branched into land development as well. As the system grew it needed a reliable source of power, and Huntington, Isaias, and the syndicate joined into a new partnership to guarantee a steady supply. The group had been working with William Kerckhoff's San Gabriel Electric Company, which operated three hydroelectric plants throughout the region. Kerckhoff now proposed to fold that company into a larger one that got power from the Kern River, more than one hundred miles away from Los Angeles. The new company would produce so much electricity it could supply the LARY, the Pacific Electric, and other businesses as well.[12]

Pacific Light and Power was incorporated on March 6, 1902, with a $10 million capitalization. Huntington, Isaias, and the rest of the San Francisco syndicate got 51 percent of the shares, with the most being held by the LARY. Kerckhoff and his partners, who included the Jewish pioneer Kaspare Cohn, the attorney Henry O. Melveny, and John Bicknell, took 49 percent of the shares. Kerckhoff was president. Isaias's Union Trust Company was retained to sell the $10 million bond issue.

Soon, Kerckhoff started construction on a ten-thousand-horsepower hydroelectric power plant on the Kern River. Two sets of 105-mile transmission lines would carry the electricity to Los Angeles.

Huntington now decided to leave San Francisco and make Los Angeles his permanent home. His marriage to Mary Huntington had long been troubled, and the couple would divorce within a few years. With the $12 million Huntington made from the sale of his Southern Pacific stock, as well as the fortune he had amassed on his own, he instantly became one of the region's richest men when he moved south. Huntington wanted a home that was worthy of a man of his stature.

Isaias knew the place for him: the remnants of what was once the region's most productive winery, Lake Vineyard, a spread near Pasadena that had been owned by Benjamin Wilson, one of the first Yankees to move to Los Angeles.

Wilson had raised grapes on his farm, grapes that made wine that was exported around the county. His daughter Maria married James de Barth Shorb in 1867, and Wilson's son-in-law immediately expanded the family's holdings. On a knoll he constructed a twenty-eight-room mansion that was lit by both gas and electricity from water power created on site. He built expansive outbuildings for dairy cattle, a large packing house to store fruit, and stables and dormitories for his ranch hands, who were referred to as "chinamen and negroes."[13] The land had almost 150 acres of oranges with more than 13,000 orange trees, another 2,376 lemon trees, 1,896 peach trees, and table-grape vines.

Over time, Shorb built the state's biggest winery, which he called the San Gabriel Winery. Isaias and other businessmen, including the senators William Gwin and F. G. Newlands, invested $500,000 in 1882 to plant six hundred acres of new vineyards and to construct a brick, steam-powered winery that could ferment 1 million gallons of wine at a time and hold another 1 million gallons of finished wine.

But the scale of the winery was too grand to ever become profitable and Shorb soon saw his debts spiraling. To stem some of the loss, he and his wife Maria took out a mortgage with the Farmers and Merchants Bank. After Shorb died in 1896, Isaias spent countless hours trying to help Maria turn around the declining business, even taking over as president of the San Gabriel Winery. Maria hired George Patton, her brother-in-law and the father of the famed World War II general, as manager, but even his intervention was unsuccessful.

As the payoff date for the mortgage neared, Maria de Barth Shorb went to court to try and unburden herself from her mortgage. At first she declared that she had no memory of signing her name to the indebture document. Then she said she had been coerced by her husband. "There isn't a lawyer in San Francisco of any standing that does not laugh at the contention of Mrs. Shorb," Isaias wrote to Herman. "It is nothing more than a crazy action of a woman who has squandered her fortune and now tries to repudiate her debts."[14]

The Farmers and Merchants Bank foreclosed on the Shorb estate in April 1901. In January 1903, Huntington, Isaias, and his syndicate bought five hundred acres of the land and an adjacent parcel known as the Winston Ranch for $328,430.[15] Huntington paid for a 60 percent share, and Isaias and his syndicate got a 40 percent share.

In the coming years, Huntington would build a magnificent estate surrounded by extraordinary gardens on the property. It is known today as the Huntington Library and Gardens.

Huntington's expansion soon began to alarm the Southern Pacific Railroad, now controlled by Edward H. Harriman. By 1902, twenty-six years after the inaugural Southern Pacific car pulled into Los Angeles, the company had not only long-haul steam trains but short lines that carried people from downtown to Pasadena. But the Pacific Electric was both faster and cheaper, and Southern Pacific soon saw a precipitate drop in riders.

Harriman was not the type to sit back and watch profits drain away. In April 1902 he came to Los Angeles in his private railcar, the Arden, to examine the situation. Huntington, who was still a director of the Southern Pacific, escorted Harriman around town in his own specially appointed Pacific Electric car. The two men went on excursions to Catalina Island and to the top of Mount Lowe and spent an evening at the theater. Huntington also hosted an elaborate lunch in Harriman's honor at the California Club. Huntington assured Harriman that he had no designs on the Southern Pacific freight business, and the two men parted convinced they could work together.

But the détente did not last long.

W̶ithin a year, the newspapers were talking about a "war" between Huntington and Harriman.

As the Pacific Electric continued to siphon passengers away from the Southern Pacific trains, Harriman decided to take a bold—and competitive— step. On April 14, 1903, he paid $1.75 million for the "Hook" line—the Los Angeles Traction Company, which operated forty-eight miles of track and held options on twenty miles more. The purchase was a declaration that the Southern Pacific intended to battle Huntington for intercity travel.

Huntington rushed north in May and confronted Harriman. Over a dinner at the Palace Hotel's court grill that lasted until almost midnight, separated from eavesdroppers and observers by only a sheet of glass, the two railroad men negotiated until they came to a truce, achieved through an equitable distribution of assets. Huntington must have realized that as rich as he was, Harriman commanded larger resources, and it was clear that Harriman was serious about retaining dominance in the Los Angeles basin.

By the time Huntington left San Francisco the next evening to catch the "owl" train to Los Angeles, the terms were public. Harriman agreed not to do anything with his Hook line purchase. Some lines were swapped back and forth. More importantly, Harriman agreed to buy 40 percent of the Pacific Electric. Huntington would get 40 percent, and Isaias and the syndicate would have a reduced stake of 20 percent. The Southern Pacific was back in the game.

T he explosion between the brothers that many had been expecting came in May 1903. Earlier in the year, Isaias had converted the Farmers and Merchants Bank from a state to a national bank, which put it under the jurisdiction of the federal government and eased its transactions with eastern financial institutions. He had taken the opportunity to give additional responsibilities to Jackson Graves, a blunt-talking, abrasive Los Angeles attorney and one of the bank's vice presidents. Graves had first met Isaias in 1875 when he was a young attorney representing someone in a suit against Isaias. Despite that rocky beginning, the two men had become close. Isaias respected Graves's business instincts and had begun increasingly to rely on his judgment in both bank and personal matters.

Herman, in contrast, was acting more independently of his brother than ever and didn't always make decisions of which Isaias approved. The latest example was Herman's decision to erect an office building on the site of his old home on Fourth and Spring streets. Herman wanted a first-class building and hired the St. Louis architect Alfred F. Rosenheim to move to Los Angeles and take over the job. Rosenheim was an advocate of using steel frame construction for structural integrity rather than the more commonly used reinforced concrete, and he employed that technique in the eight-story Herman W. Hellman Building.

Herman spent close to $1 million to construct the tower, making it the most costly building erected in Los Angeles to date. It was also one of the most magnificent, with marble floors and corridors and a Tiffany-style domed skylight in the lobby. While the newspapers praised Herman's boldness, Isaias criticized his brother for spending too much money on the building. Isaias was opposed to taking on debt and he thought the building would leave Herman dangerously leveraged.

In May 1903, Isaias traveled from San Francisco on one of his periodic inspections, this time bringing along his son-in-law, Emanuel Heller. As Isaias strolled around the bank talking to various clerks and tellers, Heller, Herman, and Graves gathered in one of the glass-walled anterooms that lined the perimeter of the bank. They were talking when Isaias marched from the safe-deposit department into the glass-walled president's office, which was dominated by a large mahogany rolltop desk covered with phones. He turned and beckoned to the others to join him. "Come in here, I want to talk to you all," Isaias demanded, according to notes taken by Heller shortly after the conversation.

Herman, Heller, and Graves got up from their seats and walked a few steps into the president's office.

Isaias turned to his brother, his face steely. "The girl outside complains that you have insulted her and says she's going to leave."

Herman looked perplexed. "That's not so," he said. "I didn't insult her."

"Well, she said to me that you have insulted her," said Isaias.

Herman appeared agitated and began to protest. "That girl must go," he said. "She must be discharged."

Herman's comment seemed to infuriate his brother. "She'll not go. I hired her, and she's going to stay," insisted Isaias.

The two brothers glared at each other, and their mutual dislike seemed to pour into the room. "I resign immediately," announced Herman.

"Don't be foolish," replied Isaias.[16]

But Herman sat down and pulled out a piece of Farmers and Merchants stationery. "To the President and Board of Directors," Herman wrote hastily, smudging some of the letters as he went. "I hereby tender to you my resignation as Vice President of the Farmers & Merchants Bank of Los Angeles to take effect without further delay. Respectfully, Herman W. Hellman.[17]

Herman had resigned numerous times before, but he had always come back to the bank after his brother pleaded with him or he reconsidered his action. This time, however, Herman meant business. He had worked directly under Isaias for thirteen years, a period that had seen him succeed financially, but suffer physically with stress-induced diabetes. He had been berated by his brother, accused of incompetence and sloth. He had had enough. By the end of the day, Herman had gathered his personal belongings. Two days later, his son, Marco H. Hellman, an assistant cashier, also resigned. This time the board of directors accepted the resignations.

The split meant war between the two brothers. All the years of accumulated hostility, bad words, and hurt feelings exploded as the brothers looked for allies and jockeyed for position. Within days, Isaias started to hear that his brother intended to reenter the banking business as soon as he completed construction on the new Herman W. Hellman Building. Herman's son, Marco, would join the new bank as well. "All sorts of rumors are floating around about H.W.," Jackson Graves wrote Isaias on July 1, 1903. "The latest is that he is going to get an interest and the presidency of the Merchants National. I do not believe this, but I do think that he is dead set on going into the banking business."[18]

Isaias didn't express concern that his brother might soon head a competing bank. "This does not bother me much," Isaias wrote to Graves the following day. "The people there will soon find out how incompetent both are, and they will have to pay for it some day just as has been the case in the Farmers and Merchants National."[19]

A few days later, Herman did become president of the Merchants National Bank. One of his first orders of business was to pay calls on many of his old contacts—men who were customers of the Farmers and Merchants Bank. Herman was frank in asking them to move their accounts to his new bank, and even pressuring those he was close to. "Uncle Herman has asked me several times to give him part of our account," Adolph Fleishman, the son of Bertha, Isaias and Herman's sister, wrote on July 29, 1903. He had a wholesale fruit and produce business. "He has gone as far as calling me ungrateful and calling my attention to the fact that he loaned me $2500 when I first went into business."[20]

Herman wrote to many former customers and friends and used the opportunity to criticize Isaias. "As you know I had been with the Farmers and Merchants National Bank of this city for nearly 14 years, but it was impossible for me to get along any longer with my brother, Isaias Hellman, who is a regular tyrant, self-conceited, and one of the most selfish men living," wrote Herman to a potential client.[21]

Many companies were happy to make the leap from the Farmers and Merchants Bank to Merchants National. Many of the accounts were sizable, like that of the Los Angeles Traction Company, recently acquired by the Southern Pacific, and Newmark Brothers, the wholesale grocers, but most were small. Still, Herman claimed that deposits at the Farmers and Merchants Bank dropped by more than $1 million after his departure, funds that found their way into his new bank.[22]

The defections pained Isaias. He was particularly annoyed when he noted that a check by Frank Shafer, who was married to the daughter of Isaias's good friend Matthew Keller, was drawn on a Merchants Bank account. After Keller died in 1881, Isaias had served as executor of the estate and guardian of the surviving children. He frequently wrote them letters, guided their education, and suggested investment strategies. He considered himself a surrogate father and offered his blessings when the two sisters, Carrie and Alice, married two brothers from San Francisco, Frank and George Shafer. Now Isaias felt aggrieved that one of the spouses would do business with Herman's bank. "I never expected these people to leave our bank since every dollar they possess has been saved by me, and I might say, given to them," Isaias wrote Graves. In retaliation, Isaias told Graves to call in the $10,000 loan the bank had made to George Shafer. "I do not want to give you any reason for this action now, but may do so when I again meet you in Los Angeles," Isaias wrote Graves. "In the meantime, I think it prudent that the Farmers and Merchants National Bank should call in its loan of $10,000 from G. Shafer & his wife. The demand should be made and enforced and no nonsense about it."[23]

As Isaias aged, he increasingly started to look at the world in black and white—those he didn't approve of and those he did. "Mr. Hellman had a shortsighted tendency to think the world was divided into good people and bad people and the good people were the ones who did business with him," recalled Frederick Lipman, who worked in the banking business with Isaias for decades. "He wouldn't have made such a silly statement but that's the way it worked. The good people did business with us, the wicked people didn't do business with us."[24]

I n the summer of 1903, the Hellmans were finally able to move into their new house at Lake Tahoe. It had taken eighteen months to build at a cost of about $44,000.

Unlike the summer homes of the newly rich in Newport, which were decorated with mirrors and gilt in imitation of the French monarchy, Isaias and Esther chose a California craftsman motif for their new home. The living room was decorated with mission-style wooden furniture arranged in a few conversational groupings. They laid a black bear rug in front of the massive granite fireplace, a gift from Louis Sloss, the president of the Alaska Commercial Company and a director at the Nevada Bank.

The dining room could seat thirty, and its walls were covered with mat woven from virgin redwood strips. The tile on the fireplace was imported from Holland.

The house quickly became the Hellmans' favorite retreat. They named it Pine Lodge for the sugar pines that covered the property, and from the first summer they spent as much time as possible there. Isaias found he was able to relax deeply at Tahoe and leave behind the demands of the business world, although he kept in touch with daily telegrams and letters. His crippling migraine headaches also seemed to go away in the clean mountain air.

The days had a rhythm that the Hellmans found soothing. Isaias would rise early every morning, dress in a light suit and his favorite white Panama hat, and set out for a long walk by the lake or through the paths he had constructed through the woods. His young grandsons—Warren, Frederick, and Edward—would often accompany him, and they could be seen tearing down the paths followed by Isaias with his walking stick.

Breakfast was served when Isaias returned around eight thirty. Many guests and family members preferred to eat in bed, so Pine Lodge's numerous servants would carry trays piled high with eggs, toast, and coffee to the upstairs bedrooms.

During the day there were many things to do. By 1903 Isaias had purchased two boats: the *Mi Dueña,* one of the fastest wooden boats on the lake, and another, thirty-foot eight-horsepower boat equipped with a tin-lined icebox to store the family's lunch or any fish they caught. Isaias spent part of each day out on the lake, often for hours at a time. Lake Tahoe brimmed with trout, and both Esther and Isaias loved to fish.

There were also horses to ride, picnics to go on, and friends to entertain. The family never completely lost its formality, however. Esther, Clara, Florence, and Frances, Marco's wife, always dressed in floor-length white high-collared summer gowns. The men stayed in lightweight suits, often substituting a bow tie for a cravat and a straw hat for a bowler. The little boys wore white cotton sailor suits.

The wide, covered porch at the front of the house was the family's favorite retreat. They would gather there in the late afternoons to play bridge or other card games and regroup before dinner for cocktails. There were wicker rocking chairs to relax in and a hanging porch swing. The eight pillars holding up the roof were tree trunks still covered with bark, creating a rustic atmosphere.

The view was the best part of Pine Lodge. As Isaias sat on the porch, breathing in air saturated with the scent of pine, he could look out onto a lake with ever-changing hues of blue. In shallow pockets along the sandy beaches the water could be turquoise, startling unnatural in the Alpine setting. As the water got deeper, it turned from blue to indigo to navy. The snow-capped mountains ringing the lake reflected on the water like an image in a mirror.

"I sit here for hours and look at it," Isaias said in a 1914 newspaper article. "I have been all over Europe and all over the United States. There is nothing to compare with it. Here I enjoy myself. Here I am at perfect rest, whether indoors or outdoors about the house, or in the forest where I love to walk."

WELLS FARGO

1903–1905

By June 1903, scarcely three years after its founding, the Pacific Electric had used $3.5 million of its $10 million bond issue for expansion. Huntington had great ambitions for the interurban line, which connected far-flung towns in Los Angeles County to the city's downtown core. While he had to change plans slightly not to compete directly with the Southern Pacific, he still constructed routes at a rapid pace. There were now about 170 miles of lines, reaching into Pasadena, Whittier, Alhambra, and Long Beach.

But Huntington's San Francisco partners were not happy with his spending spree. They had invested funds in the Pacific Electric with the expectation the company would be profitable and pay annual dividends, but these never materialized. Huntington could wait on the dividends because he owned large tracts of land around his ever-expanding lines and he knew that land prices would go up once rail ties were laid down. But Isaias, Borel, and de Guigne, the minority shareholders, were not partners in Huntington's land company. They could not look forward to those profits.

The bond market in 1903 was also depressed, and Isaias was having so much difficulty finding buyers that the Pacific Electric owners had to buy their own bonds to raise funds for the continued expansion. In frustration, Isaias wrote Huntington on June 2 and bluntly told him to stop expanding. The two roads currently under construction, one to San Pedro and one to Whittier, could proceed, but nothing else, he insisted. Isaias also requested that Huntington stop buying land for expansion.

Huntington downplayed Isaias's concerns and warned in a letter that they should "not stop in the middle of the stream." In August, he wrote an extraordinary note which revealed that he intended to keep building as fast and furiously as possible. "I think we would make a mistake if we should cut everything off at this time, and if we should stop the construction Southern California would receive quite a setback," Huntington wrote Isaias. "What we have been doing has, as you know, quite changed the general outlook there. Today everything looks prosperous and the hopes of all the people, based principally, I believe, on the rapid development of property and corresponding increase of value in and around Los Angeles, are very high. I, for one, don't want to disappoint them; but would like to go on up-building and creating as we have been doing just as far and as fast as we can do so without going beyond the safety point for ourselves and I don't think there is much danger of our doing that. As my uncle used to quote me so often (and there is no truer maxim, it seems to me) 'There is a withholding that leadeth to poverty' and in all measures looking toward retrenchment of expenditures we must of course not lose sight of the fact that in saving there is sometime loss."[1]

Isaias and the other minority partners might have been able to tolerate that expansion, but in September Huntington announced that another one of the group's companies, the Los Angeles Land Company, needed an emergency infusion of $100,000. To get this, the company's directors needed to pay an extra assessment. Isaias was suddenly presented with a $16,700 bill. A few days later Huntington decided to double the capitalization of the Pacific Electric from $10 million to $20 million.

As the assessments added up, Isaias and de Guigne headed to Los Angeles for a meeting with Huntington. They intended to demand that the expansions slow down. But the confrontation was avoided when the men, all directors of the Los Angeles Railway Company, voted to have the rail line buy the assets of the land company using bonds from the Pacific Electric. This way Isaias and the others could avoid paying the assessment.

The peace was short-lived.

In May 1904, in an apparent breach of protocol, Isaias wrote an exasperated letter to Huntington's son Howard, the general manager of the Pacific Electric, and ordered him not to spend any more than the $100,000 recently loaned by the Nevada National Bank. Perhaps Isaias felt that he needed to try a new tactic, since he obviously wasn't getting through to the elder Huntington, who was continuing to spend money rapidly as he expanded to Glendale and Newport. The elder Huntington got furious that a company director had bypassed him to communicate directly with an employee. He wrote Isaias that maybe they were at "cross-purposes."

By November of that year, Huntington still needed money, and he informed his partners that he would assess their stock 5 percent. Isaias exploded at the notion that his small group needed to come up with $48,000. "I just received your letter of Nov. 21, 1904, notifying me of the necessity of further advance of $250,000 from the stockholders of Pacific Electric Railway Company," Isaias wrote. "You know very well that I am utterly opposed to continued expenditure of money on these railways, but my views in this matter have been entirely ignored. I have concluded that I will make no further advances as a stockholder except under the compulsion of regular proceedings by way of assessment."[2] Borel and de Guigne also signed the letter.

By this time, Isaias had gotten to know E. H. Harriman, the Pacific Electric's other major shareholder. Since Harriman was a railroad man, he at first supported Huntington's rapid building, but he changed his mind as he considered how much the expanded Pacific Electric lines were cutting into his Southern Pacific business. Isaias communicated with Harriman through the general counsel of the Southern Pacific, William Herrin. For a while it looked as if the two sides would pull together on the board and order Huntington to stop his expansions. "I told Mr. Hellman that so far as the Pacific Electric Railway Co. was concerned, we could control this matter by standing together—that we could agree upon a resolution and have same passed by the Board of Directors, declaring that no further contracts should be made or obligations incurred, and that it was the policy of the Company, for the present, not to undertake any further new construction," Herrin wrote Harriman.[3]

In December, Isaias and the other minority stockholders finally gave up. Although they had been investors in Los Angeles transportation companies for years predating Huntington, they did not have the appetite to keep raising money or putting in their own funds. Isaias, Borel, and de Guigne sold their Pacific Electric shares equally to Huntington and the Southern Pacific for $1.2 million, but still retained their ownership in the LARY. "I am not a speculator," Isaias told a reporter from the Los Angeles Times. "I am strictly an investor, and I have all my life paid for things as I go along. I never borrow money. It is against my principles, and that is the reason that I could not stay with those rich fellows that are building railroads all over Southern California."

On June 30, 1904, Isaias and Esther's youngest daughter, Florence, was married in her parents' home on Franklin Street to a young attorney, Sidney Ehrman. Esther had decorated the entrance hall with towering palms, and the hundred guests invited to the wedding walked through the green bower to an altar draped in gold cloth and adorned with lilies and yellow daisies. After the ceremony the guests had a bridal breakfast in the Hellmans' upstairs ballroom.

Florence, twenty-two, was a petite woman, barely five feet tall, with luminous brown eyes and a heart-shaped face. Her groom was the thirty-year-old son of San Francisco pioneer merchant Myer Ehrman. The young man had grown up in San Francisco, attended the University of Munich for a year, graduated from the University of California, and received his law degree in 1898 from the Hastings School of Law. Ehrman was an athletic man who loved to fish, adored music, and had a warm sense of humor that nicely counterbalanced Florence's seriousness.

Ehrman had been practicing law with the firm Garret McEnerney and W. S. Goodfellow, who had their offices in the Nevada Bank Building on Montgomery. Before long, however, he joined forces with his new brother-in-law, Emanuel Heller, in the firm Heller and Powers. Within a few years, Ehrman's name would be added to the company's title.

By the time E. H. Harriman acquired a half interest in the Pacific Electric, he was already considered the most brilliant railroad man in the country. Born in Hempstead, New York, in 1848 to a financially unsuccessful preacher and his unhappy wife, Harriman went off to Wall Street when he was fourteen years old and was soon earning more than his father. By saving his meager salary from his days as a clerk and borrowing funds from a relative, Harriman was able to purchase a seat on the New York Stock Exchange. He began to trade railroad stocks, sometimes successfully and sometimes not, but soon became fascinated by the financial interplay of the railroad business. His career in railroads was helped tremendously when he married Mary

Averell, whose father was the president of the Ogdensburg and Lake Champlain Railroad, a line along the St. Lawrence River.

When Harriman purchased the controlling interest in the Southern Pacific in 1901, he assumed control of more railroad track than any other man in the country—18,500 miles west of the Missouri River. His companies included the Union Pacific Railroad, the eastern half of the first transcontinental railroad, and he employed more men than the standing army of the United States.[4]

President Teddy Roosevelt would soon start to attack Harriman publicly and cast him as one of the nation's villains, a man who ruthlessly controlled a railroad trust. But from the first time Isaias met Harriman, who was six years his junior, he found much to admire. While Harriman was not distinguished looking—he was only five feet five inches tall and preferred baggy jackets and a soft felt hat over formal suits, high collars, and a top hat—he had pluck and determination. He was also genial. After his purchase of the railroad, a San Francisco paper declared that Harriman was a "glad-hand artist" and an "amiable and banquet-loving New Yorker."[5]

When Harriman made up his mind to do something, he didn't waver from his goal, and Isaias admired that drive. Harriman differed from other railroad tycoons like J. P. Morgan and James J. Hill in wanting to upgrade and improve railroad lines rather than plunder them. Shortly after Harriman acquired the Southern Pacific, he took a ride over every inch of its rails, noting where new embankments were needed, where ties should be replaced, and where curves could be straightened. As Isaias's dissatisfaction with Henry Huntington grew, he aligned himself more closely with Harriman, a tycoon of even greater standing.

So when Harriman found himself with a banking problem on his hands, it was natural that he turned to Isaias for help.

Harriman's purchase of the Southern Pacific came with a one-third interest in Wells Fargo & Company, a business whose name was synonymous with the development of the West.

From its humble roots as a two-man agency in San Francisco in 1852, Wells Fargo had expanded into an international express and banking company that delivered goods and capital around the nation and to Europe. During the gold rush, the opening of a Wells Fargo office in a mining town signaled progress;

miners could take their nuggets and gold dust to the office, where an agent would exchange it for a paper draft. Wells Fargo would then send drafts to banks in the East in triplicate form in case any got lost during the arduous journey.

Wells Fargo began providing freight service between California and New York. Its red-and-gold stagecoaches soon traveled throughout the sparsely settled West and beyond, racing over rutted roads to reunite families, to carry businessmen to distant locales, and to bring trunks of gold to more secure city vaults. The company eventually controlled the entire overland mail route from the Missouri River to the Pacific Coast. Wells Fargo letter carriers risked their lives thundering on horseback relay during the days of the Pony Express and while shuttling bags of mail among outposts in Indian Territory. They also delivered letters faster and cheaper than the U.S. Postal Service. As the railroads began to dominate the transportation routes, Wells Fargo formed a strong partnership with the Southern Pacific and used the rail line to transport its customers' packages around the country,

By 1904, Wells Fargo & Company was a cash machine, earning hundreds of thousands of dollars in profits each month. Harriman eyed that money hungrily, scheming how he could use the funds to upgrade and improve his railroad lines.

But Wells Fargo had one underperforming unit—its bank. It had too much money idling in its vaults instead of being lent out in interest-bearing loans. Harriman knew the bank weighed down the value of the express company, and he decided to get rid of it.

Harriman approached Isaias with the idea that the Nevada Bank take over the banking part of Wells Fargo. The concept was immediately appealing. While the Nevada Bank was an economic powerhouse with $9 million in deposits and a reputation that spanned the country, its growth had slowed in recent years, particularly compared to the Farmers and Merchants Bank, which had seen its deposits skyrocket as Los Angeles's population doubled between 1890 and 1900.

Part of the trouble was that Isaias managed the Nevada Bank on an outdated business model. It was run less like a corporation and more like a one-man shop. As president, it was Isaias's responsibility to bring in new business. But Isaias was often busy with other investments. He had just helped consolidate the various utility companies in San Francisco into the Pacific Gas Company and had sold $1.2 million worth of bonds for the new concern. The Nevada

Bank had been one of three banks in the country to sell war bonds for Japan
during the Russo-Japanese War of 1904.

Isaias was also very involved with the Union Trust Company, which managed Jane Stanford's enormous trust and the money of other wealthy individuals. And Isaias had a smattering of investments to oversee. He had started a
real estate group, the Bankers' Investment Group, with his good friends Louis
Sloss, Christian de Guigne, and Antoine Borel. They had recently made the
largest single real estate purchase in San Francisco, buying the Blythe Block
on Market Street between Grant and Montgomery for $3 million.[6]

"He became more and more of a personal banker and the bank became
more and more limited to what he could personally attend to," recalled Frederick Lipman, who worked with Isaias for fifteen years. "Certainly there was
no one else in the bank that could speak for the bank and I think the time of
the merger was a time when the bank would have been at a standstill if we
had not done some kind of a new set up; because no matter how much one
man can do in a bank and how important it is to have a fountain head of authority, the amount that one man can do adequately is limited."[7]

Isaias had pleaded with the members of his board of directors to help him
bring in new business. The results were disappointing. "I regret to be compelled to mention that a number of our shareholders have been of no assistance to the Bank except that of the collection of dividends," Isaias wrote the
directors of the Nevada National Bank. "If the holdings of such shareholders
could be placed in friendly hands, those who would give up their business
and influence, I should be pleased. You are aware that your officers can do
only a certain amount of work and have a certain amount of influence but
when 300 shareholders do their duty toward an institution our business will
be much benefited by it."[8]

Isaias had also been reluctant to change the nature of his financial institution. The Nevada Bank was a commercial bank, which meant it catered to
businesses, not small depositors. Isaias consistently refused to appeal to the
ordinary man, who could offer only a small portion of his paycheck as a deposit, and this intransigent attitude indirectly led to the creation of another
bank that would soon become one of Isaias's biggest competitors.

In 1904, Isaias was chairman of the board of the Columbus Savings and
Loan Society, which served the Italian business community. In 1902, a
young man named Amadeo, also known as A.P. Giannini took a seat on the

board and soon began agitating for the bank to lend out more money to small borrowers. Giannini saw that North Beach, the Italian section of San Francisco, was growing by two thousand people a year, people who needed help settling in a new country. He argued to the board that the bank should reach out to these immigrants, some of whom would eventually become prosperous businessmen. The board balked, and Isaias flatly rejected the idea when Giannini approached him privately. Disgusted by the board's attitude, Giannini quit and went off to form the Bank of Italy. It would one day be known as the Bank of America, the world's largest bank.[9]

So the idea of merging the Nevada National Bank with Wells Fargo held allure for Isaias. Harriman even sweetened the offer by telling Isaias he would make the new merged bank the sole depository for Southern Pacific money in San Francisco. In December 1904, the board of the Nevada National Bank met in its large wood-paneled conference room and approved a merger with the Wells Fargo Bank.

Isaias was scheduled to leave on a long-planned vacation to Europe, and the directors hoped to postpone announcement of the merger until he returned in the spring, when the shareholders would have a chance to vote on the proposal. But the news was too big to contain. On, January 15, 1905, the *Chronicle* ran a headline: "Big Bank Deal Has Been Made. Stated with Positiveness That the Nevada Has Absorbed the Wells Fargo Institution."

The Wells Fargo Nevada National Bank officially opened its doors on April 24, 1905, with deposits of $16 million. Once again, Isaias turned to the city's leading businesses and businessmen to buy shares of the new bank. Levi Strauss & Company took 250 shares; William Herrin of the Southern Pacific took 1,000 shares; the banker Daniel Meyer took 500 shares; the New York financier Jacob Schiff took 500 shares; R. S. Lovett, the general counsel for the Union Pacific Railroad, took 100 shares; and Phoebe Hearst, the widow of mining magnate George Hearst and a fellow regent of the University of California, took 250 shares.[10] By far the biggest share, however, went to Harriman and the Southern Pacific, which took 200,000 shares of the new bank—a full third. Harriman also got a seat on the board, as did Herrin.

It is interesting that the merged bank's new name started with Wells Fargo rather than the Nevada Bank. Both had long histories in California—

Wells Fargo began in 1852 and the Nevada began in 1875. Both were well respected. But Wells Fargo was much better known throughout the country and was more closely associated with the settling of the West, so its name was put first.

The headquarters of the new bank was the old Nevada Bank's headquarters on Montgomery near Pine. "Our ambition is not to be the largest bank in San Francisco, but the soundest and the best," Isaias told the newspapers.

The merger reinforced Isaias's reputation as one of the most powerful men in the West. He had also just taken control of banks in Tacoma, Washington, and Portland, Oregon. "I congratulate you on your success in bringing such an immense aggregation of banking capital under your control," wrote Lyman Stewart, the president of the Union Oil Company.[11]

With his ascension to the top of the Wells Fargo Bank, Isaias had become the premier banker of the West Coast.

While Isaias was plotting to expand his banking business in San Francisco, the Farmers and Merchants Bank was operating down south out of cramped, outdated headquarters that now no longer sat in the central business district.

The bank had moved to the site more than twenty years earlier. At the time, the building on Main and Commercial streets, which was built and owned by Isaias, was modern. Now it was sorely out of date. There was no central heating; the bank rooms were warmed by a potbellied cast-iron stove in the basement. The building was originally lit with kerosene lamps and had to be jury-rigged for electricity. At first, there were no separate safe-deposit boxes for customers to store their valuables; the bank let them bring in their own tin boxes, which they could store in a spare room. That was remedied in 1895 when the bank installed a new $12,000 vault.[12]

But the more serious problem was that the business district had shifted southwest, away from its traditional center near the Plaza. Isaias grew concerned that the bank would lose customers if they had to travel too far to bank. He also worried that if the city's business core drifted too much, his downtown properties would drop in value. "If nothing is done to impede the Real Estate boomers in Los Angeles I have no doubt that before two years the business center will be about 7th Street and soon after 10th or 12th Street," Isaias wrote to Jackson Graves. "In fact, if there is no permanent business center in Los Angeles, property values will be very much disturbed."[13]

Isaias's solution was to sell the bank his old homestead on the corner of Fourth and Main. When Isaias had first built a house there in 1877, he worried it was so far out of town that his family would be lonely. But now the property lay in the heart of downtown. The Van Nuys and Westminster hotels, both popular destinations with eastern health seekers, were across the street from the site. Henry Huntington was building a massive, nine-story depot for his various transportation companies two blocks away on Sixth Street. The exclusive Jonathan Club planned to occupy the top three floors. Herman's new business building was nearby on Fourth and Spring, on a stretch that would soon be nicknamed the "Wall Street of the West" for its line of bank buildings. Streetcars ran nearby, and the sidewalks swarmed with people during lunchtime.

Isaias hired the architectural firm Morgan, Walls, and Morgan to design a granite classical revival building fronted with Corinthian columns. The central banking room was expansive with high ceilings and a vast curved skylight that let in natural light. The bank's olive walls were set off by three types of marble: white Italian marble for pillars, yellow and blue sienna marble for the wainscoting, and a green Swiss marble known as verde antique for the horizontal slabs running around the room.

The most impressive aspect of the bank was its three-level steel vault, which reached from the basement to the ceiling. The safe-deposit boxes were on the bottom floor, and the main floor of the vault was divided in half, with one section for coin and the other for records. The entire building cost $500,000.

On March 25, 1905, two days before the new building's official opening, the bank transferred $2 million from its old vaults to its new. The transfer was planned with militarylike precision. Tellers spent days counting out the coin and separating it into canvas bags holding $25,000 each. The bags were loaded into steel boxes, which were placed into waiting wagons. The caravan then made its way carefully down Main Street. Since it was Saturday, traffic was light and the transfer went smoothly. "Three of the most valuable loads that ever passed on wagons through the streets of Los Angeles were taken down

Main Street from Commerical to Fourth yesterday," read a March 26 article in the *Los Angeles Times*. "The wagons were laden with gold—$2,000,000 of it—all in glittering coins—but their sheen was not great enough to penetrate the steel sides of the large safes in which they were stored."

After the bank was completed, Isaias used Morgan, Wall, and Morgan to design a large and modern office building. Herman's office building had received critical acclaim, and no doubt Isaias wanted to retain his standing in the city. His building, the Isaias W. Hellman Building, wrapped around the new bank structure like the letter L. It was six stories high and held hundreds of small offices.

I n November 1905, Isaias was awarded the biggest bond deal he had ever handled—a $14.5 million issue for the Spring Valley Water Company, the privately owned water company that supplied San Francisco.

The Spring Valley Water Company was an amalgamation of numerous smaller water companies, the first started in 1868 when George H. Ensign received a water charter from the state legislature. Ensign ran pipes from a spring he found in San Francisco at Mason and Washington streets. The spring never supplied more than five thousand gallons a day, but it gave Ensign's company a name.

By 1905, the Spring Valley Water Company's watershed included more than twenty-three-thousand acres in nearby Alameda, San Mateo, and Santa Clara counties, four reservoirs, and hundreds of miles of pipe, making it the largest privately held utility in the state. The board of Spring Valley included some of Isaias's closest associates, including Antoine Borel, Christian de Guigne, and William Herrin. (Marco would be appointed in January 1906.)

As in Los Angeles, San Francisco residents were growing increasingly frustrated by the notion that a private company controlled its water supply. Despite that dismay, voters had repeatedly turned down attempts to buy out the private water company, citing concern over the high price.

Since the Spring Valley Water Company controlled all the local water sources, San Francisco officials began to look farther away for water, and finally settled on the crystal-clear waters of the Tuolumne River in the Sierra

Nevada, 148 miles away. Spring Valley had a history of gobbling up water rights, so the popular reformist San Francisco mayor, James Duval Phelan, put up his own money in 1901 to secure the reservoir rights at a place called Hetch Hetchy. While the city still needed to deal with Spring Valley, Phelan's act set the stage for future municipal independence.

Spring Valley directors decided to consolidate old debt and raise new funds for expansion. The company hired Isaias to sell its most massive bond deal ever. Notably, the board did not split the issue with any other banker, nor did it hand the deal to one of Isaias's banks. The arrangement was with Isaias himself, a nod to his power and reach.

People from the East Coast had been investing in California ever since the discovery of gold. But the Spring Valley Water bond drew serious attention from New York brokerage houses, which now saw new business opportunities in bringing western investments to their customers. The New York houses were also interested because they had long-standing personal relationships with Isaias. Heidelbach, Ickelheimer & Company bought $200,000 of the bonds to resell, and P. J. Goodhart & Company bought $150,000 of the bonds. (Both firms had as their leaders men who had married daughters of Meyer Lehman.)

The bulk of the bonds, however, were bought by the same small Jewish group that Isaias usually sold to, including his brother-in-law Benjamin Newgass, Levi Strauss & Company, the banker Daniel Meyer, Louis Sloss, Abraham and William Haas, M. J. Brandenstein, Phil Lilienthal, Clarence Walter, and Jacob Neustadter.[14]

"This year I have done the largest and heaviest amount of work in my whole career," Isaias wrote in December 1905 to Newgass. "In the spring, after my return from Europe, consolidating the Nevada National Bank with Wells Fargo & Co. bank, which I am pleased to inform you had been a great success. Subsequently, consolidating and disposing of the San Francisco Gas & Electric Co.'s shares to a new corporation (which has mostly been my own work) and which will finally be closed on the 2nd of January. This has also been profitable to shareholders. And last, but not least, the Spring Valley Water Comp. bond syndicate, which has taken me several months investigation, and which must be considered a fair investment, otherwise the applications for participation would not have been so large and from the best houses in New York & San Francisco. This will

take several months to complete and will finally be wound up after the first
of Sept. 1906."[15]

By the end of August 1906, money was pouring into Wells Fargo Nevada
National Bank to secure the Spring Valley bonds. Deposits went up to
$24 million—the highest ever. On September 1, Isaias handed a check for
$13,723,000 to his son, Marco, at the Union Trust, the bank that was hold-
ing the bonds. The check was so large that the newspapers ran a photograph
of it.

FIFTEEN

EARTHQUAKE AND FIRE

1906

The opening of the opera was the biggest event of the San Francisco social season, one that consumed the attentions of society women and their debutante daughters for weeks. To look perfect on the glittering night, they visited their dressmakers and demanded silk and satin creations as elegant and fashionable as those worn by the women in Paris. They took their carriages downtown into the very private vaults of the Union Trust Company or Hibernia Bank to examine their jewels and decide which diamond tiara, which pearl necklace, which gold bracelet, would most flatter their pale necks and arms.

In 1906, the opera opened on April 16, a balmy evening that hinted of the spring to come. The "smart set," as the newspapers dubbed society people, left their mansions on Nob Hill and in the newly fashionable Western Addition and made their way in open-air motorcars and horse-drawn carriages to the magnificent opera house on Mission Street, built in 1876 to show the world that San Francisco was no longer rough, but a cultivated, cultured city.

More than three thousand people, including Isaias and Esther, crowded their way into the theater, chatting and laughing and scrutinizing the bejeweled women and their handsomely dressed escorts. The city's newspaper reporters were busy writing down exactly what certain women wore; a long description would fill the pages the next day. "Some of the dresses were lovely, and oh! The diamonds and the pearls that many of the women wore," wrote a *Bulletin* reporter under the pen name of Madame La Bavard. "First of all there was Mrs. James Flood, who sat in the Flood box with her sister-in-law Miss Jennie Flood and Miss Sally Maynard. Mrs. Flood was the cynosure of all eyes. She wore an exquisite gown of white chiffon, the corsage a solid mass of pearl-studded embroidery and the most fetching elbow-length sleeves of chiffon, just caught together at intervals with basket-like effect. On her fair neck were the famous Flood pearls, the handsomest in town."

While the *Bulletin* declared Mrs. Flood the loveliest woman at the opera, the *Call* determined that the Misses de Young, the daughters of the newspaper publisher Michael de Young, were the ones to watch. "Miss Helen de Young wore a Paris gown of elaborately embroidered white lace with festoons of pink roses," wrote society reporter Laura Bride Powers in a front-page article for the next day's *Call.* "Miss Constance de Young was very beautiful in pale yellow brocade silk with white lace."

Esther Hellman was too old and too Jewish to have her gown described in any of the newspapers, but she and Isaias had secured one of the best boxes in the opera house, slightly to the left of the center of the theater. Their son, Marco, and his wife, Frances, joined them, as did their oldest daughter, Clara, and her husband, Emanuel. Somewhere in the cavernous house sat their other daughter, Florence, and her husband, Sidney.

As the lights dimmed, the crowd hushed as they eagerly anticipated the Metropolitan Opera Company's production of *The Queen of Sheba.* For days the newspapers had detailed the opera company's rail journey from New York, and the attitudes and opinions of its star tenor, the Italian, Enrico Caruso, whose hometown, Naples, had just been devastated by the eruption of Mount Vesuvius. The company was in San Francisco for an extended tour, adding a bit of sophistication to a city many on the East Coast considered raw.

To the disappointment of the audience, Caruso would not appear until the next night, as Don Jose in Bizet's *Carmen.* Instead, the opening-night crowd would hear Anton Van Rooy sing the role of King Solomon and Edith Walker perform the part of the queen. When the curtain went up, the audience was impressed by the elaborate sets and ornate costumes, but the singers' voices failed to arouse the crowd. Only one man stood up to yell "Bravo" at the end of the opera, and he quickly sat back down. The production—and the audience—were criticized in all of the city's newspapers. "They slipped into their places modestly and meekly as nuns at mass and there was no atmosphere—no passive moment that one feels and that quickens the breath and stirs the passions," reported the *Call.*

The tepid performance did not dampen the spirits of the younger Hellmans, who continued the evening's festivities by hosting a small party afterward. They left the opera and, along with hundreds of other jeweled patrons, headed a block away to hold fetes at the Palace Hotel, wining and dining until late in the night. Isaias and Esther, however, went home after the production.

T he next evening was quiet at the Hellman home on Franklin Street in San Francisco, a welcome respite after all the excitement surrounding the opera's opening. Isaias and Esther loved their evenings at home, where they ate in their wood-paneled dining room, often before a crackling fire. When it was time to go to bed, Isaias and Esther went upstairs to their bedroom, which was decorated with an ornate wooden bed and matching bureau and dresser. A cluster of family photographs in silver frames stood on the dresser. More were perched on a mantelpiece.

If Isaias had stared into the mirror that night after he took off his frock coat and loosened his cravat, he would have seen an aging man of sixty-four with bright brown hair, a gray beard, and a receding hairline. His frame carried a little paunch now, but he was healthy, aside from his recurring migraine headaches.

Isaias put on the pajamas his valet had laid out for him and then got into the ornate wooden bed nestled against his bedroom wall. He and Esther were soon fast asleep.

T he jolt came at 5:12 A.M. Deep under the ocean, miles off the coast of San Francisco, two massive tectonic plates slipped past each other, letting loose shock waves that traveled seven thousand miles an hour through rocks and dirt, swamps and hills. This break in the San Andreas Fault—it had been named only eleven years earlier by a University of California professor—let loose an initial spasm that lasted forty-five seconds, then paused, and then expelled a jolt so large it literally threw people out of their beds. The burst of energy was felt throughout most of California and into Oregon, and in no place more strongly than San Francisco, a city built partially on filled-in marshes, paved-over sand dunes, and other unstable ground. On the Rossi-Forel earthquake scale, the one used at the turn of the twentieth century, the April 18 earthquake rated a 9, with 10 being the highest. It measured 8.3 on the modern Richter scale.

On Franklin Street, the quake hit Isaias's house like a massive hammer, rocking and swaying and twisting the timbers over and over, contorting them until they groaned and snapped. Plaster showered down from the walls, pictures fell, and the roar of the earth moving shook the house so hard it was lifted from its foundation. "About five fifteen this morning, the house rocked and swayed and twisted with a terrible earthquake," Isaias's next-door neighbor John Walter, wrote his parents in Europe on the afternoon of the earthquake. "Everything that wasn't near the floor deposited itself forcibly if not gracefully upon the floors. . . . The plaster was shaken to a great extent down onto the floors & in great quantities in the halls. . . . the chimneys came down. The pillars in the front portico are twisted & in all the rooms upstairs, including bathrooms, everything that was around & in chests thrown around & broken. The kitchen was flooded and the water connections busted.— There is no water, no gas, no electricity, no telephone, no telegraph in all the town."

Isaias's house stood on a hill of rock, so it was damaged but not destroyed. In other parts of San Francisco, in houses that sat on ancient swamps or in buildings that rested on filled-in shoreline, people were not so lucky. So many buildings collapsed around San Francisco's city hall on McAllister Street that a cloud of dust obscured the sky. City hall itself, thirty years in the making, shed its walls like a snake shedding old skin. The dome still rose intact, but the steel framework below stood bare, and columns of granite and walls of plaster lay heaped on the street.

For those who could, the first inclination was to run, particularly when three aftershocks hit the city in quick succession, at 5:18 A.M., 5:25 A.M., and 5:42 A.M. Their impulse was to get out into the open, to any place free of buildings that could rain down deadly debris. For Isaias and Esther and their servants, that place was Lafayette Park, a square of greenery just a block from their home. Within minutes of the earthquake, the streets were filled with people running in distress, some half clothed, some completely dressed, lugging trunks filled with their precious belongings. "Each and every person I saw was temporarily insane," wrote an *Examiner* reporter. "Laughing idiots commented on the fun they were having. Terror marked other faces.

Strong men bellowed like babies in their furor. No one knew which way to turn, when on all sides destruction stared them in the very eye."

A crowd quickly gathered at the park, including many of the Hellmans' friends and neighbors. Isaias's thoughts soon turned to the bank. He needed to get downtown, to assess the state of the building and see if it was fit to open for business. Isaias headed down California Street, a walk he had taken hundreds of time, but on this day San Francisco was a mockery of its former self, a grotesque sideshow of mutilated buildings and crushed bodies. Bricks were strewn in the streets; entire walls had collapsed to reveal the internal workings of homes. Cable car tracks were twisted and contorted. And this was before flames broke out, sparking a conflagration that would burn for four days and destroy three-quarters of the city.

The Nevada Bank opened for business at 9 A.M. the morning of the earthquake. The building was not severely damaged, and most of the tellers had reported to work, as if it were just a routine day. The bank's cashier and number two man, Frederick Lipman, who had worked for Wells Fargo for twenty-three years, had been jolted out of bed by the earthquake, but had taken the ferry as usual from Berkeley that morning. Lipman had plans to attend the opera that night, so he lugged a suitcase with his evening clothes across the bay.

There was no cable car to greet Lipman as he stepped out of the Ferry Building at the base of Market Street. The tracks running down San Francisco's main thoroughfare were twisted and warped, and no trolleys could pass. So Lipman walked up toward the bank. He noticed smoke rising from various points south of Market, but was not greatly alarmed. He stopped at the telegraph office at Market and Montgomery and sent out a telegram to Wells Fargo's corresponding banks in New York, asking them to send $3 million to the United States mint.

At 10:30 A.M., the smell of smoke was noticeably stronger. Business was slow, but the bank remained open. Suddenly, the fire department rushed in and ordered everyone out. The small fires that had broken out because of the earthquake had grown larger and were starting to eat up large sections of the South of Market area, burning alive those who were still trapped in the rubble. There was no water to fight the flames, as the pipes from the Spring Valley

Water Company had completely failed. Many of the mains had been routed through filled ground known as "made ground" and had ruptured, leaving the city defenseless. There were a few underground cisterns in the city, but those water reserves were soon used up.

The clerks hurriedly put the bank's working books and ledgers into the massive brick and steel vault, which had been designed to withstand fire. There was $3 million worth of coin in the safe and records of the bank's depositors, information critical for running the institution. The clerks shut the steel doors tightly, and hoped they would offer protection from the flames.

Other bankers had less faith in their vaults. A. P. Giannini, the founder of the Bank of Italy, had arrived at work that morning to find that his clerks had taken out $80,000—their entire cash supply—from the vault at the Crocker-Woolworth Bank. As the fires encroached, Giannini threw the money into a horse-drawn cart and brought it to his home in San Mateo, south of the city. William Crocker, the president of the Crocker-Woolworth Bank, had hired a boat to transport his bankbooks into the safety of the bay. At the Anglo-California Bank, clerks and tellers used a wheelbarrow to transport their negotiable bonds to a boat traveling to Oakland. The tellers transferred $1 million of bonds in three hours.[1]

By the time Isaias left the Wells Fargo Nevada National Bank, the city was burning. When he looked up Market Street, the fire was already licking the back of the famed Palace Hotel, whose sumptuous wood-paneled rooms would soon burn, despite the presence of water sprinklers and large cisterns on the roof. Smoke completely obscured the sun, and the flames were creating their own wind tunnels, which lifted and spread burning ash in a whimsical, arbitrary fashion.

Meanwhile, Marco Hellman had hurried downtown to check on the Union Trust Company, located in a building on Market Street at Montgomery. He stayed until he, too, was ordered by officials to evacuate. But Marco couldn't tear himself away from the conflagration. He walked down Market toward the burning Palace Hotel, where he encountered two friends, Walter Hobart and Charles Kendrick. "The three of us took off our coats and held them before our faces as a shield against the heat," Kendrick later accounted. "As we stood there, the Grand Hotel across from the Palace burst into flames from the intense heat; and lower Market Street . . . was now a veritable inferno. We were so intent in watching this terrible yet fascinating spectacle that not until he had gone by us and was turning into Market Street did we notice a drunken man leading a white fox terrier by a rope. We all shouted to him to turn back, but apparently the noise prevented his hearing, and he moved on. As he did so, the north side of Market Street exploded into flame, engulfing the poor fellow and his dog, and we three ran for our lives down Montgomery Street. As we did so clouds of black smoke billowed down upon us until it was as dark as midnight and we lost contact with one another."[2]

Isaias knew he had to get his family out of the city. The flames would not be stopped; it seemed they would burn until the city had burned, consume until nothing was left. Lipman had indicated he was going to take the ferry back to his family in Berkeley. Boats were still running and thousands of San Franciscans were vying to get out of the disaster zone. Isaias decided to escape to Marco's new summer home across the bay in Oakland, far from the flames.

Thousands of San Franciscans had the same idea—to flee to safety. They loaded their worldly possessions into trunks, which they then lugged out into the streets. Soon, the sound of trunks being pulled over cobblestones screeched through the air, creating an incessant backdrop that many would not soon forget. Huge crowds headed to Golden Gate Park and the Presidio or down burning Market Street to the Ferry Building, where they waited hours to board boats to cross the bay. Marco and his wife, Frances, lived in a rented house on Scott Street owned by William Herrin, the powerful attorney for the Southern Pacific Railroad. Their home was far from the flames, yet with three small children they knew everyone would feel safer across the bay.

Marco decided to drive around the southern part of the bay to his summer home in San Leandro, a trip that could take half a day. He loaded a pregnant Frances, who turned twenty-six that day, and their three children, Warren, six, Frederick, four, and five-month-old Florence, into his Mathewson automobile. The family's five servants followed in a carriage. Isaias and Esther followed in their new Peerless, driven by their chauffeur.

The trip was arduous. The Hellmans drove south on the peninsula, cut across the bottom of San Francisco Bay, and then headed north through Alviso and Milpitas and along the shore until arriving in Oakland.

The Hellmans' summer home was a welcome respite from the horrors of the day. Marco and Frances had bought the estate only a few months earlier from Edna Wallace Hopper, a well-known actress.

The house had a checkered history. It had been built by a Scottish coal baron, Alexander Dunsmuir, who had come to California in 1878 to oversee his family's coal and shipping interests. Dunsmuir soon fell in love with Josephine Wallace, the wife of a business associate. She divorced her husband for Dunsmuir, but the pair could not marry because Dunsmuir's mother threatened to disinherit him. After twenty years, Alexander and Josephine finally married, and Dunsmuir built the magnificent house for his bride in 1899. Unfortunately, he died on his honeymoon in January 1900 at the age of forty-six. Josephine returned to her house, but died a year and a half later of cancer.

Marco and Frances had rented the place for a few summers and loved it so much they bought it in January 1906 for $50,000, renaming it Oakvale for the ancient gnarled trees that dotted the hills behind the house. The 1899 Edwardian Colonial revival house, which resembled a white wedding cake, sat in a hidden valley created by the Hayward Fault. Three massive Corinthian pillars in front lent the house a regal look, and a broad double-deck porch that extended across the front of the house was a wonderful place to sit on a warm day.

The mansion was huge, with a Tiffany-style glass dome and thirty-seven rooms, which would prove advantageous in the days to come. Slowly but steadily, Hellman relatives found their way to Oakvale, retreating from the fire that raged in San Francisco. Marco's sisters, Clara and Florence, and their families ventured across the bay, as did Frances's siblings and cousins, the Jacobis and Brandensteins. The grown-ups held somber discussions, openly speculating about the fate of the city. The children ran around the estate, playing on the lawns, hiding among the fruit trees, and wandering down to the creek. The day seemed more like a holiday than a disaster to them.

"A whole bunch of relatives joined us; in fact, so many that there were not beds available for everybody and some of them slept on mattresses in the attic," Isaias's grandson Warren Hellman recalled many years later. "This was quite an event."[3]

There were no working phone lines or telegraph lines, and relatives in Los Angeles and New York were anxious to know how the Hellmans stood. "Wire me immediately—Is your family well and safe," wrote Isaias's youngest brother, James.[4] "Terrified by the news but hope you and all your dear ones are safe. We are anxiously awaiting news," wired Isaias's nephew, Arthur Lehman.[5]

The fires didn't rest. By the end of the evening of April 18, flames had demolished the South of Market area and had destroyed the city's main commercial district—including the Nevada Bank Building on Pine and Montgomery. It had scorched but not burned the Union Trust Building. Most every other city landmark became a hollow, smoldering shell. The magnificent Palace Hotel was gone, as was the Grand Hotel next door. The eighteen-story Call Building, the symbol of the modern San Francisco, home to the city's most prominent newspaper, was ruined. Temple Emanu-el, the Moorish-inspired synagogue on Sutter Street, was decimated. "City a Roaring Furnace," declared the headline in the *Berkeley Reporter*. "Fires Rage in Frisco and Entire City Seems Doomed," read the *Pittsburg Post*.

The U.S. mint stood at the intersection of Fifth and Mission streets, an imposing fortress of granite and sandstone constructed in 1874. The building held more than $200 million in coin and bullion and was the financial center of the West Coast. After the earthquake, rumors began to circulate that a gang planned to attack the building and make off with some of the money. The stories prompted Brigadier General Frederick Funston, who had illegally used the army to take control of the city, to send troops to guard the building.

In the late afternoon of April 18, the fire's ceaseless march brought it close to the mint. Army officials knew that if the building burned, the flames would take the region's financial backbone with it. The resurgence of San Francisco depended on saving the coins stored in the building's thick steel vaults.

Ten soldiers and a handful of mint employees were the only ones available to fight the flames. They closed and bolted shut the building's dense iron shutters. They went up to the roof, used picks and bars to strip off the tar surface, and then painted the beams with blue vitriol to ward away the flames. One mint employee was able to repair the building's broken pump, which meant there would be water from the building's underground well to fight the flames. This small band of men got ready to beat back the fire.

Isaias's house on Franklin Street in the western part of the city survived the first day and night. It sat empty, its plaster walls cracked and destroyed, its ornate mahogany walls still gleaming when hit by the sun. But Thursday morning, April 19, the flames raced down over Nob Hill, eating up the magnificent mansions of the men who had brought the railroad to California. Charles Crocker's home crumbled. Mark Hopkins's house, then an art institute, vanished in the flames, but not before volunteers had carried out many of the institute's paintings, statues, and bronzes. Unfortunately, they brought the art across the street into the new, still unopened Fairmont Hotel, which was supposedly fireproof, a fallacy put to rest when the white edifice on top of California Street burned through.

By Thursday night the fire had reached Van Ness Avenue, the major north-south thoroughfare that was home to many of the city's most elaborate mansions. It licked the wooden frame of D. N. Walter's house. It ruined the internationally known house of Claus Spreckels, the sugar king. Desperate to keep the flames from encroaching on the Western Addition, one of the few unscathed parts of the city, Army Colonel Charles Morris gave the order to dynamite the houses one block west, on Franklin Street, the street where Isaias had his home. "Having crossed the broad avenue of Van Ness, which had been selected as the last stand by the fire department, the fire began to eat its way on several blocks west of Van Ness Avenue," Captain Le Vert Coleman recalled later. "Resuming operations on the east side of Franklin Street, we demolished all the buildings on that side of Franklin between Clay and Sutter. . . . There was no order to our dynamiting. Instead, we blew up structures in which the existing conditions of wind and the encroachment of the fire demanded as most urgent."[6]

One by one, the houses of Isaias's across-the-street neighbors blew up, sending their percussive waves throughout the neighborhood. The house of liquor magnate A. P. Hotaling was destroyed; his downtown business and its enormous thirty-thousand-gallon storage room would survive. J. F. S. Brugiere's house was soon dust, as was Job Gunn's.

By Friday, the fire was out. Isaias's house, once in the middle of a bustling, wealthy residential district, now stood on the edge of the inhabited city. Seventy feet away, across the street, devastation began. While Isaias once looked out from his front door at houses, he now had a commanding vista. Not a house stood between his and Nob Hill, and all he saw was scorched earth, twisted metal, and smoking ruins.

"The conflagration was stopped, it would seem almost providentially, directly opposite our residence," Isaias wrote to Esther's brother, Benjamin.

In the days after the disaster, there was nowhere to buy food. Any store that had survived the earthquake and fire was commandeered by the army. The mayor had banned cooking food inside for fear cracked chimneys could set off even more fires. A few bakeries remained in business, and they cooked around the clock, distributing thousands of loaves to parks and open spaces around the city. Hungry survivors lined up for food, waiting in line for hours at a time. On Saturday, after venturing from Oakvale back into the city, Isaias went to eat. Like everyone else, he stood in a food line and waited for his ration. His appearance caused a stir and made the papers as far away as New York.

"Standing in any of the many breadlines one may see curious and diversified humanity in all its forms," reported one paper. "One man, richly dressed, stood in his place, supporting himself with his gold-headed cane, shifting his weight from one foot to the other, as he waited his turn to receive food for his family. When he reached the head of the line and the soldier ordered him roughly to take his two loaves of bread, the old gentleman, with a smile of satisfaction, took his two loaves under his arm and stepped contentedly along the street toward his ruined home. He was I. W. Hellman, President of more banks and trusts corporations than any other one man on the Pacific Coast. He laughed as he said that to receive those two loaves of bread gave him more satisfaction than to sell a whole city street railroad."[7]

From the start, Isaias sensed that a bank run, rather than natural disaster, would be the bigger calamity. He had weathered many financial storms, including panics in 1875 and 1893, and he knew that conveying a sense of confidence was critical. He demonstrated this presence of mind in a letter to Jackson Graves, the man in charge of his Farmers and Merchants Bank in Los Angeles. "My dear Mr. Graves, San Francisco is in ashes—every building of consequence is demolished," Isaias wrote on April 19, 1906. "The Bank's vaults have not yet been opened, but I think the valuables are intact. The Wells Fargo Nevada & Union Trust Company have in New York over twenty Million dollars. I am stopping in San Leandro but will return to San Francisco tomorrow & the Bankers will then have to provide means, etc, etc. Our Banks are solid and I fear no inconvenience. Kind regards to all the officers & employees of our Bank—I hope none of them will ever pass through such a terrible time as we have had here."

On April 20, Isaias stood by the smoking wreckage that had once been the Nevada Bank. Two days earlier it had been a four-story granite building with arched windows, a metal roof railing, and domed dormers. Millions of dollars had flowed through the structure, money that had helped build San Francisco. Now dynamite and fire had reduced the Nevada Bank to rubble; only one side of the facade still stood.

Almost every other financial institution had also been destroyed. The Anglo-California Bank, run by Isaias's neighbor Phil Lilienthal, was a total loss. The Canadian Bank of Commerce just a few blocks away, was a heap of smoldering ruins. The Bank of California was also gone.

But one of Isaias's other banks, the Union Trust Company, still stood, giving Isaias hope that business could soon resume. The building on the corner of Montgomery and Market had been scorched by flames but was essentially unharmed, saved by its fireproof construction. The Hibernia Bank was also standing.

Most important, the vaults of Wells Fargo appeared intact. Underneath the ruins, encased in layers of brick and steel, sat the bank's books and $3 million.

"We are happy to say that the vaults of the Banks have withstood the flames and appear to be in perfect condition," Isaias wrote the corresponding banks of the Wells Fargo Nevada on Saturday, April 21, 1906. "This is particularly true of our own vaults, built originally of extra fireproof construction, the doors having been found to be entirely undisturbed and not a brick of the outer covering having been displaced."

The vaults couldn't be opened right away. They had to cool off completely. Otherwise, when the doors were opened, the rush of oxygen would ignite the hot and smoldering contents. After the Baltimore fire of 1904, some banks there had made the mistake of opening their safes too early, and many lost all their records and large amounts of cash. Isaias knew that it might be three weeks to a month before the bank could open its safe. He hired watchmen from the Harry N. Morse Detective Agency to patrol the smouldering debris twenty-four hours a day.

The downtown financial district was ruined, but business had to continue. The residents of San Francisco had fled their homes on Wednesday, saving only what they could carry. Most people had very little cash and few ways to obtain any more. The post office had announced it would redeem postal money orders sent from the East, but only for a small amount of money. Depositors were clamoring for funds. Isaias himself had fled without much money, and had some only because his younger brother James had traveled from Los Angeles after the earthquake to bring him $3,000.

Later that day Isaias, his son, Marco, Frederick Lipman, and others gathered at 2020 Jackson Street, the home of Isaias's daughter Clara and son-in-law Emanuel Heller. The house in the Western Addition had been a gift from Isaias in 1902, and its circular wooden staircase and commanding views of Alcatraz and San Francisco Bay made it a pleasant home. It would now serve as the temporary headquarters of the Wells Fargo Nevada National Bank, the Union Trust Company, and Heller and Powers, the law firm run by Heller.

But how to reopen a bank without supplies? Without records? Names of depositors? Money to hand out? The men who gathered in the house that day knew they had to get money circulating in the city, only they weren't sure how to do that.

There was no paper on which to record transactions, so a runner was sent out to a nearby stationery store for supplies. He returned with a bunch of children's composition books and set them up on a large mahogany table in the dining room. The bankers hung cotton banners on the three street-facing windows on the first floor. "Temporary Headquarters of the Wells Fargo Nevada Bank," read one banner. The others announced that the house now served as the offices of the Union Trust Company and Heller and Powers Law Offices. The Wells Fargo Nevada National Bank resumed business.

Other banks were opening wherever they could. The Anglo-California Bank opened two doors away from Isaias's Franklin Street house in Phil Lilienthal's home. There was a "Banker's Row," on Laguna Street across from Lafayette Park, where three financial institutions—the Crocker-Woolworth Bank, the Central Trust Company, and the Mercantile Trust Company—set up their headquarters.

A. P. Giannini was the first banker to hand out cash, not checks or drafts, to his customers. On Sunday, April 22, just four days after the earthquake, he returned to San Francisco with $10,000. He set up a small stand by the city's waterfront, not far from the destroyed homes of his Italian patrons, and immediately began loaning money. His gesture won him respect and admiration from many working-class families, attributes that later helped him launch the biggest bank in the world.

T he world stood poised to help San Francisco. There was nothing like disaster to bring out the best in human nature. After the devastating Chicago fire of 1871, citizens from around the country sent their carefully saved pennies and dollars, so many, in fact, that the city collected millions in relief funds.

That same instinct was stirred when news of the great earthquake and fire reached the rest of the world. The news traveled fast as brave telegraph operators stayed at their posts on April 18, sending out updates on the disaster.

Businessmen around the country wanted to help, and when they thought of whom to enlist one man came to their minds: Isaias W. Hellman. Telegrams began to pour in, offering relief, and directing Hellman to funds. "The Times fund for relief will approximate $50,000," wrote Harrison Gray Otis, the publisher of the *Los Angeles Times*, on April 20, 1906. "Shall I send it or half of it to you or use the whole here in purchase of supplies for the sufferers. Answer if possible."[8]

"My firm's services and my own entirely at your disposal for yourself or your Bank. Wire us if you can we are anxiously awaiting news," Arthur Lehman telegraphed from New York City.[9]

The governor of Massachusetts sent $100,000 and a shipment of provisions. Harriman enlisted the resources of the Southern Pacific to hurry food and blankets to the stricken city.

Men around the country communicated with Isaias because the San Francisco city government did not function in the hours and days after the earthquake. Instead, Mayor Eugene Schmitz appointed the "Committee of 50," an extralegal group of prominent citizens, to direct police, relief, and cleanup operations. Both Hellmans worked in this group: Isaias was appointed initially but gave up his post to Marco. The committee members included most of the powerful men of the city, including former mayor James Duval Phelan; Southen Pacific owner E. H. Harriman; the company's attorney, William Herrin; Michael de Young, the publisher of the *Chronicle;* and others. Few members of the committee had been elected to public office, and their command of power was controversial.

Phelan eventually emerged as the chair of the Finance Committee, a powerful subcommittee of the group with the authority to disperse the many millions of dollars that had been donated. There had been a brief, unsuccessful attempt by Harriman to wrest control from Phelan and give it to Isaias, which created bad feelings between the men.[10] Soon, Phelan started sending letters to Isaias asking him how he had disposed of relief funds donated by the *Los Angeles Times* and other groups. The disdain with which Phelan treated Isaias would soon lead to an intense rivalry.

D espite the difficulties, San Franciscans were in a generous mood. The disaster had brought them together, erased class boundaries (but not racial ones), and produced a sense of camaraderie that helped the homeless weather their misery more easily.

From the start, Isaias and Marco and other businessmen put an optimistic spin on the city's future. If they wanted investment in San Francisco to resume, they recognized, they had to talk about the glorious future of the city rather than act like victims. They downplayed talk of the number of people who died in the disaster in favor of more optimistic messages. "These ruins will be the site of a new city, one which will rival Paris in beauty," Marco Hellman told the newspapers on April 20. "The banks will weather the storm and before many weeks the city will throb with life and activity which it never knew before."

On Monday morning, April 23, five days after the earthquake, representatives from the city's largest, most established banks met in the living room of the house of Mrs. Eleanor Martin, the long-reigning queen of San Francisco society, on the corner of Buchanan Street and Broadway. The bankers were also members of the San Francisco Clearing House, an organization formed in 1874 to streamline cash transfers between banks.

From the start the bankers were anxious to prevent panic among San Francisco's terrorized citizens and they knew the best way to do this was to coordinate their actions. They uniformly conveyed a sense of calm by first announcing to the newspapers that careful examinations of the banks' vaults indicated that the contents were intact, which meant there were records of accounts. They also sought to deflect any rising sense of alarm caused by spiraling prices in a city where people had no money, and little chance of getting any. The members of the clearinghouse voted that morning to ask Governor George Pardee to declare a bank holiday for the next thirty days, which would mean that no one was obligated to pay rent, bills, promissory notes, mortgages, or anything else that relied on the exchange of money.

The U.S. mint had survived the fire intact, and most of the city's banks had ample reserves stored inside. The Wells Fargo Nevada had $9 million in coin in the mint, which meant the bank was in a strong position to give its depositors their funds as well as to make loans for rebuilding.

The whole system could collapse, however, if worried depositors started taking their funds out of a bank, causing a run that could spread to other institutions. Members of the clearinghouse decided to avoid this by acting in concert with one another. They would all open simultaneously, and preclude any panic.

In the interim, the clearinghouse set up an arrangement with the mint that let depositors draw out $500 from their accounts. A customer would go to the temporary headquarters of his or her bank, get a check, and then take it to the mint to be cashed.

On May 1, the unorthodox banking arrangement began. Long lines of penniless depositors lined up to get cash, forming a queue down the front steps of the mint, along Fifth, stretching quite a distance on Mission Street.

As president of one of the largest banks on the Pacific Coast, Isaias knew it was important to convey confidence in the city's regrowth. He was determined to bring San Francisco back to its former glory and pledged publicly to use his bank's funds for the rebuilding effort. "In the same way Mr. Hearst will use every effort for the rebuilding of San Francisco, let the whole world know what I intend doing," Isaias told the newspapers on May 4. "It will only take ⅓ of the Hellman resources to pay off the depositors of the Wells Fargo Nevada National Bank and the Union Trust Company. The Hellman surplus will be $30,000,000. Every dollar of this will be used for the rebuilding of San Francisco. It will be for the use of men of commerce in San Francisco, for loans on the reconstruction of buildings and in any way that San Francisco can be benefited."[11]

By May 9, the newspapers were projecting a rosy future. "That the financial situation in San Francisco is rapidly resuming its normal condition and that the banks will soon open as though nothing had happened is the opinion of those in close touch with money affairs," reported the *San Francisco Chronicle*.

Isaias agreed. "The financial situation is getting quieter and better everyday," he commented in a May 10 newspaper article. "The bankers are all anxious to resume and none more than I. . . . One of the encouraging features of the situation is that our deposits yesterday were ten times larger than the withdrawals."

By May 16, the vaults of the Wells Fargo Nevada National Bank had finally cooled off. Isaias had given the go-ahead to open the safes, but he took extra precautions to ensure that their contents did not burn when the doors swung open. He had requested that flame-retarding chemicals be brought to the ruins to dose any hint of fire.

A large contingent of armed men stood around the perimeter of the bank while Isaias and Frederick Lipman carefully made their way over scorched bricks and granite blocks to stand in front of the vaults. When the workmen pulled off the brick surround to reveal the safe's door, it was clear the fire had melted and distorted the frame. Had the fire gotten inside? Had the intense heat permeated? The workmen inserted a wedge along the crack of the door and began to pound it with a sledge, harder and harder, until the massive steel door finally swung open.

There was a heap of ashes at the bottom of the vault. One of the bank's massive Boston Ledgers had been entirely destroyed. But the fifteen others were mostly intact. The bottom sections had been scorched, but names and numbers were still visible, which meant that the bank had almost complete records. The city's other banks were able to rescue their records as well.

Five days later, Wells Fargo Nevada National was back in business. It had moved into the Union Trust Company Building, which had been scorched but not destroyed in the calamity. The Wells Fargo took the frontage on Market Street, and the Union Trust Company took the section that faced Montgomery.

The interior of the bank looked like it had during the gold rush. Unpainted planks had been laid down to form counters and desks. Smoke-stained and fire-scorched walls were hidden behind bolts of white cotton cloth. Despite the rough interior, Isaias was pleased. "The smile upon the countenance of the veteran financier was a sufficient guaranty of San Francisco's financial integrity," reported the *Chronicle*.

There was no panic, no rush to take out funds. In fact, San Francisco citizens ended up depositing more money than they withdrew. Banks from all over the country had sent funds, and in May and June 1906, San Francisco banks sent those moneys back. They had enough local funds to rebuild the city.

Isaias and Esther never moved back into their beloved house on Franklin Street. By May 6, they had rented it to the Union League Club for use as a gathering place, a retreat where dignified men could find a good meal, smoke a fine cigar in one of the wood-paneled rooms, and enjoy vibrant conversation. Esther and Isaias went to live with their daughter Clara on Jackson Street.

Even as Isaias was helping San Francisco rise from the ashes, he was having more troubles with his Los Angeles partner, Henry Huntington. While Isaias had sold out from the Pacific Electric in 1904, he and his syndicate had

held on to their shares of the Los Angeles Railway, the series of trolley lines
that ran throughout the city of Los Angeles. Since the population was denser,
there were more opportunities for profits—and the paying of dividends.

But with time, Isaias came to realize that Huntington would never change
his ways. He was a railroad man at heart, despite his vast riches, and would
always want to plow profits back into the tracks rather than pay them out as
dividends to investors.

Huntington expressed their differing approaches quite elegantly in a letter he sent Isaias shortly after the 1906 San Francisco earthquake. "Of course
there is always bound to be a difference of opinion between a banker and a
railroad manager as to the proper method of conducting the business of a
railroad; the former, by education and habit, looking naturally for dividends;
the latter, by *his* training and experience, being averse to the distribution of
money which he feels ought to go into the improvement of the property and
cannot be paid away in dividends without injury to the real value and standing of the property and serious check to its future development."[12]

In addition to his attitude toward spending, Huntington had begun to
encroach into an area Isaias considered his territory: banking. In 1905,
Huntington bought the Redondo Land and Beach Company, which owned
virtually the entire town of Redondo along the Pacific Ocean. While Redondo had never been a popular place to live, Huntington's purchase suddenly made the area desirable. Hundreds of people clamored to buy the
lots, and Huntington was all too happy to sell to them—and offer a loan
through a bank that he controlled. This irritated Isaias because it directly
competed with one of his banks, the Farmers and Merchants Bank of Redondo Beach.

Isaias, Borel, and de Guigne decided for the second time they wanted out.
Isaias approached Huntington and offered to sell the syndicate's shares.
Huntington turned him down. Isaias then turned to his other business partner, Harriman, who all too eagerly bought the stock for $4.75 million.[13] The
purchase meant Harriman controlled the Southern Pacific, half of the Pacific
Electric, and 45 percent of the LARY, making him the most powerful force in
the Los Angeles transportation industry.

When Huntington heard about the sale, he became furious. He once again
had started to regard Harriman as his enemy. The truce the two men had established three years earlier had dissolved, scuttled by Harriman's purchase

of the Los Angeles Pacific Railway, a 108-mile line that included routes through Hollywood and Santa Monica. That acquisition had been a public declaration that Harriman still wanted to dominate the region, prompting the newspapers to fill their columns with reports about the battle between two transportation titans. Isaias's syndicate's sale of its LARY stock fit right into Harriman's plans.[14]

Huntington regarded the sale as a betrayal and he never forgave Isaias. While Huntington stayed on the board of the Farmers and Merchants Bank for two more years, men in his employ spread tales about how Isaias had sold out Huntington, rumors that eventually made their way back to the aging banker. "Mr. Huntington, ever since [you] voted your stock with the Harriman people, has not only to me, but everywhere expressed intense bitterness toward yourself," Jackson Graves wrote Isaias.[15]

The break with Huntington was the fourth time Isaias ruptured relations with men with whom he had once been close. Each time—with Temple and Workman, with Downey, with his brother Herman, and now with Huntington—Isaias had forged a close business bond only to later feel he had surpassed his partners. Yet each time he blamed the other man, as he did now with Huntington. "I have never in my life done Mr. Huntington an injustice, simply having protected my own interests," he wrote to Graves. "If he wishes to break off business connections with me, well and good, but I would not want to be the mover nor give him the reason for doing so. I am satisfied that he will in time regret it."[16]

Years later, Isaias and Huntington met in front of Graves at the Farmers and Merchants Bank. Isaias complained about the slanderous comments Huntington's friends were making, and Huntington denied all knowledge of the disparaging remarks. Isaias asked his former partner whether he wanted "war or peace." Huntington stuck out his hand and said, "Peace." That was the last substantial contact between the two men. By 1912, Huntington no longer had any significant funds at the bank.

The earthquake was not the only calamity in 1906.

A few years after leaving the Farmers and Merchants Bank, Herman was once again at the top of the Los Angeles banking world, serving as president of one bank and director of twelve others. His sons, Marco H. and

Irving, also joined him in the business, and a new branch of the legendary Hellman bankers was born.

Herman and Isaias were not speaking, but Isaias's anger seemed to be softening. "I can only say that I pity H. W. . . . because of his disappointment, envy, and jealousy and no matter how much he speaks of revenge, I for my part, only have pity for him, and should he ever be in trouble you may rest assured that I shall not let him suffer," he wrote Graves. "That is the revenge I shall have and the feeling which I carry in my bosom toward him."[17]

Herman had grown increasingly weak during the previous few years. His physical decline began in 1895, when he had an operation for a festering sore on his foot—an indication of diabetes. Both he and his wife, Ida, were very heavy, and his weight aggravated his condition. In mid-October 1906, after a short visit to San Francisco during which he pointedly did not visit his brother, Herman took to his bed. He had not seen a doctor in more than a year, and the sugar level in his blood had risen to dangerous levels.

Herman's family determined that the stress caused by the rift with Isaias was making matters worse. His sons approached James Hellman, the youngest Hellman brother, to broker a reconciliation. "I met Dr. Kurtz and this is what he said," James wrote to Isaias in San Francisco on October 13, 1906. "Your brother Herman is in a serious condition, but there is no immediate danger. If he will follow my instructions he will be a well man but what would help him above all would be a reconciliation with the brother, I.W. . . . Mrs. H. W. and all the children including Marco are very much pleased over the probable outcome of having a family reunion."[18]

Before Isaias could respond, Herman's diabetes worsened, and four days later he fell into a diabetic coma. He lay in his bedroom, barely alive, surrounded by close friends and family. "Was to see Uncle Herman last evening and much to my regret, have to inform you, that uncle is a very sick man indeed," Adolph Fleishman wrote to Isaias. "He laid [sic] there almost lifeless and could not talk a word to me."[19]

As hope for his recovery vanished, family members hurried to bring the two feuding brothers together. It had been more than three years since they had last spoken. On the morning of October 18, 1906, Herman's family sent a telegram to Isaias at his office at the Wells Fargo National Nevada Bank: "Herman Desperately ill very little hope. Ida and children."[20]

Isaias, stuck four hundred miles away from his dying brother, wasn't sure what to think, what to do. Should he go to Los Angeles? Would he be welcomed? Shunned? He asked his son-in-law Emanuel Heller to intervene. Heller sent a telegram to James Hellman looking for advice. "Does Uncle Herman or Aunt Ida desire brother Isaias to come to Los Angeles? If either of them do, he leaves here tonight. Wire Answer."[21]

By 1:41 P.M. Isaias had his answer: "Father in critical condition. Can not be seen but entire family desire you to come down. Marco."[22]

After the last telegram, Isaias set aside any of the misgivings he might have felt about Herman to hurry to his bedside. While their feud had kept them apart for three years and driven a painful wedge in the family, Isaias still loved his younger brother. They had shared so much together—life in Reckendorf, immigration, the rigors of the frontier, business ups and downs, and the joys and sorrow of family life. They were both obstinate men, but Isaias finally understood that their mutual silence would soon extract a high price.

Isaias left the bank, rushed home to pack, and then took the ferry to Oakland to catch the Southern Pacific's Owl service to Los Angeles. It was one of the Southern Pacific's sleekest trains, with elaborate sleeping compartments and well-stocked dining cars and it covered the four hundred miles to Los Angeles in fifteen hours, traveling a little faster than thirty-three miles an hour. The Owl left Oakland in late afternoon, ran all night, and arrived into Los Angeles in the morning.

But Isaias was too late. Herman died at 1:45 A.M. The train pulled into the depot at Los Angeles six hours later.

The funeral was one of the biggest ever held in Los Angeles. More than one thousand people came to pay their respects to Herman, considered one of Los Angeles's pioneers and a link to a bygone era. Only three hundred people could squeeze into Herman's home on Hill Street, so the rest gathered outside, on the lawn and sidewalk, waiting their turn to view the body.

Herman lay in a casket in the front drawing room. Curtains hung over the windows, and long tapers cast a soft light. More than two hundred floral arrangements filled the house, including a casket piece of white lilies of the valley and wild ferns sent by Isaias and his family.

"He will be missed and he will not be forgotten," solemnized Rabbi

Sigmund Hecht of Temple B'nai B'rith, where Herman had long served as president. Herman's family, including Isaias, clustered in the drawing room to hear the rabbi reflect on the rich life of one of Los Angeles's pioneers. Hours later, Herman's casket was lowered into the earth in the new Jewish cemetery in Boyle Heights, near the graves of his dead children, Clothilde and Waldo. It was the closest Isaias had gotten to his brother since their fight.

SIXTEEN

GRAFT AND CASH

1907–1910

Harry Spoenemann steered the streetcar gingerly out of the Thirty-second Avenue barn, way on the western edge of San Francisco, looking to make sure there was no traffic in front of him. Spoenemann did not have much experience driving trolleys—he'd been hired only a few days earlier—and he was nervous about making a mistake.

Four other streetcars followed car no. 1543 and they caravanned down California Street in a long green line, keeping close together for protection. Streetcars on that route normally stopped every few blocks to pick up passengers who made their homes among the rolling sand dunes of the outer Richmond district, but traffic was light that May day in 1907. Only two women boarded Spoenemann's car in the course of eighteen blocks.

Around Fourteenth Avenue, just as the car approached the massive earthquake refugee camp stretching out on both sides of the street, Spoenemann spotted something blocking the tracks ahead. It was a bonfire heaped with chunks of wood, old furniture, railroad ties, and piles of paper. Black smoke billowed into the air, a dark mark against the midmorning spring sky.

Spoenemann braked to avoid the fire, and as the car slowed, a swarm of women dressed in long dark skirts and white shirtwaists surrounded him, their faces contorted with anger. They heaved bricks and stones at the glass windows of the trolley, sending shattered glass flying. Some poured sand on the tracks while others stood defiantly in front of the streetcars. "Scabs, strikebreakers," yelled the mob, their fury directed at Spoenemann and the other drivers. Soon, all the windows on the five trolley cars were broken.

The women were among the seven thousand residents of Refugee Camp

no. 25, which sprawled along California Street. For more than a year, ever
since the great earthquake and fire destroyed their homes, the women had
been living with their families in canvas tents and hastily constructed wooden
shacks, some cooking three meals a day, rain or shine, on outdoor cooking
fires.

Now their fathers, husbands, and sons were on strike against the United
Railroads, the city's biggest streetcar company. For the past eight days, since
May 5, 1907, more than 1,500 drivers for the Street Carmen's Union had refused to go to work, pushing for an eight-hour day and a $3 daily salary. But
the streetcar company had turned down their demands and called in scabs
like Spoenemann to break the strike.

San Francisco, which just a year earlier had witnessed numerous acts of
kindness and generosity as an entire city coped with the losses from the
earthquake and fire, had become a city at war, a city divided between labor
and business. The streetcar strike was the most violent in the city's history.
Blood and death were daily occurrences as strikers confronted scabs in sudden, unexpected outbreaks, their battles barely mediated by the police. Just
days earlier, two strikers had been shot and killed and twenty others injured
when hired guards fired at a group of men heaving bricks at some streetcars.
The papers immediately called the day "Bloody Tuesday."

The company that vowed to break the strike, the United Railroads, was a
successor to the Market Street Cable Railway. Eastern capitalists led by
Patrick Calhoun had purchased the trolley company from the Southern Pacific Railroad in 1901 and had consolidated it with other small lines that traversed San Francisco. Isaias, a major stockholder and bond seller for the
Market Street line, sat on the board of directors of the new company.

Spoenemann's trip down California Street was a direct affront to the
strikers and their families, and when the women saw the green trolley cars
approaching, they rushed to stop them. "The sounds of breaking glass and
the cries of the attacking parties aroused the entire camp and in a few minutes
several hundred persons had gathered at the scene, all of them shouting defi-
ance to the non-union Car men and inviting them to leave their posts and cast
their lot with the union men," read the next day's report in the *San Francisco
Call*.

The police hurried to California Street, whipped out their batons, and
quickly dispersed the crowd. Soon wisps of smoke and the battered skeletons

of the four trolleys were the only evidence of the riot. As punishment, the police shut down the neighborhood bars.

As the angry women stoned the streetcar, Isaias was farther east on California Street, waiting in an office under the huge dome of Temple Sherith Israel. Ever since the earthquake and fire had destroyed city hall, the imposing Jewish temple on California and Webster streets in the Western Addition had served as the city's makeshift courthouse.

On an average day, the sacred temple with its famous carved mahogany walls teemed with San Francisco's underworld—pickpockets, murderers, thieves, prostitutes—all there to plead their cases before a judge. On that afternoon, though, another dark side of San Francisco was on display, a side some argued was more corrosive than any collection of petty criminals.

Scores of spectators had come to watch the beginning of the graft trial of Abraham Ruef, the city's political boss who could—for a price—guarantee entry into city hall. For six years, Ruef, a short French Jew whose bowler hat and handlebar mustache were well known throughout San Francisco, had been the power behind San Francisco's mayor, Eugene Schmitz. If anyone wanted to do business with the city, he came to Ruef and "hired" him as his attorney. Money paid to Ruef then made its way into the pockets of Schmitz and members of the board of supervisors.

Isaias had been called down to the courthouse to testify before a grand jury looking into a $200,000 payment that the United Railroads had made to Ruef right after the San Francisco Board of Supervisors approved a controversial contract. The grand jury wanted to know if the money was a bribe, and whether Isaias and other directors of the trolley company authorized the payment. "Millions on the Stand," read the headline in the *Call* the next day. "Rich men testify before grand jury recall trolley deal."

As Isaias settled on the witness stand, dressed in his ubiquitous black vest and suit, he regarded the United Railroads a minor interest, little realizing that the graft prosecution and ensuing political battles would consume much of his attention for the next few years. Isaias owned just a small portion of the streetcar line, his bank handled less than $100,000 of the company's bonds, and he considered the company an insignificant client. As Isaias answered the grand jury's questions, he had no idea he would come to represent what many people saw as the enemy—a rich man who put his business interests before the interests of the city. But Isaias would soon be sucked into the graft scandal and see his family name smeared in the newspapers.

Petty graft had always been the cost of doing business in early-twentieth-century San Francisco and other cities around the country. A few bills here, a few there, would encourage the police department to renew a bar's liquor license or to overlook minor infractions.

But Abe Ruef and Eugene Schmitz took the practice of graft to such extremes in early 1906 that a group of irate and influential reformers set out to dismantle their illegal operations. The result was a series of highly dramatic trials that consumed the city and put San Francisco's dirty politics on view for the entire nation to see. And who could help but be captivated? During the course of numerous trials over three years the prosecutor was shot in the head in court; the police chief drowned under questionable circumstances; the house of a key witness was bombed; the editor of a crusading newspaper was kidnapped; the main defendant disappeared for an extended period; and the grandson of an American vice president became known for offering bribes. All this took place against the backdrop of a city that had been devastated by the earthquake and fire and torn asunder by labor problems.

In the end, sheer exhaustion eroded the city's will to go after the powerful businessmen who bribed Ruef and Schmitz. Ruef was the only one who went to jail, and he served just four years in San Quentin. The trials, however, helped start a reform movement that captured the state government in 1910.

At first Ruef's graft was rather minor. He had helped elect Schmitz in 1901 on the Union Labor ticket, the first time a mayor friendly to the working classes had ever captured the office. Schmitz soon appointed his cronies to the police and public works commissions, and he and Ruef started the first in a series of extortion rackets.

San Francisco still retained a flavor of the freewheeling days of the gold rush, most notably in its so-called French restaurants. Places like the Poodle

Dog on Mason near Eddy looked like respectable establishments. There were elegant, moderately priced restaurants on the bottom floors where gentlemen often brought their families to dine on some of the best food in the city. The second floors held private dining rooms elegantly furnished with couches and lounge chairs. Up higher, there were private supper rooms catering to the gentlemen interested in renting rooms by the hour. The French restaurants were such a San Francisco institution that there was no shame in being connected with them. In fact, they were somewhat of a tourist attraction. For example, the Union Trust Company, one of Isaias's banks, held the lease for one of the establishments.

These restaurants had to renew their liquor leases each quarter, a routine matter under previous mayors. After Schmitz's election, however, some of the dozen French restaurants found that their licenses were revoked. How could the restaurants get the licenses restored? By hiring Ruef, of course, to represent their interests before the police commission. Ruef soon found his legal advice was needed for many similar services. For example, he arranged for the Board of Public Works to look the other way when a group of businessmen tore down an old opium den in Chinatown and replaced it with an "apartment house," which was really a brothel.

In the fall of 1905, the Union Labor Party swept the city's elections, and for the first time Ruef totally controlled the votes on the board of supervisors. This meant that Ruef and Schmitz could milk companies that wanted lucrative city franchises. Virtually all privately held municipal utilities, including water, gas, and transportation companies, needed to get approval from the supervisors to make improvements or raise their rates.

When the companies figured out the game, they came to the table. And paid. The Parkside Realty Company, for example, wanted to build houses on four hundred acres of sand dunes in the western part of the city. The area was so remote, however, that the project would succeed only if the company could run a trolley line into the center of town. Parkside needed the approval of the supervisors for the franchise. The supervisors balked until the company hired Ruef as its attorney at a fee of $30,000 for two years. Ruef later paid Schmitz and the supervisors their "fair share."

When the Pacific Telephone and Telegraph Company saw the efficacy of using Ruef, it hired him as its consultant for $50,000. The company wanted to make sure that no rivals ever got a contract. The gas company hired Ruef and saw the rates it paid for gas decrease. And the United Railroads paid $200,000 for approval for an overhead trolley line.

When Patrick Calhoun, the grandson of the great southern orator and former Vice President John Calhoun, bought the Market Street Cable Railway in 1901, he had grandiose plans to build on Henry Huntington's vision of creating a modern streetcar company from a mishmash of cable cars and streetcars. Calhoun, who had grown up in Atlanta but later moved to New York, had already enjoyed success in that field. He had earned a fortune helping J. P. Morgan consolidate the Southern Railway and had successfully modernized the streetcar systems in Pittsburgh, Baltimore, and St. Louis. Calhoun, a tall and portly man with impeccable southern manners, now set his sights on the Market Street Cable Railway, which he and a syndicate bought for an astronomical $39 million. "It was almost universal gossip that the owners of the previous street railway companies, notably Henry H. Huntington, had forced the eastern capitalists to pay an exorbitant price," wrote historian Walton Bean.[1] Calhoun paid a premium because he was confident the population of San Francisco would grow and make the rail system even more valuable. He further leveraged the company by selling bonds, bringing its capitalization to $75 million.

The streetcar lines in the city were propelled by a number of different technologies, including Andrew Hallidie's cables, which quickly grew to be a symbol of hilly San Francisco. Calhoun wanted his trolleys to run on electricity, which was cheaper and more reliable. He proposed to string overhead electric wires along some of the busiest routes and needed permission for the change from the board of supervisors.

The Sutter Street line was one of the routes Calhoun wanted to upgrade, but his plan quickly ran into opposition. Two of the city's most powerful men, former mayor James Duval Phelan and capitalist Rudolph Spreckels (estranged son of sugar magnate Claus Spreckels), owned property along the route. Spreckels was particularly adamant that he didn't want any unsightly wires hanging in front of his home on Pacific Avenue. He suggested that the United Railroads run the electricity in underground conduits. The railway refused, saying the underground lines were costly and difficult to maintain.

When the United Railroads formed, it had immediately hired Ruef as its attorney on a $500 monthly retainer. This may have been Isaias's suggestion. "Mr. Helland, who was then the President of United Railroads, came to me to ask my advice whether Mr. Ruef should be employed as an attorney for the United Railroads, stating that by employing him peace could be secured with the Labor Unions, that he had great influence with them and there would be general peace and it was to the benefit of the railway company to have such peace," Isaias testified in one of the trials in 1907. "Mr. Ruef was then an attorney of high repute, recognized as a good lawyer, and I said if that could be accomplished it would be for the benefit of the railway company as well as for the public, and I advised yes."[2]

The United Railroads had little success getting its proposal for overhead trolley lines passed until 1906, when Ruef and Schmitz gained control of the board of supervisors. The application had been turned down in December 1905 by the old board. On May 6, 1906, eighteen days after the earthquake, Ruef left his office in the morning and had his chauffeur drive him in his distinctive green car to Fillmore and Pine streets. Ruef got out and entered a haberdashery, where he picked up an empty cardboard shirt box. His chauffeur then drove him to the headquarters of the United Railroads on Oak and Broderick streets.

When Ruef came out of the building an hour later, the cardboard box was bulging with cash, money that Ruef doled out to the mayor and the board of supervisors. Fifteen days later at an unpublicized meeting, the board of supervisors approved the overhead trolley franchise.

There were people watching Ruef and Schmitz's machinations, and they didn't approve or consider it business as usual. Fremont Older, the six-feet two-inch editor of one of San Francisco's evening papers, the *Bulletin*, had outrage in his soul. Newspapers at the turn of the century were filled with hyperbole and bombast, and the *Bulletin* was no exception. Sensational stories on murder, extramarital affairs, and any dark doings of the well-to-do filled its front pages. The *Bulletin* was also slightly corrupt. The Southern Pacific Railroad paid it $175 a month—later raised to $375—to be friendly to the railroad.

The *Bulletin*'s owner, R. A. Crothers, had appointed Older editor in 1895 with a mandate to increase circulation. The paper had been a big booster of former mayor Phelan, and had supported his successful mission to create a new city charter and his unsuccessful push for municipal control of utilities. As soon as Schmitz took office in 1901, Older's paper began to publish tirades against the new administration. Many of the accusations were guesses that turned out to be right, although the facts about bribery and extortion wouldn't be revealed for many more years. For the next five years, Older published article after article accusing the Schmitz administration of corruption.

In 1904, San Francisco native Lincoln Steffens published his *Shame of the Cities,* an exposé of municipal corruption. Steffens argued that corrupt politicians were less culpable than the rich businessmen who bribed them. The system of graft would never be shattered until the law snagged the men at the top. Despite Older's continual campaign against Ruef and Schmitz, most San Franciscans seemed content enough to reelect Schmitz in the fall of November 1905.

The election so demoralized Older that he vowed to take stronger action to rid San Francisco of Schmitz. Older approached the San Francisco district attorney, William Langdon, about prosecuting Ruef and Schmitz, but Langdon confessed he did not have enough men or money to pursue the case. In December 1905, Older traveled to Washington, D.C., where he met with Francis Heney, a San Francisco lawyer who had recently become well known for his successful prosecution of a land fraud scheme involving an Oregon senator. Older told Heney about the state of government in San Francisco, and the prosecutor expressed interest in rooting out the corruption, with certain conditions. Heney wanted to conduct the investigation under the auspices of the city's district attorney's office, and he wanted to hire Detective William Burns to assist him. Heney also needed at least $100,000 for the investigation.

The next day Older had an audience with President Theodore Roosevelt, who as a former New York police commissioner had investigated numerous illegal payoff schemes. Roosevelt listened sympathetically to Older and pledged the use of Heney and Burns as soon as they finished up the Oregon case.

Older returned to San Francisco determined to find the money to fund the investigation. He went to see Rudolph Spreckels, the president of the First National Bank. Although Spreckels came from an enormously rich family and had his own millions, he was an iconoclast, someone comfortable with breaking societal molds.

Spreckels was already familiar with Ruef's extortion tactics, and he readily agreed to raise $100,000 to fund the prosecution. Spreckels's dislike for Ruef began in 1904, when the attorney came to see him concerning a bond issue proposed by the city of San Francisco. For a variety of reasons, the banks and financiers of the country were not interested in buying the bonds, and a failure would look bad for the Schmitz administration. Ruef wanted Spreckels to bid on the bonds, and he guaranteed they would sell at a low price. When Spreckels asked how Ruef could make sure the bonds would sell below par, Ruef said he would foment a rail strike right before the bonds went on sale, thus ensuring an indifferent market. Spreckels was so taken aback by this proposition that he assumed Ruef was joking. When Ruef saw that his proposal was not well received, he changed tactics and told Spreckels that of course it was all a joke.

Former mayor Phelan also joined the "reformers," the name the group used to describe its efforts. While these men were sincerely horrified that the city government was for sale, there were also other motives to their zeal. Both Spreckels and Phelan didn't want the United Railroads to string electric trolley wire in front of their properties. Spreckels, in fact, started a rival streetcar company called the Municipal Railway Line. He planned to run its trolley on underground conduits and he wanted to thwart any of the advantages held by United Railroads.

Phelan and Spreckels also associated Ruef with the Southern Pacific political machine, which took every opportunity to meddle in politics. Ruef had worked so hard to elect some candidates friendly to the Southern Pacific in the 1906 primary that William Herrin, the political boss, paid him $14,000. Phelan had frequently spoken out against the railroad and those associated with it, and that included the Hellmans. He was also critical of the Spring Valley Water Company, with which Herrin and the Hellmans were closely associated. To Phelan, those men represented an old way of doing business, which put the interests of private corporations before those of the taxpayers.

The graft trials that consumed San Francisco for the next three years would have been farcical if so much had not been at stake. The prosecution gained the early advantage when it got almost the entire board of supervisors to agree to testify against Ruef and Schmitz in exchange for immunity. Their testimony led to indictments against Ruef and Schmitz and corporate executives of the Pacific Telephone and Telegraph Company. Ruef then agreed to turn state's witness, and in June 1907 the mayor was convicted and sentenced to five years in San Quentin Prison. (His conviction would later be overturned.)

But the prosecution unraveled there. When it became clear that Francis Heney intended to use Ruef to testify against the business elite, including Calhoun, public support for the prosecution plummeted. Many San Franciscans had approved of the way Calhoun had treated the striking car men in 1907; they saw his firm stance as an important bulwark against the socialistic tendencies of the unions. "Patrick Calhoun has rendered a very great service to San Francisco in this fight that he has made against the strikers, and I can state that in my opinion public sentiment of the community generally is strongly behind Mr. Calhoun," Isaias told the *Los Angeles Times*.[3]

Soon, weariness set in. Tirey L. Ford, the counsel of the United Railroads and the man who supposedly gave money directly to Ruef, was tried three times. The first jury could not agree on his guilt or innocence after thirty ballots; the second could not agree after six ballots; and in the third trial, it took the jury seven minutes to acquit Ford. Part of the problem came when Ruef testified that Ford was only paying him attorney's fees and had no knowledge that the money became bribes for the supervisors.

In the middle of the trial Fremont Older was kidnapped by one of the United Railroad's detectives who felt he had been libeled in the newspaper. Older was hustled on a train bound for Los Angeles, but was rescued in Santa Barbara.

Events grew even more bizarre, and then deadly. A bomb destroyed the house of the main witness, former supervisor James Gallagher, who had acted as the liaison between Ruef and the supervisors. Three other buildings Gallagher and a partner had built were also blown up. Schmitz's conviction was thrown out twice by higher courts. (He had lost his position as mayor but would go on to serve two terms as a supervisor.)

Heney and his prosecutorial team did not give up. In the summer of 1908, they brought Ruef to trial for bribing a supervisor for the trolley franchise. By that time, San Francisco had solidified into two camps: those in favor of the prosecution and those opposed. Each side was so determined to win that it went to extraordinary lengths to stack the juries. Burns sent out a corps of detectives to look into the backgrounds of all the potential jurors. Burns's men posed as members of an antiprosecution group and went to the jurors' houses and asked them to sign a petition against the graft trials. If the jurors signed, Heney knew ahead of time not to accept them for the trial. This meant it took seventy-two days to pick a jury for the trolley case; selection started on August 27 and finished on November 6, after the lawyers had spoken to 1,450 potential jurors.

A week after the trial started, a man whose criminal past had been revealed by Heney during jury questioning walked into the courtroom and shot Heney through the head. Heney survived but had to be replaced by Hiram Johnson, who would parlay his fame as prosecutor into the governorship. The would-be assassin committed suicide in jail. The prosecution blamed Police Chief William J. Biggy for the death, publicly berating him and calling for his resignation. A few nights later, Biggy mysteriously went overboard while he was sailing back from Marin County. Ruef was convicted in December 1908 of bribery and sentenced to fourteen years in jail.

Still, the trials dragged on. Calhoun came up next, and the attorneys had to interview 2,370 men before selecting a twelve-member jury. In June, that jury failed to reach a verdict.

This emotional roller coaster proved exhausting for San Franciscans, who were still struggling to rebuild the city after the April 1906 disaster. Pride at the arrest and prosecution of city officials soon turned to weariness and disgust.

It was particularly hard for San Francisco's Jewish community. Jews had been proud of Ruef, the well-educated son of successful French immigrants. While he worshipped beside them at Ohabai Shalom, the imposing temple on Bush Street, he also mingled with the city's political elite. Now he was the symbol of the city's corruption, and many Jews feared that his actions would fuel more anti-Semitism.

While some prominent Jewish leaders denounced Ruef, most notably Rabbi Stephen Wise of Cincinnati, many San Francisco Jews tried to help him. Ruef's attorney was Henry Ach, a Temple Emanu-el member active in local political circles. Rabbi Jacob Nieto of Temple Sherith Israel and Rabbi Bernard Kaplan of Ohabai Shalom became Ruef's spiritual advisers and worked closely with the prosecution to encourage Ruef to take the high moral road and confess.

But as the prosecution fumbled and lost case after case, many Jews began to wonder whether there was a strain of anti-Semitism coming from those going after Ruef. These feelings intensified after Heney canceled the immunity agreement Nieto and Kaplan had worked so hard to arrange. This led Rabbi Jacob Voorsanger, the rabbi of Temple Emanu-el and editor of the weekly, the *Emanu-el*, to denounce the trials as "a chapter of disgrace unequalled in the history of San Francisco."

Strains started to show in the upper classes as well. In July 1907 Calhoun was a guest at the city's elite Olympic Club, a club of sportsmen. Calhoun had originally been told not to talk about the graft prosecution at the club, but when he entered the dining room, members spontaneously broke out in applause. Calhoun listened for a moment, then thanked the men for their support. Not everyone was pleased by his words. Dr. Charles Clinton, a longtime member of the club, tried to interrupt Calhoun's remarks by commenting that it was not appropriate for a man under indictment to speak. Few people paid attention to Clinton, but a few weeks later the Olympic Club's board of directors voted to expel him. Older eventually resigned from the Bohemian Club, one of the city's oldest all-male clubs, because he felt the members' disapproval of his support of the prosecutors.

Soon some of the business elite refused to do business with others in their class. The new mayor appointed Phelan to raise money for a celebration of the American naval fleet, but when Phelan visited businessmen around town, including representatives for the Wells Fargo Nevada National Bank and the Union Trust Company, he found they were unwilling to contribute. It soon became clear that the city's leading businesses were boycotting the celebration because they disapproved of Phelan's support of the graft prosecution, rather than from an aversion to the White Fleet.

Isaias found himself pulled into the trials' vortex. He testified time and again about what he knew or didn't know about United Railroads' $200,000 payment to Ruef. It came out that Ruef had also approached the Spring Valley Water Company for funds but was rebuffed. "Much is being said in commendation of the Spring Valley Water Company in refusing to permit itself to be forced to bribe Ruef, Schmitz and the rest of the pack, and naturally the commendatory language says much in your praise as to your idea on such matters," wrote Isaias's son-in-law and attorney, Emanuel

Heller.⁴ No prosecutor ever suggested in any proceeding that Isaias was aware of the bribe.

In 1907, on the eve of an extended trip to Europe, Isaias resigned from the directorate of the United Railroads. He had very little invested in the trolley company, and after being called into court, he was relieved to establish even more distance from the company.⁵

Older's *Bulletin* continued to hammer Ruef, Ford, Schmitz, and Calhoun. Day after day its front pages were filled with huge headlines, pictures, comics, and articles lambasting the city's grafters and praising the prosecution's hunt.

Isaias and other businessmen determined that the continuing bad press was hurting economic reinvestment in San Francisco, which had not yet fully recovered from the earthquake. While the city's downtown was now filled with new brick buildings and towering skyscrapers, huge swaths of land stood vacant, their owners either unwilling or unable to rebuild.

Isaias finally decided to take a more direct role in putting an end to the divisive trials. On July 21, 1908, a new newspaper hit the streets of San Francisco, becoming the city's fourth afternoon daily—and a direct competitor to the *Bulletin*. It was called the *Globe*, and its motto was "Pull together and build a great city." "The cry of 'Boost!' has taken the place of the wails of the knocker and the vituperation of the schemer," read an editorial on July 24, 1908. "Hand in hand, whatever our political or religious differences may be, let us march forward and make San Francisco one of the greatest cities on the face of the Globe. Let us dwell together as brethren in peace."

From its arrival, the *Globe* garnered suspicion. Its owner on paper was Willard P. Calkins, the head of the Calkins Newspaper Syndicate. Born in Ohio, Calkins, forty, ran a chain of minor newspapers in the interior sections of California, including the weekly *Truckee Republican*, the *Fresno Herald*, the *Contra Costa Standard*, the *Grass Valley Daily Tidings*, and a number of trade papers, like the *Pacific Coast Merchant*, the *Pacific Miner*, and the *Pythian Chronicle*. But starting a daily in a major city like San Francisco took enormous resources, money that no one thought Calkins possessed.

The Calkins Newspaper Syndicate soon won the contract to print *Sunset Magazine*, a promotional travel magazine put out by the Southern Pacific

Railroad. Soon, critics were whispering that the Southern Pacific had given funds to start the *Globe*, an idea that gained strength as the Calkins syndicate went on a spending spree. It bought the *Sacramento Union* and the *Sonora Times* and acquired a state-of-the-art printing press for the *Globe*.

The *Call*, a pro-prosecution newspaper (it was owned by Rudolph Spreckels's older brother John, although the two were estranged), ran an editorial cartoon that showed a stork named "William Herrin" carrying a newborn babe, named "The Globe," toward its new home, titled "Hired Press." The cartoon plainly laid out what many suspected: the newspaper had been created as a mouthpiece to counteract the papers supporting the graft prosecution.

The *Globe* downplayed mention of the graft trials. It ran large stories that pilloried Rudolph Spreckels, "the man who arrogated to himself the astounding privilege of controlling the trial courts of the county." It also congratulated itself at every opportunity, as if to make the case that the city was waiting for a booster paper like the *Globe*. "Scores Rush Congratulations to the Office of the New and Leading Evening Newspaper," ran one headline. The *Globe* claimed to have sold thirty-six thousand copies on July 22 and thirty-eight thousand on July 23.

One of its tactics was to get prominent people to write letters complimenting the paper. "It is my opinion that a paper advocating the fair-minded and cooperative spirit of The Globe will be a great influence in bringing outside capital into our city," Isaias wrote in a letter printed on July 23. "This is noteworthy for such a condition would aid materially in the reconstruction of San Francisco."

But the paper was never a success. In December 1908, Calkins went bankrupt and sold the paper to C. H. Wilson. When a price decrease from 10¢ to 5¢ a copy didn't build readership, the *Globe* was folded in with the *Evening Post*.

The bankruptcy forced the *Globe* to file papers revealing its creditors. It soon became clear that Isaias was the puppet master. The Union Trust Company filed court documents that showed it had loaned $175,000 to the Calkins Newspaper Syndicate, making it the syndicate's major backer.[6]

Clearly Isaias and other businessmen felt frustrated by the pro-prosecution stance of the *Call* and the *Bulletin*. (By 1908 the *Chronicle* and the *Examiner* had switched sides and now opposed Heney.) They believed that

San Francisco had become a joke in the financial community, making it more difficult to attract investors in the quake-ravaged city. The purchase of the paper also reflected the businessmen's belief that they knew what was best for San Francisco, and educating the rest of the citizens would help them realize the pitfalls of the graft trials.

Hellman's purchase of the *Globe* infuriated Older. The editor, always a mercurial man, had developed an almost messianic obsession with the graft trials, putting himself in the role of savior. He regarded anyone who opposed the trial as an enemy, and Isaias would soon find himself the target of that anger.

"During many months, to my knowledge, you have been actively endeavoring to injure the business of The Bulletin," Older wrote Hellman on September 19, 1908. "You have brought persuasion and pressure to bear, I am informed, to keep advertising out of the paper. You have denounced The Bulletin as a trouble-maker and an influence hostile to the prosperity of the city."

Older went on: "It is possibly true that The Bulletin by its agitation for decency and the public improvements has indirectly impaired the value of your large investments in the Spring Valley Water Company and the United Railroads but you can hardly expect a decent newspaper to cut its cloth according to the measure of the Hellman interests. The Bulletin urges the public interest. It is not concerned about private investments when through their own fault they conflict with the public interest."[7]

Isaias rose to make a toast in honor of his wife's fifty-seventh birthday. It was January 10, 1908, and he and his family were in the dining room of the Fairmont Hotel, seated around a table draped in linen and set with silver and crystal. The room was bathed in a golden glow as light from massive crystal chandeliers reflected off the gilt walls. Tail-coated waiters hovered discreetly as the guests considered which of chef Emile Billy's signature dishes to order. The winter menu included toké points mignonette, strained chicken gumbo in cups, sweetbreads under glass, roast stuffed squab, and cold asparagus tips paprika.

The Fairmont Hotel, named for James Fair, one of the Silver Kings who had created the Nevada Bank, had come to symbolize San Francisco's rebirth. The six-hundred-room Italian Renaissance hotel, perched on the top of Nob Hill, had been days from opening in 1906 when the earthquake and fire ravaged its interior, leaving nothing but a charred white granite shell. It stood sentinel on top of Nob Hill after the disaster, a lonely reminder of the magnificence that once characterized San Francisco.

The Fairmont's original owners, Theresa Fair Oelrichs and Virginia Fair Vanderbilt, had married into two of the East Coast's most prominent families, and both ran huge houses at Newport, the preferred summering hole of the very rich. Accustomed to lives of luxury and grand architecture, the two sisters had ordered an opulent monument that would honor their father, who died in 1894. They sold the Fairmont to Herbert and Hartland Law just days before the earthquake, and the brothers were determined to rebuild the Fairmont as quickly as possible. They hired Julia Morgan, the first female graduate from the École des Beaux-Arts in Paris, to revamp the hotel. She would later go on to great renown as the architect for William Randolph Hearst's San Simeon, but she was not well known right after the earthquake and fire. Morgan was inexpensive and worked quickly, and the Fairmont reopened exactly one year after the disaster with a party celebrating the "New San Francisco." There were fireworks, three days of banquets, and a charity fete hosted by Mr. and Mrs. Michael de Young, the owners of the *San Francisco Chronicle*. San Francisco society raised $22,000 that evening. Guests admired the imported marble, the ceilings of beaten gold, the sixteenth-century Venetian mirrors and plush red rugs, all while dining on oysters, turtles, delicate cuts of meat, Champagne, and California wine.

Theresa Fair Oelrichs bought back the Fairmont in 1908, and it soon became home for many of the city's displaced rich. Residents marveled over the enormous bathtubs in every guest room. Ladies strolled through the spacious marble-columned lobby and chatted over tea in the Laurel Court. Children could attend the hotel's elementary school—and then play on its outdoor playground. Each Sunday, the Fairmont Orchestra performed.

The clammy winter night of her birthday, Esther had been feeling poorly for a few weeks, tired and feverish with a pain in her side that would not go away. She had gone to see her doctor, Morris Herzstein, at his office on Sutter Street, but neither she nor Isaias was particularly worried about her health. She had always been robust and vigorous, spending her days immersed in charity work at the hospital or at the kindergarten. Her evenings were reserved for her family, which now included seven grandchildren.

Time, however, had begun to show. Esther's petite frame now carried extra pounds, and she favored high-necked, beaded Victorian dresses to hide the soft skin under her chin. Her eyes were still a soft brown, but her nose stood out more sharply from her face than it had in her youth, and dark circles seemed permanently etched under her eyes.

Isaias stood up and looked lovingly at the woman he had married thirty-eight years ago. They had barely known each other when they stood under the huppah and recited their marriage vows, but now they were so close that Esther always wore a locket around her neck that held a picture of the two of them. "Let us drink to the health of the truest and most devoted wife, the most self-sacrificing and best of mothers," Isaias said, raising his glass in a toast. "Long may she remain with us in health and happiness."

The guests sitting around the table offered their congratulations and the party continued. No one suspected it would be Esther's last birthday.

In late July 1908, Esther was making plans for the summer at Tahoe. As usual, she expected her three children and their families to come up for a lengthy stay. She was confident Florence, her husband, Sidney, and their two children would spend two to three weeks at Pine Lodge in August. Of all the family, they seemed to enjoy Tahoe the most. Sidney would fish all day if given the chance. Marco's family enjoyed the lake, but also loved to spend time at Oakvale, their country house in the East Bay.

Esther was looking forward to the time away. The pain in her abdomen was wearing her down, its incessant pounding an unwelcome distraction. Dr. Herzstein had treated her for the ache, but he had not diagnosed anything serious. Now Esther's obligations were wrapping up for the summer. The Emanu-el kindergarten had finished another year, and Esther's duties as president had lessened. She was president of the Ladies' Auxiliary of Mount Zion Hospital, but that work was never completed. Perhaps at Tahoe she could catch up on her reading for the Philomath Club, a group of women who got together regularly to encourage literary and educational pursuits and to promote civic ideals.

The family was all collected at Pine Lodge when Esther's pains became unbearable. Her abdomen started to expand, almost as if she were pregnant. Isaias telephoned Dr. Herzstein and followed that communication with a telegram. The doctor recommended that Esther return to the city for an examination. The entire family couldn't return, so Isaias hired a private rail car to carry her from Truckee to San Francisco. Marco, Clara, and Emanuel Heller accompanied Esther.

"My dear Father," Marco wrote Isaias on August 3, 1908. "We arrived here this morning after a quiet and uneventful trip. Dear Mother stood the journey with very little, if any discomfort, and is now only anxious to return to you at the lake. Of course I can tell you nothing about the results of the examination, as it has not yet taken place. Signed, your affectionate son."

Esther returned to her suite at the Fairmont Hotel, where she immediately felt better. The men went to work, Clara went out in the fog to do a little shopping, and Esther sat down to write Isaias a four-page letter. It was the final letter she ever wrote, and Isaias kept it until his death with an inscription on the envelope: "The enclosure is the last letter written to me by my beloved wife."

Dr. Herzstein ordered Esther to come to the office for a blood test. He then recommended she drink large quantities of castor oil to ease her pain. For almost a week the family continued to believe that Esther's illness was nothing serious. "I spoke to Mother over the telephone to-day and she gave me the impression of feeling much better," Marco wrote his father on August 10, 1908. "I sincerely hope this is true."

But Dr. Herzstein's ministrations were unsuccessful. Esther's abdomen grew so distended and tender that the doctor recommended an operation.

Isaias immediately made plans to come to San Francisco. He was worried, but had no reason to suspect his wife's life was in danger. No one had mentioned the word "cancer." In 1908 the topic was avoided, as the disease was considered shameful.

Dr. Herzstein planned to operate at the Adler Sanatorium, a state-of-the-art hospital on Van Ness Avenue that catered to the upper classes. He began the operation the morning of August 17. After administering an anesthetic to dull Esther's pain and put her to sleep, he cut her open. Her insides were riddled with foreign growth, wrapped around her organs like a noose around a neck. He closed her up. He could see there was no hope.

Esther never woke up from the operation. She lay in her hospital bed surrounded by her family and finally died at 9:30 P.M. The official cause of death recorded in the city clerk's office was "Carcinoma of the Liver and Gall Bladder." A contributing factor was "ascites," or a serious accumulation of fluid in the abdomen. She was fifty-seven years old.

T he funeral was held two days later in Clara's home on Jackson Street. Two rabbis from Congregation Emanu-el led the prayer service, which was attended by family and close friends. Esther's coffin, draped in a canopy of orchids held together by purple ribbon, was transported after the service to the train station at Third and Townsend and loaded onto a private rail car for the trip to the Jewish cemetery outside of town. Isaias had purchased the best plot in the Home of Peace Cemetery, a knoll on top of a hill that offered a view of the entire place. He erected a marble tomb that resembled a Greek temple with columns and ledges and a massive iron gate that let mourners look in but kept intruders out. Location mattered in the cemetery, just as it did in San Francisco. Once again, Isaias had shown the world the scope of his wealth and power.

Isaias was devastated by Esther's death. He found himself too distracted to focus on banking matters. When he woke up in the morning, his wife was gone. When he went to bed at night, she still wasn't there. He could find no comfort, not at his beloved home in Tahoe, or at his daughter Clara's house. "It seems to me that instead of forgetting, the blow is heavier and harder on me as each day passes, but I have to do the best I can, and trust in God Almighty, for what he does is well done," Isaias wrote to Jackson Graves on September 8, 1908, three weeks after his wife's death.

Two days later, Isaias took action. He knew that Esther had been dedicated to Mount Zion Hospital and the Ladies' Auxiliary. The hospital had been conceived in 1887 at a time when patients entering the San Francisco City and County Hospital were as likely to contract tuberculosis there as get cured. The idea of a Jewish hospital proved controversial, even though a French, a German, and a Catholic hospital were already operating in the city. After much debate, the hospital organizers agreed that while Mount Zion would be a Jewish hospital, it would serve all needy patients. Its doors opened at a local doctor's clinic in 1897, and the hospital was able to buy its own building for $15,000 in 1899.[8]

By 1908 Mount Zion had outgrown its facility, and its board of directors, which included the Hellmans' good friend and fellow Reckendorfer William Haas, was trying to raise $250,000 for a new building. Isaias decided to donate $100,000 to the effort. It would go toward the erection of a wing known as the Esther Hellman Building.

"It almost seems idle for me to speak of the past loyalty and devotion of my beloved wife to the Mount Zion Hospital," Isaias wrote to the board of directors on September 10, 1908. "While charities of every kind appealed to her broad humanitarian spirit, the call of the sick, feeble and suffering touched a tenderer chord in her nature than any other. She cherished great hopes and ideals for your institution and devoted much of her spirit and intelligence to the task of realizing them."[9]

Isaias soon left on a trip to Europe with his daughter Clara, her husband, Emanuel, and their son, Edward. They visited Naples, Rome, and Florence, took the waters in Nauheim and Bad Kissengen, and visited relatives in Germany. Isaias thought of Esther all the time. "Bright sunny morning," Isaias wrote from his stateroom on the steamer *Deutschland,* which was on its way to Naples. "I feel that our trip has been the nicest which I have ever made on the ocean. Had my good wife been along, it would have been perfection. How I miss her, the dear good soul. She was the sweetest of women and dearest and most devoted of wives."[10]

The trip was a needed respite from his grief and the pressures building in San Francisco. Isaias especially enjoyed spending time with his eight-year-old grandson. "My grandson Edward has been with me the past five days, his parents are in Berlin," Isaias wrote in his diary on May 11, 1909. "He has been no trouble to me, has behaved splendidly and has been a very good boy. I shall miss him when I return home."[11]

As soon as Isaias returned on August 3, however, he was thrust back into the maelstrom of graft prosecution politics. Calhoun's second bribery trial was set to start, and reporters wanted to know how the national and international finance communities regarded San Francisco's attempts to root out graft. Isaias told them that the continuing trials were hurting business. "In New York, I found that there is still a great difficulty in securing capital for San Francisco on account of the graft prosecution, or the graft persecution as they call it there,"

Isaias said in the interview. ". . . Certain people in New York . . . were unwilling to send capital here as long as this 'graft persecution' was continued."[12]

Isaias's comments were like a spark to tinder, as they clearly reflected the sharp divisions between the city's business and working classes.

Mr. Hellman "longs for return of those conditions existing before the graft prosecutions had begun, with its calamitous effect on the mind of the financier," wrote the *Liberator*, a pro-prosecution paper published by the Citizens' League of Justice. "Those were the days the financier could help himself to the public pie, after paying Ruef and his henchmen the entrance fee. Those were great days for the financier."[13]

Isaias's return coincided with the start of the primary season, and the election promised to be a referendum on both the graft trials and municipal control of utilities. Older saw the two as inextricably intertwined: men like Phelan and Spreckels who supported the graft trials also wanted San Francisco to take over Spring Valley, the privately owned waterworks. Men like Isaias and Marco Hellman, Michael De Young, and William H. Crocker wanted the trials to stop immediately. To Older, that proved they had their own interests, not the interests of the citizens, at heart. Those men also owned Spring Valley and were resistant to ceding control.

San Francisco's district attorney, William Langdon, a Republican, had decided not to run for reelection, and Heney wanted to run for the post. He ran as a write-in candidate on the Democratic ticket.

The Hellmans, Herrin, and other businessmen formed a group called the Citizens' Alliance and put up former Stanford football star and assistant U. S. attorney, Charles Fickert, as the candidate for district attorney on the Republican ticket. They also supported the candidacy of William Crocker (no relation to the railroad family) for mayor. The labor leader P. H. McCarthy ran for mayor on the Union Labor Party ticket.

It was a nasty campaign, and the Hellmans saw their names besmirched on numerous occasions. Heney made the Hellmans a target, denouncing them from stage in front of thousands of people. Older blasted the Hellmans in editorial after editorial, holding them up as master puppeteers who wanted to put into office men who would squash the graft trials. "Most of the candidates recommended by the business men, would be owned by the corporations as absolutely as Mr. Hellman owns the negotiable instruments in the vaults of his bank," the *Bulletin* editorialized on August 3, 1909.

The incessant attacks against Isaias and his son took a toll, as Isaias grew increasingly bitter. "The San Francisco campaign is running quite high," Isaias wrote in his diary. "Heney attacks me on the platform—in fact all San Francisco citizens who are connected with quasi public corporations. That miserable dog will have his day. Rudolph Spreckels and Jim or Judge Phelan are his sponsors and Heney does their dirty work."[14]

Two weeks later he added: "The weather is very hot. Political excitement runs very high. I hope that Heney (the firebrand) will be beaten. He [Heney] is abusing me and my son both on the stump—He has no reason. I do not even know him well. He is simply playing the demagogue to the rabble."[15]

Much of the country, including President Teddy Roosevelt, still supported the graft prosecution and didn't understand why those living in San Francisco were tired of the ongoing trials.

San Francisco showed its weariness. While McCarthy, the labor candidate for mayor, defeated the Republican candidate Crocker, Fickert beat Heney by ten thousand votes to capture the district attorney's post. The graft trials would now stop. Fickert had implied throughout his campaign that he would not prosecute Calhoun, whose first trial had ended in a hung jury.

Only one man went to prison for graft—Abraham Ruef. After he was sentenced to fourteen years in San Quentin, Older reassessed his vendetta against the man. Older decided it was unfair that Ruef, rather than powerful businessmen such as Calhoun and Ford, sat in jail. He began a crusade to get parole for Ruef. Older published Ruef's memoir (which did not contain any admission of guilt) and got prominent citizens to write letters on his behalf. On August 23, 1915, after serving four years and seven months in prison, Ruef was released.

CHANGE

1911–1916

The sun was shining as Isaias's open-air motorcar pulled into Reckendorf around 9:30 A.M. on Sunday, June 4, 1911. It had been two years since he had visited his German birthplace, but Isaias made a point of coming back every time he returned to Europe. Walking the streets gave him a chance to reflect on his childhood and to pay homage to his parents, who now lay under a gleaming white marble tombstone in the Jewish cemetery a mile out of town.

Reckendorf hadn't changed much in the fifty years since Isaias left. The streets were still unpaved and geese and chickens ran freely. The Catholic church dominated the hamlet, and clusters of stucco-and-half-timbered houses ran right up to its walls. The most obvious sign of modernity was the direct railroad link to Bamberg, about ten miles away.

As Isaias meandered through the town, he was surprised to spot two of his boyhood friends, Reckendorf youths with whom he had studied Torah, chased geese, and thrown balls. Isaac Walter and William Haas, now gray and slightly stout, were wandering about Reckendorf with their relatives. Walter was Isaias's next-door neighbor in San Francisco, and Haas lived down the street, but Isaias had not known they were in the vicinity. "Met Isaac Walter and Mr. and Mrs. William Haas," Isaias wrote in his diary. "We passed a delightful afternoon together. We sat in the Schlossgarten for an hour."

The Walters and Haases, like Isaias, had come back to Reckendorf to reminisce. For them and many first-generation German Americans, Germany remained a touchstone. Even though they had fled in their youth from towns that restricted opportunities for Jews, they spoke to their children in German, regarded the culture as superior to that in America, and returned to their birthplaces regularly to visit friends and family. Isaias had just completed a monthlong stay at the nearby spa of Bad Kissengen to treat his recurring migraines. He, like many German Americans, had more faith in the water-healing cures of the famous Dr. Dappler than in the suggestions of the best-trained American doctors.

As Isaias and his friends walked through the streets, they couldn't help noticing that the vibrant Jewish community they had grown up with was all but gone. The 184-year-old sandstone synagogue where they had first recited the Torah still offered religious services, but the small Jewish school they had attended had been closed the year before because of dwindling enrollment. Only thirty-two Jews lived in Reckendorf at that point, a sharp decline from the three hundred or so Isaias had grown up with.

The group paused to have their photograph taken in front of a sprawling stone house where the Haas family had lived for generations. They posed, too, in front of the Walters' old half-timber home with its robin's-egg blue shutters, which the family had turned into a kindergarten for all of the town's children. They then retired to a nearby restaurant to talk. Perhaps they spent time remarking on how many emigrants from Reckendorf had made good— at least nine of the former Jewish residents who had gone to America had become multimillionaires.[1] They couldn't help comparing their childhood homes with the impressive San Francisco mansions they now lived in. Who would have thought fifty years ago that the skinny, shy boys who left for America with only a few dollars in their pockets would one day become some of the most powerful, influential men in California?

"Reckendorf has not changed, only getting smaller and smaller all the time," Isaias wrote in his diary. "I have an affection for the old place and am always glad to visit again."

But these dual loyalties—to Germany, the land that gave them birth, and America, the land that gave them opportunity—would soon conflict. Within a few years, the two nations would be at war, and Isaias and other German Americans would be forced to choose which land held the greater sway.

California had become less desirable to Isaias, not only because of Esther's death but because Hiram Johnson had been elected governor in 1910. Johnson, one of the prosecutors in the San Francisco graft trials, had run on an anti–Southern Pacific ticket. He was a nominee of the Progressive wing of the Republican Party, which vowed to get the Southern Pacific Railroad out of California politics. For too long, Johnson argued, the notorious Southern Pacific lawyer William Herrin had dictated who would be elected to political office. The railroad's main criterion was friendliness to business interests.

Johnson's election signaled a major shift in the power structure of California—a shift that undermined the influence of men like Isaias and his business associates. Ever since California had become a state in 1850, a tiny oligarchy of very wealthy men had dictated the state's direction. Many were friends of the Southern Pacific Railroad; at the least they represented the state's business interests. They helped shape the state's political institutions by donating generously to like-minded candidates and directly lobbying for bills favorable to their interests. At times, they paid for votes. They were on a first-name basis with the state's governor and two senators—and expected the officials to pay attention when called upon.

These influential men saw their success as a reflection of their own efforts, rather than the outcome of luck or circumstance. Since they believed that the individual had the power to shape his own life, they often blamed the poor and unsuccessful for their own fate. "Idleness is the cause of all our poverty and most of our misery," Isaias once told a San Francisco newspaper.

San Francisco's graft trials had been an attempt to expose the business elite as a group working only for its own interest. Hiram Johnson carried that message into his campaign. He relentlessly attacked the Southern Pacific Railroad and called for a new state government free from its influence and coercion. Even though the Southern Pacific's grip had been loosening, particularly after it was acquired by E. H. Harriman in 1901, Johnson's slogan resonated with an emerging middle class who clamored for more say in political life.

Isaias was dismayed by Johnson's rhetoric. He had switched from the Democratic to the Republican Party in 1896 after William Jennings Bryan won the Democratic nomination and turned the party in a more populist direction. Isaias, who had enjoyed close relations with most of the state's governors—his correspondence is peppered with letters to George Stoneman, George Pardee, Henry Gage, and Henry Markham—regarded Johnson with distaste. The feeling intensified in the next few years as the Progressives pushed through a number of new laws. In 1909, reform-minded legislators had passed a law that let the citizenry directly elect candidates during primaries. Once Johnson was elected, the Republicans initiated numerous reforms, which were then presented to voters as constitutional amendments, including the right of citizens to circulate petitions to create laws; the direct election of U.S. senators (they had previously been chosen by the legislature); the referendum process to repeal laws; and the recall system, which could remove a sitting official from office. The Progressives strengthened the notoriously ineffective railway commission and gave it the ability to regulate other public utilities.

In 1911, women in California were granted the right to vote. Only five other states offered suffrage to women. (The first woman to cast her vote was ninety-one-year-old Caroline Severance, the leader of the Women's Club movement.)

"The California legislature now in session is the most radical which has assembled in many years—a number of vicious bills are introduced and some have passed," Isaias wrote in his diary on February 10, 1911. "Governor Johnson is a radical of the worst kind."

But Isaias was most opposed to the legislature's attempts to levy corporate taxes. He strenuously believed that taxes were bad for business, once even going so far as to have the Nevada National Bank sue the city and county of San Francisco for its assessment on bank stock. Johnson and his Progressive coalition saw increased taxes as a means to fund their ambitious programs. "At the recent special session of the Legislature a new tax law was passed, which, if adopted at the coming election, will be very injurious—especially to our interests," Isaias wrote his bank's board of directors. "It raises the tax from %₀ of 1% to 1%; this would increase our taxes to such an extent as to make them almost ruinous, and would compel our bank and other large financial institutions to reduce their capital and surplus."[2]

The law was adopted and the taxes of the Wells Fargo Nevada National Bank increased from $50,000 to $150,000 in a year.[3] But the bank still managed to pay out its semiannual dividend of 8 percent to its stockholders.[4]

D espite the increasing tension Isaias felt with the governor, he had never been more powerful. The merger of the Nevada National Bank with

Wells Fargo in 1905 had created a formidable financial institution, one of the largest on the Pacific Coast. In spite of temporary downturns, like the 1907 financial panic where customers withdrew $6 million in deposits, the bank's profits increased every year. In 1911, its net earnings were $560,000, of which $480,000 was paid to the small group holding the bank's fifty thousand shares of stock. By 1915, deposits would increase to $40 million.

The Hellman family had become the premier banking family in the state. Isaias controlled institutions whose resources totaled over $100 million.[5] He was president of the Wells Fargo Nevada National Bank, the Union Trust Company, and the Farmers and Merchants Bank. He was a large shareholder and director of the Columbus Savings and Loan of San Francisco, the United States National Bank of Portland, the Fidelity Trust Company of Tacoma, the Long Beach Savings Bank, and the Southern Trust Company. He was also associated with the Security Trust and Savings Bank of Los Angeles, the Pasadena National Bank, and the Berkeley Bank, among others.

He was also president of the Bankers' Investment Group, a syndicate that included Louis Sloss, Lewis Gerstle, and Antoine Borel. The group controlled one of the largest blocks of real estate in downtown San Francisco, a parcel that stretched fifty feet along Market Street and forty feet along Kearny. The Bankers' sold part of the property in 1909 for $5 million, or more than $10,000 per front foot, the highest ever paid in San Francisco. Two of Isaias's banks occupied prime locations in downtown as well, including a new Union Trust Building on Grant and Market, designed by Clinton Day.

And despite the slew of attacks from Fremont Older's *Bulletin*, Isaias had become an almost mythical figure, lauded for his banking genius and his sagaciousness. "He has quite an extraordinary forehead, that might belong to a philosopher, a poet, or a musician," one reporter wrote. "His eyes betoken frankness and sincerity. They are large, full and gentle, and tell of neither cunning nor shrewdness."

Marco's stature had also grown considerably in San Francisco and he now ranked in prestige with his father. Marco was vice president of the Union Trust Company (he would become president in 1916), vice president of the Wells Fargo Nevada National Bank, director or official in numerous other banks, the treasurer of the University of California, a board member of the Spring Valley Water Company, and a big player in Republican politics.

Newspaper editorials against the capitalists were now as likely to attack Marco as to criticize his father.

The dynasty extended into Los Angeles. Isaias's two nephews, Marco and Irving, were also prominent bankers. After Isaias's brother Herman died in 1906, his sons became vice presidents of the Merchants National Bank, which they later renamed the Hellman Bank. For years the money poured in, letting Marco build one of the most magnificent mansions on Wilshire Boulevard. Like his father, Marco adored horses, and he kept a huge stable of them on the old family ranch in Alhambra. He often dressed them up in the silver-studded tack so popular in the days of the old Californios. He had started the Uplifters Club, which sponsored horse rides in the hills around Los Angeles, and would go on to become a grand marshal in the 1929 Tournament of Roses parade.

Other Jewish bankers in California were prominent, although not as important as the Hellmans. Herbert and Mortimer Fleishhacker, two brothers who had merged their London, Paris & American Bank with the Anglo-California Bank in 1909, were also well regarded. The Anglo-California Bank, originally organized by the prominent banking firm of J. W. Seligman and Company, was run for many years first by Eugene Meyer, Isaias's old friend, and then by Phil Lilienthal and Ignatz Steinhart. (The new combined institution, the Anglo & London Paris National Bank, was later merged with Wells Fargo.)

"Isaias Hellman was born a banker," rhapsodized an article in *Town Talk*, the East Coast society magazine, on January 15, 1914. "I do not mean to say that he came into the world with a bank on his hands, or that he had money to lend in the cradle. I mean that he was born with an instinct for estimating probabilities. . . . One seldom thinks of a banker as an empire builder. The common notion is a banker is only a money lender. This is a very narrow conception of the banking business. Without the banker, trade would have to be conducted on a primitive basis, as it was in the days when the mathematics of money-dealing was an unknown science. The banker is the refined means by which capital is moved accurately from one trade to another. It is he that turns an endless procession of written promises into money as though they were precious stones. He makes it possible for wealth to increase wealth."[6]

Even though Isaias was seventy, he had no intention of slowing down.

"Work and the pleasures of doing it well, is best for a man who has been active all his life," he told the *Los Angeles Times* on October 5, 1912. "Were I to retire I do not know what I would do with my time. It is not good for men to rust their lives away. I see the great development ahead of the Pacific Coast and I want to have a part in it."

On October 14, 1911, a huge crowd gathered in San Francisco's Golden Gate Park to watch the president of the United States turn over a shovel of earth. William Taft had come to town to break ground for San Francisco's declaration to the world that the city had recovered from its 1906 earthquake and fire: the 1915 Panama-Pacific International Exposition.

Winning the right to hold the exposition had been years in the making. San Francisco businessmen had first suggested a world's fair to Congress in 1904, shortly after work began on the Panama Canal. They trumpeted the new waterway as an innovation that would transform trade in the West and suggested San Francisco was the ideal place to celebrate. Congress turned the city down.

The idea was resurrected when debris from the earthquake and fire still covered the city. In December 1906, a small group of the city's top businessmen gathered in a temporary wooden shed in Union Square to discuss holding some kind of event that would show the world that San Francisco had not been defeated by nature. They knew that they needed to refocus the world's attention away from the city's destruction to its resurrection.

Isaias played an important role in making the fair happen. Although the planning committee included some influential men, including Isaias's son, Marco, the committee knew it needed the support of San Francisco's top businessmen. More important, the city needed to show the federal government it was serious about an exposition by raising $5 million. In February 1910, the planning committee convinced forty-two men to donate $25,000 each, which added up to just over $1 million. At first Isaias wasn't inclined to contribute, but Marco told him he would regret it later if his name wasn't on the list of major donors. A second meeting, this one in April at the Merchants Exchange Building, raised an additional $4 million in pledges.

San Francisco eventually beat out New Orleans as the site for the exposition, and President Taft came to town to formally dedicate the fair. No one was quite sure where the fair would be held—the various proposed sites included Golden Gate Park, Oakland, and a strip of land along the bay—but Taft was breaking ground anyway.

Taft's motorcade set out from Van Ness Avenue toward the park, accompanied by a long procession of National Guardsmen, military troops, police, and firefighters. More than one hundred thousand people gathered in the park's stadium to watch the burly president, dressed in a black silk top hat and dark frock coat, turn a silver spade into the ground. As he lifted the dirt, one hundred doves flew into the air, and a barrage of rifle shots went off.

"San Francisco wants to show the world how she has come up out of the ashes of her destructive fire, and she is willing to pay for that privilege," Isaias told the *San Francisco Examiner* on Sunday, April 9, 1911. "Her business men feel assured that the completion of the canal will be of tremendous benefit to the people of the state. It will put us in direct touch with European ports and bring us the kind of immigrants we need, the kind that has built up the East and the Middle West."

The committee to receive Taft included Isaias's son. Marco had been among the small group of men who had envisioned the fair in 1906, and he was now a vice president of the Panama-Pacific International Exposition board. His wife, Frances, served on the Women's Board.

The groundbreaking signaled a milestone of sorts for the Hellmans. In the past it had always been Isaias who had been invited to wine and dine with presidents, but now Marco, forty, was almost as influential as his father. Isaias, who was stinting with his compliments, expressed his appreciation for his son in a letter. The praise was so unexpected that it prompted a response. "An expression of confidence such as you have given me is the kind of thing that makes life worth living, and makes it a pleasure to try to do the very best I know how," Marco wrote his father. "Expressions of appreciation from you are doubly welcome because you are so sparing of them unless you feel they are thoroughly deserved."[7]

The group of nurses clustered on the ground floor of the building under construction. With starched white caps, immaculate bibs, and aprons, they appeared the model of the new American woman, professionals devoted to the care of others. It was three o'clock on Wednesday, August 14, 1912, and the nurses had gathered to participate in laying the cornerstone of the new Esther Hellman Building of Mount Zion Hospital. The mood was ceremonial: an American flag was draped out from the wooded framework that would one day be the second floor, policemen in their brass-buttoned blue coats held the hands of little children, and carriages and horses lined the streets.

The ceremony began with a short prayer by Rabbi Jacob Nieto, followed by other brief speeches. Then Frances Jacobi Hellman, who was married to Esther's son, Marco, hoisted a copper box containing hospital reports, photos, letters, and other keepsakes appropriate for a time capsule, into the cornerstone. She was flanked by her brother-in-law, Emanuel Heller, who addressed a few brief remarks about his mother-in-law to the crowd.

Isaias was nowhere to be seen. He could not bear to attend.

I n December 1913, President Woodrow Wilson signed the Federal Reserve Act, creating a national consortium of banks that could act in concert to regulate the nation's money supply. The Federal Reserve Act was a major modernization of the country's currency system. It acted as a stabilizing force that reduced the number of bank runs and gold shortages. The federal government would now take an active role in controlling the money supply. If there wasn't enough currency circulating, the government could release more into the system.

Isaias had served on a West Coast advisory committee that examined the strengths and weaknesses of the Federal Reserve Act. After living through bank runs in 1875 and 1893, and watching banks suffer during another panic in 1907, he was a strong supporter of increased regulation. "I am convinced that it represents a marked step forward in American finance and banking," Isaias wrote to the Wells Fargo Nevada National Bank board of directors. "There may be friction and disturbance while the country is adjusting itself to the provisions."[8]

O n February 20, 1915, President Wilson pressed a button in Washington to open the Panama-Pacific International Exposition, which had been built on filled-in ground on San Francisco's northwestern edge, an area now known as the Marina District. The fair sprawled over hundreds of acres along the bay. More than 18 million people came from near and far to walk through verdant gardens, pass by Moorish-inspired fountains, and stroll among the pastel-colored buildings that were designed by some of the country's leading architects.

The centerpiece of the exposition was the Tower of Jewels, a forty-three-story cornice-laden building decorated with 140,000 colored glass gems from Austria. It dazzled during the day when the sun refracted off the glass facets, and sparkled at night when lit by concealed lights. Visitors could find rides in the Zone, a seven-block area of amusements, including the Aeroscope, the fair's challenge to the incredibly popular Ferris wheel unveiled at the 1893 Chicago Exposition. The Aeroscope could hold five hundred people at once in a car that rose up on a crane to offer breathtaking vistas of the exposition, the bay, the city, and Alcatraz. Visitors could also gawk at the enormous Underwood typewriter or the assembly plant set up by the Ford Motor Company. Every afternoon, the line came to life for three hours, and visitors could watch as workers put together a car in ten minutes. There was a five-acre replica of the Panama Canal where visitors could see tropical vegetation and a warship "on Guard" sending out wireless messages.

When the Wells Fargo Nevada National Bank closed in the evening, Isaias often made his way down to the fair. He frequently took one of his grandchildren along, and they would spend hours exploring the exhibits in the Palace of Machinery or the Palace of Technology. "I am visiting the Exposition grounds regularly after banking hours," Isaias wrote in his diary on February 24, 1915. "Always find something to admire. It is a wonderful exhibit, the grounds and buildings. I do not think they have ever been equaled."

Like most visitors, Isaias was particularly taken with the fair at night, when thousands and thousands of lightbulbs illuminated the buildings. Electricity was still a new phenomenon, and the General Electric Company used the exposition to show off its product. It was a brilliant marketing move, as virtually every visitor was astounded by the spectacle of lights. Of particular note was "the Scintillator," a batch of searchlights located near the water. When it got dark, the Scintillator would beam colored searchlights into the air for a dazzling light show that resembled the aurora borealis, or northern lights. "We sat and watched and soon a long finger of white light swept across the sky, and then another and another of different colors, and then there was flashing and fading across the whole sky in that direction, the most beautiful northern-lights effect you could imagine," the author Laura Ingalls

Wilder wrote her husband in August 1915. "Well, this was more brilliant, more colors and very much higher in the sky. All the colors of the rainbow and some shades that I never saw the rainbow have."[9]

' Since the war in Europe prevented overseas travel, many easterners who might have gone abroad came west instead to the exposition. As one of the exposition's major donors, Isaias could host people in the Directors' Club, and he used his access to entertain some of the country's most influential financiers. He was determined to show that San Francisco, now recovered from the earthquake, was an attractive place for investment. In April he held a lunch for twenty-four to honor Jacob Schiff, the New York financier and prominent spokesman for Jewish rights, and Judge Simon Rosendale, the former attorney general of New York. On the last day of the fair, Friday, December 3, he hosted a banquet at the New York Building for Sir Edgar Meyer, the German-born, British brother of banker James Speyer, and Adolph Stahl, Guatemala's representative at the fair.

After they ate, the group watched the closing ceremonies, when the lights in all the major buildings were turned off one by one, with the fair closing for good at 12:15 A.M. More than 430,000 people had gathered to say good-bye. "The closing ceremonies were most beautiful," Isaias wrote in his diary. "Everybody pronounces the Exposition a big success and San Francisco may feel proud of it."

The fair proved to be the advertisement the city's business leaders had wished. It had been an event that paid homage to the past, with its rich display of antique sculptures and paintings, and to the present, with its emphasis on the technological wonders of the day. The fair wiped out the image of a city in ruins and replaced it with a perception of a city with energy and panache. Most important, the fair lured visitors across the country where they could see for themselves that California—long considered distant, exotic, and somehow different—was an important contributor to the United States. Like the Panama Canal for which it was named, the exposition linked old to new, the East to the West.

The closing of the Panama-Pacific International Exposition at the end of December 1915 ended the undeclared truce between San Francisco's business community and its labor unions. As soon as the tourists departed and workmen began tearing down the plaster-and-chicken-wire walls that had made up the fantasyland, San Francisco exploded. The premise that Isaias, Marco, and other businessmen had put forth—that a popular fair would improve San Francisco's economic situation—shattered with the tensions created by the war in Europe. Isaias and others had hoped the exposition would usher in a new period of prosperity after the earthquake, but they soon found that trouble was just beginning.

Working men and women were feeling the pinch of prices of wartime inflation. They wanted higher wages, but businessmen, who saw their profits compromised because of the war in Europe, resisted. Money had gotten so tight that in 1914 most eastern banks had to issue scrip for use as currency.

In June 1916, ten thousand longshoremen up and down the Pacific Coast walked out on their jobs, virtually shutting down the maritime industry. In San Francisco, the ports were even more paralyzed than those in Seattle and Long Beach because six hundred steamboat operators who navigated the rivers joined the four thousand striking Bay Area dockworkers. Since San Francisco relied so heavily on the import and export of goods—particularly to the Far East—the strike was a disaster to city businesses.

Within nine days, many of the issues were resolved and most longshoremen went back to work. But by June 22, thousands had walked out again, and the tension at San Francisco's docks was acute. Huge cargo ships sat idle, with no one to load or unload their wares. Angry picketers marched in front of the long wharves jutting out into San Francisco Bay. There were numerous confrontations, and both sides hurled rhetoric that only inflamed emotions. On July 7, several hundred longshoremen were protesting on Steuart Street just a block from the waterfront when a wagon owned by D. Ghiradelli & Company pulled up. The strikers got angry at this attempt to collect goods, and they pulled the driver from the wagon and roughed him up.[10]

The strike prompted the business community to take action. For decades unions had pushed and pushed for greater rights, higher wages, and shorter working hours through strikes, boycotts, and hard negotiations. Sometimes the business community agreed to the demands, particularly after the earthquake, when a huge number of rebuilding projects created a shortage of workers. But just as often the business community had held firm against unions, most particularly in the fight to create an eight-hour workday.

The widespread and violent strike on the waterfront presented business-men with an opportunity to reassert themselves against the unions. The presidents of the San Francisco Commercial Club and the chamber of commerce sent out letters to members, calling on them to attend a mass rally on Monday, July 10, at 3 P.M. The slogan "Law and Order Must Be Maintained in San Francisco" adorned the letters.

More than two thousand businessmen gathered in the great hall of the Merchants' Exchange Building at the southeast corner of California and Montgomery. It was an appropriate place to meet, for the structure had come to personify capitalism. The original structure had been designed in 1903 by Willis Polk, who was at that time working for the great Chicago architect Daniel Burnham, but would soon become famous in his own right. The fire gutted the building, but it had been rebuilt to its former glory, and had been the place businessmen had gathered six years earlier to raise funds for the Panama-Pacific International Exposition.

"A condition of lawlessness exists, for which there is no excuse, and you all know that due to mob intimidation, it is impossible to handle goods to and from certain wharves," Frederick J. Koster, the president of the chamber of commerce, told the crowd. "Merchants are subjected to shameful, tyrannous, and uninterrupted rule of the waterfront by officers of the Longshoreman's Union."[11] Koster referred to a "disease permeating this community," and asked the businessmen for the means to combat the increasing anarchy on the streets. He insisted that he and others were not against legitimate unions, but opposed the elements who advocated radicalism and lawlessness. He also made it clear that he thought San Francisco should be an "open-shop" town, where businessmen, not the unions, decided whom to hire. By the end of the meeting, the city's business community had pledged $500,000 to the cause.

The sheer number of businessmen reflected the fear that the union movement was being taken over by radical elements. The Industrial Workers of the World union had become increasingly popular since its founding eleven years earlier. San Francisco had also become home to a strong anarchist community, which would forever be identified as the political persuasion that drove a man to assassinate President William McKinley a decade earlier. One of the movement's most visible leaders, Alexander Berkman, who had spent fourteen years in jail for his attempted assassination of industrialist Henry Clay Frick, published his magazine, the *Blast*, in San Francisco. Berkman was also the former lover of Emma Goldman, a leading radical anarchist.

The Hellmans stood firmly on the side of the businessmen. Isaias had seen trouble like this before, in 1910, when a group of union radicals bombed the Los Angeles Times Building, killing twenty. His right-hand man in Los Angeles, Jackson Graves, often spoke out publicly—and in a very inflammatory manner—about renegade unions and the breakdown of law and order. A number of people complained about Graves's public stance, arguing that it was inappropriate for the representative of such an important bank to make such controversial comments, but Isaias never asked Graves to keep quiet. Isaias had also kept quiet when Henry Huntington crushed any attempts to unionize his trolley lines.

Marco attended the rally on July 10 and then sent a letter to the board of directors of the Wells Fargo Nevada National Bank, imploring the bank to contribute $10,000 toward the newly created Law and Order Committee. "Unorganized business has been at a disadvantage in confronting organized labor," Marco wrote. "We must all believe, that, in the long run, no class in the community can take advantage of any other class without injuring all. Therefore, on the other day, Monday July 10, a general meeting of the businessmen of San Francisco was held at the Chamber of Commerce and an organization was there effected to inquire into and handle situations arising along this line."[12] The bank's board of trustees agreed to contribute funds to the employers' cause.

The waterfront strike and confrontation between the business class and labor came at exactly the same time San Francisco was gearing up for a parade that called for the United States to prepare for war. While President Wilson had kept the country neutral, a growing number of people were pushing to get the country ready for what many saw as inevitable. San Francisco congressman Julius Kahn was one of the country's strongest proponents of military preparedness and had just recently sponsored the National Defense Act of 1915, which authorized the expansion of the army.

Anarchists like Emma Goldman and representatives from the mainstream unions regarded the conflict as a businessmen's war, one designed to increase the profits of the country's biggest industries. That perception was only enhanced with the announcement of the members of the Preparedness Day Parade committee. The grand marshal was Thornwell Mullally, the nephew of

Patrick Calhoun, the former head of the United Railroads and a central figure in the graft trials. Calhoun had been indicted—but never convicted—of
bribing Abe Ruef. Marco Hellman was the chairman of the committee,
which included some of San Francisco's other prominent businessmen, including Herbert Fleishhacker; William Crocker, the head of an eponymous
bank; Michael de Young, the owner of the *San Francisco Chronicle*; Jesse
Lilienthal; William Randolph Hearst, the owner of the *San Francisco Examiner*; and Marshal Hale, the head of a chain of department stores.

The parade became a symbol of the fight between capital and labor.
Rudolph Spreckels called the parade organizing group "grafters" and suggested they were the men who had undermined legal attempts to stop bribery
in the city. Labor leaders denounced the parade and organized a "peace
demonstration" that drew five thousand people only two days before the
event.

The Preparedness Day Parade was scheduled for July 22, 1916—just ten
days after striking laborers had shut down the waterfront for a week. Despite
the tensions, organizers were determined to proceed. New York had held its
own Preparedness Day Parade just a few days earlier without incident.

On Saturday afternoon more than twenty thousand people gathered at
the base of the Ferry Building to march up Market Street toward city hall.
Another one hundred thousand flag-waving men, women, and children lined
the parade route, ready to cheer on the veterans, the marching bands, the
women's auxiliaries, and the well-dressed officials and businessmen who
rode in cars draped in red, white, and blue bunting.

At 1:30 P.M. the parade started. Mayor James Rolph and parade grand
marshal Mullally led the way, followed by their wives. The people marched
sixteen abreast down the street, with some groups holding massive American
flags and others waving their own individual flags.

At 2:04 P.M., just as the Veteran Soldiers of the Grand Army of the
Republic—veterans of the Civil War—walked by the Ferry Exchange Saloon near Steuart Street, a street about a block from the starting place of the
parade, a lead pipe loaded with dynamite exploded. Shrapnel and flying
bullets flew in every direction, sending out a powerful concussive blast that
mowed down hundreds in an instant. Six people were killed outright, their
body parts scattered in a hundred-yard radius, and another four would die
of their injuries in the coming days. Blood and pieces of clothing littered

the street. Witnesses to the explosion rushed to pick up souvenirs, destroying crucial evidence in the process.

As police and helpers hurried to care for the wounded, the parade continued. It would take more than a half an hour for word to reach the organizers that a bomb had gone off. Still, the marchers walked on for another hour and a half.

Police immediately suspected that the anarchists had something to do with the bombing, particularly since Emma Goldman was scheduled to speak that night on "Preparedness, the Road to Universal Slaughter." She and Berkman were questioned and then released. They denounced the violence but said it was understandable. "If you saturate the very air with militarism you are bound to produce violence," Goldman told the *Chronicle*. "Incessant agitation for war and talk of bloodshed are sure to arouse people."[13]

Within days, police had arrested two union activists, Warren K. Billings and Tom Mooney, who had helped Berkman with the *Blast*. Both men had served time in jail for transporting and using explosives. In a series of trials that became celebrated around the world, they were convicted. Evidence suggests they were framed.

The bombings provided the business community with new ammunition to weaken the labor movement and turn the state back toward a more moderate Republicanism. Four days after the bombing, more than five thousand people crowded into the Civic Auditorium. While Koster, the president of the chamber of commerce, focused his speech on capturing the perpetrators of the violence, the antiunion tone of the gathering was clear. The chamber appointed a new Law and Order Committee of one hundred men, including Marco, to help restore order to San Francisco. The committee went so far as to compare itself to the notorious Vigilance Committee of the 1850s, a group of citizens who took it upon themselves to kill those they determined were unsavory elements.

A few days after the bombing, Jackson Graves made explicit a link between California governor Hiram Johnson and the radical forces. "I hear the District Attorney of San Francisco has a letter from one of the McNamaras [the men convicted of bombing the Los Angeles Times building in 1910] in which McNamara complains that Johnson is very slow in coming through with his pardon. This letter ought to get into the public print, & if there is any decency left in the people of the state of California, it ought to put an end for all time to the political aspirations of Hiram. San Francisco is at last aroused to the labor proposition. I hope she will see the necessity of battling to the last ditch for the open shop."[14]

EIGHTEEN

WAR AND ANTI-SEMITISM

1916–1919

The winds howled and rain fell, but the nastiest weather in decades did not deter thousands of people from gathering in the stately Exposition Auditorium on Grove Street in San Francisco. More than five thousand men, women, and children streamed through the doors, shook off the water that had collected on their hats and coats, and made their way into the massive exhibit hall. Enormous American flags, as well as flags from other countries, hung at the front of the stage, patriotic bunting that spectators could see from every part of the auditorium.

As people came into the hall that January 26, 1916, they were escorted to their seats by young women clad in white smocks and aprons with white caps on their heads, dubbed "the society girls" by the papers for their good looks and charm. More than three hundred businessmen, the "vice presidents" of the evening, crowded together in chairs on the mammoth platform at the front of the hall. Working-class men and women, labor union representatives, and priests, clerics, and rabbis from around the city were also in attendance.

The crowd had gathered that rainy night out of a sense of horror about what was happening to Jews caught in the crossfire between Russian and German troops battling for hegemony in World War I. Every day, it seemed, the newspapers were filled with stories of the dead, the starving, and the homeless. Though the United States remained neutral about the conflict, many Americans were just one generation removed from countries in Europe and had relatives there, making the battles almost personal. The deprivation and death toll were so terrible that President Woodrow Wilson had declared "Jewish Relief Day." Communities around the country were hosting rallies like the one in San Francisco.

Marco was one of the organizers of the massive rally. In the last ten years, he had become increasingly involved with charitable work, particularly in organizations that worked with Jews. In 1910, San Francisco leaders united many of the individual charity groups under a new umbrella organization called the Federation of Jewish Charities. Marco was elected to the executive board of the group and went on to serve as president.

"The condition of the Jews, especially in Poland, but also in the various other sections of the European war zone, beggars description," Marco told the *San Francisco Chronicle.* "In Poland they have always been regarded as an alien race. They have been driven before the army whenever the army advanced in their direction. When the Russians commenced their retreat, they attempted to follow the tactics of Napoleon when he invaded Russia by destroying all the houses and driving the inhabitants, including the Jews, before them. When the Jews reached the end of the Pale they were driven back by the police on to the bayonets of the soldiers. It was a ghastly game of battledore and shuttlecock. The consequence is that they have died, not by the hundreds and thousands, but by the hundreds of thousands. The lowest estimate is that of the six million Jews in Poland when the war broke out, more than seven percent are dead, including all the children under seven years of age. Their only hope of assistance now is from America, and we must help them."[1]

The rally started with descriptions of the chaos and mayhem in Russia, where millions were threatened with death. As speaker after speaker got up to detail the scorched-earth policies of the Russian, German, and Austro-Hungarian armies, those in the audience were moved to help.

"Every penny given here tonight will cement us together, Jew or non-Jew, into a new citizenship of an ideal republic, the watchword of which is 'Liberty,' and the hope, 'Humanity,' " Rabbi Martin Meyer of Temple Emanu-el told the crowd.

As the call for donations went out, so many people stood up to pledge that they could not all be heard at once. The white-clad ushers fanned out through the crowd with baskets and collected checks, coins, bills, and pledges.

William H. Crocker, scion of the banking and railroad family, went to the front of the auditorium and announced he would donate $5,000. His offer prompted the master of ceremonies to ask other "big fellows" to state their pledges.

Marco stood up and said that his father, Isaias, would donate $10,000, the largest single individual donation of the evening.

"Well, we have heard from the father, what about the son?" asked the MC, Lawrence W. Harris.

"The son gives twenty-five hundred dollars," replied Marco.

Donations from companies and other well-to-do people were announced. Levi Strauss & Company pledged $10,000. Michael de Young donated $1,000. Mortimer and Herbert Fleishhacker donated $10,000. Abe and William Haas gave $5,000. The popular stage actress Blanche Bates, who pioneered the lead in David Belasco's *The Girl of the Golden West* in New York in 1905, sent a telegram pledging $500.

The smaller pledges got as many cheers as the larger ones. When eleven-year-old Herbert Hinder walked to the platform and gave his entire savings—$1—the crowd roared. Hundreds of people surged after Hinder to heap their coins on the stage.

By the end of the evening, the five thousand people at the rally had donated or pledged $198,000.[2]

As World War I raged in Europe, Isaias found himself at a crossroads, forced by the fighting to reassess his identity. He had been born in Europe, was a Jew from a state that was now part of modern Germany, and had made his life and fortune in America. For more than sixty-five years, Isaias had had no trouble with this triple identity. The hostilities in Europe, though, made him feel all of those distinctions more strongly and brought them into irreconcilable proximity.

Like most central European Jews who had immigrated to the United States before 1880, Isaias considered himself as American as he was Jewish. While he attended temple regularly, he belonged to a Reform congregation that had toned down its religious rituals to better blend with American society. Men at Temple Emanu-el were not required to cover their heads with a hat either in synagogue or outside, nor to wear tefillin, the small leather prayer boxes wrapped around the head and upper arm, like their Orthodox brethren. Services were in English, and many prayers were sung by a choir accompanied by an organ, much like services in a church. These adaptations worked well for German and other central European Jews, who as a group had achieved unprecedented acceptance and prosperity.

The eastern European Jews who flocked to America in the last part of the nineteenth century did not feel the same compulsion as German Jews to fit in with the broader society. They wanted to preserve their customs and religion, which often meant wearing traditional religious garb, speaking Yiddish, and standing up proudly for their religion. As a group they were more politically radical and confrontational than the German Jews. Men like Isaias regarded their outspokenness and visibility with some distaste.

The influx of eastern European Jews had swelled the ranks of American Jews tenfold, and the United States had the second-largest Jewish population in the world after Russia. There were many vibrant pockets of Jewish learning, including theological schools in New York and Cincinnati and a world-class Jewish library in Washington, D.C. In San Francisco after the earthquake, new Jewish communities popped up in the Fillmore District and out on San Bruno Avenue near Daly City. These areas were populated by people vastly different from Isaias—more religious and working class.

While eastern European Jews dominated numerically, the central European Jews held a disproportionate amount of power and influence. Men like Jacob Schiff, the Kuhn Loeb banker, and Adolph Ochs, the owner of the *New York Times,* had the ear of presidents. Oscar Straus served as ambassador to the Ottoman Empire. Louis Brandeis became a Supreme Court justice in 1916. In San Francisco, the Hellmans, Haases, Fleishhackers, Lilienthals, and other German Jews held most of the leadership posts in Jewish organizations.

But the wave of violence against the Jews in Europe that erupted in 1903 and continued almost without pause through the first two decades of the twentieth century forced many German Jews, including Isaias, to reexamine what it meant to be Jewish in America. When on Russian Easter 1903 a mob attacked the Jewish population of Kishinev, a city in Russia that had more than fifty thousand Jews, sixteen Jewish schools, and seventy synagogues, it highlighted the continued insecurity of Jews around the world. For two days police remained in their barracks while crowds looted Jewish stores and beat and killed young men and their families. More than forty-five Jews were killed and dozens of others were badly injured.

The news made headlines around the world. "Babes were literally torn to pieces by the frenzied and bloodthirsty mob," reported the *New York Times*. "The local police made no attempt to check the reign of terror. At sunset the streets were piled with corpses and wounded. Those who could make their escape fled in terror, and the city is now practically deserted of Jews."[3]

The atrocities were enough to make the German and eastern Europeans Jews set aside their differences and work together temporarily to raise funds for the survivors. An interfaith coalition hosted a massive rally at Carnegie Hall that drew many prominent speakers, including former president Grover Cleveland and New York's two senators. After the rally raised more than $50,000, groups in fifty-one other cities hosted their own meetings.

One of the men most affected by the Kishinev pogrom was Schiff, who had always preferred to work behind the scenes in a way that would not attract attention. The pogrom, however, made Schiff and others realize that low-key diplomatic pressure was not an effective means to protect Jews around the world. In 1906 Schiff, Straus, Louis Marshall, Judah Magnes, Meyer Sulzberger, and other prominent Jews formed the American Jewish Committee to confront directly issues concerning international Jewry. While the men leading the group were exclusively central European Jews (and they proved reluctant to admit eastern European Jews into the leadership), it was the first time American Jews had formed an organization to represent their interests.

Isaias and Schiff had been friends for many years and had done a number of bond deals together. When Schiff encouraged Isaias and Marco to organize West Coast fund-raising drives to help Russian Jews, both men responded generously.

Jews in America could not help but notice that anti-Jewish sentiment seemed to be growing in the United States as well. On September 10, 1915, in a much publicized visit, Rufus Isaacs, the lord chief justice of England, and a Jew, came to the United States in search of a massive war loan that would be backed by the French and British governments. Isaacs and more than one hundred prominent financiers met in the library of the J. P. Morgan firm—the same room the famed financier had used while defusing the Panic of 1907—to talk about the possibility of the United States lending $500 million to France and England. None of the invited financiers were

Jewish, and the slight angered Isaias and other Jewish bankers, who regarded it as a declaration by the Morgan firm of its disdain for Jews. The slight, and the fact that the loan aided the Allied cause at a time when the United States was neutral, and indirectly supported the anti-Semitic czarist Russian state, may have prompted the Wells Fargo Nevada National Bank to decline to participate in the $50 million loan offering. "The Anglo-French loan now being put out has been the subject of considerable discussion, but we have not allowed ourselves to be quoted publicly," Isaias wrote to his board's directors. "Believing that our local investors would not take much active interest in it at this time we declined the invitation to participate and courteously advised Messers J. P. Morgan & Co. to that effect."[4]

World War I also forced Isaias to reconsider his loyalties toward Germany. While he considered himself an American, he retained strong ties to the country of his birth, even returning there every year for vacation. He had scores of relatives, including some of his and Esther's sisters, still living in Bamberg, Nuremberg, and Würzburg, and he regularly sent them food and money. His daughter Clara had been visiting her relatives in Germany right before the war broke out in August 1914, and got stuck for a few weeks in England before she and her family could secure passage back to New York.

When the fighting began, many Americans sympathized more with the Russian and British cause than with that of the Germans and Austro-Hungarians. Isaias felt the opposite. Besides his affection for Germany, Isaias was reluctant to support Russia because of its virulent anti-Semitism. After the Kishinev pogrom in 1903, violence against the Jews continued and the state did little to intervene. Russia also routinely denied visas to American Jews who wanted to visit the country and restrained the movements of those it did permit to come.

Isaias fought back against Russia in his own, small way. In addition to donating funds for victims of the war, he had the Wells Fargo Nevada National Bank buy Japanese war bonds from Kuhn Loeb during the 1904–5 Russo-Japanese War. The bank later resold them to California investors.

In 1914, Isaias put forward his own version of propaganda. He paid $2,500 to bring Dr. Hermann Paasche, the first chancellor of the German Reichstag, to California on a lecture tour. Germany had once been admired for its music and art but was rapidly becoming known for its military might, particularly the policy of unrestricted submarine warfare, which sent underwater boats to cruise the shores of England and shoot whatever got in their way. Paasche delivered a series of lectures at the University of California that were intended to counteract rising anti-German attitudes.[5]

Pro-German sentiment was harder to maintain after May 7, 1915, when the Germans sank the British steamer *Lusitania* in the Irish Sea. More than 1,200 passengers died, many of whom were American. Isaias had sailed on the ship on his way home from Liverpool in July 1911.

Eighteen days after the *Lusitania* sank to the bottom of the ocean, sparking a wave of anti-German hysteria in the United States, Isaias got a request in the mail. It was a letter from the German consulate in San Francisco, asking Isaias to help alleviate the suffering of German prisoners of war in Siberia.

The soldiers had been captured by Russian troops and were living in squalid conditions. Unprepared for the harsh Siberian winters that continued for months at a time, the soldiers were at risk of freezing and maybe even starving to death. Would Isaias consider donating some money to help their plight? asked the missive.

Isaias was moved by the request, since he hated to think of his former countrymen suffering at the hands of the Russians. "The German consulate made an appeal to the Germans of California for aid for the unfortunate German prisoners now held in Siberia," Isaias wrote in his diary. "It is said that great misery exists amongst 35,000 German men, women, and children now interned by the Russians in Siberia. I subscribed $500 toward this worthy cause."[6]

In November 1915, he sent 500 marks to Professor Dappler, the doctor who treated him at the Bad Kissengen spa, to help the German war wounded. He also continued to send his relatives food and money.

By 1916, the Hellman family was divided on the necessity of America's entry into the war. President Wilson had stepped up his anti-German rhetoric in December 1916 in a speech that called for a buildup of the army and navy.

Isaias became a charter member of the League to Enforce Peace, a national group headed by former president William Taft. The group, founded in Philadelphia in 1915, aimed to set up an international organization and tribunal that could mediate disputes between countries. Isaias advocated for world peace in part because he recognized that war would impede American economic expansion. "Peace," he told a newspaper, "means the end of autocracy; it means the end of absolute monarchy. It means that in the future men will be judged not by their ancestors, but what they have done themselves. It means for the USA an opportunity in the world of trade such as we have never seen."[7]

Marco, on the other hand, had started to feel that America would soon have no choice but to enter the war on the side of the Allies. Even as his father sought to emphasize a peaceful solution to the conflict, Marco advocated that the United States should strengthen its military forces and get better prepared to fight.

In the midst of all the concern about the war, Isaias continued to go to work at the Wells Fargo Nevada National Bank. In 1916 he stepped down as president of the Union Trust Company, turning the helm of the company over to Marco. But Isaias had no plans to retire, to become a mere figurehead, as he felt idleness would sap his intellectual vigor. Isaias still lived with his daughter Clara, her husband, Emanuel, and their son, Edward, on Jackson Street in San Francisco's Pacific Heights. On Sundays, the family often gathered for dinner, rotating the meal between the houses of Isaias's children or occasionally eating at a restaurant. There now were fourteen people in Isaias's immediate family. Florence had two children, Sidney and Esther, and Marco had four, Warren, Frederick, Florence, and Marco.

His daughters were particularly attentive to Isaias and often went out on motorcar rides with him or out for some other entertainment. In fact, caring for Isaias seemed to bring out their competitive instincts. They often tried to outdo one another. They would alternate hosting holiday meals, and each feast was more sumptuous than the last.

Isaias also spent time with friends, although they had started to die off. Antoine Borel died in Switzerland in 1915. William Haas died in 1916. Isaias often had his chauffeur drive him fifteen miles south to San Mateo to the Beresford Country Club, where he would play bridge in the large Tudor-style clubhouse overlooking the golf course. Jews had started the country club in 1911 after many of the older San Francisco men's clubs started to exclude Jews from membership.

Isaias also took extended trips to his thirty-five-thousand-acre Nacimiento Ranch near Paso Robles. It reminded him of his early days in California, and he tried to re-create that bucolic splendor by planting wheat and stocking the

ranch with cattle. Isaias hired Fred Bixby, the son of one of his original partners in Rancho Los Alamitos, to manage the place.

Nacimiento was a place Isaias could indulge in his passion for horses. Years
earlier, while still living in Los Angeles, he had raised Thoroughbreds,
prompting the Bixby family to nickname him "Shire." Now he made an effort
to attend the annual rodeo at Paso Robles. He also enjoyed bringing down
Marco's two oldest sons, Warren and Frederick, to ride in the oak-studded hills.

In March 1917, President Woodrow Wilson made a speech that made it
clear the United States was planning to go to war—on the side of the Allies.
At that point Isaias stopped supporting the country he was born in and
started supporting America. "Before the President's message to Congress
most of us were neutrally inclined but now we must do our duty to our government as good & loyal citizens and assist it to the fullest extent of our
power, financially and otherwise," Isaias wrote the board of directors of the
Wells Fargo Nevada National.[8]

Isaias directed the bank to buy as many war bonds as it could, and he
strongly suggested the directors do so as well. The U.S. Treasury immediately issued $2 trillion in war bonds at 3½ percent interest. Patriotic fever
swept America, and by June 15, 1917, the bonds had been oversubscribed by
50 percent. Wells Fargo Nevada National Bank customers wanted to buy $6
million worth of war bonds, but the bank could get only a $3 million allot-
ment. For the duration of the war, Isaias was intimately involved in selling
each bond issue. He was appointed to the Treasury Department's Capital Issues Committee. Marco became the chairman of the local Liberty Bond
committee. In 1918, the bank launched two bond offerings totaling $15 mil-
lion, about 33 percent of the bank's total assets.[9]

The United States' entry into the war crystallized anti-German senti-
ments, and soon Americans of German descent were under attack. A group
calling itself the "Knights of Liberty" terrorized people in the San Jose area
in 1918 and kidnapped and presumably killed an Oakland tailor, whose body
was never found.[10]

Many German Jews, sensitive to the rising anti-German hysteria, formally changed their names. Max Brandenstein and his brother Charles
changed their names to Bransten. Some Dinkelspiels became Dinels or
Dicksons. Other families stopped talking in German at home to further distance themselves from their original homeland. The German Hospital,

founded in 1856 by Joseph Brandenstein and others, became the Franklin Hospital in 1917.

On October 3, 1917, Isaias turned seventy-five and used that occasion to make a gift to the University of California, where he had served as regent for thirty-six years. Isaias had always been generous, but he stepped up his donations after Esther's death. The $100,000 he had donated to Mount Zion Hospital in 1908 had been used to construct the Esther Hellman Building. In 1909, he contributed $10,000 toward the construction of a new city hall in Los Angeles. He gave funds in 1911 to assist the expansion of the Lick Observatory on Mount Hamilton near San Jose.

Isaias wanted to leave a lasting memorial to the university, one that would be more than a monetary contribution. He decided to donate $50,000 to be used for four scholarships, two for Jewish students and two for Christian students. The students would be selected by a committee of family members and university officials and would be expected to pay back the money if they became financially successful later in life. "My long connection with your board, my interest in the growing usefulness of the university and my desire to be of some help to worthy students in the generations to come have all combined to prompt this gift," Isaias said in a letter to the university.[11]

Isaias celebrated another milestone a month later. On November 6, he threw a gala at the Palace Hotel to celebrate the Wells Fargo Nevada National Bank's twentieth anniversary as a national bank. The bank now had about 220 employees and deposits of more than $55 million. The employees dressed in dark suits and tea-length chiffon dresses for the party, dined on delectable food, and sipped champagne. The entire company, which included many more men than women, gathered for a photo in the ballroom underneath hanging crystal chandeliers. Isaias, almost bald and with a white beard streaked with a few strands of black, stands slightly in front of the group, his hands held behind him. Marco, his hair slicked back, stands slightly behind his father. Very few people in the photo are smiling.

The entry of the United States into the war made it more difficult—but no less urgent—to raise funds for the Jews displaced by the fighting. By

November 1917, Marco had been elected the California chair of the American Jewish Relief Committee. The committee had evolved from a group run exclusively by central European Jews to one that now also included Jews of eastern European descent. The group set a goal of "$10 million to save 3 million lives." San Francisco was asked to donate $350,000. In addition to holding rallies and mass meetings, San Francisco Jews adopted a more grassroots approach to fund-raising. Many Jews, including Marco's wife, Frances, tried to raise money by giving stump speeches at their synagogues and clubs. While Isaias once again gave $10,000, San Francisco failed to raise as much money as New York organizers had hoped.

The appeal for funds intensified as the war wound down. Millions were displaced and starving, living in countries without viable governments. In 1918, Schiff composed a letter addressed to the Jews of America: "I wish to sound for you the most terrible cry, the most urgent call for aid that Jewish ears have heard in 3000 years," Schiff wrote. "I wish to ask you to look with me at a scene of absolute misery and starvation that Jewish martyrdom in all its history has never equaled."

On November 26, San Francisco congressman Julius Kahn attended a luncheon for the American Jewish Relief Committee in the Italian Room of the St. Francis Hotel on Union Square. Marco was one of the organizers of the benefit, which drew one hundred people. To encourage Bay Area residents to give yet again so the region could make a $325,000 goal, the committee put a full-page ad in the city's Jewish newspaper, the *Emanu-el:*

TO THE JEWS OF SAN FRANCISCO
THE CALL OF OUR BLOOD!
SAN FRANCISCO MUST DO ITS PART—WILL DO ITS PART
THE CALL OF OUR BLOOD SHALL BE ANSWERED.

Despite the appeal, San Francisco raised only $175,000.

When the University of California opened for its fall semester in 1918, the campus resembled a military installation rather than a place of learning. Around 3,500 male students enrolled simultaneously in university classes and military classes as part of a nationwide mobilization for war. The young men wore army or navy uniforms and slept together in battleship gray wooden barracks that had hastily been erected around campus. Each barrack was steam heated and held a large mess hall and sleeping space for 250 students. The fledgling soldiers marched and drilled on the school's broad lawns and learned military tactics and procedures in Harmon Gym or the Mining Building, leading the student newspaper to characterize the campus as an "armed camp." On October 2, more than 2,000 of the students gathered to pledge allegiance to the American flag and their new masters, the military.

Women students were also asked to do their part for the war by enrolling for a degree in nursing or occupational therapy, or by taking home economics or Red Cross supply classes. About 1,800 women learned how to sew, make bandages for wounded soldiers, or treat wounds and help soldiers recover the use of their injured limbs at classes in Hearst Hall.

There was no escaping the duty to prepare for war. The student newspaper, the *Daily California,* ran first-person accounts from former students on life in the trenches in France. Each death of a former Cal student was reported, right next to an advertisement of where people could buy their military uniforms. So many men enrolled in the army that there were not enough reporters to put out the newspaper. The editors ran an ad on the front page asking for volunteers and even deigned to turn to women for help.

While the university was gearing up to fight an enemy on foreign shores, it was nearly undone by a threat on the domestic front. On October 6, two student airmen came down with aches and fever and were quickly admitted to the infirmary. Three days later, seventeen more students complained of feeling poorly. By the time a week had passed, sixty-eight students, mostly members of the Students' Army Training Corps, were ill, some with high fever and pneumonia. The infirmary was so full that university doctors took over a nearby fraternity to house the sick.

The dreaded Spanish flu had made its way to California.

The deadly strain of the influenza virus could not have found a more opportune time to make its appearance. It came to the United States just as the country had herded together hundreds of thousands of young soldiers. The men came from different parts of the country and were housed in massive barracks where beds were placed closely together. The young recruits lived practically on top of one another, and when they weren't sleeping they were marching shoulder to shoulder or eating side by side in the mess hall.

The flu first broke out in a more benign strand in the spring of 1918. Sufferers came down with the usual assortment of aches and chills but usually recovered within three days. This flu was highly contagious and spread rapidly through Europe, even affecting King George V of England and King Alfonso XIII of Spain, before quieting down. But when it resurfaced in September 1918 it had mutated into an extremely virulent and deadly strain that felled not only the very young and the very old—the flu's usual victims—but people in their twenties and thirties.

A person could wake up in the morning feeling perfectly fine and be dead by evening. A high fever would come first and was often accompanied by bouts of delirium. But this strain of the influenza virus also caused internal hemorrhaging that quickly filled the lungs, forcing a person to gasp desperately for breath until he could no longer draw oxygen into his body. For these unfortunate sufferers, death came quickly.

In other victims, high fever and an achy body were accompanied by a bluish tint that spread slowly across the face, signaling the body's inability to draw in enough oxygen. After four or five days, these patients' weakened lungs would be attacked by bacteria, and they would quickly develop pneumonia. Some recovered, but many died after an illness of a week or so.

The Spanish flu was so contagious that it spread to every continent except Australia by October 1918 and killed from 50 million to 100 million people by the time it exhausted itself. In the United States, more than 500,000 people would die.

By October 17, so many people had developed the flu that the San Francisco Board of Supervisors ordered all schools, churches, theaters, and other public gathering spots to close. Eight days later, the board ordered everyone to don gauze masks in public. The *San Francisco Chronicle*, which had been downplaying the epidemic, emphasizing Liberty Bonds instead, was finally compelled to write about influenza on its front page. It published a collage of prominent men wearing masks that covered their mouths and nostrils. "Everyone Is Compelled to Wear Masks by City Resolution," read the headline. "Great Variety in Styles of Face Adornment in Evidence." The paper showed men in hats and men with spectacles looking outward, a white swath of cloth covering the lower portions of their face.

Mayor James Rolph pleaded with residents to protect themselves: "You are face to face with a deadly epidemic," he wrote in an open letter run in the city's newspapers. "Already it has begun to make its record of death in our city. It must be stopped. It is the duty of every person to help stop it. . . . Wear these masks and save your lives and those of your children and your neighbors."

At the University of California at Berkeley, President Benjamin Wheeler had ordered all students to wear masks to protect themselves on October 21. School officials called on women students to help make the masks, and more than 650 women rallied to the call. Sewing together four layers of gauze in about fifteen minutes, the women made 8,300 masks in three days, and eventually produced close to 24,000 masks.[12] Signs went up everywhere urging people to protect themselves. "Obey the Laws. And Wear the Gauze. Protect Your Jaws from Septic Paws."

The university sold the masks for 5¢ each in stations set up around the school. Health officials recommended that the masks be boiled for five minutes each night to kill germs, but this was not practical in a university setting, so students in the Hygiene and Pathology Department set up sterilizing stations. Berkeley police threatened to arrest anyone caught not wearing a mask and fine him $500 or send him to jail for up to ten days.

The irony is that the virus that caused this deadly strain of influenza was so small it easily passed through the gauze. The masks made people feel as if they were taking measures to protect themselves, but they weren't.

San Francisco, like other cities in the country, started to resemble a ghost town as children stayed away from school, shops shut their doors, and people avoided contact with one another. Restaurants, which were permitted to remain open, saw a dramatic drop in sales. Isaias himself returned to his daughter's house every day for lunch to minimize his exposure. "The town is dull, no places of amusement open," Isaias wrote in his diary. "The merchants might as well close their doors, no business." At the Wells Fargo Nevada National Bank, forty-five employees came down with the flu. The bank started to shut its doors at 2 P.M. instead of 3 to minimize exposure to the virus.

The quarantine also meant there would be no public ceremony for the opening of the Esther Hellman Settlement House on San Bruno Avenue in the southern section of San Francisco. Isaias and his children had donated funds for the construction of a large community building in an area that had seen an influx of Jews since the earthquake. The building was designed to hold a kindergarten, a gymnasium, a lecture hall, a reading room, and a branch of the Mount Zion Hospital clinic. The building opened on October 25 with little fanfare.[13]

Around that time, Isaias got the devastating news that his grandson Edward Heller had been stricken with a strong case of influenza. The eighteen-year-old boy and his older cousin, Warren, had enlisted in the army and were stationed at the Officers' Training School at Camp MacArthur near Waco, Texas. Edward had come down with the flu, which had quickly developed into a case of pneumonia.

Clara and Emanuel Heller left immediately on the train for Texas to be by the bedside of their only child. Their departure and his distance from Texas made Isaias feel helpless, and he sent off a series of telegrams to try and assist in any way possible. He wired William Woodson, the vice president and cashier of the First National Bank of Waco, to arrange hotel rooms for the Hellers and to get any information he could on Edward.

Woodson and his wife, who had regularly invited soldiers to their house for Sunday dinners, drove out to the base hospital and spoke directly with Major Goodloe, the field director of the Red Cross. More than one thousand soldiers had come down with the flu, and they were crowded into the base hospital, tossing and turning with fever and gasping for air.[14] When Woodson told the major about Edward, the major "immediately detailed a man to look into the condition of Mr. Heller, whom I found a very sick man," Woodson wrote to Isaias. "On Saturday afternoon he passed through the crisis with two doctors and a nurse in attendance. He rested well during Saturday night and Sunday night. . . . The doctors made a thorough examination of him today [Tuesday] and state that he has pneumonia but is improving rapidly and they think he is out of danger."[15]

There was no effective medical treatment for those with the flu. Health officials invented something called the influenza diet to be fed to patients every four hours. The sickly were given a diet rich with milk products, including ice cream, sugar, bread, gruel, and pureed vegetables. Meat broth was deemed worthless, while doctors considered chilled fruit juices beneficial. Edward's mother, Clara, convinced the hospital commander to serve their son and other patients orange juice every day.[16] It took Edward more than two weeks to gain back the strength he had lost in his fight against the pneumonia. While he was recovering, Isaias sent him $50.

Edward was one of the lucky ones. By early October more than 88,000 servicemen had come down with the flu and more than 2,800 had died. The army eventually estimated that 36 percent of its soldiers got the flu. The navy's numbers were even higher, with 40 percent of the sailors sick.[17]

The flu had cut a wide swath through the Jewish community. The eleven-year-old son of John A. Walter died in the spring, as did Solly Aronson, who was married to Herman Hellman's youngest daughter, Amy.

On November 11, the Germans surrendered and the armistice was declared. Sirens rang and bells chimed all over San Francisco, and people weary of war piled out on the streets to shout and celebrate. "San Francisco has been wild with noise and excitement," Isaias wrote to his son-in-law. The flu still raged, however, and schools, theaters, and churches remained closed until November 16. Five days later, siren wails throughout the city gave the signal that people could take off their gauze masks. Everyone thought the crisis was over.

It was not. Two weeks later a slew of new flu cases convinced officials that they had been mistaken. By December, five thousand more people would come down with the disease. There would be another flare-up in January, and then the virulent form of the flu appeared to go away.

THE LIGHT FADES

1918–1920

The end of the war did not mean an end to the violence against the Jews of Europe. If anything, the attacks intensified, for the social fabric that once restrained people from acting out their worst impulses had dissolved in the detritus left in the aftermath of the fighting. Jews were targeted in the Ukraine, Hungary, and Poland. The reports of lootings, burnings, and killings were so frequent that they became difficult to distinguish from one another.

In December 1918, the American Jewish Congress held its first annual meeting in Philadelphia's historic Independence Hall. Composed of prominent Jews from around the world, the congress—an outgrowth of the American Jewish Committee—came together to call for equal civil, political, and economic rights for Jews around the world. Marco Hellman was one of two delegates elected from San Francisco to attend the congress. Judge Max C. Sloss was the other. (They were both elected representatives to the American Jewish Relief Committee.) As head of the Federation of Jewish Charities, and a force in raising funds to help Jews in Europe, Marco had become one of the most visible and outspoken Jews on the West Coast. His wife, Frances, accompanied him to Philadelphia.

Jews were not the only ones questioning their future. The breakup of the Ottoman Empire after the war put the question of Palestine front and center. The British were poised to seize control of Palestine, and the government had declared its support for "a national home for the Jewish people in Palestine" in a document called the Balfour Declaration. President Woodrow Wilson, who had initially rejected the plan for a Jewish home in Palestine, changed his mind and endorsed the expansion of the Jewish presence in Palestine in 1917.

The Great Powers planned to discuss the plight of the Jews at the Paris peace talks in April 1919. There was great support for the establishment of a Jewish state. While Jews had once pushed for emancipation in their home countries, many now believed that anti-Semitism was too ingrained to permit the Jews to be political and economic equals. The Austrian Jewish journalist Theodor Herzl had become convinced of this after he covered the 1894 trial of Alfred Dreyfus, the French Jewish artillery officer who was convicted on a trumped-up charge of treason. Herzl began to advocate that the Jews find their own homeland where they would be safe from anti-Semitism.

Isaias was strongly opposed to the idea of transforming Palestine into a new home for Jews. He thought it would be better for European Jews to receive full equality in their homelands rather than have to leave and seek it elsewhere. Besides, the idea was impractical: there were millions of Jews in Europe, and there was no way they could all fit in the Middle East. He also disagreed with the notion that one hundred thousand Jews could or should rule over six hundred thousand Arabs.

Isaias had come to the United States in search of economic and religious liberty and found that he was able to combine his faith and his business in his adopted country. He thought the creation of a Jewish state would force American Jews to have dual loyalties, which would ultimately undermine both countries. "I . . . am not at all in favor of a Jewish state to be organized in Palestine, either under English rule or independent," wrote Isaias to a business acquaintance.[1] "I am perfectly satisfied with my status and my position as a citizen of the greatest republic the world has ever seen, and feel that it is incumbent on all of us who have had the benefits of living under the Government of the United States of America to do nothing at any time, and especially at the present time, which could in any way be construed as showing a divided allegiance."[2]

Many Jews of German Jewish descent agreed with Isaias's stance on Zionism, including his son, Marco, and Abraham Voorsanger, whose late father had been the rabbi of Temple Emanu-el and who served as editor of the influential *Emanu-el* newspaper. Congressman Julius Kahn of San Francisco, one of the few Jews in Congress and a man who had pushed for America's preparedness for war, was also an ardent anti-Zionist.

But a growing group of Jews, including two of Isaias's confidants, felt

differently. They believed the continuing anti-Semitism and violent outbreaks showed that Jews would not be safe until they better controlled their
own destiny. One of the major Zionists in the Bay Area was Rabbi Martin
Meyer, who had taken over Voorsanger's position after his death. Meyer
had declared his support of Palestine during a sermon he delivered from
the bimah in January 1916. Emanuel Heller, Isaias's son-in-law, had also
come to believe that the Jews needed their own homeland. "I've gone into
the subject of Zionism very thoroughly and I'm very much in favor of it,"
Heller declared.[3]

The Jews of California had come together during the war to raise funds
for their persecuted brethren, but the Zionist question drove a wedge into the
cordial relations. Both sides vowed to push their agenda at the Paris peace
talks, where the question of Palestine would be raised.

To thwart the creation of a Jewish state, Congressman Kahn asked thirty-
one of the country's most influential Jews to sign a petition. The signers included Isaias; Henry Morgenthau Sr., ex-ambassador to Turkey; Simon W.
Rosendale, ex–attorney general of New York; Mayor L. H. Kampner of
Galveston, Texas; E. M. Baker, from Cleveland and president of that city's
stock exchange; R. H. Macy's Jesse I. Straus; New York Times publisher
Adolph S. Ochs; and Judge Max C. Sloss of San Francisco.

"Whether the Jews be regarded as a 'race' or a 'religion,' it is contrary to
democratic principles for which the world war was raged to found a nation
on either or both of these bases," read a section of the petition. "America,
England, France, Italy, Switzerland, and all the most advanced nations of the
world are composed of representatives of many races and religions. Their
glory lies in the freedom of conscience and worship, in the liberty of thought
and custom which binds the followers of many faiths and varied civilizations
in the common bonds of political union. A Jewish state involves fundamental
limitations as to race and religion, else the term 'Jewish' means nothing. To
unite Church and State, in any form, as under the old Jewish hierarchy,
would be a leap backward of 2,000 years."[4]

Congressman Kahn hoped that President Wilson would present the petition at the peace talks, and he looked for a good moment to hand the petition
to him. On March 4, 1919, he telegraphed Henry Berkowitz, the head of the
Jewish Chautauqua Society, that he had presented the petition to Wilson at

the capital. Wilson promised Kahn he would read the petition on his trip across the Atlantic.[5]

In March and May another wave of violence against Jews broke out in the Ukraine. Homes were burned, stores were looted, and hundreds were killed or maimed. On June 13, the Jews of San Francisco came together at a massive rally in the Scottish Rite Auditorium one more time to protest the murders. Isaias and Marco both served on the executive committee. It was the last time the two men would work together.

The world after the end of World War I seemed a gloomy place. The combatants quarreled incessantly at the Paris peace talks, with Germany rejecting the terms offered for surrender. People in Germany and Austria were starving. The hostilities unleashed pent-up anti-Semitism, and the Poles took the opportunity to slay thousands of Jews. "The miserable Poles have been slaughtering the. . . . Jews lately," Isaias wrote on June 10, 1919. "May heaven curse and punish them for their infamous cruelty."

Many of Isaias's friends were dying around him. The influenza epidemic had returned with a vengeance in January and San Francisco officials ordered everyone to once again don gauze masks. The flu killed Irving Otto Weiss, one of the city's most respected attorneys, in mid-January. On April 14, Phoebe Hearst, one of the great benefactors of the University of California, died. She and Isaias had served on the board of regents together for twenty-two years. They were both close to President Benjamin Ide Wheeler, who had retired from the presidency that February.

Isaias was a pallbearer at Hearst's funeral. Thousands crammed into Grace Cathedral to listen to the Right Reverend William Ford Nichols's sermon and pay homage to a woman who had been born with little and who had later heaped her husband's millions on the people of California. A funeral cortege stretched for miles as the black hearses made their way to Cypress Lawn cemetery south of San Francisco. "Mrs. Hearst's funeral was an immense affair," Isaias noted in his diary. "The Courts, the Universities and other public institutions were closed in her honor."

He received a telegram on August 27, 1919, that his sister-in-law Babette Lehman had died in New York. The next day Isaias got a letter from a friend in Germany informing him his older sister Bertha Fleishman had died the previous December after an eleven-day illness. The loss of two women he loved deeply added to his sense of the world as a less inviting place.

On July 2, Isaias traveled to Pine Lodge at Tahoe, grateful to visit the place he loved the most in the world. He found the house in good order and enjoyed a few quiet days lounging on the porch and taking long walks along the lake. While he felt a slight shortness of breath—it took him longer than normal to acclimate to the high altitude—he felt well enough to have his old friends Mr. and Mrs. Abe Haas, Joe Koshland, and Mr. and Mrs. Max Brandenstein (now known as Bransten) over for lunch and a game of bridge. His daughter Florence and her family came to Pine Lodge on July 8 with the intention of remaining there with Isaias for the rest of the summer. The next day Frances came with her children.

On July 19, Isaias received devastating news—news that he had feared half of his life. Marco had suffered a severe heart attack and had been rushed to Adler Sanatorium. For decades, Isaias had had a presentiment that he and his son would die around the same time—and now Marco was seriously ill.[6] Isaias immediately drove to Truckee and boarded a train to San Francisco, where he arrived the next morning. Frances drove down from Lake Tahoe and pulled into the city around 5 A.M.

Marco was just forty-nine years old and had always seemed in good health. He was naturally athletic and liked to ride and walk, but he was a heavy smoker and had recently been diagnosed with diabetes. He had worked hard in the last few years at the Union Trust Company and the Wells Fargo Nevada National Bank, and with various Jewish charities around the country. The toil showed on his face, which had pouches permanently perched under his eyes. But just a few weeks earlier he had seemed as happy as ever. He hosted a barbecue at Oakvale for 150 employees of the Union Trust Company—a way to say thank you for all their hard work.

At the Adler Sanatorium Marco's doctor was Dr. Morris Herzstein, Isaias's longtime physician and the doctor who had treated Esther at the end of her life. But there was not much Dr. Herzstein could do for Marco except advise him to rest and start to walk when he got stronger.

Marco seemed to improve and moved back to his home on Broadway a few days later. The summer San Francisco weather was damp and foggy, so three weeks after his heart attack Marco moved across the bay to Oakvale, where the days were much sunnier. Isaias was so concerned about his son that he decided not to return to Lake Tahoe but to remain close by in the Bay Area. He spent most of his time at Clara's house on Jackson Street or down at her country home in Atherton, with numerous day trips to the Beresford Country Club on the peninsula to see friends and play bridge. He also went into the office regularly. "I am very much worried and distressed over son Marco's condition," wrote Isaias on August 13. "He does not look well."

On Sunday, September 7, the entire family came to Oakvale to celebrate Marco and Frances's twenty-first wedding anniversary. The Hellmans spent a joyful day together, gathered on the glassed-in porch overlooking the estate's massive lawn and orchid-filled greenhouse. Three days later, Isaias moved to Oakvale for a two-week stay.

In mid-September President Wilson arrived in San Francisco to cheering crowds and massive rallies. He was stumping to raise support for the League of Nations, the international body proposed by the Great Powers as a way to avoid another catastrophic war. Congress had already rejected numerous bills put forward to create the league, but Wilson took the plan directly to the public. He marched in a parade, spoke in front of two thousand women at a luncheon at the Palace Hotel, talked to many thousands more that evening at the Civic Auditorium, and then returned to the Palace to explain the plan to a roomful of businessmen. Isaias followed Wilson's movements closely in the papers but felt the treaty set too many stringent conditions on Germany and did not pay any remuneration to the United States. "President Wilson is making speeches daily in support of the League of Nations treaty," Isaias wrote. "He is fighting hard for it, but I hope he will not succeed."[7]

The country seemed ill at ease. The end of the war brought some improvement to the economy, but working men and women soon felt squeezed by rising prices and flat wages. The women running the telephones went out on strike, followed by railcar operators and dockworkers. "Strikes and riots all over California," Isaias noted on Wednesday, October 8, 1919. "Street railways strike at Oakland, sailors & stevedores strike in San Francisco, fifty thousand men on strike in local and Oakland shipbuilding plants. What is this country coming to?"

The family celebrated Isaias's seventy-seventh birthday on October 3 at a dinner at Florence and Sidney's brick home on Broadway, overlooking San Francisco Bay. A few weeks later an era came to an end when Isaias sold the site of the old Nevada Bank building on Pine and Montgomery to an English insurance company. The price was $500,000.

In mid-December, Marco's family set out to spend a few weeks in Santa Barbara and Clara and Emanuel left on a monthlong trip to New York. While Marco was in Santa Barbara, he took a turn for the worse and was ordered to stay in bed. His sister Florence traveled south to visit him and reported that he was pale and very thin, his body having shed many pounds in a short period of time. Marco finally made it back to San Francisco on February 11 after spending more than two months at the Hotel Belvedere in Santa Barbara.

After so many prosperous years, the family, which had accomplished so much and had left its mark on the history of California, seemed to be coming apart bit by bit. Clara came down with a mild case of influenza and the doctor ordered her to bed because the virulent form of the disease had resurfaced again. In fact, Isaias's niece Amy Hellman would die of the flu in Los Angeles on February 9, just thirteen months after her husband succumbed to the disease. "The poor woman leaves her two small children," Isaias wrote. "Her husband died a year ago of the same disease, I pity . . . her little orphaned children. Peace both to her and her ashes."[8]

Florence's daughter Esther came down with the measles but quickly recovered. Her son Sidney, however, had such a high fever that he was sent to the Adler Sanatorium on February 23. Then Clara relapsed, and her mild case of influenza turned severe. For two weeks she lay in her bedroom on Jackson Street, unable to see anyone but the doctor and her husband. Isaias came to the house every day but was not allowed to visit.

Isaias now had no one to console him. All three of his children were either ill or treating sick family members and they had little time to care for their father. Isaias was used to being central in their lives, and he didn't take their inattentiveness well. He felt abandoned and discarded.

Isaias didn't want to be a burden to his children, so he decided to strike out on his own. He had been living between Clara's homes in San Francisco and Atherton, occasionally sleeping at the Beresford Country Club in San Mateo. He still worked at the Wells Fargo Nevada National Bank almost every day, although his duties were minimal. "I have made up my mind that under present conditions it will be more convenient & more satisfactory if I try housekeeping," Isaias confided to his diary on March 9, 1920. "I will not inconvenience my children who I think ought to lead their young lives. I have rented Mr. Leonard Jacobi's residence. Mr. J. will go to Europe the end of this month when I will take his house."

Before he could move into his new rental, Isaias's nephew Herbert Lehman and his family arrived from New York for a visit. Isaias felt very close to Herbert, his wife, Mary, and their two adopted children, as they reminded him of Herbert's parents, Meyer and Babette Lehman. But the happy reunion was cut short. On March 17, Marco suffered another massive heart attack. "My son Marco has had a bad relapse & is very sick," Isaias wrote in his journal. "God Almighty alone can help & I pray to the Almighty to help & restore my son to his good health."[9]

That was Isaias's last entry in his diary. The stress and loneliness that had accumulated finally broke him down. He got pneumonia and was rushed to the Adler Sanatorium. Three weeks later, he died. He was seventy-seven.

The news of Isaias Hellman's death was bannered across the tops of San Francisco newspapers. Flags were lowered to half-staff at various banks.

"In the regrettable death of Mr. Hellman, this community and the entire Pacific Coast suffers an irreparable loss," Herbert Fleishhacker, the president of the Anglo & London Paris National Bank told a newspaper. "A pioneer of Western financiers, his virile energy, sterling ability and high sense of honor were combined to wield a potent influence upon the development of the West, to make him an outstanding international figure. His public interests were as wide as his modestly unheralded private philanthropies were generous."[10]

In a letter written in 1911, Isaias had requested that his children lay out his body on a pine board for ten days surrounded by a minyan, a group of ten Jewish men, before he was buried. This was an unusual request because custom required Jews to be buried within twenty-four hours of death. Isaias never elaborated why he wanted to delay his entombment. Perhaps it was the fear, popular at the time, that some people were buried alive. Perhaps he wanted his children and friends to pay him the respect he thought he deserved. Perhaps he remembered wakes from his childhood.

His children ignored his wishes. They buried Isaias two days after his death. They had to hire—and pay—ten men to say the prayers over his body. When the funeral rites were over, Isaias was moved to the marble tomb in the Home of Peace Cemetery in Colma where his wife's body lay.

A month later his son, Marco, only forty-nine, also passed away.

Isaias Hellman's death marked a passage in California history. The frontier era with its crude, violent ways, its unregulated financial markets, and its opportunities for the quick accumulation of wealth was over, but the time was still recalled with fascination and nostalgia. Now another link to the past was gone.

From humble beginnings, Isaias had grown to be a banker with international stature, a man noted for his fiscal sobriety and his canny instincts for a good business deal. By bringing capital to the frontier, Isaias had come to symbolize the opportunities available in the West. He not only had grown enormously wealthy, but had helped create a state that was an economic powerhouse, an engine that drove the national economy. He played a major role in the creation of two cities, Los Angeles and San Francisco, and the development of eight industries—banking, transportation, oil, water, wine, land development, electricity, and education. His judgment was highly valued, and many of the country's most important businessmen sought his counsel.

When Isaias died he left a vast estate, one that would be in probate for thirty-five years. He was the president or director of seventeen banks throughout his life, was one of the largest landholders in California—his holdings in southern California were valued at more than $2 million—and a man who consulted with the top financiers in the country on everything from bond sales to the establishment of the Federal Reserve. He had $5.7 million in cash in the bank at his death, and his children paid $1.38 million in inheritance taxes to the state of California, one of the largest sums ever collected. His fortune was estimated at between $10 million and $20 million, which is equal to $1.5 billion to $3 billion today.

In his will, Isaias left $100,000 to various Jewish charities and $25,000 to the Catholic Orphan Asylum in Los Angeles. He also left $2,000 to be distributed among the poor in Reckendorf. His seven grandchildren got $50,000 each, as did his younger brother James. His daughter-in-law and two sons-in-law got $25,000 each, and his three children split the rest of his estate.

EPILOGUE

There's not much left of Rancho Los Alamitos, which once spread over 26,000 acres of pristine grassland from the Pacific Ocean up into the hills above Long Beach. The Hellman portion has been whittled down to 182 acres, its entrance hidden behind a rusting metal gate off of Seal Beach Boulevard.

I got my first glimpse of the land in 2004 when I was in southern California doing research. I rode with one of the ranch's managers up a rutted dirt road and past a sign that said, "Hellman Ranch: No Trespassing Allowed." As we drove past a concrete culvert containing the San Gabriel River, past marshes and wetlands that once nourished sugar beets, I saw the ranch's newest crop: rows of metal oil pumps. The looming derricks rose and fell with a steady whoosh, their heads resembling ants sucking nourishment out of the ground.

Oil was discovered in this region in the 1920s, right after Isaias's death. The Alamitos Land Company, controlled by the Hellmans and Bixbys, had been selling off plots of land in the area for thirty-three years at that point. While houses sprouted in Long Beach and Seal Beach, the two families had difficulty getting rid of lots on the slopes of Signal Hill, a 350-foot-high hillock that marked a point where Rancho Los Alamitos and Rancho Los Cerritos came together. A few families had purchased plots on the hill and constructed single-story wooden dwellings that they landscaped with grass and flowers.

All that changed on June 23, 1921. The Shell Oil Company, drilling on land leased from the Bixbys and Hellmans, struck a huge reservoir of oil. Their well, named Alamitos no. 1, tapped into a pool of oil formed millennia earlier by the decay of plants and animals. Oil gushed out of the well into the sky, reaching a height of 114 feet. Black oil sprayed everywhere, covering rooftops, cars, lawns, and people.

It was the largest source of oil ever discovered in California and it reignited the oil rush. Within a few years, hundreds of oil derricks crowded the top of Signal Hill, many of them jammed into the front and back yards of the people who had been lucky enough to buy a parcel from the Bixbys and Hellmans.

The two families earned 12½ percent of the profits from Alamitos no. 1. Its discovery prompted Isaias's heirs to look for oil on other parcels. It turned out that some land south of Signal Hill, right next to Seal Beach, was rich in oil as well. The family leased out that land, but took back control in 1937. It is now called the Hellman Ranch, and fifty-three oil pumps reach into the bowels of the earth. It is one of the oldest family-run oil fields in California. The Hellman family, of which there are many descendants, has pulled more than 30 million barrels of oil out of the ground since the 1920s. Adjusted for 2005 dollars, the family has earned $485 million in profits.

Not bad for a parcel that cost Isaias about $875 in 1881.[1] It definitely was the most lucrative of all his land purchases.

It's even more interesting to note that this acquisition continues today to contribute to the California economy. Building the state was Isaias's most enduring legacy, and he was extremely proud of his efforts to develop the economy. Many of his contributions continue today.

Jackson Graves took over the presidency of the Farmers and Merchants Bank after Isaias's death in 1920. The bank grew as Los Angeles grew, and the bank's continued conservatism helped it weather the real estate and oil booms of the 1920s and the Great Depression. Hellman family members continued to serve as bank directors until 1956, when the bank, with $356 million in assets and liabilities, merged with the Security–First National Bank of Los Angeles. There was irony to the merger as Isaias had lent the funds in 1889 to start the bank, then called the Security Trust and Savings Bank. The irony continued when the Bank of America later purchased the merged institution—then called Security Pacific—because A. P. Giannini had started the Bank of Italy (later the Bank of America) in response to Isaias's banking principles.

The Farmers and Merchants Bank's last building still stands at the corner of Fourth and Main streets in downtown Los Angeles. It is frequently used as a set for filming commercials

Wells Fargo Nevada National Bank absorbed the Union Trust Company in 1924 and became known simply as the Wells Fargo Bank. The institution has merged with numerous other banks over the past hundred years, but the name has remained the same. The bank now has $1.3 trillion in assets and is the United States' twenty-fifth-largest employer with 281,000 employees and eleven thousand branches.

Wells Fargo and its signature stagecoach symbol have come to embody the West and the growth of the United States. A portrait of Isaias sits in the bank's History Room in a branch on Montgomery Street in San Francisco. The Wells Fargo Archives contain many of Isaias's papers, including the 1865 ledger he used when he opened his first dry-goods store.

When Herman Hellman sold his share of his grocery, Hellman, Haas & Company, in 1890, the company became known as Haas, Baruch, and Company. In 1953 the company was acquired by Smart & Final, a discount food store that operates 280 stores in the western United States and Mexico.

A version of Lehman Brothers survived until September 2008, when the firm declared bankruptcy, the largest recorded in U.S. history. The collapse of the 156-year-old investment firm shocked the world and helped trigger the huge economic downturn of 2008. While the firm carried the name Lehman Brothers, the Lehman family had disassociated itself from the company decades earlier.

No Jews remain in Reckendorf, Bavaria. Most of them moved to larger towns like Bamberg after the German government lifted residential restrictions in 1861. There were a handful of Jews living in the small hamlet when Adolf Hitler rose to power, but they soon left or were deported. The sandstone synagogue was looted and burned during Kristallnacht, reportedly by Catholics living outside of Reckendorf. Some of Isaias's relatives were killed by the Nazis, including Otto Hellman, a cousin who was the son of another Herman Hellman, a successful banker in Bamberg. After the war, the synagogue was used as a brewery and shoe storage facility. The town of Reckendorf is in the process of restoring the synagogue for use as a cultural center, which will include a small display about the town's Jews. I took my two daughters to Reckendorf in 2003 to see where their ancestors had come from. We were greeted by the town's archivist and a former mayor who knew a great deal about Reckendorf's Jewish residents. They are proud of the accomplishments of their former inhabitants. Many descendants of the Hellman, Haas, and Walter families have gone back to visit.

With Temple B'nai B'rith, Isaias left an enduring gift to the Jewish community. The Los Angeles congregation is now known as the Wilshire Boulevard Temple and is the largest Reform synagogue on the West Coast. It is so large that it occupies two sites—its historic Moorish-inspired temple on Wilshire Boulevard and a newer temple on the west side of Los Angeles, home to most of the city's Jews. Hellmans remained as leaders of the temple even after Isaias's departure to San Francisco. Herman Hellman was president for fifteen years, until 1901. Isaias's brother James and their nephews Adolph and Isidore Fleishman served on the board until the 1930s. Los Angeles is now home to more than five hundred and fifty thousand Jews, making it the second-largest Jewish community in the United States after New York City. The first U.S. census in 1850 recorded eight Jews in Los Angeles.

The University of Southern California opened its doors in 1880 with fifty-three students. Today, more than thirty-three thousand undergraduates and graduates study on a number of campuses around Los Angeles. USC's president, Steven Sample, recently raised $100 million to improve the quality of the school's education by bringing in top professors. USC's football team has been ranked number one in the country numerous times.

The University of California, which had just one location in Berkeley during Isaias's days as regent, has grown into a nine-campus system with more than two hundred thousand students. It is generally regarded as one of the finest public university systems in the country, with numerous Nobel Prize winners on its faculty. Several of Isaias's relatives also served as regents of the university, including his sons-in-law Emanuel Heller and Sidney Ehrman, and his grandson Edward Heller. His granddaughter-in-law Elinor Heller became the first female chair of the Board of Regents. The $50,000 Isaias donated for scholarships in 1917 has ballooned into a $2 million fund.

Emanuel Heller's law firm eventually became known as Heller Ehrman and at its peak had more than seven hundred lawyers in offices in thirteen cities in the United States, Europe, and Asia. The law firm was widely regarded as instrumental in the development of the West. It continued to represent Wells Fargo Bank and played a key role in arranging financing for the Hoover Dam, the San Francisco–Oakland Bay Bridge, and Golden Gate Bridge. The law firm took Levi Strauss & Company public in 1971 and then private again in 1985. The firm dissolved in 2008 after 118 years in existence.

Clara Hellman Heller and Emanuel Heller helped start the San Francisco Symphony and endowed the International House at the University of California at Berkeley, among other causes. Their son and daughter-in-law, Edward and Elinor Heller, became influential in Democratic Party politics in California. Edward Heller, an investment banker, was an early founder of Silicon Valley. He gave generously to the Bancroft Library at the University of California at Berkeley. The Heller family has continued its philanthropic commitment to the university.

Florence Hellman Ehrman and Sidney Ehrman had two children, Esther and Sidney, who died of a brain infection in England in 1930. The parents

were so distraught that they dismantled his Cambridge study and recon-
structed it at their home on Broadway in San Francisco. Sidney was an accomplished Renaissance historian and a chair in European history at the University
of California at Berkeley is endowed in his name. Esther married Claude
Lazard of France, a distant cousin of Isaias's good friend Eugene Meyer. She
raised her four children in France until the Nazis forced them to flee.

Florence and Sidney Ehrman took over possession of Pine Lodge at Lake
Tahoe and enjoyed using it until the state of California purchased in 1965. It
is now known as Sugar Pine Point State Park, named after the large pine
trees of the region. Isaias's house was slated to be torn down to make way for
campsites, but the state changed its mind. For the last twenty-six summers
the state parks department has put on "Living History Day" at the estate.
Volunteers dress up in historical costumes and reenact different eras of the
estate's history.

Sidney Ehrman lived to 101. He and his wife were ardent lovers of the
symphony. They became the patrons of the violinist Yehudi Menuhin when
he was nine and supported his education and family for many years.

Marco Hellman was appointed president of the Wells Fargo Nevada National Bank after his father's death but died a month later. He never woke
up from a coma to learn that his father had predeceased him. Marco's widow,
Frances, lived until 1959. She spent every summer at Oakvale, their home in
Oakland, and continued to throw elaborate parties that drew high-profile
guests like the Budapest String Quartet. She endowed a swimming pool and a
music series at Mills College in Oakland. The Hellman family sold Oakvale to
Oakland in 1961 after a highway was built nearby. It is now known as the Dunsmuir Hellman Historic Estate, and is open to the public.

Marco's three sons all went into banking or finance. Warren Hellman
served as president of Wells Fargo Bank from 1943 to 1960, and his younger
brother Frederick served as vice president. The third son, Marco, bought J.
Barth and Company, an investment banking house.

Florence Hellman, Marco's only daughter, married Lloyd Dinkelspiel, an
attorney who worked at Heller Ehrman. I am their granddaughter. Florence
became the youngest woman ever appointed to the San Francisco Board of

Education. After her untimely death from stomach cancer in 1958, her husband and family endowed Dinkelspiel Auditorium at Stanford University.

James Hellman, Isaias's youngest brother, lived until 1940. He owned a hardware store in Los Angeles and married Josephina Sattler and had two children. After her death, he married Eda Kremer, a granddaughter of the Los Angeles Jewish pioneers Joseph and Rosa Newmark. They also had two children. After Eda's death, James married her younger sister, Agnes. James served on the board of B'nai B'rith for more than thirty years.

Herman Hellman's two sons, Marco and Irving, followed him into the banking business. Marco served as president of both the Merchants National Trust and Savings Bank of Los Angeles and the Hellman Commercial Bank, two institutions that played an important role in the growth of the economy. Marco was one of the principal sellers of bonds for the Owens River aqueduct. He also lent funds to the film industry at a time when other banks did not. Marco lived lavishly in a mansion on Wilshire Boulevard and owned one of the largest stables of stock horses in the country. He served as grand master in the Tournament of Roses parade.

Irving Hellman branched out into real estate and was one of the developers of Windsor Square, a residential neighborhood in Los Angeles. He was also a devoted horseman and became president of the Bridle Path Association. Frieda Hellman, their sister, married Louis Cole, a businessman. Frieda never had children, but she raised the two orphaned sons of her sister Amy. All three of Herman Hellman's children were actively involved with Jewish and other civic organizations throughout their lives.

In November 1928, the Hellmans merged two of their banks with the United Security Bank and Trust Company, which was controlled by A. P. Giannini. The new institution was named the Bank of America of California and was one of the largest banks on the West Coast with assets of more than $50 million. The Hellmans exchanged their bank stock in a complex swap for stock in Transamerica Corporation, the holding corporation for many of Giannini's financial institutions.

After the stock market crash of 1929, the price of Transamerica stock plummeted, virtually bankrupting the Hellman brothers and many of their family members. Marco was forced to sell his house, his horses, and his extensive landholdings. He was also asked to resign from many of the clubs and groups he or his father had helped start in Los Angeles.

Henry Fleishman continued to live in South America, but sometime after Isaias's death he made his way to New York, where he lived the remainder of his days eking out a living as a waiter. Fleishman reestablished relations with his son, Harrell Harrell, and wrote to him on each birthday. "Today is your birthday and memories—to me—of the past are most unhappy—for I have failed in my duty to you, as your father, for reasons beyond your control," Fleishman wrote in 1928 on his son's thirty-seventh birthday. "I made and committed one great error and crime in my life, for which, as events have proven, I have been severely punished by God Almighty, for physically, mentally, and financially, I have been unable to struggle upward and onward, as I have striven, with desire to atone for my one false step in my business and social career."[2]

Many of Isaias's descendants have led productive lives as lawyers, doctors, writers, and artists. But one has re-created, and perhaps surpassed, the financial productivity of his ancestor.

F. Warren Hellman, Isaias's great-grandson, has made an enormous fortune in his own right. Warren, born in 1934, first showed an aptitude for finance when he went to work for Lehman Brothers after graduating from the University of California at Berkeley and Harvard Business School. He was president of the firm by the time he was thirty-six.

In 1984, Warren started Hellman and Friedman, a private equity firm in San Francisco. It has been tremendously successful, investing $16 billion in capital in various companies, including Levi Strauss, NASDAQ, Young and Rubicon, Blackbaud, DoubleClick, and Axel Springer, Germany's largest newspaper publisher. Warren is now a billionaire, although he declines to specify his net worth.

Warren is a fanatical athlete who runs every morning at 4 A.M.; he has completed the hundred-mile Ride and Tie, a foot and horse race through the Sierra Nevada, and many other grueling sporting events. He and his wife, Chris, started the Stratton Mountain Ski School in the Green Mountains of Vermont in 1972, and one of their daughters skied on the U.S. ski team. Warren currently owns the Sugar Bowl Ski Resort in the Sierra Nevada. He is a prominent contributor to political causes, and sits on Governor Arnold Schwarzenegger's board of economic advisers. He is a major donor to the University of California, the San Francisco Ballet, and the San Francisco Free Clinic, which was started by his daughter and son-in-law.

In recent years, Warren has become well known for his patronage of the Hardly Strictly Bluegrass Festival, a free three-day music festival in San Francisco's Golden Gate Park. It started in 2000 with one stage and six bands. In 2007, seven hundred thousand people came to see sixty-eight bands spread over five stages. Warren pays for the entire festival, which he calls his gift to San Francisco, and he has set up an organization to make sure the festival continues after his death. When he walks through the crowd, usually dressed in a bluegrass-inspired denim jacket or some other casual attire, cries of "Warren, you rock!" or "Thanks, Warren," follow him. Warren plays the banjo, and in 2005 his group, the Wronglers, started appearing at the festival.

Warren's success begs the question of whether genius for finance can be passed on through genes. Despite Warren's achievements, he thinks of his ancestor, Isaias Hellman, every day, and feels he comes up short in comparison.

ACKNOWLEDGMENTS

When I set out to write about Isaias Hellman I never imagined the process would take eight years. Despite the length, it's been an immensely enjoyable journey, largely because of the people I have encountered along the way.

I grew up going to libraries, and one of the joys of the book was spending time in some of the country's most distinguished research institutions. There is no greater place to feel pampered as a scholar than at the Huntington Library in San Marino, California, where a reader's card not only provides access to papers from the pueblo era of California, but a discount at the restaurant and free admission to the magnificent gardens. The Bancroft Library in Berkeley holds a dizzying array of Americana, and I could spend the rest of my life happily poking through its manuscript collections. I also benefited from my visits to the Western Jewish History Center of the Judah L. Magnes Museum, where archivist Aaron Kornblum was always helpful.

Most of Hellman's papers are housed at the California Historical Society. Mary Morganti and her staff always made me feel welcome and even opened the library in off hours so I could get through the massive Hellman collection. I owe a special note of gratitude to Joe Evans, who spotted a mismarked box down in the society's archives. It contained a trove of material dealing with the controversies in Hellman's life. Opening that box was the biggest eureka moment of my research.

Wells Fargo Bank does not frequently permit independent scholars to look through its archives, but Andy Anderson and Beverly Smith made sure I had the access I needed. The archivist Keri Koehler made an extra effort to find me material, including the minute books of the Nevada Bank, and for that I thank her. I also benefited from the guidance of Marianne Babal. Robert Chandler dispensed humor and history in equal measure.

The first time I fully appreciated the complexity of the Jewish experience in nineteenth-century Germany came when I read Roland Flade's excellent history *The Lehmans: From Rimpar to the New World.* Roland not only informed my understanding of where Hellman came from, he offered to comb through the Würzburg State Archives for long-forgotten information about the Hellman family. Roland also translated when I went with my daughters to Reckendorf, where we met the town's indefatigable archivist, Heidi Waschka. Heidi dug up most of the information about the Hellmans's schooling and professional occupations. My cousin Joachim Bechtle and Oliver Bryk helped me understand old German script and German Web sites. Jim Harris deciphered the byzantine world of Jewish intermarriage for me; without his clear-eyed knowledge of "Our Crowd," I would have been much more confused.

I also want to thank the historians Bill Deverell, Ava Kahn, Fred Rosenbaum, Kevin Starr, and Karen Wilson for conversations that deepened my knowledge of California and the role Jews played in its development.

The journey to uncover Hellman's life was also an opportunity to rediscover my family, many of whom I barely knew when I started the project. Christiane de Bord not only saved about 150 German letters written to I. W. Hellman in the mid-nineteenth century, but didn't hesitate a moment when I asked if I could borrow them. Crickie, her sister Florence de Lavalette, her brother, Claude Eric Lazard, and I spent a fun evening in New York pulling out other old Hellman letters from a musty trunk. Alf and Ruth Heller and their daughters Miranda, Katherine, and Anne endured my endless requests to look through boxes and to just "get a copy" of a particular photograph or letter. Sarah and Peter Mandell opened their beautiful house in Los Angeles to me. While Sarah is a Hellman by marriage, she more than matched my fascination with Hellman and early California. She also introduced me to an unknown cousin, Carol Halperin, who spurred me on with her upbeat e-mails from Los Angeles. Katherine Hellman Black let me pore over her extensive files, no strings attached. It was her father, Warren Hellman III, who donated all of his grandfather's papers to the California Historical Society and to Wells Fargo Bank. If he had not thought to do that, this book could never have been written.

I owe a special debt of gratitude to Chris and Warren Hellman. When I was just poking around in the archives, Chris called me up and said she and Warren believed that I should, no, that I must, write this book. They followed their encouragement with financial support from the Hellman Family Foundation.

The Historical Society of Southern California provided me with a Haynes Research stipend. I also want to thank the Louis N. Littauer Foundation for its generous support.

I brought the first two chapters of *Towers of Gold* to the Community of Writers at Squaw Valley. Michael V. Carlisle was leading the nonfiction workshop, and from the time he read my first attempts at narrative, he was one of the book's biggest cheerleaders. I owe him an immense debt of gratitude for telling me to keep going, that I had a big book on my hands, and to call him when I had more. Michael eventually became my literary agent and has continued to encourage me and believe in me even in times when I doubted myself. I could not have done this without him

I also want to thank Diane Reverand at St. Martin's Press for seeing the book's potential and Michael Flamini for deftly handling the manuscript.

This book could never have been written without my writers group, North 24th. We came together as a motley collection of reporters, editors, and essay writers and with time, actually grew respectable. I want to thank Allison Hoover Bartlett, Leslie Crawford, Katherine Ellison, Sharon Epel, Susan Freinkel, Katherine Neilan, Lisa Okuhn, and Jill Storey for their red pencils and wisdom. The book is much better as a result of their insights. One member of the group, Julie Flynn Siler, headed my personal cheering section. I greatly relished our conversations about the nature of narrative.

As a working mother, I would never have been able to complete this book without my extended network of friends. Not only did they encourage me, they picked up my daughters from school, took them to various appointments, fed them, and loved them while I was at work. Thanks to Susan Helmrich, Ali and Michael Ranahan, Pamela Mazzola, Mya Kramer, Tim Choate, and Elizabeth McKoy. Another round of thanks to Jan Waldman, Daryl Austern, and Janet Traub, just for being there.

I also want to thank my family. There are no words to express my appreciation for their belief in me. My mother and stepfather, Georganne and Scott Conley, were proud of me before I wrote a single word. My brothers, Steven and Lloyd Dinkelspiel, helped me as only older brothers can: by loving me and challenging me, often in the same sentence.

Finally, a thank-you to my husband, Gary Wayne. He was the one who thought leaving my newspaper job to write a book was a great idea. He was the one who expressed confidence in my abilities. And a big hug and kiss to my wonderful daughters, Charlotte and Juliet Wayne. Charlotte started reading my pages when she was only twelve years old; even then her insights were helpful. Juliet was always ready to step in and cook when Mom was busy. This book, with its history of our family, is my gift to them.

NOTES

2. New Names, New Lives

1. I must thank Adleheid Waschka, the archivist of Reckendorf, for finding and translating the files relating to various Hellmans.

2. According to the records of the council of Reckendorf, there were seventy-seven Jewish families living in town in 1823, one under the maximum permitted by law.

3. From the transcripts of the Baunach court. Research done by Roland Flade.

4. Ava F. Kahn, *Jewish Voices of the California Gold Rush: A Documentary* (Detroit: Wayne State University Press, 2002), pp. 63–64.

5. Moses Rischin, ed., *The History, 1849–1880 Jews of the West: The Metropolitan Years* (Waltham, Mass: American Jewish Historical Society for the Western Jewish History Center of the Judah L. Magnes Museum, 1979), p. 35.

6. I. J. Benjamin, *Three Years in America, 1859–1862* (Philadelphia: Jewish Publication Society of America, 1956); vol. 1, p. 233.

7. Kahn, p. 490.

3. Coming to Los Angeles

1. Horace Bell, *Reminiscences of a Ranger* (Santa Barbara, Calif.: Wallace Hebbard, 1927), p. 26.

2. Harris Newmark, *Sixty Years in Southern California* (Cambridge, Mass.: Riverside Press, 1930), p. 31.

3. Ibid., p. 248.

4. Joseph Mesmer, "Some of My Los Angeles Jewish Neighbors," *Western States Jewish Historical Quarterly* 3, no. 3 (April 1975), p. 199.

5. Mora eventually became the Catholic bishop for a territory extending from Monterey to San Diego. He and Isaias remained friends, and Isaias became a financial counselor for the Catholic Church.

6. Michael Engh, "Charity Knows Neither Race nor Creed: Jewish Philanthropy to Roman Catholic Projects in Los Angeles, 1856–1876," *Western States Jewish Historical Quarterly* 21, no. 2, p. 162.

7. *Los Angeles Examiner*, December 2, 1917.

8. Benjamin, vol. 2, p. 101.

9. "Hebrew Benevolent Society of Los Angeles, Constitution and By-Laws, 1855," *Western States Jewish Historical Quarterly* 30, no. 2 (January 1998), pp. 145–54.

10. William M. Kramer, "The Founding of the Organized Jewish Community of Greater Angeles," *The Jews of Los Angeles: Urban Pioneers* (Southern California Jewish Historical Society, 1981), p. 17.

11. Mesmer, p. 192.

4. A SAFE AND A DREAM

1. William Brewer, *Up and Down California: In 1860–1864* (Berkeley: University of California Press, 1966), p. 20.

2. John W. Robinson, *Los Angeles in Civil War Days, 1860–1865* (Los Angeles: Dawson's Book Shop, 1977), pp. 50–51.

3. Ledger, 1865 Hellman Family Papers, 1859–1971, Wells Fargo Archives, box 24, folder 26.

4. Ibid.

5. Untitled article, *Los Angeles Herald Examiner*, December 23, 1917.

6. Ira B. Cross, *Financing an Empire: History of Banking in California* (Chicago: S. J. Clarke Publishing, 1927), p. 536.

7. John McGroarty, *The Pioneer: A Fascinating Chapter from the Pages of California History* (Los Angeles: Press Publishing, 1925).

8. Letter, June 7, 1867, Adelaide Hellman to Max Hellman, collection of the author.

9. "Income Returns of 1867 in the Second Internal Revenue District," *Los Angeles Weekly Star,* June 27, 1868. The richest man by far was Edward F. Beale, who earned more than $85,000, mostly by speculating in cattle. Beale, a Mexican War hero, had come to California in 1846, eventually amassing almost three hundred thousand acres north of Los Angeles. In 1848, he carried word of the discovery of gold to Washington, D.C., by crossing the continent in a harrowing six-week journey. In the 1850s, Beale convinced Congress to import camels into the region to test their stamina in the mountains and semiarid areas.

10. Robert Glass Cleland and Frank B. Putnam, *Isaias W. Hellman and the Farmers and Merchants Bank* (San Marino, Calif.: Huntington Library, 1965), p. 16.

5. MARRIAGE

1. Elliot Ashkenazi, *The Business of Jews in Louisiana, 1840–1875* (Tuscaloosa: University of Alabama Press, 1988), p. 128.

2. Letter, November 21, 1867, Rosa Newmark to Sarah Newmark, Rosalie Meyer Stern Personal Papers, box 9, folder 12, Western Jewish History Center, Judah L. Magnes Museum, Berkeley, CA.

3. Engh, pp. 154–65. When Isaias died in 1920, he left $5,000 to the Sisters of Charity. He had also given the sisters $5,000 in 1891.

4. "Rabbi Abraham W. Edelman—In Loving Memory," *B'nai B'rith Messenger,* June 7, 1929, p. 30.

5. "The Hebrew Congregation Ball," *Los Angeles Star,* February 10, 1872.

6. "Hebrew Synagogue," *Los Angeles Star,* August 24, 1872.

6. THE FARMERS AND MERCHANTS BANK

1. Cleland and Putnam, p. 18.
2. Jackson A. Graves, *My Seventy Years in California* "1857–1927," (Los Angeles: Times-Mirror Press, 1927), p. 425.
3. The *Los Angeles Daily News* ran a list of local incomes on June 11, 1870. Downey was at the top of that list, with an income of $13,540, followed by F. P. F. Temple, with an income of $8,954. Isaias reported an income of $6,200, while Eugene Meyer's was $3,978 and Harris Newmark's was $3,797.
4. *Farmers and Merchants Bank v. John Downey*, Los Angeles County Court Records no. 3918, filed December 28, 1877, Huntington Library, San Marino, Calif.
5. Newmark, p. 430.
6. Ibid., p. 435.
7. *Los Angeles Daily News*, May 14, 1871.
8. C. P. Dorland, "Chinese Massacre at Los Angeles in 1871," *Historical Society of Southern California Quarterly* (January 7, 1894), p. 22–26.

7. THE RAILROAD

1. "Railroad Meeting," *Los Angeles Daily News*, May 19, 1872.
2. Louisa and Louis Jungst had a number of children but never expained Junot Wattell's parentage to them. Junot Wattell moved back to Los Angeles in 1890. In 1915, he successfully petitioned the court to change his last name to Hellman, although the court turned down his request to rename himself Herman W. Hellman. Junot did not have children.
3. Neill C. Wilson, *400 California Street: The Story of the Bank of California* (San Francisco: Bank of California, 1964), p. 42.
4. Grant H. Smith, "The History of the Comstock Lode, 1850–1920," *University of Nevada Bulletin* 37, no. 3 (July 1, 1943).
5. Ibid., p. 174.
6. Ibid., p. 163.
7. Ibid., p. 176.
8. Cleland and Putnam, p. 36.
9. Letter, September 20, 1875, IWH to Esther Hellman, private collection of Christiane de Bord.
10. Letter, September, 25, 1875, ibid.
11. Cleland and Putnam, p. 39.
12. *Farmers and Merchants Bank v. John Downey*.
13. A. M. Bragg, Hubert Howe Bancroft Dictations, CD 810:43, Bancroft Library, Berkeley, Calif.
14. "The Last Spike," *Los Angeles Express*, September 6, 1876.
15. Newmark, pp. 505–6.

8. PROSPERITY

1. *San Francisco Examiner*, December 15, 1912, p. 8.
2. *Los Angeles Herald*, October 10, 1876.

3. *Los Angeles Star*, September 13, 1877.

4. Frederic C. Jaher, *The Urban Establishment: Upper Strata in Boston, New York, Charleston, Chicago, and Los Angeles* (Urbana: University of Illinois Press, 1982), pp. 577–709. This group of men, most of whom had been born in Europe and had arrived between 1850 and 1859, charted the economic course of the city. They owned the most land, sat on the boards of the water, gas, and transportation companies, controlled the banks, and held the political power. Only two were native Californios, a sad reflection of that group's displacement since the arrival of the Yankees. An astonishing 13.2 percent were Jews, and they included Isaias, his brother Herman, his cousins Isaiah and Samuel, Eugene Meyer, Harris Newmark, and others.

5. Robert Post, *Street Railways and the Growth of Los Angeles: Horse, Cable, Electric Lines* (San Marino, Calif.: Golden West Books, 1989), p. 4.

6. When Isaias died in 1920 he left more than fifty cases of port and Angelica produced in 1875 by Cucamonga Vineyards. Various family members took bottles and some sold through Sotheby's for more than $300 a bottle. In 2006, one of Hellman's great-great-granddaughters asked a friend for advice whether to recork the bottles. While he was pondering the question, he sent the wine to a temporary storage facility in Vallejo, California. In 2006, an arsonist burned down the warehouse, taking Isaias's 131-year-old port with it.

7. Benjamin Cumming Truman, *Semi-Tropical California, Its Climate, Healthfulness, Productiveness and Scenery* (San Francisco, Calif.: A. L. Bancroft & Company, 1874), p. 197.

8. Jane Aspostal, "Don Mateo Keller: His Vines and His Wines," *Southern California Quarterly* 84, no. 2 (Summer 2002), p. 101.

9. Ibid.

10. Ibid., p. 111.

11. Letter, March 31, 1879, IWH to Matthew Keller, Papers of Matthew Keller, 1851–1961, box 4, folder 3, Huntington Library, San Marino, Calif.

12. Letter, undated, Matthew Keller to IWH, ibid., box 5, ephemera.

13. Letter, undated, IWH to Matthew Keller, ibid., box 4.

14. *Farmers and Merchants Bank v. John Downey.*

15. *John Downey v. Isaias Hellman*, case no. 4285, June 12, 1878, Los Angeles County Court Records, Huntington Library, San Marino, Calif.

16. *Los Angeles Daily Herald*, July 6, 1881.

17. William W. Ferrier, *Origin and Development of the University of California* (Berkeley, Calif.: Sather Gate Bookshop, 1930), p. 376.

18. "Rancho Los Alamitos," *Los Angeles Times*, July 1, 1883.

19. Letter, April 3, 1890, IWH to Meyer Lehman, Isaias W. Hellman Papers, 1865–1922, MS 981, California Historical Society, San Francisco, Calif., vol. 8.

20. Letter, August 17, 1884, IWH to Benjamin Newgass, ibid., vol. 4.

21. Inventory, ibid., box 1, folder 7.

22. A. S. Cooper, "Oil and Gas Yielding Formations of California," *California State Mining Bureau Bulletin* no. 19 (November 1900), p. 216.

23. *Pacific Petroleum Record*, February 1919.

24. Letter, April 25, 1894, Harrison Gray Otis to IWH, Isaias W. Hellman Papers, MS 981, box 4, folder 23.

25. Ibid., vol. 2., p. 264.

26. Post, p. 47.
27. Ibid., p. 78.
28. Ibid., p. 80.
29. *Porcupine,* January 6, 1883.
30. Notes on John G. Downey, Hubert Howe Bancroft Manuscript Collection, Bancroft Library, University of California, Berkeley, Calif.
31. Cleland, p. 49.
32. J. R. Douglas, *The Bank and the Community—a History of Security Trust and Savings Bank of Los Angeles, 1889–1929* (Los Angeles, 1929).
33. "The Bar Mitzvah of a Banker's Son in Los Angeles—1884," *Western States Jewish Historical Quarterly* 3, no. 3 (April 1973), p. 188–89.
34. *San Francisco Blue Book,* 1890 edition. (San Francisco: Bancroft Company).
35. Letter, April 18, 1888, Eda Kremer to Rosalie Meyer, Rosalie Meyer Stern Personal Papers, box 1, folder 9.
36. Ella Giles Roddy, ed., *The Mother of Clubs: Caroline M. Seymour Severance, an Estimate and Appreciation* (Los Angeles: Baumgardt Publishing, 1906), p. 45.
37. Herman Frank, *Scrapbook of a Western Pioneer* (Los Angeles: Times-Mirror Press, 1934), p. 137.
38. Letter, November 20, 1884, E. Bengough to Rosalie Meyer, Rosalie Meyer Stern Personal Papers, box 1, folder 4.
39. Letter, January 4, 1885, IWH to Benjamin Newgass, Isaias W. Hellman Papers, MS 981 vol. 4, p. 211.

9. TRANSFORMATION

1. Letter, March 6, 1886, IWH to George Stoneman, Isaias W. Hellman Papers, MS 981, vol. 5.
2. Unidentified clip in scrapbook, March 25, 1886, Stephen Mallory White Papers, 1853–1901, box 96, p. 108, Stanford University Special Collections, Stanford, Calif.
3. Letter, October 2, 1886, Stephen White to William D. English, ibid, p. 29.
4. Edith Dobie, *The Political Career of Stephen Mallory White: A Study of Party Activities Under the Convention System* (Stanford, Calif.: Stanford University Press, 1927), p. 77.
5. Letter, November 26, 1886, Stephen White to William D. English, Stephen Mallory White Papers, outgoing correspondence book 1, p. 119.
6. Letter, November 23, 1886, IWH to Benjamin Newgass, Isaias W. Hellman Papers, MS 981, vol. 6.
7. Letter, September 9, 1886, E. McDonell to IWH, private collection of Katherine Hellman Black.
8. Letter, January 2, 1887, Stephen White to IWH, Stephen Mallory White Papers, outgoing correspondence book 2, p. 20.
9. Letter, January 5, 1887, Stephen White to IWH, ibid.
10. Letter, January 12, 1886, Stephen White to IWH, ibid.
11. Letter, January 14, 1887, Stephen White to J. D. Lynch, ibid., p. 102.
12. Letter, February 27, 1888, IWH to Stephen White, Isaias W. Hellman Papers, MS 981, vol. 7.
13. Letter, February 28, 1888, Ella Newmark to Rosalie Meyer, Rosalie Meyer Stern Personal Papers. box 1, folder 9.

14. Letter, May 5, 1886, IWH to H. H. Markham, Isaias W. Hellman Papers, MS 981, vol. 5.
15. Newmark, p. 570.
16. Tax assessments for years 1884 and 1889, Hellman Family Papers, Wells Fargo Bank Archives, box 13, folders 6–7.
17. Cleland and Putnam, p. 52.
18. Letter, October 4, 1887, IWH to Benjamin Newgass, Isaias W. Hellman Papers, MS 981, vol. 5.
19. Kaye Briegel, "A Centennial History of the Alamitos Land Company, 1888–1898," reprint from *Historical Society of Southern California Quarterly* (1988), p. 10.
20. "Real Estate and Improvements owned by I. W. Hellman on May 1, 1887, Hellman Family Papers, Wells Fargo Archives," box 3, folders 6–7.
21. Glenn S. Dumke, *The Boom of the Eighties in Southern California* (San Marino, Calif: Huntington Library 1944), p. 267.

10. THE NEVADA BANK

1. Letter, November 30, 1889, IWH to Sigmund Lehman, MS 981, box 28, vol. 7, p. 369.
2. Letter, October 4, 1887, IWH to Benjamin Newgass, Isaias W. Hellman Papers, MS 981, vol. 5.
3. Letter, December 6, 1889, Benjamin Newgass to IWH, Hellman Family Papers, Wells Fargo Archives, box 2, folder N.
4. Letter, January 8, 1890, Benjamin Newgass to IWH, ibid., box 2, folder N.
5. Letter, undated, Eugene Germain to IWH, ibid., box 2, folder 8.
6. "Banker Hellman. His Views in Regard to the Nevada Bank," *San Francisco Chronicle*, February 21, 1890.
7. Letter, March 4, 1890, Meyer Lehman to IWH, Hellman Family Papers, box 2, folder N.
8. Undated, *Los Angeles Herald*, Isaias W. Hellman Papers, MS 981, box 1, folder 6.
9. Letter, March 28, 1890, IWH to Benjamin Newgass, ibid., vol. 9, pp. 21–22.
10. Letter, April 2, 1890, IWH to Benjamin Newgass, ibid. v. 9, p. 45.
11. Letter, August 25, 1887, William Reid to IWH, ibid., box 16, folder 103.
12. Letter, September 23, 1888, IWH to Marco Hellman, ibid., vol. 7, p. 89.
13. Letter, June 16, 1888, IWH to Marco Hellman, ibid., p. 39.
14. Letter, July 6, 1892, Hannah Walter to IWH, ibid., box 3.
15. Letter, April 3, 1890, IWH to Meyer Lehman, ibid., vol. 8.
16. Letter, February 14, 1891, IWH to Benjamin Newgass, ibid., vol. 13, p. 75.
17. Letter, April 7, 1891, IWH to Nevada Bank Board of Directors, ibid., vol. 18, p. 231.
18. Letter, April 7, 1891, IWH to Herman Hellman, ibid., vol. 11, p. 247.
19. Letter, January 5, 1892, IWH to Nevada Bank Board of Directors, ibid., vol. 13, p. 87.
20. Letter, June 29, 1892, IWH to Esther Hellman, ibid., MS 981A, box 1, copybook, p. 142.
21. Letter, June 18, 1892, IWH to Esther Hellman, private collection of Christiane de Bord.
22. *Wave*, April 3, 1892, p. 4.
23. Letter, April 19, 1892, IWH to Benjamin Newgass, Isaias W. Hellman Papers, MS 981 box 30, vol. 11, p. 385.
24. Letter, July 28, 1892, IWH to Esther Hellman, ibid., MS 981A, box 1, copybook, p. 227.
25. Letter, September 27, 1892, IWH to Abraham Stern, ibid., pp. 482–83.

26. Letter, June 13, 1891, IWH to Benjamin Newgass, ibid., MS 981, box 30, vol. 11.
27. Letter, October 8, 1891, IWH to Benjamin Newgass, ibid., vol. 12, p. 265.
28. Letter, July 1892, IWH to Esther Hellman, MS 981A, box 1, copybook, p. 212.
29. Letter, November 7, 1892, IWH to Esther Hellman, MS 981, box 31, vol. 14.
30. Letter, December 30, 1892, IWH to Meyer Lehman, ibid., vol. 14, pp. 340–41.
31. Letter, July 23, 1892, IWH to Esther Hellman, MS 981, box 1, copybook, p. 200.
32. Letter, September 6, 1892, IWH to Esther Hellman, ibid., pp. 390–91.
33. Letter, September 12, 1892, IWH to Esther Hellman, ibid., p. 440.
34. Sig and Rosalie Stern's daughter Elise would go on to marry Walter Haas, the son of Herman's old partner, Abe Haas, and Fannie Koshland. Walter Haas would later take over Levi Strauss. The Haas family continues to operate the business and is one of the most philanthropic families in California.
35. Letter, May 24, 1893, IWH to Meyer Lehman, Isaias W. Hellman Papers, MS 981, vol. 15, p. 310.
36. Letter, June 17, 1893, IWH to Herman Hellman, ibid.
37. All the telegrams are in ibid., box 3, folder 18.
38. Letter, July 3, 1893, IWH to Meyer Lehman, ibid., vol. 15, p. 349.
39. "Mr. Hellman Talks," *Los Angeles Times,* July 9, 1893.
40. Letter, July 1, 1893, IWH to Herman Hellman, Isaias W. Hellman Papers, MS 981, box 31, vol. 15, p. 343.
41. David L. Clark, *A History of the California Club, 1887–1997* (Los Angeles, Calif: California Club, 1997).
42. Letter, July 26, 1893, IWH to Meyer Lehman, Isaias W. Hellman Papers, MS 981, vol. 15, p. 449.
43. Margaret Leslie Davis, *Dark Side of Fortune: Triumph and Scandal in the Life of Oil Tycoon Edward L. Doheny* (Berkeley: University of California Press, 1998), p. 27.
44. Ibid., p. 19.
45. Letter, September 30, 1919, IWH to Casper Whitney, Isaias W. Hellman Papers, MS 981, box 24, vol. 51.
46. Letter, March 28, 1894, IWH to Herman Hellman, ibid., vol. 17, pp. 59–60.
47. Letter, July 21, 1894, IWH to Meyer Lehman, ibid., p. 291.
48. Letter, March 17, 1894, Collis Huntington to IWH, ibid., box 4 folder 23.
49. Letter, October 12, 1894, IWH to Harrison Gray Otis, ibid., vol. 17, p. 466.
50. Cleland and Putnam, p. 66.
51. Letter, June 15, 1892, Herman Hellman to IWH, private collection of Katherine Hellman Black.
52. Letter, November 17, 1891, Herman Hellman to IWH, ibid.
53. Letter, August 24, 1893, IWH to Herman Hellman, Isaias W. Hellman Papers, MS 981, vol. 16, p. 9.
54. Letter, April 11, 1894, Marco Hellman to IWH, ibid., box 4, folder 23.
55. Letter, June 23, 1894, ibid, folder 24.
56. Letter, October, 29, 1894, Herman Hellman to IWH, private collection of Katherine Hellman Black.
57. Letter, October 30, 1894, Marco Hellman to IWH, ibid.
58. Letter, November 9, 1894, IWH to Marco Hellman, Hellman Family Papers, box 5.
59. Minutes, Board of Directors, Farmers and Merchants Bank, ibid., box 20, p. 12.

11. A DEATH THREAT

1. "Shot At, President Hellman of the Nevada Bank Narrowly Makes Escape," *San Francisco Daily Report*, February 9, 1895.

2. Telegram, February 9, 1895, John Mackay to IWH, Isaias W. Hellman Papers, MS 981, box 5, folder 26.

3. Letter, January 21, 1898, IWH to Louis Hellman, ibid., box 34, vol. 23.

4. Letter, January 22, 1898, IWH to Mr. and Mrs. Frederick Jacobi, ibid., MS 981A, box 4.

5. Letter, June 29, 1897, Sigmund Lehman to IWH, ibid., box 32.

6. Letter, July 2, 1897, IWH to Emanuel Lehman, ibid., vol. 22, p. 141.

7. Letter, March 17, 1898, IWH to Arthur Lehman, ibid., vol. 23, p. 231.

8. George Wharton James, *The Lake of the Sky* (Las Vegas, Nev.: Nevada Publications, 1992), p. 26.

9. Edward B. Scott, *The Saga of Lake Tahoe: A Complete Documentation of Lake Tahoe's Development over the Last One Hundred and Fifty Years* (Crystal Bay, Nev.: Sierra Publishing, 1957), p. 11.

10. Gary Noy, "The UltimateThrill: The Great Flume Ride of 1875 Celebrates Its 130th Anniversary," *Union*, Sacramento, Calif.: October 22, 2005.

11. Ibid.

12. Susan Lindstrom, "Early Historic Period, 1844–1899, Sugar Pine Point," report prepared for California State Parks, Sierra District, 2002, p. 15.

13. Edna Robinson, 1904 article in scrapbook of the Jewish Council of Women, Western Jewish History Center, Judah L. Magnes Museum, Berkeley, Calif..

14. *Emanu-el*, December 23, 1904, p. 5.

15. Howard M. Sachar, *A History of the Jews in America* (New York: Vintage Books, 1993), p. 131.

16. Ibid., p. 123.

17. Fred Rosenbaum, *Visions of Reform: Congregation Emanu-el and the Jews of San Francisco, 1849–1999* (Berkeley, Calif.: Judah L. Magnes Museum, 2000), p. 89. *Emanu-el*, June 17, 1904, p. 5.

18. Sachar, p. 126.

19. Rosenbaum, p. 90.

20. "Emanu-el Kindergarten" in the *Annual Report of the Emanu-el Sisterhood for Personal Service*. Emanu-el Sisterhood Papers, WJHC 1970.011, Western Jewish History Center, Judah L. Magnes Museum, Berkeley Calif., p. 34.

21. Ibid., p. 35.

22. "The Women's Club," *Los Angeles Times*, October 29, 1886, quoting Sarah B. Cooper from "The Golden Gate Kindergarten Association of San Francisco's 1886 Annual Report."

23. Sachar, p. 129, quoting Abraham Cahan. Cahan was the Russian-born editor of the Yiddish paper the *Jewish Daily Forward*.

12. TROLLEYS AND WATER

1. Letter, January 4, 1899, IWH to Herman Hellman, Isaias W. Hellman Papers, MS 981, vol. 24, pp. 228–29.

2. William B. Friedricks, *Henry E. Huntington and the Creation of Southern California* (Columbus: Ohio State University Press, 1992), p. 50. I owe a debt to Friedricks, whose book provides an illuminating narrative of the business genius of Henry Huntington.

3. "Crowd Cheer Eaton," *Los Angeles Times*, November 24, 1898.

4. Letter, November 1898, William Perry to IWH, Isaias W. Hellman Papers, MS 981, box 7, folder 38.

5. Letter, April 28, 1899, IWH to Andrew Hallidie, ibid., vol. 25, p. 29.

6. "The Huntington Type," *Los Angeles Times*, April 28, 1899, reprint of *Chicago Journal* article.

7. "Approaching Collapse," *San Francisco Call*, April 27, 1899.

8. Letter, March 31, 1899, IWH to Nevada Bank, Isaias W. Hellman Papers, MS 981, box 34, vol. 24, p. 440.

9. Letter, October 31, 1895, William Lacy to Farmers and Merchants Bank, Wells Fargo Archives, box 6, folder 10.

10. Letter, October 12, 1900, Marco Hellman to IWH, Isaias W. Hellman Papers, MS 981, box 8, folder 47.

11. Letter, October 8, 1900, Marco Hellman to IWH, ibid., folder 47.

12. Ruth Teiser and Catherine Harroun, *Winemaking in California* (New York: McGraw-Hill, 1983), p. 157.

13. Paul Lukacs, *American Vintage: The Rise of American Wine* (New York: W. W. Norton, 2000), p. 59.

14. Letter, June 19, 1903, IWH to Farmers and Merchants Bank, Hellman Family Papers, vol. 29.

15. Letter, September 22, 1900, IWH to James Speyer, Isaias W. Hellman Papers, MS 981, vol. 26. p. 399.

16. January 2, 1901, IWH letter book, ibid., vol. 26.

17. Letter, May 21, 1901, IWH to Henry Huntington, ibid., vol. 27, pp. 270–71.

18. Letter, May 3, 1901, W. H. Holabird to Henry Huntington, ibid., box 8.

19. Friedricks, p. 57.

20. "Pacific, Electric Sets Swift Pace," *Los Angeles Times*, February 25, 1903.

21. *Los Angeles Almanac*, www.laalmanac.com.

13. BETRAYAL

1. Catherine Mulholland, *William Mulholland and the Rise of Los Angeles* (Berkeley: University of California Press, 2000), p. 76.

2. Telegram, November 21, 1901, IWH to Herman Hellman, Isaias W. Hellman Papers, MS 981, vol. 29, p. 202.

3. Telegram, December 10, 1901, IWH to Charles Elton, ibid., MS 981, box 4, folder named "Fleishman."

4. Letter, December 18, 1901, Herman Hellman to Marco Fleishman, ibid.

5. Letter, November 20, 1902, Henry Fleishman to IWH, ibid.

6. Ibid.

7. Letter, undated but around 1868, Flora Hellman to IWH, translated from the German by Wolfgang Fritzche, private collection of Christiane de Bord.

8. Letter, November 17, 1901, IWH to Herman Hellman, MS 981, vol. 29, p. 185.

9. Letter, November 20, 1902, Henry Fleishman to IWH, Isaias W. Hellman Papers, MS 981, unmarked box.

10. Fleishman's accusation first became public in 1908 with the publication of the book *Looters of the Public Domain* by S. A. D. Puter and Horace Stevens. The book was written by Stephen A. Puter, the mastermind of a massive land fraud in Oregon around the turn of the century. After defrauding

the government in Oregon, Puter came to southern California, where he became involved in the oil industry.

Horace Stevens, a government inspector, got the tale from Fleishman before he fled, and wrote an account for the book. When petroleum was discovered in Bakersfield, oil companies rushed to file claims on the land. They were beaten by men called "scrippers" who invoked an arcane federal law that permitted them to swap federal land they already owned for other federal parcels, but only if they planned to use the land for agricultural purposes. If the land contained minerals or petroleum, the scrippers were not allowed to claim it. Millions of dollars from oil revenues were at stake, and the oil companies and the scrippers went to court over who owned the land. Judge Erskine M. Ross, the circuit court judge of the Ninth District Court, ruled in June 1900 that the scrippers had a right to claim the oil-rich land. But he later reversed himself, handing a huge victory to the oil companies and men like Doheny and Canfield, who would earn millions of dollars from their claims.

Fleishman apparently told friends Judge Ross switched his ruling after he received a $20,000 loan from the Farmers and Merchants Bank. Ross allegedly took the money after a meeting with Hellman, Canfield, Doheny, and Fleishman and used the funds to buy shares of Canfield Oil stock for 15¢ a share. After Ross issed a ruling that favored the oil companies, the stock went up to 55¢ a share, netting the judge a nice profit.

It is difficult to assess the veracity of this story. Fleishman, while never convicted, did steal money from Isaias's bank and had a motive to sully his reputation. While Stevens mentions in the book that he did file a report on the accusations, nothing came of them. Judge Ross went on to a long and distinguished career. Doheny's oil corporation went on to control by 1920 one-tenth of all the oil production in the United States. Doheny, however, was accused but never convicted of bribery in the famous Teapot Dome Scandal of the 1920s. Isaias continued to do business with Doheny and was appointed in 1910 to the board of one of Doheny's companies, American Oil Fields. He resigned less than a year later because he could not attend meetings. Doheny was appointed in 1909 to the board of the Farmers and Merchants Bank.

11. Letter, June 3, 1903, Henry Fleishman to IWH, Isaias W. Hellman Papers, MS 981A, box 4.
12. This company eventually became the basis for Southern California Edison.
13. Letter, March 25, 1887, George Patton to C. H. Jordan, Isaias W. Hellman Papers, MS 981, box 34, vol. 24.
14. Letter, January 19, 1900, IWH to Herman Hellman, ibid., vol. 25, p. 362.
15. January 12, 1903, agreement between Isaias Hellman and Henry Huntington, Henry Huntington Manuscript Collection, HEH no. 12713, Huntington Library, San Marino, CA.
16. Memorandum, May 23, 1903, Hellman Family Papers, Wells Fargo Archives, box 9, folder 5. The blowup most have been so explosive that Emanuel Heller decided it was worth recording. He wrote down the brothers' exchange, which Isaias filed with his papers.
17. Memorandum, May 23, 1903, Herman Hellman to the Farmers and Merchants Bank Board of Directors, ibid.
18. Letter, July 1, 1903, Jackson Graves to IWH, Isaias W. Hellman Papers, MS 981, box 19, folder 131.
19. Letter, July 2, 1903, IWH to Jackson Graves, ibid.
20. Letter, Adolph Fleishman to IWH, ibid., box 10, folder 64.
21. Letter, January 29, 1904, Herman Hellman to General J. G. C. Lee, Herman Hellman letterbook, Irving H. Hellman Papers, UCLA Special Collections, p. 50.

22. Ibid.

23. Letter, April 28, 1904, IWH to Jackson Graves, Isaias W. Hellman Papers, MS 981, box 17, folder 110.

24. Interview with Frederick Lipman, Frederick Lipman Papers, Wells Fargo Archives.

14. WELLS FARGO

1. Letter, August 18, 1903, Henry Huntington to IWH, Isaias W. Hellman Papers, MS 981, box 10, folder 62.

2. Letter, November 25, 1904, IWH to Henry Huntington, ibid., box 11, folder 66.

3. Letter, February 17, 1904, William F. Herrin to E. H. Harriman, MS 981A, box 4, folder 1871–1915.

4. Rudy Abramson, *Spanning the Century: The Life of W. Averell Harriman, 1891–1986* (New York: Morrow, 1992), p. 22.

5. *Town Talk*, May 17, 1902, p. 16

6. "Blythe Block Sold," *Los Angeles Sunday Times*, June 10, 1901.

7. Interview with Frederick Lipman, Frederick Lipman Papers, Wells Fargo Archives.

8. Letter, January 12, 1904, IWH to directors, Nevada National Bank minute book, 1897–1911, Wells Fargo Archives, p. 144.

9. Marquis James and Bessie R. James, *The Story of Bank of America: Biography of a Bank* (New York: Harper & Brothers, 1954), p 10.

10. Letter, March 8, 1905, Edward Heller to IWH, Isaias W. Hellman Papers, MS 981, box 11.

11. Letter, May 26, 1905, Lyman Stewart to IWH, ibid.

12. Cleland and Putnam, pp. 64–65.

13. Letter, January 18, 1904, IWH to Jackson Graves, Isaias W. Hellman Papers, MS 981, box 17, folder 135.

14. Memorandum of new investors, August 4, 1906, ibid., box 11, folder 70.

15. Letter, December 22, 1905, IWH to Benjamin Newgass, ibid., vol. 30, p. 132.

15. EARTHQUAKE AND FIRE

1. Gordon Thomas and Max Morgan Witts, *The San Francisco Earthquake* (New York: Stein & Day), 1971.

2. Charles Kendrick, Charles Kendrick's Eyewitness Account of the 1906 Earthquake, Virtual Museum of the City of San Francisco, www.sfmuseum.net/1906/ew17.html.

3. "Oakvale," date unknown, oral history done of, Warren Hellman, property of the author.

4. Telegram, April 18, 1906, James Hellman to IWH, Isaias W. Hellman Papers, MS 981, box 11, folder 7.

5. Telegram, April 19, 1906, Arthur Lehman to IWH, ibid.

6. Eric Saul and Don Denevi, *The Great San Francisco Earthquake and Fire, 1906* (Millbrae, Calif.: Celestial Arts, 1981), p. 80.

7. "Broke, But Happy," *New York Times*, April 14, 1906.

8. Telegram, April 19, 1906, Harrison Gray Otis to IWH, Isaias W. Hellman Papers, MS 981, box 11 folder 70.

9. Telegram, Arthur Lehman to IWH, ibid.

10. Philip L. Fradkin, *The Great Earthquake and Firestorms of 1906* (Berkeley: University of California Press, 2005), p. 203.

11. Undated newspaper clip from I. W. Hellman's personal scrapbook, Hellman Family Papers, box 16.

12. Letter, May 17, 1906, Henry Huntington to IWH, Isaias W. Hellman Papers, MS 981, box 12, folder 71.

13. Contract between Hellman syndicate and Harriman, July 20, 1906, Isaias W. Hellman Papers, MS 981, box 12, folder 72.

14. Memorandum, July 20, 1906, ibid.

15. Letter, January 19, 1912, Jackson Graves to IWH, MS 981, box 13, folder 82.

16. Letter, January 20, 1912, IWH to Jackson Graves, vol. 47, ibid.

17. Letter, April 28, 1904, IWH to Jackson Graves, box 19, folder 138.

18. Letter, October 13, 1906, James Hellman to IWH, box 12, folder 73.

19. Letter, October 17, 1906, Adolph Fleishman to IWH, ibid.

20. Telegram, October 18, 1906, Ida Hellman to IWH, ibid.

21. Telegram, October 18, 1906, Emanuel Heller to James Hellman, ibid.

22. Telegram, October 18, 1906, Marco H. Hellman to IWH, ibid.

16. GRAFT AND CASH

1. Walton Bean, *Boss Ruef's San Francisco: The Story of the Labor Union Party, Big Business, and the Graft Persecution* (Berkeley: University of California Press, 1972), p. 109.

2. Testimony of IWH before grand jury May 13, 1907, Special Collections, Subject Files, Hellman Related Materials, Wells Fargo Archives.

3. "Among Men of Action: Hellman on Calhoun," *Los Angeles Times*, June 29, 1907.

4. Letter, April 1, 1907, Emanuel Heller to IWH, Isaias W. Hellman Papers, MS 981, box 12, folder 74.

5. Isaias had to deal with another problem during this time. In 1907, the country suffered another economic tightening, which came to be known as the Panic of 1907. Gold was in such short supply that banks in Los Angeles had to issue scrip for depositors to use in daily transactions. To encourage the use of scrip, the banks agreed to pay 7 percent interest on the notes. Several banks in Los Angeles closed, but the Farmers and Merchants Bank withstood the crunch. Wells Fargo Bank saw its customers withdraw $6 million over six weeks. Once again, Isaias had insisted on keeping as much as 45 percent of the bank's deposits in coin, so the bank survived.

6. Case no. 6116, Calkins Newspaper Syndicate, April 16, 1909, U.S. Bankruptcy Court, National Archives and Records Administration, San Bruno, Calif.

7. Letter, September 19, 1908, Fremont Older to IWH, Hellman Family Papers, box 9, folder 21.

8. Barbara S. Rogers and Stephen M. Dobbs, *The First Century: Mount Zion Hospital and Medical Center, 1887–1987* (San Francisco: Mount Zion Hospital and Medical Center, 1987).

9. Letter, September 10, 1908, IWH to Board of Directors of Mount Zion Hospital. Isais W. Hellman Papers.

10. IWH diary, February 16, 1909, private collection of Alan Mandell.

11. IWH diary, May 11, 1909, ibid.

12. "Hellman Back from Trip Abroad," *San Francisco Chronicle*, August 4, 1909.
13. "The Financiers and Graft Prosecution," *San Francisco Liberator*, August 7, 1909, vol. 1, no. 35.
14. IWH diary, October 11, 1909, private collection of Alan Mandell.
15. Ibid., October 25, 1909.

17. CHANGE

1. Author's calculations. Isaias and Herman Hellman became millionaires, as did Emanuel, David, and Isaac Walter, and perhaps Nathan Walter; Kalman Haas; Abraham Haas; and William Haas.
2. Letter, October 10, 1911, IWH to Wells Fargo Nevada National board of directors, Wells Fargo Nevada National Bank, minute book, August 1911–January 1924, p. 377.
3. Letter, October 26, 1912, IWH to Jacob Schiff, Isaias W. Hellman Papers, MS 981, box 39, vol. 42.
4. Minutes, December 26, 1911, Wells Fargo Nevada National Bank minute book, August 1911–January 1924, Wells Fargo Archives.
5. *Western Banker*, August 12, 1914.
6. "Kings of Finance," *Town Talk*, January 15, 1914.
7. Letter, August 10, 1914, Marco Hellman to IWH, Isaias W. Hellman Papers, MS 981, box 40, book 46.
8. Letter, December 23, 1913, IWH to Wells Fargo Nevada National board of directors, Wells Fargo Bank minute book, August 1911–January 1924, Wells Fargo Archives.
9. Laura Ingalls Wilder, *West from Home: Letters of Laura Ingalls Wilder to Almanzo Wilder*. (New York: Harper & Row 1974), p. 31.
10. *San Francisco Chronicle*, July 8, 1916.
11. "Two Thousand at Chamber of Commerce Meeting," *San Francisco Chronicle*, July 11, 1915.
12. Letter, July 18, 1916, I. W. Hellman Jr. to Wells Fargo Nevada National Bank board of directors, Isaias W. Hellman Papers, MS 981, vol. 48. p. 161.
13. "She Blames Militarism," *San Francisco Chronicle*, July 25, 1916.
14. Letter, July 31, 1916, Jackson Graves to IWH, Isaias W. Hellman Papers, MS 981, box 15, folder 92.

18. WAR AND ANTI-SEMITISM

1. "All Religions and All Races to Take Part," *San Francisco Chronicle*, January 25, 1916.
2. "San Francisco Makes Wonderful Response To Humanity's Needs," *San Francisco Chronicle*, January 27, 1916.
3. "Jewish Massacre Denounced," *New York Times*, April 28, 1903.
4. Letter, October 5, 1915, IWH to Wells Fargo Nevada National board of directors, Wells Fargo Nevada National minute book, August 1911–January 1924, Wells Fargo Archives.
5. Isaias Hellman private scrapbook, Wells Fargo Archives, box 16.
6. IWH diary, May 25, 1915, private collection of Alan Mandell.
7. Untitled article, *San Francisco Examiner*, November 11, 1914.
8. Letter, March 3, 1917, IWH to Wells Fargo Nevada National Bank board of directors, Isaias W. Hellman Papers, MS 981, box 41, vol. 50.

9. Wells Fargo Bank minute book, August 1911–January 1924, Wells Fargo Archives.
10. Mary Ann Irwin, "The Air Is Becoming Full of War," *Pacific Historical Review* 74, no. 3 (2005), p. 75.
11. Untitled article in IWH scrapbook, *Star-Bulletin*, November 14, 1917, Hellman Family Papers, Wells Fargo Archive, box 16, folder 2.
12. Rex Adams, "The 1918 Spanish Influenza, Berkeley's Quinta Columna," *Chronicle of the University of California*, Spring 1988, p. 56.
13. "San Bruno Settlement House Is Now Completed and Awaits Its Formal Dedication and Accupancy." *Emanu-el*, October 25, 1918.
14. Public Health Reports, United States Public Health Service, vol. 33, no. 51 (December 20, 1918), p. 2278.
15. Letter, October 22, 1918, William Woodson to IWH, Isaias W. Hellman Papers, MS 981, box 15, folder 93.
16. Alfred Heller, great-grandson of IWH. Interview conducted by author, October 2000.
17. Gina Kolata, *Flu: The Story of the Great Influenza Pandemic of 1918 and the Search for the Virus That Caused It* (New York: Farrar, Straus & Giroux, 1999), p. 7.

19. THE LIGHT FADES

1. Letter, June 10, 1918, IWH to Sylvan L. Bernstein, Sylvan Bernstein Vertical File, Berkeley, Calif., Western Jewish History Center.
2. Letter, June 11, 1918, IWH to Sylvan Bernstein, Isaias W. Hellman Papers, MS 981, box 4, folder: letters and reprints to I. W. Hellman Sr. and Jr., 1916–1918.
3. *Emanu-el*, April 11, 1919, p. 9.
4. "Protest to Wilson Against Zionist State," *New York Times*, March 5, 1919.
5. Telegram, March 4, 1919, Julius Kahn to Henry Berkowitz, San Francisco Zionism Collection, Western Jewish History Center, Berkeley, Calif., folder 1.
6. Cleland and Putnam, p. 87.
7. IWH diary, September 8, 1919.
8. Ibid., February 9, 1920.
9. Ibid., March 17, 1920.
10. "I. W. Hellman, San Francisco Financier, Dies," *San Francisco Chronicle*, April 10, 1920.

EPILOGUE

1. The entire twenty-six-thousand-acre Rancho Los Alamitos cost $125,000, which comes to about $4.80 an acre.
2. Letter, April 28, 1928, Henry Fleishman to Harrell Harrell, property of Gloria Hovey.

BIBLIOGRAPHY

Abramson, Rudy. *Spanning the Century: The Life of W. Averell Harriman, 1891–1986*. New York: Morrow, 1992.

Ashkenazi, Elliot. *The Business of Jews in Louisiana, 1840–1875*. Tuscaloosa: University of Alabama Press, 1988.

Aspostal, Jane. "Don Mateo Keller: His Vines and His Wines." *Southern California Quarterly* 84, no. 2 (Summer 2002): pp. 93–114.

Ayers, James J. *Gold and Sunshine: Reminiscences of Early California*. Boston: R. G. Badger, 1922.

Armstrong, Leroy, and J. O. Denny. *Financial California*. San Francisco: Coast Banker Publishing, 1916.

Bancroft, Hubert Howe. *Chronicles of the Builders: A History of the Life of John G. Downey*. San Francisco: History Company, 1889.

Bean, Walton. *Boss Ruef's San Francisco: The Story of the Labor Union Party, Big Business, and the Graft Prosecution*. Berkeley: University of California Press, 1972.

Beaton, Kendall. *Enterprise in Oil: A History of Shell in the United States*. New York: Appleton-Century-Crofts, 1957.

Bell, Horace. *Reminiscences of a Ranger*. Santa Barbara, Calif.: Wallace Hebbard, 1927.

Benjamin, I. J. *Three Years in America, 1859–1862*. Translated from the German by Charles Reznikoff. Philadelphia: Jewish Publication Society of America, 1956.

Booth, Gerald. *The Fairmont Hotel: A Pictorial History*. San Francisco: Sequoia Communications, Fairmont Hotel Management, Somerset Van Ness, 1986.

Black, Esther Boulton. *Rancho Cucamonga and Doña Merced*. Redlands, Calif.: San Bernardino County Museum Association, 1973.

Bonnet, Theodore. *The Regenerators: A Study of the Graft Prosecution of San Francisco*. San Francisco: Pacific Printing, 1911.

Brewer, William, *Up and Down California: In 1860–1864*. Berkeley: University of California Press, 1966.

Caughey, John, and LaRee Caughey, eds. *Los Angeles: Biography of a City*. Berkeley: University of California Press, 1976.

Chambliss, William H. *Chambliss' Diary, or Society As It Really Is*. New York: Chambliss, 1895.

Chandler, Robert. *San Francisco Clearing House Certificates: Last of California's Private Money*. Reno, Nev.: McDonald Publications, 1986.

Chernow, Ron. *The Death of the Banker: The Decline and Fall of the Great Financial Dynasties and the Triumph of the Small Investor*. New York: Vintage Books, 1997.

Clark, David L. *A History of the California Club, 1887–1997*. Los Angeles: California Club, 1997.

Cleland, Robert Glass. *Cattle on a Thousand Hills: Southern California, 1850–1870*. San Marino, Calif.: Huntington Library, 1941.

Cleland, Robert Glass, and Frank B. Putnam. *Isaias W. Hellman and the Farmers and Merchants Bank*. San Marino, Calif.: Huntington Library, 1965.

Cogan, Sarah G. *The Jews of San Francisco and the Greater Bay Area, 1849–1919, an Annotated Bibliography*. Berkeley, Calif.: Western Jewish History Center, 1973.

Cohen, Naomi W. *Encounter with Emancipation: The German Jews in the United States, 1830–1914*. Philadelphia: Jewish Publication Society, 1984.

————. *Jacob H. Schiff: A Study in American Jewish Leadership*. Hanover, N.H.: Brandeis University Press, 1999.

Cross, Ira B. *Financing an Empire: History of Banking in California*. Chicago: S. J. Clarke Publishing, 1927.

Crump, Spencer. *Ride the Big Red Cars: How Trolleys Helped Build Southern California*. Los Angeles: Crest Publications, 1962.

Davis, Margaret Leslie. *The Dark Side of Fortune: Triumph and Scandal in the Life of Oil Tycoon Edward L. Doheny*. Berkeley: University of California Press, 1998.

Decker, Peter. *Fortunes and Failures: White Collar Mobility in Nineteenth-Century San Francisco*. Cambridge, Mass.: Harvard University Press, 1978.

Diner, Hasia R. *A Time for Gathering: The Second Migration, 1820–1880*. Vol. 2 of *The Jewish People in America*, edited by Henry L. Feingold. Baltimore: Johns Hopkins University Press, 1992.

Dobie, Edith. *The Political Career of Stephen Mallory White: A Study of Party Activities Under the Convention System*. Stanford, Calif.: Stanford University Press, 1927.

Dorfman, Elaine. *Edward Bransten: Historic Early Twentieth Century: San Franciscans, Family, and Travels*. Berkeley, Calif.: Western Jewish History Center, Judah L. Magnes Museum, 1989.

Doti, Lynn Pierson. *Banking in an Unregulated Environment: California, 1878–1905*. New York: Garland, 1995.

Doti, Lynn Pierson, and Larry Schweikart. *Banking in the American West: From Gold Rush to Deregulation*. Norman: University of Oklahoma Press, 1991.

Douglas, J. R. *The Bank and the Community: A History of the Security Trust & Savings Bank of Los Angeles, 1889–1929*. Los Angeles: Security Trust & Savings Bank, 1929.

Dumke, Glenn S. *The Boom of the Eighties in Southern California*. San Marino, Calif: Huntington Library, 1944.

Egan, Ferol. *Last Bonanza Kings: The Bourns of San Francisco*. Reno: University of Nevada Press, 1998.

Engh, Michael. "Charity Knows Neither Race nor Creed: Jewish Philanthropy to Roman Catholic Projects in Los Angeles, 1856–1876." *Western States Jewish Historical Quarterly* 21, no. 2, pp. 154–165.

The Farmers & Merchants National Bank of Los Angeles: April 10, 1871, to April 10, 1921; Fifty Years of Banking Service Under Conservative Management. Los Angeles: Farmers & Merchants National Bank, 1921.

Ferrier, William W. *Origin and Development of the University of California*. Berkeley, Calif.: Sather Gate Bookshop, 1930.

Fick, Roland G. *San Francisco Is No More: The Letters of Antoine Borel, Jr., 1905–1906*. Menlo Park, Calif.: Fick, 1963.

Flade, Roland. *The Lehmans: From Rimpar to the New World; a Family History.* Würzburg, Germany: Konigshausen & Neumann, 1996.

Fogelson, Robert M. *The Fragmented Metropolis: Los Angeles, 1850–1930.* Berkeley: University of California Press, 1967.

Fradkin, Philip L. *Stagecoach: Wells Fargo and the American West.* New York: Simon & Schuster, 2002.

———. *The Great Earthquake and Firestorm of 1906: How San Francisco Nearly Destroyed Itself.* Berkeley: University of California Press, 2005.

Frank, Herman. *Scrapbook of a Western Pioneer.* Los Angeles: Times-Mirror Press, 1934.

Friedricks, William B. *Henry E. Huntington and the Creation of Southern California.* Columbus: Ohio State University Press, 1992.

Gartner, Lloyd P., and Max Vorspan. *History of the Jews of Los Angeles.* San Marino, Calif.: Huntington Library, 1970.

Glazier, Ira A., and P. William Filby, eds. *Germans to America: Lists of Passengers Arriving at U.S. Ports.* Wilmington, Del. Scholarly Resources, Vol. 12, November 1857–July 1859.

Graves, Jackson A. *My Seventy Years in California, 1857–1927.* Los Angeles: Times-Mirror Press, 1927.

Guinn, J. M. *Historical and Biographical Record of Los Angeles and Vicinity.* Chicago: Chapman Publishing, 1901.

Harris, James F. *The People Speak! Anti-Semitism and Emancipation in Nineteenth-Century Bavaria.* Ann Arbor: University of Michigan Press, 1994.

Hawley, A. T. *The Present Condition. Growth, and Advantages of Los Angeles City and County, Southern California.* Los Angeles: Chamber of Commerce, July 1876.

Hichborn, Franklin. *The System: As Uncovered by the San Francisco Graft Prosecution.* San Francisco: Press of the James H. Barry Company, 1915.

Hicke, Carole. *Heller, Ehrman, White & McAuliffe: A Century of Service to Clients and Community.* San Francisco: Heller, Ehrman, White & McAuliffe, 1991.

Hill, Laurance L. *La Reina: Los Angeles in Three Centuries.* Los Angeles: Security Trust & Savings Bank, 1929.

Hittell, John S. *The Resources of California, Comprising the Society, Climate, Salubrity, Scenery, Commerce, and Industry of the State.* San Francisco: A. L. Bancroft, 1879.

Hungerford, Edward. *Wells Fargo: Advancing the American Frontier.* New York: Random House, 1949.

Hunt, Kathleen O'Donnell. *Downey's Destiny: Odyssey of an Irish Immigrant.* Dublin, Ireland: Libra House, 1997.

Hunt, Roxwell Dennis, and William Sheffield Ament. *Oxcart to Airplane.* Los Angeles: Powell Publishing, 1929.

Issel, William, and Robert W. Cherney. *San Francisco, 1865–1932: Politics, Power and Urban Development.* Berkeley: University of California Press, 1986.

Jaher, Frederic C. *The Urban Establishment: Upper Strata in Boston, New York, Charleston, Chicago, and Los Angeles.* Urbana: University of Illinois Press, 1982.

James, George Wharton. *The Lake of the Sky.* Las Vegas, Nev.: Nevada Publications, 1992.

James, Marquis, and Bessie R. James. *The Story of Bank of America: Biography of a Bank.* New York: Harper & Brothers, 1954.

Kahn, Ava F. *Jewish Voices of the California Gold Rush: A Documentary History, 1849–1880.* Detroit: Wayne State University Press, 2002.

Kahn, Edgar M. *Cable Car Days in San Francisco.* Stanford, Calif.: Stanford University Press, 1944.

Kendrick, Charles. *Charles Kendrick's Eyewitness Account of the 1906 Earthquake*. Virtual Museum of the City of San Francisco. www.sfmuseum.net/1906/ew17.html.

Klein, Maury. *The Life and Legend of E. H. Harriman*. Chapel Hill: University of North Carolina Press, 2000.

Kolata, Gina. *Flu: The Story of the Great Influenza Pandemic of 1918 and the Search for the Virus That Caused It*. New York: Farrar, Straus & Giroux, 1999.

Lavender, David. *California: Land of New Beginnings*. Lincoln: University of Nebraska Press, 1987.

Lecouvrer, Frank. *From East Prussia to the Golden Gate*. New York: Angelita Book Concern, 1906.

Levy, Harriet Lane. *920 O'Farrell Street: A Jewish Girlhood in Old San Francisco*. Berkeley, Calif.: Heydey Books, 1966.

Lukacs, Paul. *American Vintage: The Rise of American Wine*. New York: W. W. Norton, 2000.

McGroarty, John. *The Pioneer: A Fascinating Chapter from the Pages of California History*. Los Angeles: Press Publishing, 1925.

Mesmer, Joseph. "Some of My Los Angeles Jewish Neighbors." *Western States Jewish Historical Quarterly* 3, no. 3 (April 1975), pp. 191–99.

Meyer, Eugene. "My Early Years." *Western States Jewish Historical Quarterly* 2 (1973): pp. 87–99.

Mowry, George. *The California Progressives*. Berkeley: University of California Press, 1951.

Mulholland, Catherine. *William Mulholland and the Rise of Los Angeles*. Berkeley: University of California Press, 2000.

Nadeau, Remi. *City-Makers: The Story of Southern California's First Boom*. Corona Del Mar, Calif.: Trans-Anglo Books, 1965.

Narell, Irene. *Our City: The Jews of San Francisco*. San Diego, Calif.: Howell North Books, 1981.

Newmark, Harris. *Sixty Years in Southern California*. 3rd ed. Cambridge, Mass.: Riverside Press, 1930.

Nissenbaum, Stephen. *The Battle for Christmas: A Cultural History of America's Most Cherished Holiday*. New York: Vintage Books, 1997.

Odell, Kerry A., and Marc D. Weidenmier. *Real Shock, Monetary Aftershock : The San Francisco Earthquake and the Panic of 1907*. Cambridge, Mass.: National Bureau of Economic Research, 2002.

O'Flaherty, Joseph S. *An End and a Beginning: The South Coast and Los Angeles, 1850–1887*. New York: Exposition Press, 1972.

———. *Those Powerful Years: The South Coast and Los Angeles, 1887–1917*. Hicksville, N.Y.: Exposition Press, 1978.

Older, Fremont. *My Own Story*. New York: Macmillan, 1926.

Peninou, Ernest, and Sidney Greenleaf. *Winemaking in America*. San Francisco, Calif.: Peregrine Press, 1954.

Peninou, Ernest, and Gail G. Unzelman. *The California Wine Association and Its Member Wineries, 1894–1920*. Santa Rosa, Calif.: Nomis Press, 2000.

Pinney, Thomas. *A History of Wine in America: From the Beginnings to Prohibition*. Berkeley: University of California Press, 1989.

Pitt, Leonard. *The Decline of the Californios: A Social History of the Spanish-Speaking Californians, 1846–1890*. Berkeley: University of California Press, 1970.

Pitt, Leonard, and Dale Pitt. *Los Angeles A to Z: An Encyclopedia of the City and County*. Berkeley: University of California Press, 1997.

Post, Robert. *Street Railways and the Growth of Los Angeles: Horse, Cable, Electric Lines*. San Marino, Calif.: Golden West Books, 1989.

Puter, S. A. D., and Horace Stevens. *Looters of the Public Domain: Embracing a Complete Exposure of the Fraudulent System of Acquiring Titles to the Public Lands of the United States*. Portland, Ore.: Portland Printing House Publishers, 1908.

Quinn, Charles Russell. *History of Downey: The Life Story of a Pioneer Community, and of the Man Who Founded It—California Governor John Gately Downey—from Covered Wagon to the Space Shuttle*. Downey, Calif.: Quinn, 1973.

Rawls, James J., and Walton Bean. *California: An Interpretive History*. New York: McGraw-Hill, 1993.

Rischin, Moses, ed. *The Jews of the West: The Metropolitan Years*. Waltham, Mass: American Jewish Historical Society for the Western Jewish History Center of the Judah L. Magnes Museum, 1979.

Robinson, John W. *Los Angeles in Civil War Days, 1860–1865*. Los Angeles: Dawson's Book Shop, 1977.

Roddy, Ella Giles, ed. *The Mother of Clubs: Caroline M. Seymour Severance, an Estimate and Appreciation*. Los Angeles: Baumgardt Publishing, 1906.

Rogers, Barbara S., and Stephen M. Dobbs. *The First Century: Mount Zion Hospital and Medical Center, 1887–1987*. San Francisco: Mount Zion Hospital and Medical Center, 1987.

Roland, Carol. "The California Kindergarten Movement: A Study in Class and Social Feminism." PhD diss., University of California, Riverside, 1980.

Rosenbaum, Fred. *Visions of Reform: Congregation Emanu-el and the Jews of San Francisco, 1849–1999*. Berkeley, Calif.: Judah L. Magnes Museum, 2000.

Rothmann, Frances Bransten. *The Haas Sisters of Franklin Street*. Berkeley, Calif.: Judah L. Magnes Museum, 1979.

Sachar, Howard M. *A History of the Jews in America*. New York: Vintage Books, 1993.

San Francisco Blue Book; the Fashionable Private Address Directory, San Francisco–Oakland–Berkeley–Alameda. San Francisco: C. C. Hoag, 1888–1898.

Saul, Eric, and Don Denevi. *The Great San Francisco Earthquake and Fire, 1906*. Millbrae, Calif.: Celestial Arts, 1981.

Scharlach, Bernice. "Abe Haas: Portrait of a Proud Businessman." Reprinted from *Western States Historical Quarterly* 28, no. 1 (Oct. 1979).

———. *House of Harmony: Concordia-Argonaut's First 130 Years*. Berkeley, Calif.: Western Jewish History Center, Judah L. Magnes Museum, 1983.

Schweikart, Larry, ed. *Encyclopedia of American Business History, "Banking and Finance, to 1913*. New York: Facts on File, 1990, pp. 249–60.

———, ed. "Isaias Hellman." In *Banking and Finance to 1913*, Encyclopedia of American Business History and Biography. Columbia, S. C., 1990, pp. 249–260.

Scott, Edward B. *The Saga of Lake Tahoe: A Complete Documentation of Lake Tahoe's Development over the Last One Hundred and Fifty Years*, vol. 1. Crystal Bay, Nev.: Sierra Publishing, 1957.

Sherwood, Midge. *Days of Vintage, Years of Vision*. San Marino, Calif.: Orizaba Publications, 1982.

Sichel, Caroline Meyberg. "Los Angeles Memories." *Western States Jewish History* 7, no. 1 (1974): pp. 49–58.

Sinclair, Upton. *The Brass Check, a Study of American Journalism*. Pasadena, Calif.: published by the author, 1920.

Smith, Grant H. *The History of the Comstock Lode, 1850–1920. University of Nevada Bulletin* 37, no. 3 (July 1, 1943).

Starr, Kevin. *Inventing the Dream: California Through the Progressive Era*. New York: Oxford University Press, 1985.

Stern, Norton B. "Jews in the 1870 Census of Los Angeles." *Western States Historical Quarterly* 9, no. 1, pp. 71–86.

———. "Location of Los Angeles Jewry at the Beginning of 1851." *Western States Historical Quarterly* 5, no. 1, pp. 25–32.

———. "Toward a Biography of Isaias W. Hellman–Pioneer Builder of California." *Western States Jewish Historical Quarterly* 2, no. 1 (October, 1969): pp. 27–43.

Swift, Fletcher Harper. *Emma Marwedel, 1818–1893: Pioneer of the Kindergarten in California.* Berkeley: University of California Press, 1931.

Teiser, Ruth, and Catherine Harroun. *Winemaking in California.* New York: McGraw-Hill, 1983.

Thomas, Gordon, and Max Morgan Witts. *The San Francisco Earthquake.* New York: Stein & Day, 1971.

Thorpe, James. *Henry Edwards Huntington: A Biography.* Berkeley: University of California Press, 1994.

Truman, Benjamin Cummings. *Semi-tropical California: Its Climate, Healthfulness, Productiveness, and Scenery.* San Francisco: A. L. Bancroft & Co., 1874.

Turner, Justin. *The First Decade of Los Angeles Jewry: A Pioneer History (1850–1860).* Philadelphia: Press of Maurice Jacobs, 1964.

Van Dyke, Theodore S. *Millionaires of a Day: An Inside History of the Great Southern California Boom.* New York: Fords, Howard & Hulbert, 1892.

Vorspan, Max, and Lloyd P. Gartner. *History of the Jews of Los Angeles.* San Marino, Calif: Huntington Library, 1970.

Warner, J. J, Benjamin Hays, and J. P. Widney. *A Historical Sketch of Los Angeles County.* Los Angeles: Louis Lewin & Co., 1876.

Wilder, Laura Ingalls, *West from Home: Letters of Laura Ingalls Wilder to Almanzo Wilder.* New York: Harper & Row, 1974.

Williams, Hal R. *The Democratic Party and California Politics, 1880–1896.* Stanford, Calif.: Stanford University Press, 1973.

Workman, Boyle. *The City That Grew.* Los Angeles: Southland Publishing, 1936.

Wright, Benjamin C. *Banking in California, 1849–1910.* San Francisco: H. S. Crocker, 1910.

INDEX